Fourth Edition

Interpreting Educational Research

An Introduction for Consumers of Research

Daniel R. Hittleman

Professor Emeritus
The City University of New York/Queens College

Alan J. Simon

Metis Associates, Inc., New York

PEARSON

Merrill
Prentice Hall

Upper Saddle River, New Jersey
Columbus, Ohio

Library of Congress Cataloging-in-Publication Data

Hittleman, Daniel R.
  Interpreting educational research: an introduction for consumers of research / Daniel R. Hittleman, Alan J. Simon.—4th ed.
     p. cm.
  Includes bibliographical references and index.
  ISBN 0-13-170731-0
  1. Education—Research. 2. Research—Methodology. 3. Education—Research—Evaluation. I. Simon, Alan J. II. Title.

LB1028.H537 2006
370'.072—dc22   2005000257

Vice President and Executive Publisher: Jeffery W. Johnston
Publisher: Kevin M. Davis
Editorial Assistant: Sarah Kenoyer
Production Editor: Mary Harlan
Production Coordination: Thistle Hill Publishing Services, LLC
Design Coordinator: Diane C. Lorenzo
Cover Designer: Thomas Borah
Cover Image: SuperStock
Production Manager: Laura Messerly
Director of Marketing: Ann Castel Davis
Marketing Manager: Autumn Purdy
Marketing Coordinator: Brian Mounts

This book was set in Meridian Roman by Carlisle Communications, Ltd. It was printed and bound by R.R. Donnelley & Sons Company. The cover was printed by R. R. Donnelley & Sons Company.

Pearson Education Ltd.
Pearson Education Singapore Pte. Ltd.
Pearson Education Canada, Ltd.
Pearson Education–Japan

Pearson Education Australia Pty. Limited
Pearson Education North Asia Ltd.
Pearson Educación de Mexico, S.A. de C.V.
Pearson Education Malaysia Pte. Ltd.

10 9 8 7 6 5 4 3 2 1
ISBN: 0-13-170731-0

To Carol and Carole,
our dearest wives and lifelong supporters

Educator Learning Center: An Invaluable Online Resource

Merrill Education and the Association for Supervision and Curriculum Development (ASCD) invite you to take advantage of a new online resource, one that provides access to the top research and proven strategies associated with ASCD and Merrill—the Educator Learning Center. At **www.educatorlearningcenter.com**, you will find resources that will enhance your students' understanding of course topics and of current educational issues, in addition to being invaluable for further research.

HOW THE EDUCATOR LEARNING CENTER WILL HELP YOUR STUDENTS BECOME BETTER TEACHERS

With the combined resources of Merrill Education and ASCD, you and your students will find a wealth of tools and materials to better prepare them for the classroom.

Research

- More than 600 articles from the ASCD journal *Educational Leadership* discuss everyday issues faced by practicing teachers.
- A direct link on the site to Research Navigator™ gives students access to many of the leading education journals, as well as extensive content detailing the research process.
- Excerpts from Merrill Education texts give your students insights on important topics of instructional methods, diverse populations, assessment, classroom management, technology, and refining classroom practice.

Classroom Practice

- Hundreds of lesson plans and teaching strategies are categorized by content area and age range.
- Case studies and classroom video footage provide virtual field experience for student reflection.
- Computer simulations and other electronic tools keep your students abreast of today's classrooms and current technologies.

LOOK INTO THE VALUE OF EDUCATOR LEARNING CENTER YOURSELF

A four-month subscription to Educator Learning Center is $25 but is **FREE** when packaged with any Merrill Education text. In order for your students to have access to this site, you must use this special value-pack ISBN number **WHEN** placing your textbook order with the bookstore: 0-13-225926-5. Your students will then receive a copy of the text packaged with a free ASCD pincode. To preview the value of this website to you and your students, please go to **www.educatorlearningcenter.com** and click on "Demo."

Preface

This edition of *Interpreting Educational Research: An Introduction for Consumers of Research* can be used in introductory, postbaccalaureate research courses that prepare people as consumers rather than as producers of educational research. Such people include elementary and early childhood education teachers, reading/literacy specialists, special education teachers, content-area teachers at the middle and secondary school levels, administrators, and curriculum specialists. We provide preservice and in-service teachers with basic knowledge and skills for reading, interpreting, and evaluating both quantitative and qualitative educational research, so that they can make program, curriculum, and instructional decisions based upon those research results. This knowledge base is useful for teachers who collaborate in research projects with college and university faculty and other teachers. In addition, we provide a guide for composing teacher-as-researcher research projects and syntheses of research.

Our text presentation guides learners in activities based on current integrated language arts principles and practices for reading and writing content-area discourse. We lead readers to independence in the use of techniques for reading, interpreting, evaluating, and writing about education research. Our approach to understanding and evaluating education research is to direct educators to become research consumers by understanding the underlying methodological and procedural assumptions used by other educators who are research producers. In essence, teachers are guided in research literacy, learning to think as research producers.

NATURE OF THE REVISION

Our revisions consist of updating information about how research is produced. We explain various theoretical perspectives that researchers have about learning and research and how those perspectives influence the nature and design of their research. We provide examples of research method and methodology, as well as exemplary quantitative and qualitative research studies and research syntheses and meta–analyses. We have retained the current standards for producing action or program evaluation research. The discussions throughout the text are supported with examples of what we feel are good, curriculum-based, quantitative and qualitative research reports representing the fields of elementary-, middle-, and secondary-school general and content-area education, school administration, teacher education, and gifted and special education. A very important and extensive revision we made in this fourth edition is the expanded explanation and interpretation of qualitative research. We have added additional information about the use of effect size in analyzing quantitative results. The discussion about interpreting and evaluating research syntheses has been revised and updated. Information and strategies for locating research reports through the use of electronic databases and the Internet have been updated and expanded. Because we feel that all educators, whether consumers or producers of research, should know and appreciate the criteria for conducting instructional program evaluations, we have retained the program evaluation standards that have been established by professional associations.

ORGANIZATION

In this revision, we have maintained the organization and chapter topics of the previous editions. The text is organized into eleven chapters and two appendixes. In chapters 1, 2, and 3, we lead the reader to an understanding of theoretical perspectives underpinning both quantitative and qualitative research, research designs, research methods and methodology, the general procedures of research producers, and a plan for reading research reports. In chapters 4 through 9, we present extended discussions of the aspects of research design and methodology and illustrations of the manner in which research producers present these aspects in research reports. We have put information about understanding the procedure sections and the results sections of quantitative research in two sections within chapter 7. We have devoted an entire chapter to the discussion of interpreting and evaluating procedures and findings of qualitative research. In chapters 10 and 11, we provide information about reading and writing reviews of research and about sources for locating research reports. At the end of the book are a glossary of key terms, citations of model research studies and both syntheses and meta-analyses of research in print and online sources, and ethical standards for conducting educational and program evaluation research.

As we did in previous editions, we begin each chapter with a graphic overview of the content and focus questions so readers can attend to the key ideas of the chapter and the interrelationships portrayed in the structured overview. In the main body of the chapters, we provide techniques for reading, interpreting, and writing about specific sections of research reports. In the activities section at the end of each chapter, we present ways for the reader to gain greater understanding of the key concepts and proficiency in applying the evaluative techniques. For many of these activities, we provide the reader with feedback in which we give samples of how we might respond to our own students' work. Feedback for other activities, we feel, should come from other students and the course instructor.

SPECIAL FEATURES

Special features of the text are as follows:

- The text is intended for teachers with a range of backgrounds: generalists, content-area teachers, reading/literacy specialists, administrators, special educators, and middle- and secondary-school teachers.

- The examples used throughout the text are drawn from current curriculum-based research literature that these teachers will find relevant to their specific instructional situations. All research designs and methodology are illustrated with published research.

- The material is conceptualized for consumers of educational research.

- The text is intended to teach preservice and in-service teachers, in a non-threatening supportive manner, to read and write about educational research. A step-by-step process leads teachers to understand and use research reports.

- Information is included about strategies for reading the various types of quantitative and qualitative research.

- The chapters begin with a structured overview of the content showing each chapter's focus in relation to the overall content of the text.

- Specific strategies that have been shown to be effective for the reading of typical content-area texts and the writing of content-area-related expository prose are applied to the reading of research reports and the writing of research evaluations.

- Ample practice is provided for developing readers' skills in evaluating educational research.

- The text provides readers with an understanding of syntheses of research and research meta-analyses and gives guidance in the preparation of teacher-as-researcher syntheses of research.

- A glossary contains the definitions of all key terms presented in the text. Within the text, key terms are highlighted the first time they are introduced.

- Appendix A contains citations of research reports in both print and electronic form for additional practice in evaluating research or for use in in- and out-of-class assignments.

- The text is intended to provide teachers with the knowledge and skills to act as teacher-researchers and to create classroom-based research projects and syntheses of research.

Acknowledgments

No book is published without the support, input, and assistance of others, and we continue to be indebted for the help and assistance of many people. We appreciate the encouragement and support of many of our colleagues at CUNY/Queens College, especially those who have used the previous editions and have provided us with invaluable insights for this revision. We appreciate the comments and critiques of our students and have incorporated many of their ideas in this revision. We also thank our colleagues at Metis Associates, Inc., New York, for their support.

We are again fortunate for the opportunity to have had Suzanne Li's assistance in the preparation of chapter 11. She provided extensive knowledge and insight about both traditional and electronic searches of library resources, as well as numerous recommendations for revising and modifying the chapter's content.

We are extremely pleased that Margo Hittleman shared with us her knowledge and insights about research perspectives and qualitative research methods and methodology. She focused our attention on key issues related to understanding and interpreting qualitative studies and critically examined our interpretations with a caring mind. The final form of those ideas, however, is ours, and we lovingly take responsibility for any possible misinterpretations.

We appreciate the constructive comments and reviews by Lamont Flowers, University of Florida; Teresa Cabal Krastel, University of Maryland; Denise Smith, Indiana University at South Bend; Ronald Weiss, Minnesota State University at Mankato; and Klaus A. Witz, University of Illinois. We have given extensive consideration to their concerns and questions and have incorporated many of them in the revision. We also have kept in mind comments and reviews of previous editions by Maurice R. Berube, Old Dominion University; J. Kent Davis, Purdue University; Thomas D. Dertinger, University of Richmond; Karen Ford, Ball State University; Joe L. Green, Texas Tech University, Anthony Manzo, University of Missouri, Kansas City; and Thomas J. Sheerman, Niagara University. However, we ultimately take responsibility for the interpretations and perspectives about research presented in the text. We also are extremely grateful for the help and assistance of Kevin Davis, Margaret Wright, Mary Harlan, and Kathy Termeer at Merrill/Prentice Hall, and Amanda Hosey at Thistle Hill Publishing Services.

Brief Contents

Contents

Chapter 3   **READING AND EVALUATING RESEARCH REPORTS**   **75**

PART II   **UNDERSTANDING THE RESEARCH REPORT**

Chapter 4   **READING AND EVALUATING INTRODUCTORY SECTIONS: ABSTRACT, BACKGROUND, AND PURPOSE**   **89**

Chapter 5   **READING AND EVALUATING SUBJECT/PARTICIPANT SECTIONS**   **100**

Chapter 8   **READING AND INTERPRETING QUALITATIVE
PROCEDURE AND FINDINGS SECTIONS**   **183**

Chapter 9   **READING AND EVALUATING DISCUSSION SECTIONS**   **199**

Chapter 10   **READING AND INTERPRETING REVIEWS OF RESEARCH**   **208**

PART III   UNDERSTANDING HOW TO FIND RESEARCH REPORTS

Chapter 11   LOCATING INFORMATION ABOUT RESEARCH REPORTS   267

Figures and Tables

Figures

Tables

Note: Every effort has been made to provide accurate & current Internet information in this book. However, the Internet & information posted on it are constantly changing, so it is inevitable that some of the Internet addresses listed in the textbook will change.

The Research Process

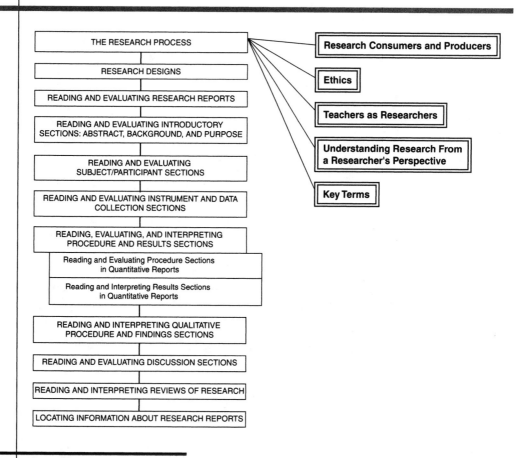

FOCUS QUESTIONS

1. Why do educators conduct research?
2. What is the distinction between research *consumers* and research *producers*?
3. What is research, from a researcher's perspective?

Teachers continually make decisions about instruction, such as curriculum, teaching techniques, classroom management, and assessment of student learning. They base these decisions on their experiences, other teachers' experiences, and their understanding of accumulated knowledge about education. Teachers' instructional decisions are also influenced by the social, cultural, historical, and political factors common in their schools; that is, by the prevailing ideas about how to help children learn, and the kinds of instruction favored by school boards, administrators, and parents. Further, their decisions are influenced by the availability of funding from federal and state agencies.

Much of the knowledge about teaching and learning comes from educational researchers who seek answers to educational questions or who try to clarify some existing educational issue. One sign of a "productive" profession, such as education, is the systematic attempt by its researchers and practitioners to examine the knowledge base upon which the profession functions. For the purposes of this book, the systematic attempt to examine a knowledge base is called *scientific research.*

For us, **scientific research** is an investigative activity that makes possible (*a*) the discovery that our world is (or is not) organized as our preconceptions lead us to expect and (*b*) the suggestion of theoretical means of understanding our world. Scientific research documents both the investigative processes and conclusions arising from them in sufficient detail for other interested parties to be able to evaluate the information and interpretations offered (Greenwood & Levin, 2000, p. 68). Specifically, **research** is the systematic attempt not only to collect information about an identified problem or question, but also to analyze that information and to apply the evidence thus derived to confirm or refute some prior prediction or statement about that problem. Like research in any other field, educational research is the application of generally accepted systematic procedures. Akin to educational research is *educational evaluation,* the use of research techniques to judge the effectiveness of existing in-place programs of instruction. In this book, educational evaluation will be considered a subarea of educational research.

Six characteristics are common to professions whose members research its knowledge base.

1. Professionals work at verifying ideas and practices believed to be effective. Often, teachers read about a "new" teaching technique in a professional journal and say, "We've known that all along!" But teachers cannot rely entirely on a common-sense approach; intuition needs to be supported and substantiated through research (Berliner, 1987).

2. Professionals work at discovering new ideas and practices. The need for research-derived new ideas and practices is almost self-evident. For example, consider the idea of reciprocal teaching, which has been extensively researched and is now common in schools. The application of reciprocal teaching features guided practice in applying learning strategies (Rosenshine & Meister, 1994).

3. Professionals clarify ideas that are designed to simplify teaching. Take, for example, the illustration of research results about cooperative learning procedures when they are applied to problem solving in various subject areas (Qin, Johnson, & Johnson, 1995).

4. Although professional educators try to simplify teaching, they often express ideas that may complicate everyone's teaching. An example of this effect is the body of research findings indicating how the learning of many students with disabling conditions is improved in mainstream classes as opposed to self-contained classes (Leinhardt & Pallay, 1982; Madden & Slavin, 1983).

5. Professionals discover ideas and practices that are counterintuitive. For example, many educators assume that grouping in self-contained classes according to students' ability permits students to work more effectively with peers and to have instruction adapted to their performance level. Regarding mastery learning, however, research evidence does not seem to support this contention. Instead,

research shows that students may achieve more when they are in classes of mixed ability for most of the day. Cross-grade assignments also may increase students' achievement. Limited grouping of students at the same level seems effective only when that strategy is employed for specific skill instruction (Slavin, 1987a, 1987b).

6. Professionals engage in a collective activity carried out by members of research teams within a larger scientific community. The larger community provides the literature on which the research is built to some degree, as well as the resources used to carry out the research. Research teams are complex, dynamic social systems of people acting on phenomena. Such teams share their thoughts within the pragmatic limitations set by the availability of key resources and the dynamics of the human relationships involved. Scientific research is more than just being objective and rigorous, using statistical tests, and using experimental controls (Greenwood & Levin, 1998).

All good researchers attempt to be systematic, rigorous, and account for personal biases in the conclusions they reach. At the same time, research is a collective activity that is carried out within the complex politics of the social world. Researchers work with finite energies and budgets. Their educational training has emphasized certain approaches to research over others. The particular educational institutions in which they work (and the colleagues whose respect they want to earn) value some kinds of research more than others. Their research projects are often paid for by someone (often, by the government or large corporations). These entities influence the topics and methods of research based in part on intellectual concerns and in part on political and social priorities. Researchers' background, life experiences, and personality all contribute to their worldview, and thus, to their beliefs and assumptions about what we can know about the world, how, and to what end. These factors influence all parts of the research process—from the problem to be considered and the questions that are asked, to the research designs that are chosen and the way data are analyzed and interpreted.

RESEARCH CONSUMERS AND PRODUCERS

This book is intended for research consumers—the people who read, interpret, and apply the information systematically collected and examined (researched) by others. Like research producers, research consumers are interested in answering educationally related questions; however, they do so by reading and applying research producers' results, rather than by conducting research themselves.

Research consumers need to read research with a mindset *similar* to that of research producers—similar, but not the same. Research producers need certain skills to put different phases of educational research into operation. They need technical competence in applying research strategies. Research consumers, on the other hand, need to understand decisions facing research producers, possible alternatives the researchers may consider at those decision points, and the implications of researchers' results and conclusions. Also, consumers need a means of judging the adequacy of research producers' work.

We believe a research consumer can more fully understand educational research by reading research as a research producer does. The research consumer can read research by reconstructing the researcher's message and by constructing a meaning from the information on the page—much as students reconstruct a message during an instructional session and then construct its meaning for themselves. The reader may create meanings different from those intended by the writer (as may a listener, in response to a speaker). Research consumers reach understanding by reconstructing the ideas of research producers as well as by constructing meanings of their own. A consumer's understanding is constructed from that person's prior knowledge and prior experiences, combined with that person's maturity and his or her proficiency in manipulating research ideas.

ETHICS

Research consumers need to understand the ethical standards by which research producers should be guided in their activities. The American Educational Research Association (AERA) and the American Evaluation Association (AEA) have adopted sets of ethical standards for conducting educational research and evaluation. Although research producers' compliance with these standards is voluntary, researcher consumers should be aware of the existence and content of standards. The standards of both associations are found in Appendix B.

TEACHERS AS RESEARCHERS

The concept of teachers as researchers is not new, but we are now more aware of how important it is for classroom teachers to collaborate with research producers and to produce research themselves about their lives in classrooms (Bissex, 1994; Burton, 1991; Burton & Seidl, 2003; Donoahue, Van Tassell, & Patterson, 1996; Erickson, 1986; Goodson, 1993; B. Johnson, 1993; R. W. Johnson, 1993, McFarland & Stansell, 1993; Olson, 1990; Santa, 1988; VanDeWeghe, 1992). This text is not intended to create research producers. Even so, the concept presented here of "understanding research as a researcher does," and the ideas about research methods and research evaluation presented in subsequent chapters, will provide teachers with the background knowledge and understanding they need to participate in such research projects.

Teachers need to assume the responsibility of examining their own practices (Erickson, 1986; Patterson & Shannon, 1993). Teachers need to question what they and their colleagues know about teaching and students, and they need to see the meaning and sense that each student brings to a learning situation (Ballenger & Rosebery, 2003). Because teachers are increasingly being held responsible for what and how they teach, they need to take leadership in determining what insights about learning and teaching should be systematically applied in classrooms. It is especially important that classroom teachers collaborate with researchers when changes in curriculum and instructional procedures are being evaluated. Curriculum and instructional leadership should not be expected to come solely from university research centers and state and federal agencies. Instead, teachers must participate in research that will significantly affect what happens in the classroom. Through the teacher-researcher experience, individuals can serve the larger educational community as well as their own classrooms by engaging in the examination of the challenges and instructional questions that are part of the demanding context of the classroom (Burton & Seidl, 2003).

Collaborating in this research

(1) reduces the gap between research findings and classroom practice, (2) creates a problem solving mindset that helps teachers when they consider other classroom

dilemmas, (3) improves teachers' instructional decision making processes, (4) increases the professional status of teachers, (5) helps empower teachers to influence their own profession at classroom, district, state, and national levels, and (6) offers the overriding and ultimate advantage of providing the potential for improving the educational process for children. (Olson, 1990, pp. 17–18)

Teacher-researcher studies are attempts to explain and understand the experiences of teachers and students as such events are enacted in actual classrooms. For example, in a study describing the evolution of research questions among elementary- and secondary-school teachers (Baumann, Allen, & Shockley, 1994), teachers posed initial questions about the following classroom-related concerns: motivation, interests, and attitudes; home-school-community links; content reading and learning from text, or functional literacy; assessment; technology; linguistic, racial, and cultural diversity; and instructional strategies and interventions.

*Classroom
Conditions*

Inquiry, reflection, and action characterize the work of teacher-researchers (Burton, 1991; Patterson & Shannon, 1993). *Inquiry* is the purposeful observation of all aspects of classroom life. *Reflection* is the systematic attempt to understand the multiple layers of meaning of what happens in classrooms. *Action* is the altering of classroom practice as a result of the "new" classroom life. These might even be considered a "re-searching" experience (Burton, 1991, p. 230) in that they are not used to create educational laws, but to reexamine the often hidden dynamics of teaching and learning, look at them in a new light, and take an instructional stance based on what is seen.

UNDERSTANDING RESEARCH FROM A RESEARCHER'S PERSPECTIVE

Educational research producers approach the systematic study of school-related matters from different perspectives. A basic principle of all educational research is that it begins with one or more important questions or focuses of study; then methods and procedures are selected to match the questions (Gall, Gall, & Borg, 2002). Broadly, there are two dominant perspectives that influence the approaches taken by educational researchers: **positivism** and **constructivism.** What we are discussing are the beliefs researchers have about the world. Those beliefs influence the type of research they choose to do and the methodology of their research. Whatever perspective researchers take, the search for and reporting of so-called facts are always intertwined with ideological and political choices. So, as these perspectives are considered, educators should keep in mind:

a. Science has emotional, political, and cognitive elements.
b. Scientific knowledge is not objective or neutral.
c. All theoretical positions have unconscious assumptions about the world and are based on the assumption that scientists know what the world is like.
d. Language is never neutral.
e. In modern science there are conflicting assumptions underlying people's reasoning.
f. It is not important to argue the superiority of any particular theoretical position, but to consider multiple perspectives and their underlying assumptions (Kuhn, 1970, as cited in Giangreco & Taylor, 2003, p. 133).

Positivism and constructivism are differing perspectives of the world. What we present here are general explanations of these perspectives. Within each of them, there are differing understandings. Also there are other positions besides these about the nature of the world and reality.

Positivism

Researchers with a positivist perspective look at knowledge as an awareness of objects that are independent of any subject (Fieser & Dowden, 2004; Sauvage, 2003; Trochim, 2001). According to this view, objects and events have intrinsic meaning, and knowledge is an explanation of an association with what is real. A statement is meaningful to positivists if it can be shown to be supported by means of the experience; this rule is considered the verifiability principle. Positivists consider a statement as supportable only when the conditions under which the statement is verified is known. In this way, knowledge should represent a real world that is thought of as existing (that is, separate and independent of the researcher). This knowledge should be considered true only if research results accurately explain that independent world. The understanding gained from research is from information outside the researcher; that is, meaning is determined by the structure of the research event and not by the researcher. Positivists can be sure that the meaning of a question is clear when they are able to exactly describe the conditions within which it is possible to answer "Yes," or the conditions in which it is necessary to answer "No." A question's meaning is defined only through the detailing of those conditions. Positivists generally require empirical evidence to determine the answer to their questions.

Constructivism

Researchers with a constructivist perspective argue that knowledge and reality do not have an objective or absolute meaning (Abdal-Haqq, 1998; Applefield, Huber, & Moallem, 2000–2001; Brooks & Brooks, 1999; McBrien & Brandt, 1997.) Knowledge is constructed, not reproduced. Goals and objectives of a research project are derived by the participants in negotiation with the researcher. To constructivists, an individual interprets and constructs a reality based on his or her experiences and interactions with the environment. Rather than thinking of what is true in terms of being equal with the so-called real world, constructivists have the idea that things and events vary. The environment, context, and research activities represent the natural complexities of the real world. Ideas and theories are feasible only if they appear adequate in the contexts in which they were created. Further, multiple perspectives and representations of ideas and events are presented and encouraged. The participants have a central role in the design and implementation of the research project. Activities, events, and information are provided by researchers to encourage self-analysis, self-regulation, self-reflection, and self-awareness by themselves and the participants. Constructivists generally use nonempirical (qualitative) evidence to answer their questions.

The terms *constructivism* and *social constructivism* refer to two related perspectives. The term *constructivism* is used in two senses: the first and more general sense embraces the perspective that our understanding of reality is not a one-for-one representation of what is "out there," but rather the result of both individual and social processes (mediated by way of language) that alter, select, and transform our experience. In this sense, *constructivism* is an "umbrella" term that includes a broad spectrum of positions. The second and more restrictive sense of *constructivism* refers to the notion that individual persons or intelligent agents actively fashion or interpret their experience via various processes. Here the emphasis is on the personal and agentive aspects of experience as constructed. *Social constructivism* designates the understanding that human beings are born into a social world and from earliest moments live their lives inextricably bound to the social matrix, most especially by language, which serves as an a priori interpretative framework for experience. Thus, social life has a (preponderantly) determinant role not only in establishing what experience an individual will have, but also in how that experience will be interpreted (Hevern, 2003).

These differing perspectives (about how researchers can create knowledge) influence the way in which research producers conceptualize, develop, implement, and report their research. To illustrate the process, the following sections show the ways in which research teams with differing theoretical perspectives might develop projects. Although the process is presented linearly for illustrative purposes, it is important to remember that the process actually does not often unfold in such a clear sequence, especially for researchers with a constructivist perspective. The researchers may start and stop several times, reject questions and possible solutions, and encounter many pitfalls. Table 1.1 contains a summary of these ideas.

The Researchers Select a Problem Area and Specify Research Questions.   First our hypothetical research teams select a problem area for study from personal experience, professional readings, historical trends, current policy deliberations at the local, state, or federal level, possible funding availability, or discussions with colleagues. For example, thoughts arise about the writing performance of middle-school students who are learning disabled. (The differing and often confusing definitions of *learning disability* will be disregarded here.) These thoughts flow from an array of concerns, many based on the theoretical perspectives previously discussed. A few of these ideas follow.

First, many students with learning disabilities are included in regular classes for particular academic studies. Second, writing skill has increasingly become an issue in the teaching and learning of content areas other than language or communication arts. Third, different writing skills may be needed in different content areas (e.g., science, social studies, mathematics, or technology).

Researchers with a positivist position might be concerned about the use of the resolutions of these issues. These "use" concerns lead to other questions. Are the answers to be applied only to the students in one specific school, grade level, or class? Are the answers to be used for the students in an entire district, state, region, or nation? Should the writing skills of students with learning disabilities be compared with that of students who do not have such disabilities? Positivists' next set of concerns deals with the teaching and learning of writing. The researchers wish to know the following: What is the writing performance of students with learning disabilities? How does it compare with that of students without disabilities? What can be done to help students with disabilities write effectively in content areas? Of equal importance to researchers is whether these questions are interrelated (or, can any one of them be answered without answering the others?).

The question "Why do students with learning disabilities write the way they do?" is also of concern. However, seeking answers to that query moves the researcher away from the primary concern of instruction.

Table 1.1

Positivist and Constructivist Approaches to Research

Aspect of Research	Positivist Approach to Research	Approaches Common to Both Positivist and Constructivist Research	Constructivist Approach to Research
Identify Perspective of Research	• Information exists to be found and verified • Meaning is inherent within the situation being researched • Generally requires empirical evidence	• Approaches exist on a continuum of perspectives	• Understanding and meaning results from multiple interpretations of information • Knowledge is constructed, not reproduced • Goals derived in negotiation with participants • Generally uses nonempirical, qualitative evidence
Select Problem	• Develop questions prior to study	• The selection comes from personal experience, professional readings, historical trends, current policy deliberations at local, state, or federal level, possible funding availability, or discussions with colleagues	• Might be concerned about use of findings, or about social conceptions of students' performance, What is "disability"? • Concern with matters of process • Develop additional questions during study
Search Research Literature	• Use literature to relate the study to larger, ongoing dialogue among researchers about the chosen topic	• Gain insights from professional journals, books, educational encyclopedias, and electronic databases about other researchers' findings and conclusions	• Literature primarily used for establishing theoretical framework for research • Used at end to help interpret and give meaning to findings
Formulate Questions	• Keep questions the same throughout study	• Decide which questions to answer	• Poses more general, open-ended questions • May refine research questions during study
Select Research Designs and Methods	• Include common aspects of studies, which include efforts to determine methods such as (*a*) where and when research is to occur—the setting or location, (*b*) with whom specifically research will be done—subjects or participants, (*c*) with what device students' characteristics and their writing will be assessed—instruments or data collection devices, and (*d*) how to analyze the information		• Considers several possible designs: observing, interviewing, analyzing documents • May use "participant observation" • Repeating cycles of observation; also reflection and action are used by action-oriented researchers

Table 1.1
Continued

Aspect of Research	Positivist Approach to Research	Approaches Common to Both Positivist and Constructivist Research	Constructivist Approach to Research
Select Subjects or Participants	• Use randomly selected subjects • Include subjects with and without a specific characteristic	• Include subjects within school or district, with wide variety of teacher and student demographics and performances	• Selects participants through interviews • Participants representative of a wide range of diversity and skills
Select Tests	• Use standardized tests and/or evaluation systems • Produce data in numerical form		• Analyzes data in nonnumeric form • Uses inductive procedures to examine process
Conduct Study	• Proceed to answer questions in linear fashion • No changes made to design during study • No analysis made during study		• Cycles back and forth between data collection and analysis • Includes discussions with colleagues and participants • Constant reflecting and interpreting data during study • Creating tentative explanations and interpretations, which are revised as study progresses
Analyze Data	• Analyze data after study concludes in statistical or nonstatistical manner		• Analyze data during study (see "Conduct Study" section)
Report Results	• Reports and publication manuscripts prepared in formalized manner	• Produce written reports, submit report for publication, and/or report findings at conferences	• Reports and publication manuscripts prepared in less formal manner

Researchers conducting their work from a constructivist paradigm are also concerned about many of these same issues. However, our hypothetical constructivist researchers are also concerned with *social conceptions* of "disability" performance. These concerns lead to questions such as how teachers, parents, and even the students' differing views about "learning disabilities" affect student writing performance and impact efforts to help students write more effectively. Further, in asking "What is the writing performance of students with learning disabilities?" they are likely to mean, *how* do these students construct that performance? That is, what is the *process* by which LD students approach writing tasks? How do they conceptualize that process? Does the process differ for students without disabilities? If so, how?

Some constructivists are more concerned with *action*. They, together with a local professor of education, may be more concerned with practical educational problems of teaching and learning. The issue of how to improve the writing performance of students with disabilities in inclusion classrooms is of foremost concern to them. They want to understand and improve upon pedagogical practices in their own classrooms. However, they are also interested in learning about things that may help other middle-school teachers in situations similar to theirs.

Other constructivist researchers bring still other concerns. For example, researchers working from critical or feminist paradigms are concerned with issues of social relationships and power; that is, questions of who is labeled as "learning disabled" and why. They ask questions like How have these definitions changed throughout history? Whose interests do such definitions serve? How do conceptions of "learning disability" intersect with social positions such as race and class? How are schools and classrooms organized as social systems? To a critical research team, these concerns are crucially relevant to the understanding of writing performance and effective instruction. For the feminist researchers, questions of gender within cultures loom central. They wish to know how girls' experiences, perceptions, and performance differ from that of boys. They ask whether what constitutes as effective instruction will differ depending on the gender of the students. They may also want to look at how differing social expectations about girls' and boys' intelligence, school performance, behavior, and so forth, impact writing performance and instructional strategies.

Like the other researchers, constructivist researchers are also concerned about the use of the "answers." Of course, our positivist (and most of our constructivist researchers) might argue that their job is merely to do good research and that it is up to educational policy makers to determine the ways in which those results translate into public policy. But additionally, these researchers see themselves as having an advocacy role, intentionally hoping their research will change social norms and, in particular, help promote greater equality and justice for groups historically marginalized or oppressed. These concerns also "factor in" to the questions they want to answer.

The Researchers Examine and Search Journals, Books, and Databases to Review Existing Research Results and Define Terms.   All researchers try to find out what other researchers have already done to answer these or similar questions. By consulting professional journals, books, educational encyclopedias, and electronic databases, researchers gain insight about what other researchers have found and what conclusions have already been drawn. This literature review helps them to relate their study to the larger ongoing dialogue among researchers about their chosen topic. They discover the gaps in existing knowledge, identify ways to extend prior work, or develop a framework for establishing the significance of their study.

Although research teams look at how a wide range of other researchers have studied a selected problem, they will pay particular attention to how the problem has been studied by those who share their paradigmatic perspectives.

After reviewing the material from these sources, our positivist researchers conclude that the meaning of certain terms requires clarification. For example, they realize that several terms are defined differently by different researchers: *learning disability, language arts, communication arts, content-area classes, writing, composing, mainstreaming,* and *regular education.* The researchers select an accepted definition or create a new one to enhance communication with other researchers and users of the research.

Our constructivist researchers want to help other researchers and practitioners gain a deeper, more robust understanding of the teaching and learning *processes* related to students' writing performance. After reviewing the literature, they conclude that most previous studies have been conducted within a positivist inquiry paradigm. While those studies have looked at specific variables that may affect writing performance, these researchers find few studies that adequately portray the dynamic interaction of the many factors involved in a complex *process* like writing. They also may note that other researchers have predominantly studied the performance of boys with learning disabilities, with limited consideration as to whether girls' writing performance is similar or different.

Because our action researchers want to improve their own practice, in addition to reading research studies, they look for articles in professional journals about interventions that other teachers have tried. Because several members of this hypothetical team are new to research, they also read about how other teacher-researchers have studied classroom practice, looking for ideas that might be applicable to their own work.

The Researchers Formulate Researchable Questions.   Now the positivist researchers return to the questions about the teaching and learning of writing. A decision must be made about answering one or more of these queries. They decide to answer three questions and must now determine whether those questions need to be answered in a specific order. The answer is yes, because the answer to the question "What can be done to help students with learning disabilities write effectively in the content areas?" presupposes answers to the others. So, the researchers decide to first answer the questions "What is the writing performance of students with learning disabilities?" and "How does that performance compare with the performance of students without learning disabilities?" (This last question is of major concern, because the researchers wish to examine the writing of students with learning disabilities in mainstream classes.)

The constructivist researchers decide to answer the same three questions. However, they pose them in a more general, open-ended way, without defining specific hypotheses or predictions. They know that their research questions will be refined—and new research questions may emerge—during the course of their study. They, too, decide to focus first on the process by which students with disabilities approach writing tasks, because that answer will inform the study of effective interventions. They also generate a series of subquestions: What can be observed about how students with disabilities approach writing tasks? How do the students themselves characterize their writing processes? How do these processes relate to actual writing performance? How do these processes and outcomes compare to those of students without disabilities? As the members of this team also see themselves as gender-concerned researchers, they add two additional questions: How are these processes and outcomes similar or different for girls and boys? How do the students' approaches to writing and self-characterizations of their writing processes relate to gendered social expectations?

Our action-oriented researchers begin with a very general question. They choose the issue of central concern: How can we improve the writing performance of students with disabilities in mainstreamed classrooms? Do effective strategies for improving writing performance differ between students with and without learning disabilities? Based on their reading, they develop some further questions about whether and how specific instructional interventions will help improve student writing performance. Too, they know that their questions will evolve considerably—and may even change completely—as their study progresses.

The Researchers Select Research Designs and Methods.   Our positivist researchers now have three possible studies. (It is possible for the researchers to conduct these three studies as one; but in our discussion, the three different research plans are separate.) For each, they need a different research plan, or design. **Research designs** are methods for answering questions. Just as skilled craftspeople and artisans have several methods for manipulating their raw material, so do researchers. Some research designs are more appropriate or effective for answering certain questions. Also, more than one plan may be appropriate or effective for answering a particular question.

In the first possible study, our hypothetical positivist researchers want to describe the writing performance of students with learning disabilities. The description is to be in statistical and in nonstatistical form (see **quantitative research, qualitative research,** and **statistics** in the Glossary). They decide on several activities. They decide to describe the students' processes for beginning a writing task, their topics and organization of ideas, the maturity of their vocabulary and sentence structure, the grammatical form of their works, and the physical aspects of their writing.

To compare (in a second possible study) the writing of students with learning disabilities with that of students who do not have such disabilities, the researchers will collect the same data from both groups. They plan a statistical and nonstatistical comparison of the two types of students.

They consider the third possible study, "What can be done to help students with learning disabilities write effectively in the content areas?" The researchers decide to set up one or more instructional programs and look at them singly, and in combination, to see which has the greatest effect (or any effect) on the writing performance of these students.

For our positivist researchers, the three studies have both common and unique aspects. The common aspects include efforts the researchers must make to determine the methods they will use. That is, they consider (*a*) where and when the research is to occur—the setting or location, (*b*) with whom specifically the research will be done—the subjects or participants, (*c*) with what assessment device the students' characteristics and their writing will be evaluated—instruments or data collection devices, and (*d*) how they will analyze the information they collected (see **data** in the Glossary).

In selecting a location, the positivist researchers think about conducting the studies in a special site, such as a college educational clinic or a middle-school classroom. Both sites have advantages and disadvantages. An educational clinic allows the researchers better control of the data collection environment and the opportunity to make unobtrusive observations and recordings. However, the setting is not educationally natural, because the students need to be brought to it under special circumstances. A classroom allows the researchers to observe and collect data in the setting where the students usually learn and work. However, a classroom has distractions that might influence the data collection and the students' performances in ways the researchers may not recognize. After weighing the pros and cons, the researchers decide to conduct all three studies in middle-school classrooms, fully aware that they must make some effort to reduce or eliminate the possible influence of certain distractions.

Our constructivist researchers also have a number of different ways to approach these studies. They consider several possible research designs and discuss whether to emphasize observation, interviewing, and analyzing documents, such as portfolios of student writing. To collect several different kinds of data to compare, they decide to include a combination of these approaches in their research. They decide to begin with **participant observation,** working in the classroom, observing how students go about their work, taking notes on what they see, and writing memos to themselves on what they think these observations mean. The team will begin to talk with and question students, to learn about the students' thought processes as they write. They will also gather documents, such as samples of the students' writing and teachers' assessments of those students' performance, in order to analyze them. To answer the comparison questions, they will gather this information about boys and girls with and without disabilities. For the third study, they will consider one or more instructional programs and use similar methods to see how the interventions change students' writing processes, conceptions about writing, and performance. However, just as they expected their research questions to develop throughout the study, so also do they know that their design will evolve as insights arise that seem worth exploring further.

The action-oriented research team chooses a design based on repeating cycles of observation, reflection, and action. A college professor may serve as a consultant for this team, helping them think through the implications of different research designs and providing them with information about methods that may be unfamiliar. They talk about whether to take a more statistical approach like the positivist team, or an approach more like that of the constructivists. They decide the latter is more consistent with their beliefs and the kinds of information they want to gather. They decide to begin with a period of observation and reflection, then choose specific actions (e.g., interventions) to try. So they, too, will combine observation and note taking, questioning students about their thought processes, and collecting students' writing portfolios to analyze. They also decide to keep personal journals and to engage in some structured autobiographical writing to capture and reflect on their own experiences, beliefs, and feelings. Finally, they may ask the college professor/consultant to help by videotaping classroom interactions for later analysis. This group of teacher-researchers will meet monthly, over the course of the year, to share with each other the information they are collecting and producing and to discuss what they are learning. Transcribed recordings of their discussions will give them additional material that they can refer to later as they formulate answers to their questions.

The Researchers Describe and Select the Students and Participants to Be Part of the Study.   All our researchers are interested in doing the study with middle-school students in an urban center. The positivist team uses the nearby middle school affiliated with a college because its total student population reflects the range of ability and performance test scores and demographic characteristics of the region as whole. They include all students classified as *learning disabled* in grades five through eight, in mainstreamed, inclusion, and self-contained classes. They also want to collect data about the writing performance of students who do not have learning disabilities. However because it is impractical to collect data about the several hundred students in the middle school, they decide to *randomly* select, at each grade level, a portion of the students without learning diabilities.

The researchers must describe the students for others, so they collect relevant data normally found in students' permanent records—information such as age, sex, grade level, educational history, and attendance.

The constructivist team also likes the middle school near their college because it is typical of many other schools on a variety of demographic and performance measures. Further, other educational researchers from their college have worked with some teachers in this school before, and these teachers recall those experiences positively. This history will help the researchers build the trusted relationships they need to carry out this work. Because of the in-depth data that this team will be collecting, they use a set of initial interviews to choose a small number of teachers and students to participate. To help them explore the issues they want to understand, they choose a small group of about a dozen students, pupils who are representative of the diversity of students in the school, including both boys and girls, with a range of writing skills; half have learning disabilities, half do not.

Our action researchers, of course, will carry out their research within the middle-school classrooms, too. The teachers will gather some information about all of the students in their class, but they will pay particular attention to a small subset of students (half with learning disabilities), selected to ensure that the group includes students with a range of writing abilities.

All the researchers must now get approval from the school administrators. They must also submit a description of their research plans to the university's institutional review board (which oversees the ethics of any research involving "human subjects,") and receive approval. Finally, they must also get written consent from the parents of all the students, as well as from any other teachers involved in the study.

The Researchers Select Devices to Evaluate the Students' Performance.   All researchers also begin to document the students' writing performance. To do this documentation, samples of the students' writing in content-area classes are obtained and scored or analyzed by some accepted system (e.g., a rubric). The positivist researchers have the option of using one or more standardized achievement tests or scoring system (such as holistic scoring and rubrics) to measure students' writing performance. Or, they may analyze the students' compositions by nonnumeric analysis. Some constructivists use these devices to collect information about students' writing, while others use a variety of other procedures that allow them to examine how students compose their work, or to identify features that may be involved with students' composings.

The Researchers Conduct the Study.   The positivist researchers now have enough information to answer the first question, "What is the writing performance of students with learning disabilities?" To answer the second question, "How does that performance compare with the performance of students without learning disabilities?" the researchers collect the same data about students who do not have learning disabilities. Because it is impractical to collect data about all such students in the middle school, the researchers decide to randomly select a portion at each grade level of the students without learning disabilities.

As the positivist researchers proceed, another question arises. The researchers want to know "Are teachers using any instructional strategies and techniques that seem to enhance the learning of students who are learning disabled?" To answer this question, they set up a series of classroom observations and teacher interviews. They wish to determine possible answers to this question by collecting information about what occurs in classrooms while teaching and learning are happening. As they collect this information, they sort it and seek out patterns of teacher-learner interactions.

To answer their last question, "What can be done to help students with learning disabilities write effectively in the content areas?" the posivitist researchers select and prepare instructional activities and collect additional data. Using the information gleaned from other research, from professional sources, and from their classroom observations and teacher interviews, the researchers create or select three instructional programs that have shown promise for teaching students who are learning disabled. The researchers' question now becomes "Which of these instructional programs help the students who are learning disabled to write effectively in content-area classes?" or "Which of the programs cause the students to write effectively?" The researchers decide how long (for how many days, weeks, or months) the instructional program will last and who will do the actual teaching. They plan to have all content-area teachers in the middle school participate in a special 8-week after-school workshop about implementing one of the instructional programs. The teachers are to use the techniques for the 12 weeks following the workshop.

Additional data about students' writing performance are collected during and after the instructional programs. The researchers now conduct the studies.

The constructivist research team cycles back and forth many times between data collection and analysis. They read through the rapidly growing number of pages of narrative many times. A computer software program designed for this purpose may be used to help them label different sections of these texts and look for recurring themes. They periodically talk to the classroom teachers, as well as to their academic colleagues, sharing the interpretations and conclusions they are generating and asking for feedback. Do their interpretations make sense to others? Do the classroom teachers have similar or different interpretations for their tentative research findings? They also explore with each other—through writing and discussion—the ways that their own life experiences and beliefs may be related to the interpretations they are making. They will continue this process of data collection and analysis for many months, until they decide that further observations and interviews are not yielding many new insights.

The action researchers begin by writing autobiographical statements describing their own learning experiences, how they came to become teachers, and their own views about learning disabilities. They also begin to collect notes on what they observe in their classroom. At their monthly meetings, they share their writing, talk about what they are seeing, and decide what they think it means. Further, they look for recurring themes and new interpretations.

After several months, they reach some tentative conclusions and choose a particular instructional approach that they think will address some of the parts of the writing process giving the students trouble. They decide to try using the approach in their classrooms for the next several months, continuing to observe, question students, keep notes, and assess writing portfolios. As they come together each month, they share what they are learning. They talk about ways to adapt their instructional approach so that it might be even more effective. Then they return to their classroom to put their new plan into action and continue their observations. They find this process of continued reflection-on-action and regularly scheduled dialogue with colleagues to be so helpful, that they decide they want to continue it in some form throughout their teaching careers. But meanwhile, once they have completed their agreed-upon 18 months of work, they conclude that they have enough information to report on what they have found.

The Researchers Analyze the Data and Determine Implications of the Research.
Our positivist researchers, after conducting the study and collecting the data, analyze
the data using appropriate statistical (quantitative) and nonstatistical (qualitative)
methods. Then, they determine what implications the results have for other researchers and teachers.

The Researchers Publish Their Results.   After conducting their research, the teams
produce written reports. In those reports, all of our researchers describe their reasons
for conducting the study, how it relates to previous research that they read about in
the literature, the steps they took to select the students and teachers studied, how
they went about collecting and analyzing information, what they found, and the
conclusions they reached.

The research teams meet to talk about who will get these reports. Both the
positivist and constructivist researchers plan to submit their report in the form of
a research article to a prestigious academic educational journal; they talk about
the various options and choose journals that have published research similar to
theirs in the past. The positivist research team, however, may present their information in a more prescribed manner than the constructivist team, including specific sections dealing with (*a*) their reason for conducting the study; (*b*) the
conclusions they and others have made about previous research; (*c*) the steps they
took to select the students, the writing scoring procedure, and the instructional activities; (*d*) the in-service workshop, the instructional programs, and the way the
programs were used in the content-area classes; and (*e*) the statistical and nonstatistical results.

They will also present this same article at an upcoming educational research conference. Our action research team, in addition to preparing an article to submit to an
academic journal, also wants to prepare a written report for their own school administrators. Further, they decide to hold an evening presentation about their research to which they will invite school administrators, school board members, and
the parents of students with learning disabilities. Finally, they prepare a presentation
for an upcoming professional conference.

KEY TERMS

Most key research terms are defined as they occur in this book. They are identified
by being highlighted in bold print. The Glossary contains all key terms discussed in
this book. Additional information about these and other key terms is given elsewhere
in the book. Key locations where these terms are explained are found through the
Subject Index.

OVERVIEW

The ideas in this book are organized to reflect the phases of research as research
producers would go through them. In Table 1.2, the phases of research undertaken by the research team in the example are linked to the information in later
chapters.

Table 1.2

Overview of the Research Process and Location in This Text

The Research Team's Activity	Phase of Research and Location of Information within This Text
The researchers formulate researchable questions.	• "The Research Process," chapter 1 • "Reading and Evaluating Introductory Sections: Abstracts, Background, and Purpose," chapter 4 • "Locating Information about Research Reports," chapter 11
The researchers select research designs and methods.	• "The Research Process," chapter 1 • "Research Designs," chapter 2
The researchers describe and select the students and participants to be included in the study.	• "Reading and Evaluating Subject/Participant Sections," chapter 5
The researchers select devices to score the students' performance.	• "Reading and Evaluating Instruction and Data Collection Sections," chapter 6
The researchers conduct the study.	• "Reading and Evaluating Procedure Sections in Quantitative Reports," chapter 7, section I • "Reading and Interpreting Qualitative Procedure and Findings Sections," chapter 8
The researchers analyze the data and determine implications of the research.	• "Reading and Interpreting Results Sections in Quantitative Reports," chapter 7, section II • "Reading and Interpreting Qualitative Procedure and Findings Sections," chapter 8
The researchers report or publish their results.	• "Reading and Evaluating Research Reports," chapter 3 • "Reading and Interpreting Reviews of Research," chapter 10

ACTIVITIES

Each chapter has an activities section in which the book's readers are asked to apply the chapter's content. Two sources of feedback are available to the reader. The first consists of the authors' ideas immediately following the activities. The second consists of the course instructor's feedback.

Activities in this book can be done with another class student. This process of interacting can follow a simple format:

- Each student reads and does an activity.
- Each student explains to the other what the response is and why that response is chosen.
- The students' responses are compared with the authors' feedback.
- If there are differences between peer responses (or between peer responses and the authors' feedback), students should refer to the text or to the course instructor for verification.

Activity 1

Write a summary of the key ideas found in the chapter. Use the focus questions at the beginning of the chapter as a guide to structure your summary.

Activity 2

Scan—as opposed to intensively reading—the two research reports following this chapter: "Effects of Classroom Structure on Student Achievement Goal Orientation (Self-Brown, 2003), pp. 19–26; and "Images of America: What Youth Do Know About the United States" (Cornbleth, 2002), pp. 27–51. Note how we have annotated the reports to indicate the location of the different kinds of information found in a quantitative research report (Self-Brown, 2003) and a qualitative research report (Cornbleth, 2002).

Then select one quantitative and one qualitative research report of your own choosing, or select them from the resources in Appendix A. Scan the reports and locate the particular sections in which the researchers have placed information. Do not be concerned with fully understanding the reports. Just locate where the different types of information are placed.

FEEDBACK

Activity 1

Why do educators conduct research?   Educators produce research to verify the effectiveness of teaching and learning ideas and practices already in use. They may discover new ideas and practices and develop practices that simplify people's lives, to introduce practices that complicate people's lives and discover counterintuitive practices.

What is the distinction between research consumers *and research* producers?   Research producers need technical competence in applying research strategies—the procedures for conceptualizing, developing, implementing, and reporting research. Research consumers need skills in understanding how researchers undertake research, and in reading, interpreting, and applying others' research results.

What is research, from a researcher's perspective?   To understand research "as a research producer does" means understanding research with the mindset of a research producer. To do that, research consumers need to understand that different educational research producers (*a*) approach the systematic study of school-related matters from differing theoretical perspectives; (*b*) approach the research process and the decisions facing them with differing research paradigms; (*c*) consider different possible alternatives at those decision points; and (*d*) formulate differing implications of their results and conclusions (or of their explanations and understandings).

Activity 2

Verify your responses with a peer or with feedback from the instructor.

Chapter 1 Appendix A

> **Introduction and Background Section With Related Research**

(1)

Effects of Classroom Structure on Student Achievement Goal Orientation

Shannon Self-Brown

(2) Over the last 35 years, considerable research and writings have addressed the relationship between the classroom learning environment and student goal orientation. However, only a paucity of research has focused on establishing a link between the classroom evaluation structure, differences in students' goal orientation, and classroom strategies for the creation

> *Statement of Purpose*

(3) of specific goal orientations within the classroom (Ames, 1992c). In this study, we addressed those issues.

> *Related Research*

(4)   Students' goal orientation has been linked to contrasting patterns that students exhibit when they attend to, interpret, and respond to academic tasks (Dweck & Leggett, 1988). One leading model of goal orientation focuses on two goal orientations—performance goals and learning goals. According to the model, students who set performance goals are focused on demonstrating their abilities to outside observers such as teachers, whereas students who set learning goals seek to increase their competence regardless of the presence of outside observers (Kaplan & Migdley, 1997). Researchers have found consistent patterns of behavior that are related directly to the types of goals that students establish (Dweck, 1986; Nicholls, 1984; Schunk, 1990).

Generally, researchers have concluded that a negative relationship exists between performance goals and productive achievement behaviors (Greene & Miller, 1996; Zimmerman & Martinez-Pons, 1990). Adoption of a performance goal orientation means that ability is evidenced when students do better than others, surpass normative-based standards, or achieve success with little effort (Ames, 1984; Covington, 1984). Consequently, those students often avoid more difficult tasks and exhibit little intrinsic interest in academic activities (Ames, 1992c; Dweck, 1986; Nicholls, 1984). Students with a performance goal orientation can become vulnerable to helplessness, especially when they perform poorly on academic tasks. That result occurs because failure implies that students have low ability and that the amount and quality of effort expended on tasks is irrelevant to the outcome (Ames, 1992c).

In contrast, researchers have consistently found evidence for a positive relationship between learning goals and productive achievement behaviors (Ames & Archer, 1988; Greene & Miller, 1996; Meece, Blumenfeld, & Hoyle, 1988). Students who are focused on learning goals typically prefer challenging activities (Ames & Archer, 1988; Elliot & Dweck, 1988), persist at difficult tasks (Elliot & Dweck, 1988; Schunk, 1996), and report high levels of interest and task involvement (Harackiewicz, Barron, & Elliot, 1998; Harackiewicz, Barron, Tauer, Carter, & Elliot, 2000). Those students engage in a mastery-oriented belief system for which effort and outcome covary (Ames, 1992a). For students who are focused on learning goals, failure does not represent a personal deficiency but implies that greater effort or new strategies are required. Such persons will increase their efforts in the face of difficult challenges and seek opportunities that promote learning (Heyman & Dweck, 1992). Overall, researchers have concluded that a learning-goal orientation is associated with more adaptive patterns of behavior, cognition, and affect than is a performance-goal orientation (Ames & Archer, 1988; Dweck & Leggett, 1988; Nicholls, Patashnick, & Nolen, 1985).

In several empirical studies, researchers have established a relationship between the salience of certain goal orientations and changes in individual behavior (Ames, 1984; Elliot & Dweck, 1988; Heyman & Dweck, 1992; Schunk, 1996). Previous laboratory studies have

Source: The Journal of Educational Research, 97(2), 106–111, 2003, Reprinted with permission of the Helen Dwight Reid Educational Foundation. Published by Heldref Publications, 1319 Eighteenth St., NW, Washington, DC 20036-1802.
Copyright © 2003.

created learning and performance goal conditions by manipulating the instructions provided to children regarding the tasks at hand (Ames, 1984; Elliot & Dweck, 1988). Results from those studies indicate that children who participated in performance goal conditions, in which instructions made salient the external evaluation of skills and/or competitive goals, most often attributed their performance on tasks to ability. Those children also exhibited reactions that were characteristic of a helpless orientation, giving up easily and avoiding challenging tasks. In contrast, children exposed to learning-goal conditions, for which instructions focused on improving individual performance and further developing skills, typically attributed their performance to effort. Those children demonstrated mastery-oriented responses toward tasks by interpreting failures as opportunities to acquire information about how to alter their responses in order to increase their competence.

Schunk (1996) conducted a study in a classroom setting to investigate the influence of achievement goal orientation on the acquisition of fractions (Schunk, 1996). Similar to the laboratory studies, learning and performance goal conditions were established through a distinction in teacher instructions. Results indicated that students in the learning-goal condition had higher motivation and achievement outcomes than did students in the performance-goal condition. The results of that study suggested that varying goal instruction within the classroom can influence students' goal perceptions and achievement-related behavior on academic tasks.

Given that achievement-goal orientation is an important predictor of student outcomes in educational settings, researchers must attend to the classroom environment variables that are necessary so that children orient toward a learning-goal orientation versus a performance-goal orientation (Church, Elliot, & Gable, 2001). Researchers have suggested that such variables as the instructional and management practices that teachers use can influence the type of achievement goals that students set (Ames & Ames, 1981; Kaplan & Maehr, 1999; Meece, 1991). One major element of instructional and management practices within a classroom is the structure of classroom evaluation that teachers use in their daily practices. A focus on the type of evaluation, that is, striving for personal improvement or performing to attain a teacher's goal for external reward may be related to students' goal orientation (Ames, 1992c).

Typical evaluation in elementary classrooms compares students against a normative standard, such as that required to pass a course or to receive a reward within a token economy system (Brophy, 1983). Token economy systems provide students with tangible reinforcers and external incentives for meeting normative standards. Although token economy programs have received empirical support for improving student behavior and academic responding in a variety of school subjects, this classroom structure can have paradoxical and detrimental effects when applied with no regard for the varying degrees of students' capabilities (Lepper & Hodell, 1989). For instance, a student who has a learning disability in mathematics will not be motivated by the same amount of tokens to complete mathematics assignments as other students in the same classroom who have average abilities in this subject. In addition, the type of evaluative structure that stems from a token economy tends to increase the perceived importance of ability and public performance in the classroom, which makes performance-goal orientation salient to students (Ames, 1992c).

To promote a learning-goal orientation, Ames (1992c) suggested a type of classroom structure in which student evaluation is based on personal improvement and progress toward individual goals. The use of contingency contracts as an evaluative tool likely would place emphasis on these variables. Contingency contracting creates an agreement for learning and performing between a student and teacher. Success is based solely on each student's individual performance, according to the goal that he or she sets (Piggott & Heggie, 1986). Contracting allows each student to consider his or her unique needs and competencies when setting goals and places responsibility for learning and performing on the student (Kurvnick, 1993). The use of contingency contracting has been an effective intervention for improving students' academic behavior in a variety of academic subjects (Murphy, 1988). It encourages students to become active participants in their learning with a focus on effortful strategies and a pattern of motivational processes that are associated with adaptive and desirable achievement behaviors (Ames, 1992c). One question that remains, however, is whether an intervention such as

Statement of Purpose

contingency contracting will lead to an increase in learning goals relative to performance goals. (5) In this study, we addressed that question.

(6)   We manipulated classroom structures to assess the effects on student goal orientation. Each intact classroom was assigned randomly to either a token-economy classroom structure, contingency-contract classroom structure, or a control classroom structure. We assessed student goal orientation by comparing the number of learning and performance goals that students set according to the classroom-structure condition. On the basis of previous research, we hypothesized that the type of classroom structure would be linked directly to the achievement goals that students set. Our prediction was as follows: (*a*) the token-economy classroom structure would be related positively to student performance-goal orientation, (*b*) the contingency contract classroom structure would be related positively to student learning-goal orientation, and (*c*) the control classroom structure would be unrelated to student goal orientation.

Statements About How Study Was Conducted

Statement of Purpose as Hypothesis

Method Section: Subjects

(8)   **METHOD**

Participants

Students from three classrooms at a local elementary school participated in this study. Participants included 2 fifth-grade classes and 1 fourth-grade class. Each of the three intact classrooms was randomly assigned to one of the three classroom evaluation structure conditions. Twenty-five 5th-grade students were assigned to the token economy condition, 18 fourth-grade students to the contingency contract condition, and 28 fifth-grade students to the control condition.

Subjects Are Labeled as Participants

Method Section: Materials

(9) *Materials*

Materials varied according to the classroom evaluation structure condition. The conditions are described in the following paragraphs.

Token Economy.   Students in this condition were given a contract that (*a*) described explicitly how tokens were earned and distributed and (*b*) listed the back-up reinforcers for which tokens could be exchanged. Students received a contract folder so that the contract could be kept at their desk at all times. Students also received a goals chart that was divided into two sections: token economy goals and individual goals. The token economy goals section listed the student behaviors that could earn tokens and the amount of tokens that each behavior was worth. The individual goals section allowed students to list weekly goals and long-term goals for mathematics. Other materials used for this condition included tokens, which were in the form of play dollars, and back-up reinforcers such as candy, pens, keychains, and computer time cards.

Contingency Contract.   Students in this condition were given a contingency contract that described the weekly process of meeting with the researcher to set and discuss mathematics goals. Students received a contract folder so that the contract could be kept at their desk at all times. Participants also received a goals chart in which they listed weekly and long-term goals for mathematics. Gold star stickers on the goals chart signified when a goal was met.

Method Section: Design

Control.   Students in this condition received a goals chart identical to the one described in the contingency contract condition. No other materials were used in this condition.

Identification of the Independent and Dependent Variables

(10) *Design*

In the analysis in this study, we examined the effect of classroom evaluation structure on students' achievement goals. The independent variable in the analysis was classroom structure, which consisted of three levels: token economy, contingency contract, and control. The dependent variable was goal type (performance or learning goals) that students set for mathematics. We used a two-way analysis of variance (ANOVA) to analyze the data.

<table>
<tr><td>

**Method
Section:
Procedure**
*(data
collection)*

---

*Data Collec-
tion (instru-
ment)*

---

*Data Collec-
tion (instru-
ment)*

---

*Treatment #1
(instruction
or teaching
condition)*

</td><td>

(11) *Procedure*

Each of three intact classrooms was assigned randomly to one of three classroom evalua-
tion structure conditions: *token economy, contingency contract,* or *control.* We applied those class-
room evaluation structure conditions to mathematics. The mathematics instruction in each
classroom was on grade level. Throughout the study, teachers in the participating classrooms
continued to evaluate their students with a traditional grading system that included graded
evaluation of mathematics classwork, homework, and weekly tests.

Student participants in each classroom structure condition completed a mathematics goal
chart each week during a one-on-one meeting with the first author. The author assessed goals
by defining them as performance goals or learning goals, according to Dweck's (1986) defini-
tions. Further procedures were specific to the classroom structure condition. The treatments
are described in the following paragraphs.

(12)   *Token Economy.*   The first author gave a contract to the students, which she discussed indi-
vidually with each of them. When the student demonstrated an understanding of the terms of
the contract, the student and author signed the contract. Reinforcement procedures were writ-
ten in the contract and explained verbally by the author, as follows.

"For the next six weeks you can earn school dollars for completing your math assignments
and/or for making *A*'s or *B*'s on math assignments. For each assignment you complete, you will
earn two school dollars. For every *A* or *B* you make on a math assignment, your will earn four
school dollars. At the end of the five weeks, if you have an *A* or *B* average in math and/or have
turned in all your math assignments, you will earn ten school dollars. These are the only be-
haviors for which you can earn school dollars. Your teacher will pay you the dollars you earn
on a daily basis following math class."

</td></tr>
</table>

Tokens were exchanged on a weekly basis when students met with the author. The process
was explained to students as follows: "Once a week you can exchange your school dollars for
computer time, pens, markers, keychains, notepads, or candy. You must earn at least ten
school dollars in order to purchase an item."

<table>
<tr><td>

*Data Collec-
tion (instru-
ment)*

</td><td>

A goals chart also was provided for the students in the token economy condition. At the top
of the goals chart, target behaviors that could earn tokens were identified. Beneath the token
economy goals, a section was provided in which students could write their own mathematics
goals. During the weekly meeting time that students met with the author, they (*a*) traded to-
kens for back-up reinforcers, (*b*) received reminders of the target behaviors that could earn to-
kens, and (*c*) wrote individual mathematics goals on the goals chart.

</td></tr>
<tr><td>

*Treatment
#2*

</td><td>

(13)   *Contingency Contract.*   Students who participated in this condition received a folder with a
contract provided by the author. The terms of the contract were presented verbally by the au-
thor, as follows:

"Each week we will meet so that you can set goals for math. You will be allowed to set
weekly goals and long-term goals. When we meet we will look over the goals you set for the
previous week. We will identify the goals you have met and place a gold star beside them on
your goals chart form. We will discuss the goals you did not meet and you can decide whether
to set those goals again or set new ones."

</td></tr>
</table>

Contracts were discussed individually with each student, and once the student demonstrated
an understanding for the terms of the contract the student and the author signed the contract.

<table>
<tr><td>

*Data Collec-
tion (instru-
ment)*

</td><td>

Students in the contingency contract condition received a goals chart, which was divided
into sections according to the week of the study. Below the weekly sections, a long-term goals
section was provided. During the weekly meeting time, the previous week's goals were re-
viewed. Students received gold stars and positive verbal feedback, contingent on effort when
they met a particular goal. Students then set weekly and long-term mathematics goals for the
upcoming week.

</td></tr>
<tr><td>

*Treatment
#3*

</td><td>

(14)   *Control.*   Students in this condition received an individual goals chart identical to the one
used in the contingency contract condition. The author met one-on-one with students on a
weekly basis so they could write short-term and long-term goals for mathematics on their goals

</td></tr>
</table>

*Data Collec-
tion (instru-
ment)*

chart. The students did not discuss their goals with the author. Furthermore, the students did not receive verbal feedback or external rewards for achieving their goals from the teacher or author. Thus, this condition simply served as a control for goal setting and time spent with the author.

**Results
Section**

(15) *Results*

Findings

We computed an ANOVA by using a two-factor mixed design (classroom structure by goal type) to determine the frequency of learning and performance goals set according to classroom structure condition. Table 1 shows the cell means for learning and performance goals that students set as a function of classroom structure. Results indicated a significant main effect for classroom structure, $F(2, 67) = 36.70$, $p < .0001$, as well as a significant classroom structure-by-goals interaction, $F(2, 67) = 31.35$, $p < 0.0001$.

Table 1   Means and Standard Deviations for Learning Goals and Performance Goals, by Classroom Structure

Classroom structure	Learning goals		Performance goals	
	M	SD	M	SD
Token economy	.75	1.59	4.95	2.15
Contingency contract	14.27	3.98	5.55	3.95
Control	5.36	5.39	5.61	1.96

Findings

We computed a Tukey post hoc test to determine the significant differences between classroom structure-by-goals on the ANOVA. A summary of post hoc results are shown in Table 2. In our post hoc analysis, we concluded that students in the contingency contract condition set significantly more learning goals than did students in the other conditions. Students in the control condition set significantly more learning goals than did students in the token-economy group. There were no significant differences between the numbers of performance goals that students set according to classroom structure conditions.

Table 2   Summary of Tukey Post Hoc Test for Classroom Structure-by-Goals Interaction

Classroom structure results	
Token economy	Performance goals > learning goals
Contingency contract	Learning goals > performance goals
Control	Performance goals = learning goals

Goals results	
Learning goals	Token economy < control < contingency contract
Performance goals	Token economy = control = contingency contract

Findings

Within the contingency contract group, students set significantly more learning goals than performance goals. In the control group, there were no significant differences between the number of learning and performance goals that students set. In the token-economy group, students set significantly more performance goals than learning goals.

Discussion Section	⑯ *Discussion*

Findings

Results from the goal analyses indicated significant differences within and across classroom structure conditions. Those results were consistent with the theoretical relationship predicted by Ames (1992c) and the hypothesis in this study that the type of classroom evaluation structure would influence student goal orientation. Students who were in the contingency-contract condition set significantly more learning goals than performance goals and significantly more learning goals than did students in the other classroom structure conditions. Students in the token-economy condition set significantly more performance goals than learning goals. There were no significant differences within the control classroom for the number of learning versus performance goals that students set. However, students in that classroom did set significantly more learning goals than did students in the token-economy condition. There were no significant differences for the amount of performance goals that students set across classroom-structure conditions.

Results Related to Other Research Findings

Our results support the idea that a contingency contract classroom structure, in which students were evaluated individually and allowed to determine their own achievement goals, led students to adopt a learning-goal orientation versus a performance-goal orientation. In this classroom structure, student evaluation was focused on individual gains, improvement, and progress. Success was measured by whether students met their individual goals, which creates an environment in which failure is not a threat. If goals were met, then students could derive personal pride and satisfaction from the efforts that they placed toward the goals. If goals were not met, then students could reassess the goal, make the changes needed, or eliminate the goal. A classroom structure that promotes a learning-goal orientation for students has the potential to enhance the quality of students' involvement in learning, increase the likelihood that students will opt for and persevere in learning and challenging activities, and increase the confidence they have in themselves as learners (Ames, 1992b).

In contrast, students in the token-economy classroom structure were rewarded for meeting normative standards and tended to adopt a performance-goal orientation. That is an important finding because token economies have been successful in changing student behavior in classrooms, so teachers may implement this intervention without concern for the special needs of students (McLaughlin, 1981). Students are not motivated by the same amount of tokens for given assignments because of individual differences. Students with lower abilities will likely become frustrated and helpless. According to Boggiano and Katz (1991), children in that type of learning environment typically prefer less challenging activities, work to please the teacher and earn good grades, and depend on others to evaluate their work. As a result, the token-economy classroom evaluation structure makes ability a highly salient dimension of the learning environment and discourages students from setting goals that involve learning and effort.

The number of performance goals that students set did not differ across classroom structure conditions. Students in the contingency-contract and control conditions set similar numbers of performance goals as compared with those in the token-economy condition. That result likely occurred because throughout the study teachers continued to evaluate all students on their schoolwork with a traditional grading system. It would have been ideal if a nontraditional, individually based evaluative system could have been implemented in the contingency-contract condition to assess whether this would have altered the results.

Identification of Research Limitations

There were limitations to this study. One limitation was that it did not control for teacher expectancies and how these may have influenced students' goal setting. Another potential limitation was that mathematics was the only subject area used for this study. Further studies should include additional academic areas, such as social studies, humanities, and science to investigate whether similar results will ensue.

Summary of Findings and Implications

This study provides strong evidence that the classroom evaluation structure can influence student achievement goal orientation. Specifically, we demonstrated that in a classroom structure that emphasizes the importance of individual goals and effort, learning goals become more salient to students. That result can lead to many positive effects on elementary students' learning strategies, self-conceptions of ability and competence, and task motivation (Smiley & Dweck, 1994). Students' achievement goal orientation obviously is not contingent on any one variable, but it is comprised of the comprehensive relationship between classroom processes and student experiences. Understanding the influence of classroom evaluation structure on student goal orientation provides a foundation for further research of other potentially related variables.

⑰ **NOTES**

We would like to thank Lucas Ledbetter for assisting in data collection. We would also like to thank the teachers and students at Jim Allen Elementary for participating in the project.

Source: The Journal of Educational Research (Washington, D.C.) 97 no2 106–11 N/D 2003.

⑱ **REFERENCES**

Ames, C. (1984). Achievement attribution and self-instructions under competitive and individualistic goal structures. Journal of Educational Psychology, 76, 478–487.

Ames, C. (1992a). Achievement goals and the classroom motivational environment. In D. L. Schunk & J. L. Meece (Eds.), Student perceptions in the classroom (pp. 327–343). Hillsdale, NJ: Erlbaum.

Ames, C. (1992b). Achievement goals, motivational climate, and motivational processes. In G. C. Roberts (Ed.), Motivation in sport and exercise. Champaign, IL: Human Kinetics Books.

Ames, C. (1992c). Classroom: Goals, structures, and student motivation. Journal of Educational Psychology, 84, 261–271.

Ames, C., & Ames, R. (1981). Competitive versus individualistic goal structures: The salience of past performance information for causal attributions and affect. Journal of Educational Psychology, 73, 411–418.

Ames, C., & Archer, J. (1988). Achievement goals in the classroom. Student learning strategies and motivation processes. Journal of Educational Psychology, 80, 260–267.

Boggiano, A. K., & Katz, P. (1991). Maladaptive achievement patterns in students: The role of teachers' controlling strategies. Journal of Social Issues, 47, 35–51.

Brophy, J. E. (1983). Conceptualizing student motivation. Educational Psychologist, 18, 200–215.

Church, M. A., Elliot, A. J., & Gable, S. L. (2001). Perceptions of classroom environment, achievement goals, and achievement outcomes. Journal of Educational Psychology, 93, 43–54.

Covington, M. C. (1984). The motive for self worth. In R. Ames & C. Ames (Eds.), Research on motivation in education: Student motivation (Vol. 1, pp. 77–113). San Diego, CA: Academic Press.

Dweck, C. (1986). Motivational processes affecting learning. American Psychologist, 41, 1040–1048.

Dweck, C., & Leggett, E. L. (1988). A social-cognitive approach to motivation and personality. Psychological Review, 95, 256–273.

Elliot, E. S., & Dweck, C. S. (1988). Goals: An approach to motivation and achievement. Journal of Personality & Social Psychology, 54, 5–12.

Greene, B., & Miller, R. (1996). Influences on achievement: Goals, perceived ability, and cognitive engagement. Contemporary Educational Psychology, 21, 181–192.

Harackiewicz, J. M., Barron, K. E., & Elliot, A. (1998). Rethinking achievement goals: When are they adaptive for college students and why? Educational Psychologist, 33, 1–21.

Harackiewicz, J. M., Barron, K. E., Tauer, J. M., Carter, S. M., & Elliot, A. J. (2000). Short-term and long-term consequences of achievement goals: Predicting interest and performance over time. Journal of Educational Psychology, 92, 316–330.

Recognition of Others Who Worked on Project

References Section

Heyman, G. D., & Dweck, C. S. (1992). Achievement goals and intrinsic motivation: Their relation and their role in adaptive motivation. Motivation and Emotion, 16, 231–247.

Kaplan, A., & Midgley, C. (1997). The effect of achievement goals: Does level of perceived academic competence make a difference? Contemporary Educational Psychology, 22, 415–435.

Kaplan, A., & Maehr, M. L. (1999). Achievement goals and student well-being. Contemporary Educational Psychology, 24, 330–358.

Kurvnick, K. (1993). Contracting as a motivational teaching tool: An agreement for learning offering simplicity, flexibility, and opportunity. Journal of College Science Teaching, 22, 310–311.

Lepper, M. R., & Hodell, M. (1989). Intrinsic motivation in the classroom. In C. Ames & R. Ames (Eds.), Research on motivation in education (Vol. 3, pp. 73–105). San Diego, CA: Academic Press.

McLaughlin, T. F. (1981). An analysis of token reinforcement: A control group comparison with special education youth employing measures of clinical significance. Child Behavior Therapy, 3, 43–50.

Meece, J. L. (1991). The classroom context and children's motivational goals. In M. Maehr & P. Pintrich (Eds.), Advances in achievement motivation research (pp. 261–286). Greenwich, CT: JAI.

Meece, J. L., Blumenfeld, P. C., & Hoyle, R. H. (1988). Students' goal orientation and cognitive engagement in classroom activities. Journal of Educational Psychology, 80, 514–523.

Murphy, J. J. (1988). Contingency contracting in schools: A review. Education and Treatment of Children, 11, 257–269.

Nicholls, J. (1984). Achievement motivation: Conceptions of ability, subjective experience, task choice, and performance. Psychological Review, 91, 328–334.

Nicholls, J. G., Patashnick, M., & Nolen, S. (1985). Adolescents' theories of education. Journal of Educational Psychology, 77, 683–692.

Piggott, H. E., & Heggie, D. L. (1986). Interpreting the conflicting results of individual versus group contingencies in classrooms: The targeted behavior as a mediating variable. Child & Family Behavior Therapy, 7, 1–15.

Schunk, D. H. (1990). Goal setting and self-efficacy during self-regulated learning. Educational Psychologist, 25, 71–86.

Schunk, D. H. (1996). Goals and self-evaluative influences during children's cognitive skill learning. American Educational Research Journal, 33, 359–382.

Smiley, P. A., & Dweck, C. S. (1994). Individual differences in achievement goals among young children. Child Development, 65, 1723–1743.

Zimmerman, B. J., & Martinez-Pons, M. (1990). Student differences in self-regulated learning: Relating grade, sex, and giftedness to self-efficacy and strategy use. Journal of Educational Psychology, 82, 51–59.

(1)

Images of America: What Youth Do Know
About the United States

Catherine Cornbleth

(2)

Activity

Findings

Additional Findings

Interpretation of Findings

ABSTRACT

Interviews with a diverse group of juniors and seniors from three secondary schools in the northeastern United States revealed substantial agreement in their images of America. Three themes predominated: inequity associated with race, gender, socioeconomic status, or disability; freedom including rights and opportunities; and diversity based on race, ethnicity, culture, and geography. Three additional themes were voiced by at least one third of the students: America as better than other nations, progress, and the American Dream. Crosscutting these themes were a sense of individualism or personalization and an incipient critique and or activism expressed by more than 30% of the students. Sources of or influences on students' images of America also were investigated as were changes over time. Although not overly positive, what students do know about the United States is both realistic and generally supportive of the nation-state. There are, however, grounds for concern insofar as the major themes about which students agree play out differently for different individuals and groups, masking deep societal tensions and fissures.

(3)

American Dream is just a joke to me. . . . I think it was all a facade. . . . People in despair want something to wish for. (Sheldon, 2)[1]

Introductory Section

Quotations From Students Used as Introduction

In some countries a woman is discriminated against. . . . Here I can be the same as a man. . . . I might have to work harder . . . but I have the same opportunities. . . . We've come from racial prejudice to equality. We've come from sexual discrimination to women's rights. (Carrie, 2–3)

I'd say that there are opportunities. . . . America, it's the land of the free, but it's not everything it's cracked up to be because there are a lot of limitations. . . . There's very few like amazing success stories. . . . There are definitely like racism and prejudice. . . . There are some limitations, especially on minorities. (Melissa, 1)

Better than I think other countries. Like you don't read about like the Nazis over here, that we ever killed anybody. The only thing maybe is the slaves. But, other than that we've always had good presidents who did good things and not really bad things. So it's pretty good. We have more freedom and stuff. (Marissa, 3)

I see, well I see a lot of like things haven't changed too much. Like some of the laws have changed. But people—you still see like racism everywhere you go. It's—I don't know— bad. (Richard, 4)

. . . free people . . . those who can pursue their desires . . . I know there's been discrimination against certain minority groups in the past, but I like to think that's changing. (James, 1)

(4)

Initial Statement of Research Purpose

These are a sampling of comments from urban and suburban high school juniors and seniors in response to our questions about their images of America. Overall, their images are more personalized and localized than the images of America conveyed in their U.S. history classes (Cornbleth, 1998); in some ways, they also are more complex, mixing critique with pride, misrepresentation, and hope. These students' understandings of America and the implications of those understandings are the focus of this article.

Source: From Cornbleth, C. (2002). Images of America: What youth do know about the United States. *American Educational Research Journal, 29* (2), 519–552. Copyright 2002 by the American Educational Research Association. Reprinted

Explanation of Terms

As in related work, I use America rather than the more specific United States of America when referring to questions of U.S. national identity and (re-)definition because, unfortunately, the terms of the continuing "America debate" (Cornbleth & Waugh, 1995/1999) already have been set by conservatives who have tended to cast the issues in the language of American and un-American. It also is less awkward to ask what it means to be an American than, for example, a "U.S.A.-ean." This also is true for American as an adjective as in American character. The United States is, as an academic colleague born in Mexico remarked, the only nation in North or South America without a name of its own.

Background and Related Research Literature

Over the past decade in the United States, there has been renewed argument about what kind of national history the public schools should teach. The arguments could be heard in public, professional, and educational policymaking circles. Reports of various test results (e.g., National Assessment of Educational Progress; Ravitch & Finn, 1987) provide some data about what students do not know, but very little about what they do know and believe about the United States, the nation's history, and their own and the nation's future. In response to Ravitch and Finn's (1987) claim that U.S. 17-year-olds knew shockingly little about American history, Dale Whittington (1991) offered a careful analysis of what previous generations of U.S. 17-year-olds have known and a critique of testing methods. She concluded that, with respect to "objective" test scores, "for the most part, students of the 1980s are not demonstrably different from students in their parents' or grandparents' generation in terms of their knowledge of American history" (p. 776). Given continuing disagreements about what history the schools should teach and students should learn, and about national pluralism and unity, I sought to move beyond questions of how much students know or what they do not know to what the increasingly diverse population of U.S. high school students does know and believe about America.

A four-page NAEPFacts report, "U.S. History: What Do Students Know, and What Can They Do?" (National Center for Education Statistics, 1996), is a rare exception to the "don't know" emphasis in the literature, noting, for example, those 12th-grade students scoring near the 50th percentile could "show general knowledge of historical chronology, especially 20th century history" (p. 3). Barton and Levstik (1998) provide access to middle school students' knowledge and beliefs about significant individuals, events, issues, documents, and time periods in U.S. history. Their analysis of major themes in students' responses offers glimpses of images of America characterized by progress, including the expansion of individual rights and opportunities. Although suggestive, these glimpses do not necessarily add up to the broader view sought here.

Schooling plays a key, but not exclusive, role in shaping students' knowledge and beliefs about the nation. Public schooling has been charged with a major role in nation-building at least since the mid-19th century in the United States (see, e.g., Elson, 1964; Foner, 1998). First, the schools were to transmit a recently created national identity. Later, they were to Americanize large numbers of immigrant children. A celebratory, nation-building, and assimilating history—what Stern (1956, p. 6) calls "history as a national epic"—still appears to predominate in U.S. school curricula and textbooks (e.g., History—Social Science Curriculum Framework and Criteria Committee, 1987–88, 1997; New York State Education Department, 1999; Appleby, Hunt, & Jacob, 1994; Fitzgerald, 1979). Trends within academic history and historiography (e.g., emergence of conflict theoretical frameworks, work in social history) may appear as sidebars or special features in school textbooks, but there is no evidence that they have altered the main contours of school history nationwide. There is evidence, however, that the celebratory grand epic of U.S. history has begun to crack under the weight of contrary evidence, the struggles of marginalized groups to be fairly represented, and the decisions by some teachers to include more of the histories, cultures, experiences, and perspectives of the peoples who make up the United States (see, e.g., Cornbleth, 2000).

Explanation of Personal Position on the Topic

Because school curriculum is a key means by which visions or versions of the nation are transmitted to the next generation, schools have been the arenas where Americans have debated social values and national priorities (see, e.g., Cornbleth & Waugh, 1995, 1999, chap. 2). Too often lost in this curriculum contestation has been recognition that students are not simply blank tapes upon which the schools' or other institutions messages are forever imprinted.

Societal messages are mediated by schools in at least two interrelated ways—institutionally and individually. By mediation I refer to the interpretive process by which people make sense of or create meaning from experience. Mediation is an intervening and linking process between messages on the one hand and meanings and actions on the other. Schools as institutions mediate between local community and national preferences on one side and the daily curricular and other experiences arranged for students on the other; "External interests are thus filtered through institutional arrangements" (Cornbleth, 1984, p. 32). Further mediation occurs both by teachers as professionals and individuals and by students as individuals and group members.

Underlying this conception of mediation is the assumption that people, students included, are active participants in the creation and interpretation of their social environments and actions. But students are not independent agents, they are shaped by history and culture, through prior personal experience in that history and culture (or cultures), and by the immediate social relations and practices of schooling. Students, like others, are situated agents. Their social locations are neither unidimensional nor mutually exclusive. They carry racial-ethnic, socioeconomic, gender, and other addresses, each of which is more salient, or influential, in some situations than in others, and for some students more than others. The relationship of individual, history, and setting is a dynamic one that is neither mechanistic nor predetermin-

Research Purpose

(5)ing (Mills, 1959). Consequently, it is wrong to assume that intended school messages are, first, transmitted and then received and interpreted as intended by their advocates. If one wants to know what teachers are teaching and students are learning regarding American national iden-

Statement of Research Belief

(6)tity, one needs to examine curriculum practice and student knowledge directly. And what one finds carries political and social as well as pedagogical implications.

Although some or many students lack information that some or many adults believe that they should know about the United States and its history (e.g., Ravitch & Finn, 1987), high school students do know something about the United States. What students know and/or believe is important because it influences their understanding and acceptance of what they learn in school and elsewhere (e.g., Epstein, 1997; Seixas, 1993). Existing beliefs also are important because they influence actions. Changing or extending people's knowledge and beliefs is not simply a matter of addition or exchange as cognitive psychological research has shown for several decades (e.g., Greeno, Collins, & Resnick, 1996; Shuell, 1996). It is a matter of working with and building on what people already "know," whatever that might be.

Consequently, my purpose in undertaking this study and the significance of its findings and interpretations are twofold: (a) to identify some of what high school juniors "do know" about the United States for consideration in curriculum planning in history-social studies education and perhaps in other arenas; and (b) to test the extent of disagreement about the United States among students, given the dire warnings of conservatives such as Ravitch (1990) and Schlesinger (1991) that the increasingly diverse U.S. population is in danger of disunity if history-social studies curriculum does not stress unity and encourage assimilation, allowing for only "modest multiculturalism."

Personal Orientation Toward Research

(7)   My approach to these issues can be characterized as critical pragmatism, which I have described more fully elsewhere (Cornbleth & Waugh, 1995, 1999, chap. 2). For the present study, the most salient aspects of this theoretical perspective are its bringing together of critical and pragmatic traditions, linking "the contextual emphasis and equity goal of critical theory with the self-questioning and pluralism of pragmatic philosophy" (Cornbleth & Waugh, 1995, 1999, p. 33) and its "opposition to efforts to limit or close off debate, either by putting topics or issues out of bounds or by a priori rejecting particular viewpoints or the participation of particular individuals or groups" (p. 34).

> The critical perspective gives depth and direction to pragmatic inquiry and dialogue. Pragmatism, in turn, reminds us that cultural critique encompasses us all; none of us or our cherished beliefs, individually or collectively as a member of one or another group, is above or beyond question. Emergent and oriented toward action, this critical pragmatism eschews materialist and theological determinisms on one side and postmodernist quicksands on the other. (p. 33)

The first aspect is evident in inviting students' images into the America debate and doing so at several school sites by means of open-ended questions. The second aspect is evident in data interpretation that probes beneath the surface agreement among students to consider implications of apparent similarities in students' images of America across school sites.

Context of Research and Restatement of Research Purpose

(8)   In sum, the present study complements and extends prior work about students' understanding of history and the influence of their background or family experience as well as my own investigation of the images of America actually conveyed in urban and suburban, elementary, middle, and high school U.S. history classes (Cornbleth, 1998). High school juniors and seniors were interviewed regarding their images of America and the sources of those understandings.[2] The focus here is on the students' reported images of America—the meanings they have made of their experiences in school and elsewhere.

SEEKING STUDENTS' IMAGES OF AMERICA

Participants *and Researcher's Relationship With Participants*

(9) Students' images of America were obtained by means of individual interviews lasting from approximately 20 to 45 minutes each.[3] Students were volunteers, interviewed at their schools by myself, another faculty member, or a graduate student member of the research team, toward the end of the larger project of which the present study is a part. Interviews were conducted during 1996 and 1997 in conjunction with observations of the students' 11th-grade U.S. history and government classes; consequently, we were not strangers to the students, and they appeared to feel reasonably comfortable talking with us (all of us are of European descent). Interviews usually were conducted during a study hall period, following a semi-structured, open-ended interview protocol. All of the interviews were taped and transcribed to facilitate analysis.

Characteristics of the Participants and Their Schools

(10)   The sample consists of 25 high school juniors and seniors (ages 16–19) from three secondary schools in upstate New York. The two districts and three schools were selected to provide a range of student socioeconomic and racial-ethnic backgrounds, excluding demographic extremes, within the public education system and reasonable commuting distance for the research staff. The four 11th-grade U.S. history teachers within these schools were those who agreed to work with us and invited us into their classrooms. As previously noted, the students we interviewed also were volunteers.

Lincoln, an urban secondary magnet school with a "traditional academic" program, draws students primarily from working class families; 60% of the students are of African descent, and 37% are of European descent. Most of the White students travel to the school from beyond its immediate neighborhood. Johnson, a predominantly Hispanic-Puerto Rican urban high school, has the most diverse student population in the region—linguistically and racially-ethnically—and a higher proportion of students from poor families than the other two schools. Eisenhower, a suburban high school, is predominantly White (92%) and upper middle class. Three of the four teachers whose classes we observed and whose students we interviewed are of European descent and male (Peter, Stephen, and George); one of the Eisenhower teachers is of African descent and female (Lindy). More information about the teachers and their classes is provided as it appears directly relevant to students' images to avoid suggesting that there is (or ought to be) a one-to-one relationship between classroom practice and student belief when U.S. history classes are only one of several influences on, or sources of, students' knowledge and beliefs about the nation.

The median household income in the suburban district is reported (by the New York State Education Department in 1998 at their web site www.nysed.gov) as more than two and one half times that in the urban district. At Johnson, 71% of the students were eligible for free lunches in 1995–96, compared to 64% at Lincoln and 1% at Eisenhower. In 1995–96, 5% of the students at Johnson and 13% of the students at Lincoln earned Regents (rather than local) diplomas compared to 73% at Eisenhower.

In presenting the results of the data analysis, pseudonyms are used to protect anonymity. Students usually are identified by school because of school-related differences in their images of America. District, racial-ethnic, gender, and teacher-class identifications also are noted

<table>
<tr><td>

Research Method-ology ⑪

Analysis of Collected Information

</td><td>

when relevant; to note them routinely would perpetuate the assumption of group differences unsupported by the present data. Appendix A on page 51 presents a roster of the 25 students.

Consistent with the norms of ethnographic interview research (e.g., Bogdan & Biklen, 1992; Erickson, 1986), data analysis has been inductive. I read, reread, and marked the transcripts in the process of constructing, testing, and refining interpretive themes in response to the research questions about images of America and change over time. The question about sources of images involved a simple tally of student responses noting of their explanations or examples. Initial interpretations also were shared with other members of the research staff who had participated in the data collection and were working with some of the same data for different purposes. Major themes are emphasized in what follows, drawing on the interview transcripts for illustration and the tenor of students' talk about America.
Bottom of Form

</td></tr>
</table>

Data Collection ⑫ — block label

Data Collection ⑫

Questions Asked of Participants

Data Interpretation

Identification of Major and Other Themes

STUDENTS TALK ABOUT AMERICA

"What youth do know about the United States" refers to what they believe or think is true about U.S. history and contemporary society and how they feel about or evaluate that knowledge. We asked specifically about their images of America, for example, "When you hear the word U.S. or America, What comes to mind?" and "Imagine a fill-in-the-blank question. America is like _____. What would you say?"

Three themes predominated in students' reported images of America: inequity associated with race, gender, socioeconomic status, or disability (18 of 25 students); freedom including rights and opportunities (14 students); and diversity based on race, ethnicity, culture, and geography (14 students). Three additional themes were voiced by at least one third of the students: America as better than other nations, progress, and the American Dream. Finally, beyond negative descriptors or isolated complaints, nine students offered more a general critique of America. Like the inequity theme, critique typically was associated with the promise of America, as in Langston Hughes' 1930 poem. "Let America Be America Again." For most of these students, America is more complex than a soundbite, a banner slogan, or a bicentennial minute.

Theme 1 Interpretation ⑬

INEQUITY: "AMERICA'S NOT LIKE IT SHOULD BE"[4]

Inequity of some kind, past and or present, is part of the image of America held by 71% of the students at Lincoln and Eisenhower high schools and 76% of the students at Johnson. More than half of the students mentioning inequity made specific reference to racism or to racial-ethnic prejudice or discrimination. Racism seemed particularly salient to two Black male students at Lincoln, a Johnson male student who described himself as Native American and Black, and three White Eisenhower students (two male and one female) who had just completed an 8-day civil rights unit including a video revealing the era's violence.

Theme 1 Supporting Examples

An articulate, young Black man, who prefers to be described as "a person first . . . a human being" (1), Blake echoed Langston Hughes,[5] saying,

> America's not like it should be . . . it hasn't been for a long time. And until America decides that it's going to be, or live by the principles that it was built on, it will never be what it should always have been. [JM: Was it ever like that?] It may have been at one point in time. . . . This country wasn't built to be segregated. It says. "All men are created equal." Then where does segregation come in? And then they said, "separate but equal." Okay, the country was built on equality, but it wasn't equal. It was separate, but it was not equal. . . . I believe it wasn't because when the principles that were made to build this country, the principles were not in place for all Americans.
>
> I believe it was only put aside for a certain group of Americans. At that time, you had, you were White or you were Black, and the principles really were set for the White Americans. . . . It was not, "You're an American, I'm an American. We're supposed to be equal." You were either Black or White. (4, 5)

Later, Blake described feeling like an outsider:

In some ways it makes me feel cheated. Sometimes I feel like I don't belong here. Like I was born here, I was raised here, but it doesn't feel like I belong here. Sometimes I feel like a stranger, a foreigner.... Why can't I just be an American just like anybody else? Why can't I just be treated fairly like anyone else? That's what it's supposed to be. That's what you say it should be.(7)

Despite his feelings of inequity and alienation, Blake is not without hope for America or himself:

America's not all bad, but there's too much wrong with it, you know? There are a lot of things that are right about America. It's a good place to be. One thing that is good is the many cultures that are here. And the many different backgrounds that are here. Um, there's a lot to learn, a lot to experience. Um, a lot of places to go in the country. Um, many things that are good. Those are some of the good things, but there are too many wrong things that are outweighing the good things, which makes it very unbalanced. So what we need to do is eliminate the bad things, tip the scale. (6)[6]

Three Eisenhower students, lacking firsthand experience as targets of racism or negative discrimination, expressed surprise and disgust with what they had learned recently about the history of racism and discrimination in a civil rights unit. Particularly informative and unsettling, the students reported, was the video, "The Shadow of Hate," produced by the Southern Poverty Law Center. Ned described knowing something of the events of the 1950s and 1960s civil rights movement but not having had direct experience or seeing the film clips of White violence (e.g., clubs, hoses, dogs) against mostly Black civil rights demonstrators before:

When you hear something, it's different than if you actually can see it, witness it.... I wasn't there, but you saw the footage of it, in the film, and that was, I believe it. They really, I mean, the teachers I've had in the past really never said, you know, "This is how it was," and showed us. (2)

He also spoke for his peers in this regard:

I never saw that till then. I never learned that till then. And a lot of kids in class were like that too. They didn't know that. I got that just from talking to the kids. So I think that. I think that just the past couple of weeks has really turned my mind about stuff. That there is stuff like that that can happen.... I never thought that. I mean, the United States would ever let something like that happen.... Really, when I saw that video, that was really. I never knew . . . how bad it was and how they were treated. I mean, that was really, really cruel. I don't know . . . somebody that could live them . . . could live through that.... it was bad.... I'm glad I saw it though. (2)

Ned also thought that the video might incite Blacks to hostility toward Whites, saying, "If I were Black and I saw that, I'd be, I'd hold a grudge against the Whites" (2).
James echoed Ned, saying,

Just recently, we did a unit on discrimination against Blacks, and, you know, we've been shown on TV films about how they were beaten. Blacks were lynched, and, and unjust discrimination that Whites have demonstrated against certain minority groups. And, it just makes me nauseous, some of what I see. (2)

Melissa, the only Eisenhower student to offer a more general critique of America, was more introspective:

When I went into the class in the beginning of the year, I had a much more positive image of America than I did now, getting through it. Um, I found that there is a lot of hidden things in our past that many people don't know about. . . . And um, I think there's a lot of people that don't know, you know, about our past and how it was not a great past. It was something that I think Americans should look at and not be proud of. . . .

I still think America is a good country. I'm not gonna like move away because I don't like what we did in the past. There's nothing I can do about that now. But, it kind of disappoints me that, um, this country that, in our Constitution is, you know, equal for everyone, and they tried to be different from the other countries by not limiting anyone, and they were, you know, hypocritical, went back on their word and did. . . . destroy these people's lives just because of their race and color. (3)

She also related her own personal experience to what she was learning:

This year like I have a lot of friends who are minorities [*apparently referring to Asians and Asian Americans*], and I see how they're treated. And how, you know, it's really uncomfortable for me when I go to their, when I like go to their family gatherings and they've got all Koreans there and I'm the only, only White person there. And I feel uncomfortable. I told my one friend that, and she said, "Well, how do you think I feel everyday?" And I, you know, it just blew my mind, and then we started something about, um, civil rights movement and everything, and I realized that our country is a little more backward than I thought. You know, for being so modern, their thoughts are backward maybe. Not as modern. (3)

Only one of the four Eisenhower students in the other class mentioned racism, which she attributed to "all the different cultures." Alice commented that, "we have so much more racism here 'cause we have so many different . . . Blacks, and different races" (3).

The contrasting comments about racism from the students in the two Eisenhower U.S. history classes are one indicator that teachers and curriculum can make a difference, at least temporarily, in what students come to know and believe. In addition, two of the three students in Lindy's class (the one that had recently completed a civil rights unit) but none of the students in the other class commented in general terms about effects of living in the suburbs, especially that it limited their opportunities to learn about people different from themselves. Melissa, for example, said,

"I don't like to think that I'm racist. I really try, you know, but coming from [a suburb] I don't know how to deal with people . . . people accuse me of being racist like, and you know, I'm not doing anything. . . . it's kind of embarrassing to me but I don't have like good public relations like that. I don't know how to act." (5)

Similarly, James assumes that he is isolated in the suburbs and that people who live in cities are more aware of, or knowledgeable about, America. He noted changes in his image of America, saying, "I knew discrimination, for example, existed but I didn't know it, ah, quite to the extent that I've learned this year" (6). In this context, however, neither student specifically referred to the social class and racial differences that separate their relatively affluent, predominantly White suburb from the poorer, more racially and ethnically diverse city. My impression is that their seeming naivete stems from being sheltered from urban and world realities by both family and school as well as physically removed in their suburb.

Fewer students mentioned inequity associated with socioeconomic status or gender, and only one mentioned disability. Compared to their statements about racism, students' comments about class or gender inequity tended to be equivocal like Carrie's comment at the beginning of this article that she has the same opportunities and can be the same as a man but she might have to work harder. Carrie's statement also illustrates students' tendency to personalize their images of America.

<table>
<tr><td>*Theme 2*
Interpretation</td></tr>
</table>

⑭

FREEDOM, RIGHTS, AND OPPORTUNITIES

Despite, or alongside, the cited inequities, freedom (including rights and opportunities) was a major part of students' images of America: 57% of the students at Lincoln and Eisenhower, and 55% of the students at Johnson. Freedom is what distinguishes the United States from other countries. "We're free here . . . not like other countries," Ann said (1). Similarly, Magdalena asserted that "In some countries the government tells you what to do, and you have to do it. Here we have a choice of how we want things" (4).

Theme 2 Sup-
porting Ex-
ample

For some students, this freedom is not always equally distributed or accessible, as illustrated in Melissa's and Marissa's comments at the beginning of this article. Two Johnson students, Kaylee and Yolanda, and Lincoln's Mary seemed to recognize the apparent discrepancy between freedom and inequity saying that, unlike other countries, the United States was fair—except sometimes. As will be described in relation to the progress theme, several students saw unfairness or limits on freedoms, rights, or opportunities as primarily in the past.

Although students frequently mentioned freedom, often as their first response to our questions about what comes to mind when you hear the word *U.S.* or *America*, few had much to say about it. Most commonly, freedom was described as simply having the right, or being able, to do what you want. For some students, freedom meant having opportunities and choices, for example, about what to do with their lives. Manuel elaborated more than most students, saying,

> Freedom . . . A Hispanic has all his rights to be a Hispanic. To have a second language. To talk about our culture and stuff Americans—everybody has the same quality of who they want to be, you know, how they want to be. It's like, you make your life of it. Not nobody else, you know. (5)

Although a few students mentioned freedom of speech, none mentioned other first amendment freedoms or the Bill of Rights. Overall, freedom seemed to be a symbol or slogan for most students, something they took for granted but gave little thought.

Theme 3
Interpretation

⑮

DIVERSITY

Theme 2
Supporting
Example

Theme 3
Supporting
Examples

The third major theme in students' reported images of America, diversity, was mentioned by 71% of the students at Eisenhower, 57% at Lincoln, and 45% at Johnson. Students mentioned regional or geographic diversity (seven) and multiple perspectives (two from Eisenhower) as well as racial-ethnic-cultural diversity. Interestingly, students at the most racially-ethnically diverse school were least likely to mention diversity as part of their image of America. Johnson students did, however, more often mention the diversity of their school population and that it was a plus. Reminiscent of Grant and Sleeter's (1986) findings from their study of a heterogeneous, midwest junior high school, Arthur, for example, said "it's fun . . . because you get to meet a lot of people" (2).

Students mentioning regional diversity usually compared large cities such as New York City, Los Angeles, and Chicago unfavorably with midsized cities such as their own, largely because of crowding and crime. A few of Johnson's Puerto Rican students said they preferred the diversity and dynamism of New York City. Rural areas in the midwest and south were portrayed less favorably than urban and suburban areas in the northeast.

Theme 3
Supporting
Examples

Very few students described the United States in specific ethnocultural terms. For most students who mentioned it, racial-ethnic-cultural diversity seemed almost decorative. Illustrative student comments include, "all different kinds of people . . . different kinds of cultures" (Carl, 8), "a melting pot . . . you're aware of all the diversities, different racial groups, religions, and stuff" (James, 1); "a box of chocolates . . . filled with different people, different languages, different everything" (Kate, 1). Alice provided a slightly different view, saying "America is like a whole bunch of pieces put together, as a whole . . . different states, different cultures, different ethnic groups, different people" (1). Blake, in contrast, talked at greater length about America's diversity of backgrounds and cultures offering a lot of experience and opportunities for learning. He used to think diversity was bad because it would lead to conflict, Blake said, but now he sees it as good. If there were no diversity, "It would be like nothing really to talk about because you know you're gonna agree on the same thing and think the same way" (8). He continued,

> So I feel now that diversity is good because I feel if we disagree on something, we can talk about it. You know, because you can give your viewpoint, I can give my viewpoint, and as long as we don't offend each other by what we say, that we don't take it to heart, but we can just talk. . . . I talked to somebody who, about racism and everything, and she had different viewpoints, I had different viewpoints. We sat down and talked for, I don't know how long, it was last summer. It was like, we had a good conversation because, I mean, she was different, I was different, and we had different back-

grounds. I learned a lot from her. She learned some from me. So I think different is, diversity is good because diversity means learning. And difference means learning. (8)

Although most students saw racial-ethnic-cultural diversity positively if superficially, a few were more critical. Julian and Alice suggested that diversity was responsible for prejudice and racism while Melissa blamed immigration for increasing economic competition. She said that because there are more people competing for jobs, you need more education and college costs more. Rather dramatically, Sheldon said, "I picture a mongrel dog . . . America as a melting pot of all the nations' worse. Their worse ideas. Their worse thoughts, everything" (1). As examples, he offered racism, White supremacy, and ignorance.

Diversity, like freedom, although a dominant part of students' images of America, seems lacking in depth of meaning for most students.

<table>
<tr><td>

Additional Themes

</td><td>

(16)   **IMPERFECT BUT BEST**

</td></tr>
</table>

The three additional themes drawn from student interviews—America as better than other nations, progress, and the American Dream—fit within the parameters of the major image of America conveyed in the observed U.S. history classes: America as the best nation in the world despite past problems and current difficulties (see Cornbleth, 1998). Nine students, six of them from Johnson, described America as better than other nations in one way or another. Only one student from Lincoln (Carrie) and three from Eisenhower (all from George's class) shared these sentiments. Students at Johnson were more likely to be immigrants to the mainland United States (e.g., Simon whose family emigrated from India) or to know recent immigrants who spoke positively about coming here, which may explain the high proportion of students who shared this image.

Additional Theme 1 Interpretation and Supporting Examples

Simon, who had been in the United States about 6 months at the time of his interview, said, "From all over the world people come here. Straight to America. Better than any other country" (3). Julian commented, "A lot of people come here because we live a better life over here than other people do in other places" (2). Johnson students also mentioned freedom from government constraint and "rules" (Magdalena, Manuel) and America's wealth and opportunities (Richard, Marissa) as reasons why the United States is better than other nations. Magdalena, for example, compared the United States to Cuba where "you have a dictatorship and whatever Fidel Castro says goes" (4). Freedom and opportunity were echoed by students at Lincoln and Eisenhower. Alice, for example, told about her grandparents coming to the United States from Italy. "People came here for peace and . . . new ideas, and new ways of life," she said (1).

Additional Theme 2 Interpretation

Nine students, five of them from Eisenhower, mentioned progress—that things are getting better in the United States. The United States has had its problems but is resolving them. Most of the students who talked about progress as a part of their image of America referred to that message as being part of their social studies classes. All three students in Lindy's class at Eisenhower, for example, referred to the civil rights unit they had just completed, indicating both that they had not realized the extent of discrimination and racism back then and that things are better now (cf. Blauner, 1992). Progress for two of the students in George's class was primarily economic and technological, since the Great Depression.

Carrie, in contrast, while referring to her social studies class, spoke more personally:

> It seems like we've come a long way. Like, um, we've come from racial prejudice to equality. We've come from sexual discrimination to women's rights. There's a lot of things done to better our country, but there a lot of things that hinder from being a better country. . . . Me being a minority and a woman, seeing what I could have been into, what I have now. Just, it's nice to know that somebody cared way back then. (3)

Although not prominent in any of the student comments, struggle for change was more evident in the comments of two of the Johnson students. Progress did not just happen; people worked for it. Referring to African Americans, Arthur said that people have come a long way to get their rights (3). Magdalena talked about the struggles of women and African Americans:

It was hard. I mean people had problems with it. They didn't like how things were going. I mean women had to fight to get rights. To get recognized as we have a voice. We want to be able to vote too. . . . [Enslaved Africans] had to fight to become free. Because they were owned. They were like, it was your dog or something practically. I mean they went through a lot. Especially for African Americans. . . . Glad that I, you know, that I live now, not then, because then—I don't know how it would be. I would be scared. (4–5)

Additional Theme 3 Interpretation

For Marissa, past progress provides grounds for hope that current problems will be resolved. "Things aren't good," she said, "but they will get better. Like the gangs . . . the smoking and the drugs . . . nobody is gonna let that control the America because it's not good" (10). Asked how she has come to believe that, Marissa said,

'Cause all the things that have happened, like the slaves, like that's gone away. The Black and White, you know, that they couldn't be together. That went away. That got better. You know, it took time and people had to go through certain things, but it went away. (10)

Marissa's hopefulness provides a link to the last of the themes to emerge from the student interviews: the American Dream. Although a number of student comments can be seen as reflecting belief in the American Dream of individual opportunity and material betterment as a result of hard work, eight students more directly mentioned this image, three each from Lincoln and Eisenhower (43%) and two from Johnson (18%).

All three of the Lincoln students were African American and were in Peter's U.S. history class during the second year of the study. Even one of the most critical students, Sheldon, was not ready to turn his back on the American Dream. Early on he said,

Um, the American Dream is just a joke to me. It's not even feasible to achieve anymore I feel. [*CC: Say a bit more if you would about the American Dream, what it means to you, what it used to mean.*] That everybody is equal, everybody can get a house, a picket fence, and raise a family. That's no longer possible. Virtually. [*CC: When do you think things changed?*] . . . I think it was all a facade. I don't think it was ever really possible. [*CC: How do you suppose that the image caught on?*] People in despair want something to wish for. I mean they want something to achieve. Even if it's not achievable. (2)

Later, in seeming contradiction, Sheldon said, "I'm optimistic. I'm gonna make it. I'm determined to be all I can be in America" (7). In this and other student comments about the American Dream, the optimism is personal or individualistic. Individualism is a thread that loops through several of the students images of America.

Additional Theme 3 Supporting Examples

Mary volunteered, "There's no such thing as the American Dream anymore" (9). She continued,

The American Dream, what is that? There's no such thing. . . . A man and a woman getting married, buying a house, buying a car, that's not true. We don't even have health benefits anymore. . . . By the time you're 40, you've already switched your occupation three times. It's so unstable now. . . . I mean, we get just enough to survive. And after that, you're just living. (9)

But Mary has not given up hope. In response to my question, "So how does this affect your plans and your hopes for your life?" Mary said,

It doesn't affect my planning at all because I know what I want. As long as I believe in God, everything is gonna be all right. I just know what I want. And I'm gonna stay in school. And all the resources that are open to me, scholarshipwise, things like that. I'm gonna take the advantage. And I'm gonna move on. And one day I do, I want a family. I want to be married. I want children. . . . I want what's left of the American Dream, the little bit. (9–10)

Although not using the language of the American Dream, Carrie emphasized a combination of freedom and individual effort, saying, "I can be just anything anyone else can be" (2). She explained,

Well, you have the freedom to get your opportunities. You have your own abilities as a person, but whether you want to work for an opportunity is your own business. It's not like anyone is forcing you not to or forcing you to go for what you want. It's up to you. Your own freedom to do what you want to do. (3)

For the Eisenhower students, the American Dream was something to be earned by hard work. The Protestant work ethic was very much in evidence. The two Johnson students who seemed to have a sense of the American Dream expressed optimism that things will get better and that their lives will improve.

Themes
Crossing the
Main Themes

Crossing
Theme 1

(17) **CROSS-CUTTING THEMES: INDIVIDUALISM AND CRITIQUE AND/OR ACTIVISM**

Two themes that cut across the substantive themes of inequity, freedom, diversity, and imperfect but best in some students' images of America were an individualist bias and an assertion of critique and or activism. Individualism took two general forms in the students' talk about America. One reflects legendary, American competitive individualism, rugged or otherwise, where one advances on the basis of merit and effort.

Crossing
Theme 1
Supporting
Examples

Three Eisenhower students, for example, commented on how difficult it is for a person to get by or to "make it" now because of increased competition for good jobs and "the good life." Kate commented on how now you "gotta work to succeed" as if to suggest that in some time not too long past one did not have to work as hard. Success is largely economic, and the competition is individual in these views. Whereas Lincoln and Johnson students tended to believe that they could get ahead if they worked hard, and they did not seem to mind the prospect of hard work, Eisenhower students were less likely to volunteer optimism. These Eisenhower students seemed resentful of what they perceived as diminished opportunities for economic success. Melissa explained,

> I think there is less opportunity. I mean, before there was not so many immigrants and now it's, you know, second and third generation of immigrants, and it's becoming overpopulated and the opportunities for jobs is becoming less and less, and if you want to get a good job you've got to go to college for what seems to be an exorbitant amount of time. And you also have to have enough money to pay for all this graduate school and, you know, just to make it so that you can support yourself and then support your own family and put your kids through college. (2)

In contrast, Lincoln's Kirk said that despite poverty, drugs, and violence in the area surrounding his school,

> there's places where people are owning businesses, doing the right thing, raising families. Ya know, even myself, going on to college. Most of the seniors in this building are going on to do something. So it shows it's not all bad. . . . [*other people*] got to see that it's not all bad, that you can actually push out of this and become better. (6)

Across schools there is little or no sense of collective in the students' comments and if they are aware of structural changes in the economy or society, they rarely mention them directly. Even Carrie's seemingly contradictory comment about having the same opportunities as a man but maybe having to work harder does not recognize structural dynamics. Acknowledging that she "might not be treated the same way" as a man, Carrie claimed, "But that's a personal issue. It's not about the whole country" (2). Individual merit and effort are emphasized. For a few students, individual greed or selfishness are prevalent. "Everyone's all out for themselves now," Mary stated matter-of-factly (5). Sheldon was more vehement, describing the United States as an "evil, maniacal, dog-eat-dog nation" (3). Concurrently, he was very proud of his first paycheck from a part-time job—and unhappy about the several deductions.

A related, more frequently expressed form of individualism is personalization or students describing their images of America in terms of personal experience, perception, or future expectations. Mary's comments about the American Dream and wanting and working for the little bit that is left illustrate both personalization and belief in meritocracy. She is not talking about high school students, young women, or African Americans as a group. Also highly personalized are students' comments about freedom in terms of being able to do what you want. Because most of these students were in the midst of or had recently completed the state-required, 11th-grade U.S. history and government course, I expected some reference to the Bill of Rights or, at least, first amendment freedoms as such.

Bill, a student at Eisenhower, took personalization another step, insisting that he could not really understand U.S. history or "know what it feels like" (4) unless he had lived through it personally.

> I don't know. I can't really feel a part of it [*America. U.S. history*] just from seeing everything that's happened. And me being like 16-years-old, nothing's. I mean besides from like the Gulf war, whatever, nothing's really happened that's affected me. (3)

Crossing Theme 2 Interpretation

A second cross-cutting theme in students' images of America is an emergent social critique and or activism expressed primarily by students from Lincoln (five, both African and European American, male and female) but also by two students from Eisenhower (both female) and two from Johnson (an Hispanic female and a mixed race male). Although critique was expressed primarily by males, activism was expressed entirely by females. Social critique as used here refers to more than complaint about or disapproval of a particular circumstance or event (e.g., past discrimination and violence against African Americans). Emergent rather than fully formed among these students, critique involves linking two or more instances of inequity so as to suggest a pattern (but not yet structural properties) and or recognizing and attempting to understand causes or reasons for the situation(s) deemed undesirable. It involves being proactive, at least intellectually, beyond passing judgment as in (dis-)liking, accepting, or rejecting.

Crossing Theme 2 Supporting Examples

Most critical were Blake and Sheldon from Lincoln and Richard from Johnson. All three spoke about racism. Recall, for example, Blake's critique of inequity, "America's not like it should be," and his feeling sometimes of not belonging because he is treated differently than White Americans. Recall also Sheldon's assertion that the American Dream is a "facade" and his references to racism and White supremacy. Observing that "it looks like it's [America] starting to fall apart" (2). Richard noted drugs, crime, and racism as significant problems in the United States. Richard said, "to be American should be like a privilege" (2), but there are problems and "we can't get along" (12).

Less bitter than these three young men were Lincoln's Mary and Kirk. Mary was clear that opportunities were not equal in the United States:

> 1996 has nothing to do with whether you're Black or you're White or you're Vietnamese. It's what you want to do. Anything that person wants to do they can do because there's opportunities out here. . . . But it's just some things are just unfair. . . . I guess they say, you know, we help the ones that want to help themselves. But what about the ones that want to help themselves but can't get started on helping themselves? [*a reference to school dropouts about whom she had talked at length*] So that's a problem. (7)

Mary also noted, "Many of us, we don't have those opportunities" (9), referring to the President's daughter attending a private school. Yet, although she claimed that the American Dream no longer exists, she wants the little bit that is left.

Hopefulness clearly is evident alongside Kirk's relatively extended critique of poverty in the United States, especially the gap between rich and poor—in addition to violence, drugs, and self-serving politicians. But it is not all bad, he insisted; there are grounds for hope. Although Sheldon's and Mary's hopefulness was personal, Blake and Kirk were more generally hopeful for their community and/or country; Richard, in contrast, expressed pessimism and frustration. Reasons for the absence of explicit statements of hopefulness (or despair) among Eisenhower students are not at all clear. Hope may be taken for granted among the more privileged. Alternatively, what have been the implicit entitlements of White, middle and upper-middle class status now may be less certain as there are fewer grounds for expectation that each generation will be better off than the last. Support for the latter interpretation comes from the previously cited comments of Eisenhower students about how you have to work harder to succeed now.

Johnson's Magdalena noted that throughout U.S. history people have fought for their rights. Improvement has had to be struggled for. In talking about and endorsing others' activism, Magdalena seems to bridge the critique and activism strands of this theme. She also is one of the few students who explicitly indicated understanding that historical events do not "just happen."

Activism here refers to suggesting or participating in some way of responding to or resolving the undesirable situation(s). It may or may not be associated directly with critique as used here. Both critique and activism, as expressed by these students, seem to suggest hopefulness. Although they were not content with America as they saw it, these students seemed to assume that problems could and should be resolved.

Three White female students, Lincoln's Linda and Eisenhower's Melissa and Ann, were clear that it was time to "do something" about America's problems, not just complain. Linda was tired of the negativity, especially what she hears in her family; she would like to focus on good things and deal with the problems—get on with it. She explained,

> everybody focuses on, you know, the decline of America. . . . violence . . . morals decline, the budget, the corruption. Nobody really looks at the good things either, you know. There's always, for every dark moment, there's a bright spot too, but nobody likes nobody likes good news. . . . There's too much focus on the bad things. It's getting kind of stale. . . . Everybody's complaining, nobody is trying to do anything. (4)

Instead of the media focus on controversy, Melissa said that it would be better to deal with the problems that Americans can do something about. Ann also referred to the mass media, particularly portrayals of violence. There are always problems, she said, "so you just gotta deal with those and go on" (7). She mentioned having been a member of Amnesty International for a year at the time of the interview. It is noteworthy that two of these three young, White women seemed to qualify or apologize for their strong views. Ann said that she tends to be optimistic while Linda said that she tends to avoid conflict and that "A lot of people think that I'm naive or I think too simply or something. I don't know. Why does it have to be so complicated? I mean it really isn't. I mean, people really aren't that different" (5). These young women may well be naive about how change can be accomplished insofar as they seemed not to recognize the nature of systemic change and the role of broad-based social movements. Even their "activism" seemed individualistic.

Summary of Theme Findings and Interpretations

(18)

AS YET UNFULFILLED PROMISE

In sum, these students' images of America are characterized by themes of inequity (72%), freedom (56%), diversity (56%), and imperfect but best (36%). Cross-cutting these themes are a sense of individualism or personalization and an incipient critique and or activism expressed by more than 30% of the students. Generally similar images were offered by a smaller sample of urban and rural western New York middle school students who mentioned freedom most often (67%) followed by danger (58%) and diversity (50%): only 2 of the 12 students, both urban, mentioned inequity. Like the older students, the middle schoolers also offered mixed, positive and negative, descriptions of America. Their images, however, tended to be more localized, more often citing direct experience in their communities, for example, the fear or threat of personal danger (Lawrence-Brown, 1998). Also similar is the major theme in a study of Kentucky middle school students' explanations of historical significance, what the authors characterized as America's "progressive expansion of rights, opportunity, and freedom" (Barton & Levstik, 1998, p. 486). These rough similarities across studies both lend credence to the findings reported here and suggest the desirability of testing their generalizability to other locales and student groups.

*Interpretation
of Themes in
Relation to
Other
Research*

Despite differences in emphasis, the high school students' reported images of America are not inconsistent with the two major themes derived from an analysis of the images actually conveyed in 5th-, 8th-, and 11th-grade U.S. history classrooms: imperfect but best—America as the best nation in the world despite past problems and current difficulties—and multiple perspectives (Combleth, 1998).[7] That the students interviewed here put more emphasis on the "imperfect" is consistent with both our classroom observations showing more consideration of multiple, including critical, views of the nation in the upper grades and students' reports of change over time in their understandings. It is also the case that students report multiple influences on their thinking about America of which school experience is only one. Sources of and influences on their thinking as well as change over time are considered in the next section.

Although these young people may be as attuned to discrepancies between democratic ideals and realities as their elders, they do seem less willing to accept America's imperfections as inevitable or incurable. Their loyalty to or stake in the nation appears to come much less from celebration of heroes, military victories, or inventions than from belief in—or desire to believe in—America's promise of opportunity and equality, of freedom and justice for all. A diverse group, they appear much less wary of diversity than older Americans of European descent who express concern that too much diversity threatens national unity (and, at least implicitly, social stability). In contrast to "ordinary citizens" or the much-polled U.S. electorate, which frequently has been characterized as frustrated and/or distrustful (especially of the federal government, e.g., Uchitelle and Kleinfeld, 1996), these students—like their U.S. history classes—tended to be more positive. Instead of alienation, I heard disappointment alongside still high expectations for America (cf. Hochschild, 1995).

(19)   **SHAPING STUDENTS' UNDERSTANDING OF AMERICA**

*Obtaining
Evidence for
Participants'
Beliefs and
Ideas*

We asked students about the major sources of their ideas about America. If students did not mention family, friends, school, TV, movies, newspapers, and magazines, we asked about each of these possible influences. For the most part, students spoke about influences on their images of America in general terms, and it was not possible to link particular images with particular sources.

*Interpretation
of Informa-
tion About
Source of Par-
ticipants' Be-
liefs and
Ideas With
Supporting
Examples*

Overall, school, including specific courses, was the most frequently noted source of students' images of America (23 of 25 students). This was not surprising insofar as all the interviews were conducted in the students' schools, and in most cases we asked specifically about images of America conveyed in social studies and English classes that the students were currently taking or had recently completed. Images that students reported as having been conveyed in classes were not attributed to the students unless they explicitly indicated their agreement with or adoption of the image. The students in the Eisenhower class that had completed a civil rights unit just prior to the interviews seem to have incorporated the new information about racism into their images of America—a clear cut indication of the potential influence of teacher and curriculum practice. The Lincoln students, in contrast, displayed a greater range of images of America and seemed to be offering their own interpretations of images conveyed in class and elsewhere. The Johnson students showed the least evidence of classroom curriculum impact on their images of America except perhaps for a leaning toward a "great man" view of history. It also was the only school in which any student claimed not to have learned much if anything in his or her 11th-grade U.S. history and government class. Representative of comments from several students were, "we really don't do nothing in that class" (Magdalena, 5) and "cause he don't really teach. He don't do nothing" (Kaylee, 2)

Generally, students' comments about sources of and influences on their images of America are consistent with the findings of Ehman's (1980) review of two decades of political socialization research about the effects of schooling on political knowledge, attitudes, and participation. Although schooling generally and curriculum practice in particular are important sources of students' political information, and more so in secondary than elementary school, secondary civics and government curriculum "appears not to be an impressive vehicle for shaping political attitudes or participation orientations" (p. 113).[8]

After school, personal experience was the next most frequently cited influence (15 students), followed by family and or older people and TV and other news media (11 students each). Interestingly, one Lincoln student described her views as a reaction to her family's bigotry; the same student, Linda, and Eisenhower's Kate described TV as a negative influence, meaning that they either discounted it or reacted against what they saw as over-statement or misrepresentation. Kate referred to sitcoms depicting the "perfect" American family, which she implied does not exist, while Linda cited "the overkill of things on TV" and "all the big thing about the O. J. Simpson case" (5).

Reading and books were mentioned as sources of images of America by five male students, three of whom were non-White (one Native and African American and two African Americans) who challenged conventional, largely positive versions of U.S. history. These are the same three previously described as offering the strongest social critique. Blake, for example, said,

> what I learned in school throughout grammar school and everything. America's been painted as such a great country, and it's been painted as a country that could do no wrong. The government's so good and it works, and the system is so great. But as I grew older and began to read things outside of what they taught in school, I found out that it is not so great. It's not so flowery as it's been painted to look, as it's been painted to be. And so, and then, like I've said, the encounters I've had, also show, this country's not so great and it's not so good and as flowery as it's said to be. (6)

He mentioned reading "a history of the Negro in America" and *The Autobiography of Malcolm X*, saying, "And he [Malcolm X] kind of had the same somewhat feeling about America also, that it is not what it is or what it should be, and has not treated people fairly" (6–7).

Blake, Sheldon, and Richard mentioned family (and or older people) as well as books and reading as influencing their images of America and leading them to be more critical of America past and present. In this respect, they resemble the African-American students in Epstein's (1998) study of the historical perspectives of 11th-grade students in an urban high school in the Detroit area. Epstein attributed the different choices and explanations of significant actors, events, and themes in U.S. history offered by African- and European-American students to "race-related differences in the lived experiences of the adolescents themselves and their family members" (p. 397). Although evident, as just noted, race-related differences in the current study were neither as clear cut nor as pervasive as in Epstein's analysis.

Lastly, movies were mentioned as a source of images of America by three students and peers by two.

School differences in the reporting of sources of images of America were evident in only two instances. Eisenhower students were less likely to cite personal experience (one of seven students) and more likely to cite TV (six of seven) as influencing their images of America. Recall the two Eisenhower students who commented about being isolated in their suburb insofar as they saw themselves as having limited opportunity to learn about people different from themselves. One of these, Melissa, was the only Eisenhower student to mention personal experience, saying,

> I've seen enough of the United States to know that things aren't always the way they seem. You know, I've been up and down the east coast and, you know, we, when we do go on vacation we do the touristy things but reality always slips into it. . . . we have relatives in Long Island, so we drive through New York City every, every uh year, and somehow every year we end up going the wrong way and end up in one of the worst neighborhoods of New York City. And uhmm, it's kind of, I mean it's scary. . . . And you see the houses and how run down they are. And me coming from [suburb], I don't see this stuff very often. I mean, I'm used to like white picket fences. So, we go down to New York City and, uh, it's just reality right there staring you in the face. (4)

In contrast, all the Lincoln students cited personal experience as a source of their images of America. Blake said, "My sources are the encounters that I've had. The encounters that my family has gone through. Um, history. Um, what my grandparents and great-grandparents have gone through" (6). Kirk described his experience on the streets:

I've seen a lot. It doesn't really seem it, but in 18 years I've seen a lot. I've seen people get in fights. I've seen people pull out guns. I've seen good things happen. . . . If you were like, let's say, in a, in a better area, you know, you don't see a lot of homeless people or people that pull guns or drug dealers, you know. Those are the kinds of things you really, ya know, those are the kinds of things that people want to shield you from. But you, I think you got to see 'em in order to realize it's going, that it is there, it's going on and something has to be done about it. . . . I've had five people in 18 years that I've known that have gotten murdered by a weapon, by some form of firearm. . . . you gotta think to the future and think before you do, ya know, instead of just going out and being, doing something stupid. It could be your life right there. So it's kind of what has shaped me. Seeing those kinds of, seeing the negatives actually, that made me work harder so I could be positive. (5–6)

Johnson's Mercedes described more specific experience with segregation in the city:

when you travel around [*the city*] itself, how it's so segregated. You know? It's like the west side is mostly Hispanic. The east side is mostly Black Americans. And then you got the south part which is mostly . . . So I see when I'm in the streets, when I go to different places in [*the city*], it's there in my face. . . . I don't like it. I really don't. . . . And I'm not used to living like that. In the City [*New York City*] we used to, you know, everybody lived together. . . . I'm pretty sure it [*segregation*] happens all around the United States of America. . . . I'm pretty sure it happens in New York too, you understand? But I don't. I never experienced it over there until I came to [*the city*]. . . . It's good to learn about other people and their culture and the way they live. You learn interesting things. But it's real segregated over here. (5–6)

Mercedes' experience with racial-ethnic segregation in the city has led her to see America as segregated. It was not unusual for students to generalize from their personal experience to "America." And, as students' experiences have changed, in and out of school, so have their images of America.

(20)   **CHANGE OVER TIME**

*Additional
Interpreta-
tions of Infor-
mation About
Source of Par-
ticipants' Be-
liefs and
Ideas With
Supporting
Examples*

Students' comments about change over time in their images of America also shed some light on what shapes those images. Except for the three Eisenhower students who had just completed the civil rights unit that had a major impact on their images of America, students who noted changed images tended to attribute change to personal experience.[9]

With the exception of Lincoln's Blake, who reported more hopeful, positive images of America compared to a year or two ago, despite his learning that "this country's not so great . . . as it's said to be" (6), the students reported change toward more realistic (i.e., less positive) images of America. The three Eisenhower students who said the civil rights unit changed their images of America said that it provided information new to them. James said he learned more about discrimination, "how difficult it was [for blacks in the United States] and how degrading" (3), while Ned said he learned about the extent of racism and "how bad it was" (2) for Blacks before then. Both were particularly taken with the video, "The Shadow of Hate." Ned, as did a few other students, suggested without prompting that students should learn about prejudice, discrimination, and racism earlier, before 11th grade:

I don't think you should show that [the video] to elementary kids because they really wouldn't understand the point of it, but . . . like, eighth grade and on. I think the kids should know, because I think that might be able to stop racism in the U.S. if they see that. I mean, not that it's totally going to solve it, but, just give you a different perspective on what it was like. (2)

Melissa, as described earlier, characterized her image of America as less positive than at the beginning of the academic year, because of the extent of prejudice in the United States that she did not know about before. In retrospect, she described her seventh- and eighth-grade U.S. history classes as superficial.

Uhm, seventh and eighth grade, the only thing that I really thought about was, uh, the way the Indians were treated. And how they were forced to move. But even then we didn't go into that enough, you know, just they said, oh um, you know, the Indians had to move. They had to go to the other side of the country and, you know, reservations and stuff like that. But we didn't really get into anything of detail. . . . We did the whole Martin Luther King, Jr., uh, you know, how he fought for civil rights but we didn't hear about the people being beaten on buses and, you know, the busses being burned and, uhm, the actual, the actual hate that went on. (3–4)

In contrast, Melissa characterized the civil rights unit as "graphic":

It was graphic . . . I mean it was disturbing to me, but it wasn't, it wasn't overboard like sometimes some groups will make things look worse than they are, just you know, to get attention I think. This was really the, the videos that we saw and the, uh, worksheets that she handed out about actual people, uh, it was really moving to me to see that. You don't know that, you don't know their names. And she handed out a worksheet that had the names and the, you know, how they died and what date they died on, and it was, you know, it was kind of, you could put a name to some of the faces maybe. (4)

Only one of the four students in the other Eisenhower class mentioned any change over time in images of America. Alice attributed the change to TV's showing an America where "there are like terrible things about it, and different things that are bad in our society and stuff" (6). She cited greed and killing as examples.

At Lincoln, none of the four female students mentioned changes in their images of America while all three male students did. Kirk talked about change accompanying his move from a neighborhood Catholic elementary school 4 years ago to Lincoln in a poorer, city neighborhood. He emphasized meeting and getting along with people different from himself and learning about social problems:

I grew up in [city neighborhood] all my life. Uh, I went to the neighborhood school, ya know, so I didn't experience too many things. . . . Basically everybody knew each other. You hung around in your own neighborhood. You stuck with your own, ya know. It was, it was, ya know, it was nice. . . . So when I came here it was like a learning experience on my own. I learned that life isn't so nice and sweet and perfect. It's not like that everywhere. Some people got it harder. And it seems. I feel lucky that I still have both my parents and that I have a family that cares about me. So that's why, ya know, it all fits in somehow . . . if you know what's going on . . . (7)

Like Ned, Kirk believed that younger students should not be sheltered from all the rougher and nastier aspects of life:

when you're growing up and you're little, ya know. I think you should be exposed a little bit to everything. Ya know, you should know what's going on. . . . If you don't know what's out there, you don't know that, that if you're doing drugs it's gonna screw your life up, ya know, because you never really knew about it. . . . Or you didn't know about even sex and all that, pregnancy. AIDS, all that. You don't know about it, you're going to go ahead and do it. . . . You gotta know those kind of things so you can see [*inaudible*]. I feel that information is the key to everything. Knowledge is the key. (7)

Whereas Kirk remained hopeful, Sheldon described change toward largely negative images of America. He attributed change to learning and "just experiences" (7), which probably include some of his reading outside of school. Sheldon described the change as follows:

when I was a freshman I used to say the, say the Pledge of Allegiance and things like that. But not anymore. . . . I'm not really proud to be an American. After realizing some of the things that we did as a people. Some of the things that we did to ourselves and to other nations and things. Our whole frame of thought is just polluted. America has polluted itself. (7)

At the same time, he described himself as more open than he used to be:

> I used to be real, real stubborn. If everybody didn't think like me, then they were wrong, but now I'm open. . . . I've got a job now. And since I've been open to different people and things like that. . . . I believe everybody as a person should be respected. But I still hold strongly about different things that I know is not right. (7)

In contrast, Blake, who expressed rather critical images of America and how he had become more critical since elementary school, also said that he recently found reason for hope. As noted earlier, he described thinking that diversity was bad because it led to conflict but now thinking it is good because he had found that you can talk things through and learn from one another. Blake also referred to an extended partner project with students from a suburban high school (in the same district as Eisenhower) as having a major impact on him. On the basis of that experience he said,

> America has a bright future, because just the youth in that group as a whole [from the suburban high school], um, were very positive. I didn't feel any racial tensions while I was there. It felt like a family, basically, because you know, everyone was entertaining, laughing, talking together, and some of them had some of the same ideas and viewpoints. And so I feel that America has a bright future because that group alone of young people who could work together to bring America back or take it to what it should have been all the time. (7)

Blake rather poignantly reflects the mix of critique and hope evident in several students' images of America. Moreover, the changes that he and other students described suggest that their images of the nation may well undergo further change as societal circumstances, their experiences, and their knowledge changes. To expect stable images of America in the face of changing circumstances is unrealistic unless those images are abstract (e.g., ideals, principles) or limited to what Melissa called the "symbols" such as the flag and the Statue of Liberty.

Discussion and Conclusion Section

㉑

CONCLUDING CONSIDERATIONS

It is not my intent to pass judgment on these students' images of America beyond noting that, although not overly positive in the way of 1950s TV sitcoms, they are both realistic and supportive of the nation-state. There are no grounds here for either super-patriotic lament or celebration.

That varied images of America are reported by this group of high school juniors and seniors is not surprising given the racial-ethnic and socioeconomic diversity of the sample as well as district, school, and teacher differences. They simply have not experienced "America" similarly, in or out of school. And, like other school messages, the images of America communicated by school curriculum and culture are not necessarily received by students or understood as intended (e.g., Cornbleth, 1984).

Moreover, a number of students appear to hold inconsistent, even contradictory, images concurrently. That their images of America tend to be disparate may be an appropriate reflection of the nation and its history. Such images can be seen as reflecting changing interpretations and differing sources of information about the United States as well as the differing experiences and views of various participants. It seems, for example, that to several Johnson and Lincoln students, America means freedom and equal opportunity in the abstract or in principle alongside their experience of discrimination in local stores and other situations—a general good alongside nasty particulars. A mix of acceptance and dissent was evident in the images of America put forward in the western New York elementary, middle, and high school classrooms we observed (Cornbleth, 1998, pp. 641–643), especially in the upper grades. Partial, unconnected images predominated, with an overall effect that was more a complex, multifaceted America than a fragmented one. The seeming disjointedness of both curriculum and student images of America, whether or not a reflection of contemporary sensibilities akin to MTV, provides openings for alternative images and questions about the nation's history and possible future.

Given this mix, the similarities in students' images may be more noteworthy than the differences. Either way, Epstein's (1998) suggestion that U.S. history curriculum and teaching should better accommodate students' differing historical perspectives, such as those brought to class by the African- and European-American students in her study, merits serious consideration here. The prior knowledge and perspectives that students bring with them shape what they make of what is offered in history classes and what they take away (e.g., Seixas, 1993). To ignore student mediation of teaching and learning is to undermine its potential positive effects. One means of accommodation is to invite and incorporate student perspectives, and the evidence on which they are based, into the classroom dialogue. Then, consider these perspectives and their supporting evidence as historical strands to be braided with others (e.g., textbook version) in constructing fuller, more authentic historical accounts (Cornbleth, 1997).

*Relevance of
the Current
Research*

 SOCIAL AND POLITICAL CONSIDERATIONS

As noted previously, the present work is one of very few studies of the substance of students' knowledge and beliefs about the United States and its history. The findings carry implications left undisturbed by analyses over the past several decades of how much students know (e.g., a lot, some, very little), how politically supportive or cynical their attitudes, or how similar or different their social and political beliefs. With respect to the latter, it has been asserted by numerous commentators, especially those of moderate and conservative bent, that similarities are good, contributing to national unity and well-being. Differences, in constrast, are seen as actually or potentially dangerous, leading to dissension and disunion: with disunion comes disaster. Thus, we are offered language in state history curriculum standards such as,

> the study of New York State and United States history requires an analysis of the development of American culture, its diversity and multicultural context, and the ways people are unified by many values, practices, and traditions. (Standard 1—History of the United States and New York, NYSED. 1996, p. 2)[10]

Without rehashing or entering into the pluralism-unity or common culture arguments prevalent since the mid-1980s (see e.g., Cornbleth & Waugh, 1995, 1999), my intent is to suggest that they are dangerously simplistic insofar as they obscure substantial tensions underlying the surface similarity or agreement in adult opinion or in young people's beliefs about America.

Looking for similarities, one could be reassured by the extent of unprompted agreement within this racially-ethnically and socioeconomically diverse group of young people. We asked open-ended questions rather than multiple-choice questions that limit respondents to predetermined choices. Even so, more than two thirds of the students (72%) agreed that inequity was part of their image of America whereas a majority (56%) agreed that freedom and diversity were part of their image of America. In addition, more than a third (36%) agreed on an image of America that I have characterized as "imperfect but best." It is when we examine what is agreed upon, not merely the extent of agreement, and how it plays out for various individuals and groups, that agreement becomes problematic.

Inequity, part of the image of America past and/or present described by more than two thirds of these students, provides the most striking example. By school, there was agreement among 71% of the students at Lincoln and Eisenhower and 76% at Johnson, which does not indicate differences along racial-ethnic, socioeconomic, or urban-suburban lines. Two aspects of the inequity theme bear repeating: more than half of the students mentioning inequity specifically referred to racism or to racial-ethnic prejudice or discrimination, and inequity often was mentioned in relation to U.S. ideals or constitutional promises (e.g., "America's not like it should be").

It is one thing for students of European descent, whether or not from a relatively affluent suburb, to acknowledge racial inequity and another for students of African, Puerto Rican, or other ancestry. Clearly, racial inequity plays out very differently in their lives. For example, students from Eisenhower told of only recently learning of the extent and viciousness of racism prior to and during the post–World War II civil rights movement—none mentioned personal experience of racial discrimination—whereas students from Johnson told of recent personal experiences of racial inequity and discrimination. Rarely do White students directly experience racial inequity except insofar as they benefit from it. It is something to be deplored but need not be faced on a daily basis. Inequity divides the advantaged and disadvantaged.

Pointing to the discrepancies between U.S. ideals and realities—"America's not like it should be"—could feed cynicism about the nation's hypocrisy, resignation, or hope that conditions will improve. Progress, implicit in the "imperfect but best" theme, and direct student statements of hopefulness suggest but do not guarantee the latter. Cynicism or alienation, however, ought not to be ruled out as a possibility. The prominence of individualism in students' talk with us; the absence of evidence of structural understanding (e.g., social class, institutional racism); and the limited recognition of struggle as an integral if not essential aspect of the expansion of civil rights all suggest that these young people are likely to remain outside the social movements that might alleviate racial-ethnic and other inequities. Some may be or become vulnerable to the promises of extremist organizations.

There also is evidence in the Eisenhower students' interviews (but not those of the White students at Lincoln) to suggest that, in the present highly competitive economy, they do not welcome more competitors. Recall, for example, Melissa's comment about diminished opportunity and increased competition from immigrants. Although deploring inequity, she seems uneasy about playing on a level field. Her Eisenhower peers, who appear to have given the issue less thought, may react even more strongly.

A focus on similarity or agreement in this instance clearly masks underlying fissures. Similar lines of argument could be laid out for students' agreement on the themes of freedom and diversity. Freedom, including rights and opportunities, was part of the images of America described by 57% of Lincoln and Eisenhower students and 55% of Johnson students. Although some students pointed to limits on freedom, specifically unfair distribution or access, these problems were viewed as occurring primarily in the past. In the turn of the century United States, however, freedom plays out differently for relatively affluent young people of European descent than it does for young people of African, Puerto Rican, and other ancestry or for any working class or poor young person. In effect, because they face less prejudice and discrimination, higher socioeconomic status Whites have more freedom or privilege (see, e.g., McIntosh, 1992, for examples of everyday, unearned White privilege).

Diversity, too, plays out differently depending upon who one is. Here, school differences were apparent with 71% of Eisenhower students, 57% of Lincoln students, and 45% of Johnson students mentioning diversity as part of their image of America. The less racial-ethnic diversity at the school or in the neighborhood, the more students noted diversity as characteristic of America. Diversity may be taken-for-granted, or less noteworthy, in more diverse settings. In any event, diversity in the contemporary United States tends to refer to non-Whites, to "others"—White is not a color; it is the norm. For example, a recent Sunday *New York Times* "Careers in Education" ad announced a "Career Fair for Culturally Diverse Educators" sponsored by several suburban New York City school districts. The most specific statement about the meaning of diversity read, "In response to the changing demographics of students within the . . . school districts, we are building a team of culturally diverse educators" (January 31, 1999, Week in Review, p. 10).

Recall Melissa's story about feeling uncomfortable being the only White person at her Korean friend's family gathering and her friend's reaction. Racial-ethnic diversity may be interesting to young people of European descent, but it usually is outside themselves, out there. Not so for the African, Puerto Rican, and other young people in our study who are diverse, that is, different. They are diversity's objects.

Even this brief examination of some of the social and political implications of apparent agreement in students' images of America indicates that similarity is no guarantor of solidarity or peaceful coexistence—especially when the agreement masks and deflects attention from significant group disparities in current circumstance and future prospects. Expecting school curriculum and culture to remedy these societal fissures and social-political-economic tensions with positive images or common symbols is naive at best.

*Implications
for Teaching
and Learning*
㉓   **PEDAGOGICAL CONSIDERATIONS**

These students are learning the traditional patriotic mythology (cf., Frisch, 1990, chap. 3). Our interviews with juniors and seniors indicate, however, that by this point in their formal education even the Eisenhower students, who might be expected to be most accepting, know at least vaguely that it is myth and symbol, and their images of America reach deeper. For example, in response to the question about images of America, Melissa responded,

> the Statue of Liberty and the American flag, just because they're such symbols of America . . . When you say America I think first of those two things and then I realize that, like, those probably aren't the best examples, and I start thinking of other, like, actual people that live in the United States. (1)

Ann suggested that these symbols are taught early on. She told us,

> Uh, the Statue of Liberty. . . . Mount Rushmore, the presidents, George Washington. *[SG asks, "Why do you think those things came to mind?"]* Well, they're like monumental. . . . George Washington is the first president, you know . . . everyone knows that, I mean, you learn that, like, in kindergarten. *[Ann and SG laugh.]* Just, like the Statue of Liberty. (1)

The traditional patriotic mythology and symbolism may backfire, however, when students' own experiences or other sources they trust provide counterevidence. The danger here is twofold. Students might become unnecessarily cynical, having come to expect an America that's "such a great country . . . that could do no wrong" (Blake, 6). Not only might young people become distrustful of the nation—and perhaps join the growing ranks of apathetic nonvoters or followers of extremist gurus—but schooling also might lose credibility as a source of information and an activity worthy of one's effort (e.g., Epstein, 1998). Teachers and school subjects then, instead of nurturing the intended political loyalty and efficacy, may prompt disdain or rejection. Alternatively, students might just dismiss the school's messages as irrelevant. Johnson's Julian, for example, related,

> It's like the things we talk about in school are way different from what happens in real life. *[AS: "Tell me more about that."]* Well, at school they talk about, know what I'm saying, everything you can be in life, but out in the street it's something different because you get caught up in different types of things . . . They just don't connect. (4)

When asked for a specific example, Julian mentioned that "A lot of people can't even afford to go to college. . . . They try to tell you to go to school and be all that you can be when you can't even go to college"(4).

The potential for various forms of backlash appears to be among the most serious pedagogical implications of the present study. Perhaps policymakers and educators would do well to heed the advice of students like Ned and Kirk who advised letting younger students know more about the real world and the nation's history sooner rather than later. Despite the urging of conservatives, neither students nor America seem to benefit from partial, highly positive portrayals of society and history as "flowery" or "sweet."

Clearly, times have changed since the 1950s, prior to which the schools apparently played a major role in nation-building, communicating a consistent if not comprehensive and coherent message about America's provenance and mission (e.g., Foner, 1998). In addition to the diversification of the population, the unwillingness of previously silenced and or marginalized groups to remain so, technological advances in communication and transportation, and much broader historical and social science research, the relatively recent explosion of mass media has severely undercut K–12 schooling as a source of information and influence about America and most everything else. Our data indicate that some school messages are getting through to students—frequently modified by other sources and interpreted through students' lenses. Schooling, specifically history-social studies curriculum and instruction, however, may be missing opportunities to exert more constructive influence on young people's knowledge and beliefs about who "we" are.

To the extent that school history focuses on people, places, and events, it not only competes with other, often more powerful sources, but also misses opportunities to help students comprehend and think critically about the information they encounter in and out of school. Instead of "one damn thing after another," school history also might help students to see connections and longer term processes (e.g., industrialization and post-industrialism) and struggles (e.g., civil rights, environmental protection). Examination of structural dynamics and collective experience (e.g., social class and gender-related) as well as individual accomplishments and frustrations will enable students to see both the societal forest and its various groves and trees—as will examining these from varied perspectives past and present. Rather than being told a single story, students would be encouraged to braid the several strands. Moreover, studying how specific groups have worked for recognition and expansion of their constitutionally guaranteed rights and opportunities can offer students realistic expectations and assist their empowerment to constructive public action. It can counter other press toward cynicism and alienation or extremism.

A final consideration here stems from students' comments about diversity in America. Recall that Johnson and Lincoln students were more vocal than Eisenhower students about liking and learning from experiences with people different from themselves in school or in their neighborhoods. Eisenhower students seemed less opposed to such interaction than apprehensive because of limited contact with young people outside their largely White and affluent suburban area. None of the students suggested the desirability of Americans becoming more alike; there were no self-described common culturalists in our sample. Instead, several students talked about accommodating diversity, of talking and working across differences. A strong case could be made here for more cross-cultural education and experience, especially for students in largely White schools.

America and its peoples might well benefit from nurturing continuing "dialogue among differences" (Cornbleth & Waugh, 1995, 1999, p. 198) in and out of school. Social connection and coherence are more likely to emerge from interaction and participation in the public sphere than from school attempts to impose commonality of any stripe. There are grounds for optimism in these young people's images of America and willingness to talk.

ENDNOTES

(24)

1.   All names are pseudonyms. Interview transcript page numbers are provided for direct quotes. Because racial-ethnic differences in images of America, although evident, were not all-encompassing, students' racial-ethnic identities are not routinely reported. To do so would suggest racial-ethnic difference when it is not apparent in these data. Racial-ethnic, school (a rough proxy for socioeconomic status and, to some extent, race-ethnicity), and gender differences are reported as relevant. Appendix A provides a who's who of participating students.

2.   The study reported here grows out of the cross-disciplinary Fallingwater research project co-directed by S. G. Grant, Suzanne Miller, Barry Shealy, and myself. My thanks to Lois Weis for feedback on an earlier draft of this article and to research project staff members who contributed to the data and interpretation for it: S. G. Grant, Diana Lawrence-Brown, Julia Marusza, and Angela Stevenson. Research support from the Professional Development Network, Graduate School of Education, University at Buffalo should not be construed as concurrence with the interpretations offered and positions taken here.

3.   The shorter interviews occurred at Johnson High School. Interviews at this school were shorter because of time constraints and, possibly, the preferences of students as well as the relative inexperience of the interviewer.

4.   Blake (4).

5.   The poem, "Let America Be America Again," had been read and discussed in an English class project in which Blake participated.

6.   The suggestion that Americans "do" something about our problems is offered by three other students as well (White female students from Lincoln and Eisenhower) and is considered in conjunction with the cross-cutting theme of critique and/or activism.

7.   These classrooms included five at Lincoln and six at other schools in the Eisenhower suburban district.

8.   Classroom and school climate, and student participation in school-related activities, however, were found to be related to political attitudes.

9.   Because of interview time limits, most Johnson students were not asked about changes in their images of America. No data from Johnson are presented on this question.

10.   Elementary students are expected to "explain those values, practices, and traditions that unite all Americans" (p. 2) whereas middle school students are expected to "explore the meaning of American culture by identifying the key ideas, beliefs, and patterns of behavior, and traditions that help define it and unite all Americans," in part by identifying "ideas of national unity that developed amidst growing cultural diversity" (p. 4). It is only at the secondary level that specifics are offered. Here, students are to "analyze the development of American culture, explaining how ideas, values, beliefs, and traditions have changed over time and how they unite all Americans," in part by exploring "the meaning of the United States motto, 'E Pluribus Unum,'" by identifying both those forces that unite Americans and those that potentially divide Americans. "Based on a study of key events in U.S. history, such as the American Revolution, the Civil War, the women's suffrage movement, and the civil rights movement, discuss how at least two core civic ideas, such as individual rights and the consent of the governed, have been forces for national unity in this diverse society" (p. 6).

㉕   **REFERENCES**

Appleby, J., Hunt, L., & Jacob, M. (1994). *Telling the truth about history.* New York: W. W. Norton.

Barton, K. C., & Levstik, L. S. (1998). "It wasn't a good part of history": National identity and students' explanations of historical significance. *Teachers College Record, 99*(3), 478–513.

Blauner, B. (1992). Talking past each other: Black and White languages of race. *American Prospect, 10,* 55–64.

Bogdan, R. C., & Biklen, S. K. (1992). *Qualitative research methods for education* (2nd ed.). Boston: Allyn & Bacon.

Cornbleth, C. (1984). Beyond hidden curriculum? *Journal of Curriculum Studies, 16*(1), 29–36.

Cornbleth, C. (1997). Birds of a feather: People(s), culture(s), and school history. *Theory and Research in Social Education, 25*(3), 357–362.

Cornbleth, C. (1998). An America curriculum? *Teachers College Record, 99*(4), 622–646.

Cornbleth, C. (2000). National standards and curriculum as cultural containment? In C. Cornbleth (Ed.), *Curriculum politics, policy, practice: Cases in comparative context* (pp. 211–238). Albany, NY: State University of New York Press.

Cornbleth, C., & Waugh, D. (1999). *The great speckled bird: Multicultural politics and education policymaking.* Mahwah, NJ: Erlbaum. (Reprinted from original St. Martin's Press 1995).

Ehman, L. H. (1980). The American school in the political socialization process. *Review of Educational Research, 50*(1), 99–119.

Elson, R. M. (1964). *Guardians of tradition: American schoolbooks of the nineteenth century.* Lincoln, NE: University of Nebraska Press.

Epstein, T. (1997). Sociocultural approaches to young people's historical understanding. *Social Education, 61*(1), 28–31.

Epstein, T. (1998). Deconstructing differences in African-American and European-American adolescents' perspectives on U.S. history. *Curriculum Inquiry, 28,* 397–423.

Erickson, F. (1986). Qualitative methods in research on teaching. In M. C. Wittrock (Ed.), *Handbook of research on teaching* (3rd ed., pp. 119–161). New York: Macmillan.

Fitzgerald, F. (1979). *America revised: History schoolbooks in the twentieth century.* Boston: Little, Brown.

Foner, E. (1998). History forum: Teaching American history. *American Scholar,* Winter, 94–96.

Frisch, M. (1990). *A shared authority: Essays on the craft and meaning of oral and public history.* Albany, NY: State University of New York Press.

Grant, C. A. & Sleeter, C. E. (1986). *After the school bell rings.* London: Falmer.

Greeno, J. G., Collins, A. M., & Resnick, L. B. (1996). Cognition and learning. In D. C. Berliner & R. C. Calfee (Eds.), *Handbook of educational psychology* (pp. 15–46). New York: Simon & Schuster Macmillan.

History-Social Science Curriculum Framework and Criteria Committee. (1997). *History-Social Science Framework.* Sacramento, CA: California State Department of Education. (Original work adopted and published 1987–88).

Hochschild, J. L. (1995). *Facing up to the American dream: Race, class, and the soul of the nation.* Princeton, NJ: Princeton University Press.

Lawrence-Brown, D. (1998). Middle school students' views of America. Unpublished manuscript, SUNY at Buffalo.

McIntosh, P. W. (1992). White privilege and male privilege. In M. L. Andersen & P. H. Collins (Eds.), *Race, class, and gender* (pp. 70–81). Belmont, CA: Wadsworth.

Mills, C. W. (1959). *The sociological imagination.* Oxford, UK: Oxford University Press.

National Center for Education Statistics. (1996). U.S. history: What do students know, and what can they do? NAEPFacts, *1*(4).

New York State Education Department. (1996). *Learning standards for social studies* (revised ed.). Albany, NY: Author.

New York State Education Department. (1999). *Resource guide and core curriculum.* Albany, NY: Author.

Ravitch, D. (1990). Multiculturalism. E pluribus plures. *American Scholar,* Summer, 337–354.

Ravitch, D., & Finn, C. E., Jr. (1987). *What do our 17-year-olds know?* A report on the first national assessment of history and literature. New York: Harper & Row.

Schlesinger, A. M., Jr. (1991). *The disuniting of America.* Knoxville, TN: Whittle Direct Books.

Seixas, P. (1993). Historical understanding among adolescents in a multicultural setting. *Curriculum Inquiry, 23,* 301–327.

Shuell, T. J. (1996). Teaching and learning in a classroom context. In D. C. Berliner & R. C. Calfee (Eds.), *Handbook of educational psychology* (pp. 726–764). New York: Simon & Schuster Macmillan.

Stern, F. (1956). *The varieties of history: From Voltaire to the present.* New York: Meridian.

Uchitelle, L., & Kleinfield, N. R. (1996, March 3). On the battlefields of business, millions of casualties. *New York Times,* pp. A1, 16–29.

Whittington, D. (1991). What have 17-year-olds known in the past? *American Educational Research Journal, 28*(4), 759–780.

APPENDIX A

Roster of Participating Students

Lincoln Secondary School

Blake	African American	male
Carrie	African American	female
Kirk	European American	male
Linda	European American	female
Maggie	African American	female
Mary	African American	female
Sheldon	African American	male

Eisenhower High School

Lindy's class with two-week civil rights unit:

James	European American	male
Melissa	European American	female
Ned	European American	male

George's class without separate civil rights unit

Ann	European American	female
Alice	European American	female
Bill	European American	male
Rate	European American	female

Johnson High School

Anhur	African American	male
Carl	Native & European American	male
Julian	Hispanic	male
Kaylee	African American	female
Magdalena	Hispanic	female
Manuel	Hispanic & African American	male
Marissa	Hispanic	female
Mereedes	Hispanic	female
Richard	Native & African American	male
Simon	Indian recent immigrant	male
Yolanda	Hispanic	female

(At Johnson, we asked students to identify their racial ethnic background and we use their self-identifications. All the Hispanic students are Puerto Ricans.)

CHAPTER *2*

Research Designs

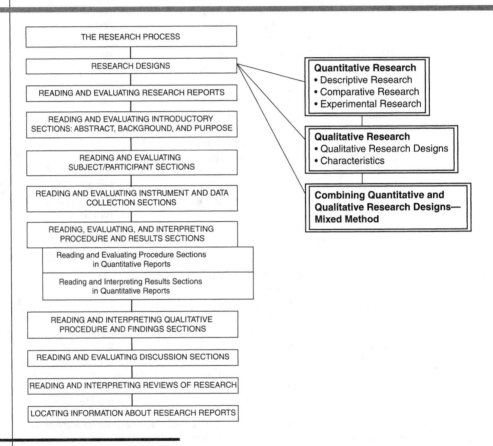

FOCUS QUESTIONS

1. What are the major designs used to conduct educational research?
2. What are these types of quantitative research: descriptive, comparative, and experimental?
3. What distinguishes the three types of quantitative research designs from each other?
4. What are the instruments used to collect quantitative data?
5. How are data analyzed in each of the three types of quantitative research designs?
6. What are central tendency and variability, and how are they measured?
7. What are the major purposes for conducting qualitative research?
8. What are the major features of qualitative research?
9. Why might quantitative and qualitative research be combined?

When researchers pose questions about educational problems, there are simultaneous concerns with one or more plans for obtaining answers. The plans, or **research designs,** structure researchers' methods for answering their questions and conducting studies. The distinction between *research methodology* and *research design* (or *methods*) is important. In chapter 1, we discussed belief systems or perspectives (positivism and constructivism), which are the way researchers view the knowledge and information they will collect and analyze. In this chapter, we discuss research designs, which are researchers' overall strategies for answering their research questions. In later chapters, we discuss **research methods,** which are the activities researchers use within their research design. Two broad categories of research designs are **quantitative research** and **qualitative research.** Keep in mind that researchers with a positivist perspective may use both quantitative and qualitative methods. Researchers with a constructivist perspective, however, usually use only qualitative methods.

Despite those differences, qualitative and quantitative research can be considered complementary. The approaches may be combined in a single research project (Lancy, 1993; Slavin, 1992). The two research perspectives share at least four procedural aspects (Hillocks, 1992). Quantitative and qualitative researchers share concerns in "problem finding, in explaining the relationships of data to claims, in theory building, and in explaining particular cases in light of established knowledge and theory" (p. 59). However, such researchers can (and do) focus on different kinds of problems. For example, quantitative methods cannot deal directly with historical problems of cause and effect, or the interpretation of unique social phenomena. On the other hand, qualitative researchers find it difficult, if not impossible, to represent the responses of large numbers of individuals to different kinds of stimuli (e.g., different methods of teaching, or attitudes toward social conditions or political events). The two sets of methods are complementary in the sense that they allow researchers to deal with problems of different dimensions in different contexts (Hillocks, 1992, p. 59).

QUANTITATIVE RESEARCH

Quantitative research uses statistical analysis. Three basic quantitative research purposes are to *(a)* describe, *(b)* compare, and *(c)* attribute causality. Each of these purposes is fulfilled through the assignment of numerical values to variables and the mathematical analysis of those values. Quantitative research is predicated on the belief that variables should be mathematically measured, and adherents to this approach stress that data should be repeatedly verified.[1]

- In quantitative **descriptive research,** the researchers' purpose is to answer questions about a variable's status by creating numerical descriptions of the frequency with which one variable (or more) occurs.
- In **comparative research,** the researchers' purpose is to examine numerical descriptions of two or more variables and make decisions about their differences or relationships.

---

[1] Some researchers, mostly those with a positivist perspective of research, consider that this aspect of *verifiability* makes research *scientific* and *objective*. We believe that there is a subjective aspect to all research and that objectivity is a reflection of a researcher's value system, not a characteristic of research. No group of researchers of any conviction have an exclusive right to consider only their research as *scientific*.

- In research to attribute *causality,* or **experimental research,** the researchers' purpose is to draw conclusions about the influence of one or more variables on another variable. They seek to answer "if . . . then" questions: If they do something, then what change will occur in a particular variable?

From the results of experimental research, researchers establish the influence, or **effect,** of one variable on another. Quantitative descriptive and comparative research may show status, patterns, and associations among variables; but studies of those types cannot be used to say that one variable or combination of variables probably does cause a change in, or influence, another variable. Only when researchers follow the plan for attributing causality can they establish that a particular variable may be the reason for a change in another. Causation research, or experimental research, is different from descriptive and comparative research, and that distinction cannot be overstressed (Gall, Gall, & Borg, 2002).

Descriptive Research

Researchers use descriptive research when they want to answer the question "What exists?" The quantitative descriptive research method is a procedure involving the assignment of numerical values to variables. For example, Table 2.1 contains partial results from a questionnaire used in a descriptive study to determine the extent to which teachers use content-area instructional practices and activities that are consistent with current views of reading and learning from text (Gillis, Olson, & Logan, 1993). These researchers collected data by asking teachers to circle one of five choices

Table 2.1

Proportion of Teachers Reporting Percentage of Time They Use Practices and Activities in Content-Area Instruction

	Practices and Activities				
	Never	1–25%	26–50%	51–75%	76–100%
Instructional context					
Ability groups	34.9	39.4	6.1	10.6	9.1
Cooperative groups	2.9	33.8	30.9	26.5	5.9
Whole class	4.4	10.3	2.1	29.4	33.8
Textbooks	4.6	15.1	21.2	45.5	33.8
Prereading					
Activate prior knowledge	—	28.4	13.4	14.9	43.3
Set purpose	—	28.4	13.4	13.4	44.8
Predict/preview	1.5	37.9	15.2	21.2	24.2
During reading					
Students read silently	9.2	35.4	30.8	18.5	6.2
Students read orally	4.5	23.9	31.3	23.9	16.4
Postreading					
Computer support	34.9	36.4	18.2	7.6	3.0
Workbook/skills center	7.6	45.5	33.3	9.1	4.6

Source: Adapted from "Are Content Area Reading Practices Keeping Pace with Research?" by M. K. Gillis, M. W. Olson, and J. Logan, 1993, p. 118. In T. V. Rasinski and N. D. Padak (Eds.), Inquiries in Literacy Learning and Instruction, The Fifteenth Yearbook of the College Reading Association, *Pittsburg, KS: College Reading Association. Copyright 1993 by the College Reading Association. Adapted with permission of the publisher.*

to indicate the percentage of time they used various types of student groupings and instructional materials.

Another research team might wish to know "What is the average intelligence of students in gifted programs in a particular county or state?" They collect and tabulate data and find that the average intelligence score of gifted program students is 129. Still another team affiliated with a county library system might wish to know "What is the average reading achievement test score of a sample of beginning sixth-grade students using the public libraries in three local communities?" They collect and tabulate the data and find that the average achievement test grade equivalent score is 6.2.

However, having these two bits of information (average intelligence and average reading achievement score) does not allow the separate teams of researchers to create accurate pictures of the subjects. Average scores may give a limited picture, because we know that not *all* gifted students had an intelligence score of 129, and not *all* sixth-grade students in each community had scores of 6.2. Also, anyone who observes gifted students and sixth-grade students sees that they differ in many ways other than intelligence or reading performance: personality, preferences, interests, and learning style, to name a few.

Two premises, then, underlie quantitative researchers' collection of descriptive information. First, they should collect and average information for several relevant variables. For the sixth-grade students, other variables relevant to library usage might be age, sex, intelligence, ethnicity, reading interest and preference, proximity of home to the library, and frequency of library usage. Second, after determining the average score for each variable, researchers should determine the extent to which the subjects' scores (for each variable) cluster near to, or spread away from, the average score. Two patterns of clustering are common: *(a)* a clustering of scores near the mean (average) and *(b)* a clustering of scores either further above or below the mean (average). The reporting of this clustering or spreading gives a picture of the subjects' similarity or dissimilarity.

All researchers use descriptive data. Quantitative researchers apply statistical procedures to answer questions about similarities and differences among variables, whereas qualitative researchers apply verbal analyses to answer similar questions.

Representative descriptive research reports are cited in Appendix A.

Statistical Descriptions of Data.   After researchers collect data, they often tally them. Table 2.1 shows the response categories for each answer and the percentage of the total group they represent. From these data, it is possible to get a sense of how most teachers responded and whether there was uniform agreement among them.

However, most researchers following quantitative procedures use other descriptive measures of data, which are **central tendency** and **variability.** Although two common measures of central tendency that researchers use in research reports are the mean and the median, the mean is the measure of central tendency they most often use. The measure of variability of a set of data most often used, and the one associated with the mean, is the **standard deviation (SD).** The following discussion is only an introduction to these measures. Chapter 8, "Reading and Interpreting Qualitative Procedure and Findings Sections," contains additional information about statistics and criteria for determining whether researchers' use of the mean, median, standard deviation, and other statistics is appropriate. Understanding the concepts of central tendency and variability is essential to understanding quantitative research designs.

Both the mean and median give researchers—producers and consumers—a sense of the middle or average score for a variable. The **mean** is an arithmetical average derived from adding up individual scores and dividing by the number of scores. The **median** is the middle score of a group of scores arranged in ascending or descending order. The mean and median may not be the same for a particular group of scores. For example, the median (middle) score of the following groups is the same (25), but the means (arithmetic averages) of the two groups are different—the median is 33.57 and the mean is 40.86:

10, 15, 20, 25, 40, 50, 75

4, 17, 24, 25, 26, 91, 99

The standard deviation (SD) is used with the mean to show how the other scores are distributed around the mean. The use of the SD lets research producers and consumers see how homogeneous (alike) or heterogeneous (varied) a group is. For example, the children entering the kindergarten classes in one school might have a mean age of 64 months (5 years, 4 months) and an SD of 4 months. In this group of kindergartners, most children (approximately two-thirds) would be between 60 and 68 months in age. For another group of children entering kindergarten in another school with the same mean age (64 months) but an SD of 7 months, two-thirds of the children would be between 57 and 71 months in age. The first group of kindergarten children would be more homogeneous in their ages than would be the second group.

Table 2.2 shows an example of mean and standard deviation reporting. The table reports information from an investigation of the effect of reading placement on reading achievement of at-risk sixth-grade students with reading problems (Homan, Hines, & Kromrey, 1993). The two groups of readers were "disabled reader" and "slow learner." They were tested with two instruments: a vocabulary test and a comprehension test. The table gives the number of subjects *(n)*, the mean scores *(M)*, and the standard deviations *(SD)* for both pre- and posttesting and for groups at three levels of reading performance: Instructional Level, Frustration 1, and Frustration 2. The table shows that on the vocabulary test, a group of 84 disabled readers had an average instructional level pretesting score of 636.56. The standard deviation was 25.40, resulting in the scores of about two-thirds of the students being clustered between 661.96 and 611.16. The same group of students had a posttesting average of 660.77, and about two-thirds of them had scores between 686.38 and 635.16.

Comparative Research

In comparative research, researchers examine relationships, including similarities or differences among several variables. These variables might represent characteristics of the same group of subjects or those of separate groups. That is, researchers might compare the writing performance and self-concept of members of a single group of subjects, or they might compare the writing performance and self-concept of two groups. Comparative research is more common than is pure descriptive research, but comparative research depends on knowledge generated from descriptive research. All researchers use descriptive data. Quantitative researchers apply statistical procedures to answer questions about similarities, differences, and relationships among variables, whereas qualitative researchers apply verbal analyses to answer similar questions.

Also, researchers can use the statistical comparative data to make predictions. When researchers find two variables that are strongly statistically related, they can

Table 2.2

Example of Mean and Standard Deviation Reporting: Means and Standard Deviations
of CTBS Test Scores by Group

| | | Testing | | | |
| | | Pre | | Post | |
	Group *n*	M	SD	M	SD
		Vocabulary Test			
Disabled reader					
Instructional level	84	636.56	25.40	660.77	25.61
Frustration 1	88	633.60	27.98	660.02	25.95
Frustration 2	25	630.80	26.80	644.48	35.05
Slow learner					
Instructional level	42	622.76	33.95	641.12	45.55
Frustration 1	51	615.78	39.76	642.27	32.43
Frustration 2	14	604.79	35.31	617.21	48.32
		Comprehension Test			
Disabled reader					
Instructional level	84	637.90	50.77	692.33	41.40
Frustration 1	88	645.75	48.92	692.99	41.76
Frustration 2	25	622.90	61.08	662.40	60.47
Slow learner					
Instructional level	42	603.02	50.06	651.40	49.81
Frustration 1	51	609.65	41.39	652.58	66.38
Frustration 2	14	593.79	45.61	643.64	55.56

*Source: From "An Investigation of Varying Reading Level Placement on Reading Achievement of Chapter 1 Students,"
by S. P. Homan, C. V. Hines, and J. D. Kromrey, 1993,* Reading Research and Instruction 33*(1). Copyright 1993 by the
College Reading Association. Reprinted with permission of the publisher.*

use one variable to predict the occurrence of the other. They cannot, however, use
relationship information to show that one variable is the cause of change in another.
For example,

> a group of researchers conducted a comparative study of lsraeli preschool, remedial, and
> elementary-school teachers' teaching performance. They found consistent differences
> among the three groups of teachers in affective variables but not in direct, actual teach-
> ing behavior. The preschool teachers were seen to be the most flexible, democratic, and
> expressive in warmth (Babad, Bernieri, & Rosenthal, 1987). The essential aspect to this
> comparative research is that researchers made no attempt to determine causality. In fact,
> the researchers state "the results provide no hint as to what might have caused the ob-
> served pattern." (p. 414)

Representative comparative research reports are cited in Appendix A.

Statistical Comparisons of Data.   After researchers following a quantitative procedure collect data, they calculate measures of central tendency (the mean) and variability (the standard deviation), as they do in descriptive research. These measures

by themselves, however, do not provide evidence of difference or relationship. One or more statistical procedures can be used to determine whether differences exist between or among groups. Many statistical procedures used in comparative research are similar to those used in experimental research. Research consumers must realize that statistical procedures are tools for answering research questions; they are not *the* research. Tools help researchers determine whether an apparent difference or relationship is large enough to be considered real. Tools also help researchers determine the extent to which they can be confident about their research conclusions. (Chapter 7, section II, "Reading and Interpreting Results Sections in Quantitative Reports," contains an extended discussion about the research reality, or significance, of differences and relationships.)

One statistical procedure used in descriptive research is the **chi-square.** Table 2.3 contains an example of a chi-square analysis. The information is from a study that examined how teachers responded when students made miscues (deviant oral-reading responses; Lass, 1984). Two types of miscues (*[a]* attempted pronunciation of word even when wrong and *[b]* refused or hesitated response) were compared with two types of teacher responses (*[a]* supplied word and *[b]* all other kinds of responses). The analysis showed that teachers who dealt with unattempted miscues supplied words more often than they used all other responses combined.

A statistical procedure used extensively in comparative research is **correlation.** Correlations show whether two or more variables have a systematic relationship of occurrence. That is, they help researchers answer questions about the scores: Do high scores for one variable occur with high scores for another (a positive relationship)? Do high scores for one variable occur with low scores for the other variable (a negative relationship)? The occurrence of low scores for one variable with low scores for another is also an example of a positive relationship.

Table 2.4 shows an example of correlation reporting. The table contains information from a study about the relationships between topic-specific background knowledge and measures of total writing quality (Langer, 1984). It shows the obtained relationships among four ways of evaluating students' writing: *(a)* teachers' marks, *(b)* a measure of coherence, *(c)* counting the words and clauses, and *(d)* a ho-

Table 2.3

Example of Chi-Square Reporting: Attempted Miscues vs. Refusals/Hesitations and Teacher Response

	Miscues				
	Attempts		Refusals/ Hesitations		Raw Total
	EO[a]	AO[a]	EO	AO	
Teacher response					
Supplied word	105.5	93	13.5	26	119
All other	237.5	250	30.5	18	268
Total		343		44	387

Note:[a] EO = expected occurrences; AO = actual occurrences.
   χ^2 = 19.83 with 1 degree of freedom (p = 0.001).

Source: Based on Lass (1993).

Table 2.4

Example of Correlation Reporting: Relationships
Among Writing Measures

	Correlations (*n* papers)		
	Teacher's Mark	Coherence	Words/Clause
Holistic score	0.44[a] (57)	0.06 (99)	0.25 (96)
Teacher's mark	0. 27 (22)	−0.15 (20)	
Coherence	−0.10 (96)		

[a] $p < .01$.

Source: Based on Langer (1984).

listic scoring method. The relationship between the holistic scoring method and the teachers' marks is positive and significant—high coherence scores were given to the work of the same students who received high teacher marks. On the other hand, the relationship between coherence and the number of words and clauses, which is negative, was not significant. Therefore, the relationship between these two scoring methods can be said to be unrelated (or nonsignificant). (A detailed explanation of significance is in chapter 8, "Reading and Interpreting Qualitative Procedure and Findings Sections.")

Researchers also use correlations in comparative studies to make predictions. Researchers can predict the existence or occurrence of one variable when a strong relationship has been established between that variable and another. For example, the high positive correlation shown in Table 2.4 between the holistic scoring method and teachers' marks of students' papers might be used to make this prediction: Students' writing that receives high scores through holistic scoring procedures most likely will receive high marks from teachers. Holistic scoring is not the cause of students receiving high marks from teachers. Whatever characteristics make students' writing receive high scores in one scoring method probably are responsible for high scores in the other, but the research data reported in Table 2.4 give no inkling what that third, causative variable is. Thus, researchers' use of one variable as a predictor of another variable or event is not justification for considering the first variable as a causative factor.

Frequently, the same statistic (e.g., *t* test, analysis of variance [ANOVA], chisquare) can be used to analyze the data in descriptive and comparative research as well as in experimental research. It is not the statistic that is the distinguishing feature of a research design. Rather, it is the research question, or hypothesis, and the characteristics of the design that distinguish among the three types of quantitative research. Researchers select a statistical procedure that they think will help them answer their research question. Research consumers, then, should not use the type of statistical procedure for determining a researcher's design.

Experimental Research

In experimental research, researchers set out to answer questions about causation. They wish to attribute the change in one variable to the effect of one or more other variables. For example, one group of researchers (Team A) may be concerned with finding answers to questions such as "Will students who receive one type of reading aid (text with focusing questions interspersed every three paragraphs) have better comprehension than students who have a second reading aid (text with key ideas underlined)?" Another research team (Team B) may want to know "Will students who are taught to use calculators for solving mathematical problems do better on final tests than students who do not receive that instruction?"

The influencing variable—the one to which researchers wish to attribute causation—is called the **independent variable.** Independent variables are measurable human and nonhuman characteristics. For example, these factors can be independent variables: age (years or months), intelligence (average, above average, or superior), sensitivity to noise (high or low), intensity of light (high or low), frequency of an occurrence (never, sometimes, or often), and teaching style (democratic or autonomous), to name a few. Sometimes the independent variable is called the *experimental variable.* When this kind of independent variable is an activity of the researcher, it is called a *treatment variable.* Researchers manipulate or subcategorize all independent variables; they can study the effects of two or more aspects of the variable by subcategorizing it. In the previous questions of Team A and Team B, the treatment, or activity, in Team A's research is type of reading aid (focus questions or underlining). Team B's treatment is type of mathematics instruction (with a calculator or without a calculator). When nontreatment characteristics, such as age or intelligence, are used as independent variables, researchers can also subcategorize them (e.g., 6-year-olds or 8-year-olds; average or above-average intelligence).

The acted-upon variable—the one being studied for possible change—is called the **dependent variable.** Not all human characteristics can be used as dependent variables. Reading ability is something that researchers might wish to change, as is degree of self-concept or teachers' comprehension-questioning behavior. Something such as age, obviously, cannot be a dependent variable, because individuals' ages are not subject to modification—people will age according to their biological clocks. The dependent variable for Team A is comprehension performance, and for Team B is problem-solving performance on tests.

The study "Effects of Classroom Structure on Student Achievement Goal Orientation," pp. 19–26, is an example of an experimental study. At [10], the author explains the independent and dependent variables. Other representative experimental research reports are cited in Appendix A.

An example of the attribution of causality is found in the research of a team that studied special-education students.

Statement of Causality

Fuchs, Fuchs, and Fernstrom (1993) wanted to find out the effect of implementing a process for readying students to transition successfully from special-education resource rooms to regular classrooms for mathematics instruction. They found that special students who received instruction that involved the use of curriculum-based measurement and transitional programming had substantially reduced time spent in special-education math classes and significantly greater math achievement on posttests. In this study, the transitional programming (identifying needs through curriculum-based measurement and teaching needed skills) was the independent variable; math progress was the dependent variable.

Identifying Variables

The following is an example of the attribution of causality in a study without a treatment. The causal variable (the independent variable) was a preexisting condition (family structure).

<table>
<tr><td>

Statement of Causality

</td><td>

Thompson, Entwisle, Alexander, and Sundius (1992) studied how parent configuration (two-parent, mother-extended, or solo-mother) and number of siblings affect, or is the cause of, first graders' conformity to a model of student role as measured by their absences, latenesses, and conduct marks. Here, differences in first graders' roles as students (dependent variable) were examined to see if they changed as a result of the children's family structure (independent variable, or causal factor). However, the researchers did not engage in an activity or treatment.

</td></tr>
</table>

Researchers can study the individual or combined effect of several independent variables on a dependent variable, or of one independent variable on two or more dependent variables.

<table>
<tr><td>

Identifying Variables

</td><td>

Here is an example of experimental research in which two independent variables were examined. The research had the purpose of testing the effects on students' comprehension by providing them with relevant background knowledge and two versions of a content-area text (McKeown, Beck, Sinatra, & Loxterman, 1992). In the study, the two independent variables were *(a)* provision of background knowledge and *(b)* coherence of the text. The dependent variable was comprehension of the text.

</td></tr>
</table>

In a study in which one independent variable was examined for its effect on several dependent variables, the researcher can conclude that something (text explicitness) caused a change in other things (various students' reactions to stories).

<table>
<tr><td>

Four Dependent Variables

</td><td>

Sundbye (1987) examined how text explicitness would enhance children's *silent reading rates, their ratings of story interest, their abilities to recall stories and answer questions about them*, and *ratings of their overall understanding of stories*. [Italics added for identification purposes.]

</td></tr>
</table>

Researchers can make causative conclusions because they make decisions about the control of variables that are not of concern in descriptive or comparative research. **Control** is the use of procedures by the researchers to limit or account for the possible influence of variables not being studied. They use these controls before the research is done (a priori). The control of these **extraneous variables** can be done in one or more ways. In the following paragraphs, two ways to develop control in experimental studies are presented. (Extended discussions of these and other ways to control extraneous variables are found in chapter 5, "Reading and Evaluating Subject/Participant Sections," and chapter 7, section I, "Reading and Evaluating Procedure Sections in Quantitative Reports.")

In the study about the use of relevant background knowledge and two versions of content-area text (McKeown et al., 1992), a variable that might possibly affect students' reading comprehension is reading ability. The researchers controlled for the possible effect of students' reading ability by dividing them equally into two groups based on the results of a standardized reading test. This way, the researchers had two groups of comparable readers, and the results could be determined to be the result of factors other than reading ability.

However, other variables might account for researchers' results. One might wish to control for the possible effect of such things as students' interest, learning style, general learning ability, and possible researcher bias in selecting the subjects. So researchers can use **randomization** to group the subjects in the treatment groups (those to whom the independent variables were applied). Randomization is an unbiased systematic selection or assignment of subjects. When researchers use randomization, they assume that most human characteristics are evenly distributed among the groups.

In the prior examples, researchers had the opportunity to manipulate the independent variable before doing the research. Sometimes, however, researchers want answers to questions but cannot manipulate the independent variable for practical or ethical reasons. They realize a condition exists and are unsure about what might have been its cause. For example, researchers might be interested in why some children develop autistic tendencies after birth. They question whether prenatal conditions might account for the development of the autistic tendencies. In such a case, it would be unethical to create an experimental study in which researchers manipulate the prenatal environment. But, by starting with the effect (children with autistic tendencies) and identifying possible causes (nutrition, mother's age, ingestion of abusive substances, or illness), researchers can try to establish a cause-effect relationship. This ex post facto research (after-the-fact) is called *causal-comparative research*.

The name **causal-comparative research** can be confusing when discussing experimental research. This type of research is comparative because researchers compare possible independent variables to see which variable, if any, has a strong relationship with the already known outcome. The method itself is "more" than comparative research, because the data analysis procedures do more than compare or correlate; the researchers analyze data with the purpose of establishing causality. Because researchers cannot establish a cause-effect relationship experimentally, they do so rationally. They take already intact groups—mothers whose children show autistic tendencies, and mothers whose children do not—and compare the groups statistically under controlled conditions. The groups already differ on the independent and dependent variables. The researchers do not induce differences; they seek to identify one or more preexisting conditions (independent variables) in one group, that exist to a lesser degree in the other. When researchers identify one or more conditions, they can attribute causality; however, this attribution may be less strong than in an experimental design where the researchers can control all of the variables.

An illustration of causal-comparative research in education is given in a study about reading comprehension and creativity in the use of English by Blacks. The preexisting condition is the independent variable.

Preexisting Condition	DeLain, Pearson, and Anderson (1985) explored the hypothesis that the rich and varied experience of Black youth with figurative language outside school would enhance the pupils' understanding of figurative language in school texts. Results confirmed that for Black students, "sounding" skill, as well as general verbal ability, has a direct influence on figurative language comprehension. Black language ability influences figurative language comprehension indirectly, through its effect on sounding skill. For White students, only general verbal ability affects figurative language comprehension.
Dependent Variable	

In this exploratory study, the independent variables, "sounding" or "playing the dozens" and general verbal ability, already existed within and varied between Black and White students. The researchers could not manipulate the variables, nor could they teach the ritual-insult verbal play in a school setting. Also, differences existed in the dependent variable and the understanding of figurative language. The researchers, in an ex post facto study, examined the possible causative linkage. They used causal-comparative research to draw conclusions about the positive influence of Black youths' ability to "sound" and their ability to understand school-based figurative language.

A limitation of causal-comparative research is that researchers cannot have the same assurance that they do in experimental research about cause-effect linkage. Often, and whenever possible, causal-comparative results need to be confirmed by experimental research. Causal-comparative research also lacks other controls used by researchers in experimental research. It is usually not possible to have randomization of subjects among treatments, or the creation of closely comparable groups. Also, researchers cannot control the quality of students' previous experiences that relate to the independent variable. Further, the people selected for the study may differ on some other variable that the researchers did not consider. These limitations show up in causal-comparative research as an estimate of unaccounted-for influence. When there is a large unaccounted-for influence, researchers must seek and test other independent variables for the possible cause of a recognized result.

Analysis of Experimental Statistical Data

After data are collected in experimental studies, measures of central tendency (means) and variability (standard deviations) are created. This descriptive information forms the basis of other statistical procedures. When researchers conduct simple one-variable studies, they often use a common statistical procedure known as the **t test.** The *t* test is used to determine whether the difference between the means of two groups on a dependent variable is significant; that is, whether the examined results could have happened by chance or whether the researchers can reliably attribute the difference to the influence of the independent variable.

But, as discussed previously, single-variable studies provide limited insight about educational questions. Multiple-variable research requires the calculation of many *t* tests, which is awkward, possibly misleading, and limiting, because the interaction among multiple variables cannot be shown by *t* tests. To overcome this limitation, researchers often use the **analysis of variance (ANOVA).** Results of an ANOVA are reported in **F ratios.** ANOVAs are used to determine whether differences can be attributed to one or a combination of independent variables.

Table 2.5 contains a common form for reporting ANOVA results. The information is taken from a study about the effect of reading placement (instructional level versus above-instructional level) and reading potential (disabled reader versus slow learner). The topic was the reading achievement of at-risk sixth-grade students with reading problems (Homan et al., 1993). The results show that there were significant differences for vocabulary achievement based on potential and placement. There was no difference shown in vocabulary achievement when potential and placement were considered together (Potential 3 Placement). On comprehension tests, only potential showed significant differences. (Chapter 8 contains a more detailed discussion of the concepts of significance and ANOVA.)

Table 2.5

Reporting of ANOVA Results: Summary Tables for a Two-Way
Analysis of Variance

Analysis of Variance of Vocabulary Achievement Scores
by Potential and Placement Level

Source	df	MS	F
Potential (A)	1	9236.14	10.45**
Placement (P)	2	4107.70	4.65*
Potential 3 Placement (AP)	2	167.09	0.19
Error (S/AP)	298	884.12	
Total	303		

Analysis of Variance of Comprehension Test Scores
by Potential and Placement Level

Source	df	MS	F
Potential (A)	1	38070.15	17.11**
Placement (P)	2	4083.84	1.84
Potential 3 Placement (AP)	2	1434.62	0.67
Error (S/AP)	298	2224.74	
Total	303		

* $p < 0.05$; **$p < 0.01$.

*Source: From "An Investigation of Varying Reading Level Placement on Reading
Achievement of Chapter 1 Students," by S.P. Homan, C.V. Hines, and J. D. Kromrey,
1993,* Reading Research and Instruction *33(1). Copyright 1993 by the College
Reading Association. Reprinted with permission of the publisher.*

QUALITATIVE RESEARCH

Qualitative Research Designs

Qualitative research is a term used for a broad range of research strategies and designs that have roots in the research of the social sciences, especially the field research of anthropology and sociology (Bogdan & Biklen, 2003; Denzin & Lincoln, 2000; Eisner, 1991; Firestone, 1987, 1993; Guthrie & Hall, 1984; Jacob, 1987, 1988; LeCompte, Millory, & Preissle, 1992; Lincoln & Guba, 1985; Marshall & Rossman, 1995; Smith, 1987; Smith & Heshusius, 1986; Van Maanen, Dabbs, & Faulkner, 1982; Wilson, 1977). While quantitative researchers rely on numerical (statistical) analyses of how often things happen, qualitative researchers examine people (such as students, teachers, and administrators) in natural contexts, interacting with other people and objects in their surroundings (Hatch, 1995). Some researchers use the term *interpretive research* to avoid the connotation of defining research as "nonquantitative," because some sort of quantification *can* be used (Erickson, 1986). The emphasis in qualitative research is on a value-packed form of research with a stress on the *how* (the process) of the creating and carrying out of social actions and events, rather than on a type of measurement and statistical analysis stressing causal relationships between and among variables (Denzin & Lincoln, 2000).

Characteristics

Qualitative research is characterized not by the use of numerical values but by the use of text—written words—to document variables and the inductive analysis of the collected information. Qualitative researchers are not concerned with numerical (statistical) analysis of the frequency of when or how things happen. They look to *inductively answer research questions* by examining students and others who influence them in natural contexts, in interaction with other people and objects in their surroundings (Hatch, 1995). Subjectivity, to qualitative researchers, is a strength of the research. Subjectivity is based on broad and comprehensive theoretical positions. (A fuller explanation of the so-called *objectivity*, that is, the "validity" and "reliability," of qualitative research, is found in chapter 8.)

The purposes of qualitative research are to *describe, interpret, verify,* and *evaluate* (Eisner, 1991; Marshall & Rossman, 1995; Peshkin, 1993).

- In descriptive analysis, the researcher gives an account of a place or process. The purpose is to visualize a situation as a means for understanding what is happening.
- In interpretive analysis, the researcher explains or creates generalizations. The purpose is to develop new concepts or elaborate on existing ones. The researcher provides insights that might lead to teachers changing their behavior, refining their knowledge, or identifying problems. Interpretive analysis also can be used to develop new theories.
- In verification analysis, the researcher confirms assumptions, theories, and generalizations.
- In evaluative analysis, the researcher provides judgments about policies, practices, and innovative instructional practices. The researcher tries to answer questions such as "Has an instructional procedure been implemented? With what impact? What has the process of implementation been like? How has it worked? For whom has it worked? Are there any exceptions?"

Qualitative research has several distinct features, and our discussion is a synthesis of ideas from authorities in this area. (See Bogdan & Biklen, 2003; Creswell, 1998; Eisner, 1991; Firestone, 1987; Gay & Airasian, 2003; Guthrie & Hall, 1984; Jacob, 1987, 1988; Lancy, 1993; Lincoln & Guba, 1985; Maxwell, 1998; Putney, Green, Dixon, & Kelly, 1999; Smith, 1987; Smith & Heshusius, 1986; Van Maanen et al., 1982; Wilson, 1977.)

- Qualitative researchers are concerned with the *process* of an activity *rather than only the outcomes of that activity*. In educational settings, qualitative researchers look at instructional activities within the total context of classrooms and schools. They want to understand the ongoing interactions occurring during instruction rather than to note only whether the students have increased their test scores.
- *The issue of context is central to qualitative research*. People do not act in isolation. Qualitative researchers believe that because people's behavior and actions occur in specific social contexts or situations, these behaviors and actions must be studied in natural settings. This belief means that researchers wishing to study educational questions must collect relevant information at the data source through direct observation and personal interviews. Ideally, the researcher becomes an accepted member of (and participant in) that setting, not

just an "observer." Further, *context* does not just refer to the individual class-room or school being studied. Contexts can also be considered as the life situations of students and teachers. Contexts are not static; contexts shape and are shaped by the people involved (teachers and students) as well by as the intentions of instruction, the resources available, and the particular time in which the events are happening (Graue & Walsch, 1995). Finally, researchers must consider the conceptual, or theoretical, context—that is, the theories, assumptions, biases, and beliefs—that they bring to their work. These personal factors must also be made an explicit aspect of the study.

- In qualitative research, data, or collected information, are *verbal, not numerical.* Although qualitative researchers may use checklists to count the frequency of occurrences of educational events, behaviors, and activities, these quantifications are for noting trends and not for presenting averages and determining statistical relationships. Verbal data helps researchers find out what participants are thinking when performing a task. Such data provide a basis for investigating the underlying mental process of complex tasks that cannot be studied in any other way.

- Qualitative researchers analyze the data *rationally rather than statistically.* The outcomes of much qualitative research are the generation of research questions and conjectures, not the verification of predicted mathematical relationships or outcomes. Because some qualitative research is descriptive, many of its data collection procedures are similar to those found in quantitative descriptive research. A distinguishing feature between the two is the use in qualitative research of the search for logical patterns within and among aspects of the research setting. (Chapter 8 contains discussion about the trustworthiness of information in qualitative research.)

The qualitative researcher must

attempt to maintain a non-judgmental bias throughout the study. The researcher's goal is to observe and describe group patterns, similarities, and differences as they occur. Preconceptions or expectations of an individual or group's behavior interferes with the researcher's ability to tell the group or culture's story in a fair and accurate manner. In addition, preconceived expectations preclude the researcher from observing subtle nuances of character and speech that may be important to understand group behaviors or interactions. While absolute objectivity is impossible, it is paramount that researchers enter the field or study group with an open mind, an awareness of their own biases, and a commitment to detach from those biases as much as possible while observing and representing the group. (Writing @CSU, 2004)

Qualitative researchers view classroom behavior "in the larger context of cultural standards and patterns of behavior, goals of participants, behavior settings, and social influences beyond the classroom. The implications are significant for our understanding of education" (Jacob, 1987, p. 38). From qualitative research, educators can obtain extensive knowledge about educational processes within classrooms, schools, and communities. For example, qualitative research helps educators to gain insights about *(a)* classroom life and how students function within the particular situation of that classroom, *(b)* the knowledge and cultural understandings members of a classroom need to participate in social and academic tasks with that environment, *(c)* the individual and group perspectives and points of view that should be considered for understanding learning within a classroom, and *(d)* the actions and interactions of students and teachers as they create teaching and learning situations (Putney et al., 1999).

Qualitative research is considered by some researchers to have several distinct research designs: ethnographic, narrative, grounded theory, action or participatory action, and feminist (Esterberg, 2002).

Ethnographic Research.   Educational researchers have borrowed practices of ethnographic research from researchers in cultural anthropology and sociology. Ethnographic research, like other qualitative inquiries, emphasizes firsthand field study. Ethnographic research designs stress the study of "culture" within a group that shares a culture, examining "shared patterns of behavior, belief, and language" (Creswell, 1998). Researchers may choose an ethnographic approach to try to understand how the culture of a district, school, classroom, or other educational environment affects teaching and learning. They will attempt to provide a detailed, close, rich portrait of a group, within its own setting.

An illustrative research study that is ethnographic in nature involved a field investigation of classroom management from the perspective of high school students (Allen, 1986). (See also chapter 8, "Reading and Interpreting Qualitative Procedure and Findings Sections.")

Purpose	Allen's (1986) study was based on the assumption "that classroom contexts interact with students' agenda and result in variations in students' perspectives of the management of the classroom" (p. 438). Data were gathered *(a)* from the students' perspective, *(b)* from different classroom management situations, *(c)* by uncovering the students' agendas, and *(d)* by analyzing the underlying theoretical constructs. To become part of the groups, the researcher enrolled in a ninth-grade schedule so that he could learn about the students' perspective by taking the role of a student. He wished to gain the students' confidence, so he asked the teachers to treat him as any other student. After the classes began, he avoided contact with the teachers. The researcher attended four morning classes each day and did not volunteer information about himself to the students until they questioned him. Then, he emphasized his student role, de-emphasized that of being a researcher, and participated in classwork, activities, tests, and homework assignments. During class he took observational notes under the guise of taking class notes.
Data Collection	
Participant Observer	
Procedure	

Narrative Research.   Researchers taking a narrative inquiry approach focus on people's lives and experiences. They point to the "storied" nature of human understanding, arguing that stories have always been one of the most basic ways that people make meaning of the world. They consider the deliberate attempt to story and restory experiences (including educational experiences) a good way to understand human experiences and their meaning for those who participate in them (Connelly & Clandinin, 1990; Clandinin & Connelly, 2000). Narrative researchers collect and tell stories of people's lives, describe people's experiences, and analyze participants' explanations of what they do, why, with whom, and in what context. They attempt to understand and portray the complexity of these experiences and to interpret them in ways that can help make those experiences relevant and meaningful to others. Many narrative researchers in education see their work influenced by John Dewey's writings about the importance of inquiring into experience, both personal and social. They postulate that human activity and experience are filled with "meaning." For them, the stories people provide, rather than logical arguments or lawful formulations, are the vehicles by which meaning is communicated. Their research projects are concerned with analyzing the participants' explanations of what the participants do.

Some representative themes and topics that have emerged in the use of narrative approaches within the field of education include (*a*) the development of narrative competence by preschool and school-age children; (*b*) the relationship between narrative competence and learning disabilities; (*c*) storytelling as a pedagogical tool in moral and language development; (*d*) the professional development of the classroom teacher and the role of stories in the formation of an identity as an educator (Hevern, 2003; Connelly & Clandinin, 1990).

Grounded Theory Research.   Researchers using a grounded theory approach apply a set of systematic guidelines to the information they collect. They hope to identify key themes and patterns in order to inductively build theoretical frameworks. This strategy is in contrast to one in which a theory is the consequence of deduction; that is, the creation of a theory before information or data is collected (and then a search is undertaken for evidence to support it) (Corbin & Strauss, 1990; Glaser & Strauss, 1967; Glazer, 2004; Pandit, 1996; Strauss & Corbin, 1998). Grounded theory was first developed by Glaser and Strauss to challenge what they saw as an arbitrary division between theory and research, to encourage theory development in qualitative research, and to develop more "rigorous" methods for qualitative research (Charmaz, 2000). Grounded theory has evolved, with different researchers emphasizing different strands. In general, however, grounded theorists use an extensive coding system, applying tags and labels to the primarily narrative data collected. Such coding enables the data to be "interrogated" (Delamont, 1992), or systematically explored. Researchers use these coding labels to group their data into categories and develop conceptual relationships among categories, looking for commonalities, differences, patterns, and themes. Although many researchers use qualitative methodology in grounded theory research, some researchers (Glazer, 2004) feel grounded theory is a general methodology that can be used with either quantitative or qualitative data, or with both in combination.

Action Research or Participatory Action Research.   *Action research, teacher research, collaborative inquiry*, and *participatory action research* are all terms to describe a systematic inquiry in which professional (i.e., academic) researchers conduct research *with*, rather than *on* (or *for*) teachers, administrators, and even parents and students. It is a research process that weaves together both professional research knowledge and "local" (for example, teacher or practitioner) knowledge. The professional researchers and other participants collaborate in setting research concerns and share in the control of the research processes and products (Borgia & Schuler, 1996; Feldman & Capobianco, 2000; Johnson, 1993; Masters, 1999).

Action research helps teachers or administrators to study educational problems that they face and to improve professional practices. Action research also attempts to remove the "artificial" separation between "knowing" and "doing." The research process consists of spiraling cycles of problem identification, systematic data collection, reflection, analysis, data-driven action, problem redefinition, more data collection, and so on.

Finally, many action researchers also aim to produce social change through their research. For some educational action researchers, the change they seek may be to improve curriculum, teaching, and learning. For others, the change may be more systemic; for example, trying to change how resources are allocated to those traditionally underrepresented or disenfranchised.

Researchers using the participatory action research strategy believe that any research in social situations (and schools are social institutions) is not possible without the active participation of all of the participants (Seymour-Rolls & Hughes, 1999; Wadsworth, 1998). Depending on the researchers, the degree of action and participation in the research process will vary. In some cases, the "action" in action research may refer to interventions by the researcher(s). In other cases, the action may involve participation by parents, students, and/or other people involved in schools.

Feminist Research. Researchers using a feminist strategy believe that what makes feminist research unique are the motives, concerns, and knowledge brought to the research process (Anderson, 2003; Ardovini-Brooker, 2002; Brayton, 2004; Esterberg, 2002). These diverse group of researchers study the ways in which gender does and ought to influence people's conceptions of knowledge, the information known to the subject of the research, and practices of inquiry and justification.

Feminist researchers come from a perspective, not a method. They see the organizing of the social world by gender. For them, the belief underlying their research is that, worldwide, women encounter some oppression and/or exploitation. Their research is aimed at undercovering and understanding the causes of these factors and at working toward their elimination. It actively seeks "to remove the power imbalance between research and subject; it is politically motivated and has a major role in changing social inequality; and it begins with the standpoints and experiences of women" (Brayton, 2004). Feminist researchers do not seek a single "truth"; rather they seek out multiple truths that exist, which are found in researching women's oppression (Ardovini-Brooker, 2002). Thus, feminist researchers generally believe that participatory action research is more appropriate and responsive for explaining and understanding their research issues.

Research consumers should not assume, however, that all feminist research is approached from a singular perspective. Within this approach to research, there is "no single set of claims beyond a few generalities that could be called 'feminism' without controversy among feminists" (Harding, 1991, p. 6). Yet, feminist researchers' considerations seem to be enriched as well as constrained by the various political and conceptual perspectives that are brought to their research.

An example of using a feminist perspective to examine an educationally related question is a research project undertaken by Rolón-Dow (2004), who approached her study from a Black, critical, feminist framework. Note that she combines feminist research, participatory action research, and grounded theory research.

Purpose	Rolón-Dow addressed the issue of differential and inequitable educational achievement along race/ethnic, class, and gender lines through a contextual exploration of the schooling of Puerto Rican low-income girls. She chose this perspective to analyze her data because she felt that deterministic views of identity (that dichotomize Puerto Rican females' sexuality against their intellectual development) do not adequately account for the influential role that the school context holds in mediating identities and subsequent schooling outcomes. The study took place in the northeastern United States. The urban neighborhood was ethnically diverse. She focused on a middle school. The participants were nine second-generation Puerto Rican, low-income girls. The researcher, herself of
Rationale for Research Perspective	
Setting and Participants	

*Information
Collection and
Analysis*
Puerto Rican heritage, visited and made observations in the school. She also visited the
girls' homes. Her study was over a two-year period. Information was collected through
interviews and focus groups using open-ended questions. Interviews and field notes were
transcribed and coded using categories derived from the research questions and theoretical framework. In her grounded theory approach, she used categories and codes drawn
from the data. Additionally, she obtained feedback from the participating girls on preliminary findings; and analysis during the last months of fieldwork.

COMBINING QUANTITATIVE AND QUALITATIVE RESEARCH DESIGNS—MIXED METHOD

Currently, many researchers combine the use of quantitative and qualitative research
methods. Although there may be purists at either extreme, the use of both methods
within a research project can incorporate the strengths of both these types of research. For example, the results from two studies on essay writing were contrasted
using qualitative and quantitative data analysis methods (Hartley & Chesworth,
1998). The two studies provided different information about essay writing and indicated that both methods can have their limitations, whether they come first or second. The researchers felt that each method might "feed" into the other, in a
sequential reflective chain (or spiral) of assessment.

A mixed methods approach (Jones, 1997) may be of benefit to a researcher for
the following reasons:

- Qualitative methods, especially observation or unstructured interviews, allow
  the researcher to develop an overall "picture" of the subject under investigation. This picture may guide the initial phases of the research.
- Quantitative analysis may be more appropriate to assess behavioral or descriptive components of a topic.
- The descriptive analysis, such as the sociodemographic profile of the subjects,
  may allow a representative sample to be drawn for the qualitative analysis.
  Quantitative research may confirm or deny the representativeness of a sample group for such qualitative research. Thus, the mixed methodology could
  guide the researcher who is carrying out qualitative research, so that his or her
  sample has some representativeness of the overall population.
- Any topic involves cognitive and affective characteristics, as well as overt behavioral aspects. Thus, a qualitative "core" is appropriate to investigate these
  aspects by examining the informant's point of view.
- Much research on many topics is still largely exploratory. The use of qualitative methods allows for unexpected developments that may arise as part of
  such research (i.e., serendipity).
- Quantitative analysis may complement the findings of qualitative methods by
  indicating the extent of their existence within the subject population.
- Quantitative analysis may confirm or disconfirm any apparently significant
  data that emerge from the study. Thus, for example, if the level of subject performance, as measured by existing standardized tests, appears to be related to
  (or result from) subject behavior, quantitative methods might be used to enable statistical testing of the strength of such a relationship or causative factor.
- If such a relationship is determined, then quantitative methods are weaker in
  providing explanations. Qualitative methods may assist the researcher in understanding the underlying explanations of significant outcome and the underlying process involved in producing that relationship.

	Quantitative Research	Qualitative Research
Words used to describe	positivist experimental hard data empirical statistical objective	constructivist ethnographic fieldwork naturalistic descriptive participant observation soft data subjective
Key concepts	variables operationalize reliability validity statistical significance replication prediction	contextualization process field notes triangulation insider/outsider perspective meaning is of chief concern making judgments
Design	structured predetermined	descriptive flexible narrative grounded theory participatory action feminist
Data	statistical operationalized variables measure overt behavior	descriptive field notes documents interviews
Sample or participants	randomized control for extraneous variables size is important	nonrepresentative can be small
Techniques or procedures	experiments standardized instruments structured interview structured observation independent variables dependent variables	observation open-ended interview review of documents participant observation researcher as instrument
Data analysis	deductive statistical	ongoing inductive verbal
Problems with approach	control of extraneous variables validity	time consuming data reduction is difficult reliability generalizability nonstandardized procedures

Figure 2.1

Comparison of Key Terms Related to Quantitative and Qualitative Research

Figure 2.1 compares quantitative and qualitative research. It should be again noted that constructivist researchers use qualitative methodology, whereas empiricist researchers tend to use quantitative methodology. However, qualitative research methodology and data analysis methods can be used by both empiricist and constructivist researchers. The choice researchers make about using qualitative methodology is independent of their underlying theoretical perspective (Meyers, 1997). The research consumer needs to examine researchers' explicit or implicit statements about research to determine which perspective is being applied. That is, research consumers should look for evidence as to whether qualitative methodology is being used within a positivist or constructivist approach to research.

SUMMARY

Note that the summary is constructed in a question-and-answer format using questions from this chapter's Focus Questions section.

What are the major designs used to conduct educational research?   Quantitative research and qualitative research designs are based on the way information, or data, are collected and analyzed.

What are these types of quantitative research: descriptive, comparative, and experimental? Descriptive research hopes to answer questions about a variable's status. Comparative research attempts make decisions about two or more variables' differences or relationships. Experimental research tries to draw conclusions about the cause-effect relationship between two or more variables.

What distinguishes the three types of quantitative research designs from each other? Descriptive and comparative research may reveal status, patterns, and associations among variables; but only experimental research can be used to attribute causality.

What are the instruments used to collect quantitative data?   Data are collected with instruments, which include direct-observation forms, tests, and surveys (questionnaires and interviews).

How are data analyzed in each of the three types of quantitative research designs?   In descriptive research, information most often is described with means and standard deviations. In comparative research, in addition to the descriptive measures of data, two common statistical procedures are correlation and the chi-square. In experimental research, common statistical procedures are the _t_ test and analysis of variance, or ANOVA.

Frequently, the same statistic (e.g., _t_ test, ANOVA, chi-square) can be used to analyze the data in research that is descriptive and comparative, as well as in experimental research. It is not the statistic that is the distinguishing feature of a research design. Rather, it is the research question or hypothesis and the characteristics of the design that distinguish among the three types of quantitative research.

What are central tendency and variability, and how are they measured?   Central tendency is the average or middle score in a group of scores. The middle score is called the _median;_ the arithmetic average score is called the _mean._ Variability is the extent to which other scores in the group cluster about or spread from the measure of central tendency. The variability of a set of data whose average is the mean is usually reported as the standard deviation.

What are the major purposes for conducting qualitative research?   The basic qualitative research purposes are to describe, interpret, evaluate, and verify.

What are the major features of qualitative research?   Qualitative research is characterized by these facts: *(a)* data are collected within natural educational settings and the major data collection instrument is the researcher observer; *(b)* data are verbal, not numerical; *(c)* researchers are concerned with process rather than outcomes alone; and *(d)* data are analyzed rationally, not statistically.

Why might quantitative and qualitative research be combined?   The use of both quantitative and qualitative research methods within a research project can incorporate the strengths of both types of research and enhance the researcher's results.

ACTIVITIES

Activity 1

Each of the following research purposes, questions, and hypotheses are from empiricist, quantitative research. For each, indicate *(a)* the type of research design (descriptive, comparative, experimental, causal-comparative, mixed-method) and *(b)* the research variables. For experimental or causal-comparative designs, differentiate between the independent and dependent variables. Note that some of the studies have more than one research purpose.

1. The purpose of this study was to describe the procedures that elementary-school principals and teachers use to create classrooms and to examine the effect of these procedures on class composition (Burns & Mason, 1998).
2. Science-talented, rural, adolescent females were the subjects of this study. Researchers examined relations among parent attitudes, intrinsic value of science, peer support, available activities, and preference for future science careers (Jacobs, Finken, Griffin, & Wright, 1998).
3. Two primary research questions framed the investigation. First, what working knowledge of narrative and informational genres do kindergarten, first-grade, and second-grade children demonstrate in text-production tasks? Second, how does their demonstration of this knowledge vary as a function of differential levels or modes of cultural scaffolding?
4. This study looked at one wage earner from each household in a small town. The hypotheses were that *(a)* higher levels of education will be associated with higher volumes of certain (but not all) content of reading, compared with lower levels of education and *(b)* occupational category will be associated with different volumes of certain (but not all) content for reading (Guthrie, Seifert, & Kirsch, 1986).

Activity 2

1. Using a quantitative research report of your own choosing (or one that is cited in Appendix A), *(a)* locate the research hypothesis, purpose, or question; *(b)* indicate the research design; and *(c)* identify the research variables. For experimental or causal-comparative research, indicate the independent and dependent variables.

2. Using a qualitative research report of your own choosing (or one that is cited in Appendix A), *(a)* locate the researcher's purpose or question; *(b)* locate the section(s) in which the researcher indicates how and where the information will be collected and from whom; *(c)* locate the section(s) in which the information is collected and analyzed.

FEEDBACK

Activity 1

1. The study had two parts, a descriptive and an experimental part. The signal to experimental research was "effect . . . on." In the descriptive part, the researchers were concerned with identifying procedures for arranging classes. In the experimental part, they examined how class-creation procedures (independent variable) affected class composition (dependent variable).
2. The study was comparative. The signal was "relationships." The five aspects were compared to see how they related (compared) to each other.
3. The study had two components, descriptive and experimental. The signal to experimental research was "vary as a function of." In the descriptive component, the researchers were looking for what knowledge the students had. In the experimental component, they examined what change (vary) of that knowledge (dependent variable) resulted from differential levels or modes of cultural scaffolding (independent variable).
4. The study was causal-comparative because both the independent variables, "higher levels of education" (Hypothesis *a*) and "occupational category" (Hypothesis *b*), were in existence prior to the study. The dependent variable in both parts of the study was "content of reading." Causality was presumed—level of education and occupational category would cause differences in reading content.

Activity 2

Discuss your responses with other students with whom you have collaborated and/or your course instructor.

Reading and Evaluating Research Reports

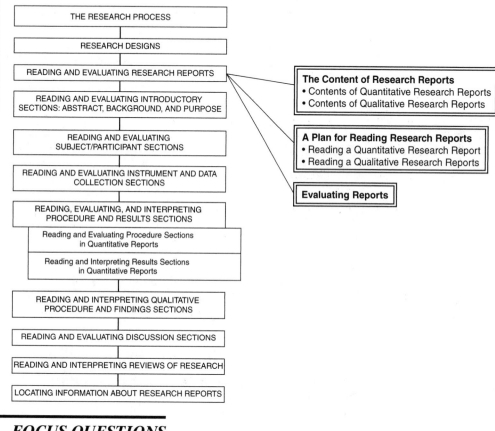

The Content of Research Reports
- Contents of Quantitative Research Reports
- Contents of Qualitative Research Reports

A Plan for Reading Research Reports
- Reading a Quantitative Research Report
- Reading a Qualitative Research Reports

Evaluating Reports

FOCUS QUESTIONS

1. What are the major sections of research reports?
2. What is an effective strategy for reading reports?
3. What are the criteria for evaluating the quality and appropriateness of reports?

Research reports help consumers to know more about educational practice, to acquire knowledge that they can apply, and to gain insight about effective instruction.

Obviously, a research report is not research. *Research* is conducted by a professional who systematically collects information about an identified problem or question, analyzes the data, and, on the basis of the evidence, confirms or disconfirms a prior prediction or statement. In comparison, a research *report* is a summary of researchers' activities and results. After reading such reports, consumers can judge the effectiveness of the researchers and the appropriateness of their results and conclusions.

Research reports are "pictures" of research. In the reports, researchers explain their studies and present their procedures. Reports can show (*a*) good research methodology, well reported; (*b*) good research methodology, poorly reported; (*c*) poor research methodology, well reported; and (*d*) poor research methodology, poorly reported. It is up to consumers to identify the quality of the report and its findings. In situation (*b*), researchers might have conducted appropriate research and reported it inappropriately; in situation (*c*), they might have conducted inappropriate research and dressed it in the "garb" of an appropriate research report.

This chapter explains the contents of research reports and presents examples of well-written ones. The chapter discusses reading strategies and presents a format for evaluating the quality of reports. These evaluative questions form the basis for reading and analyzing research methodology and methods, which will be discussed further in subsequent chapters.

THE CONTENT OF RESEARCH REPORTS

Reports should contain information related to research producers' questions and their research activities. This information reviews the researchers' efforts in selecting a problem area and specifying theoretical positions and research questions. Consumers will see sections that

Describe subjects or participants

Describe data collection devices, including instruments

Explain procedures, activities, events, and treatments (if appropriate)

Present findings or results based on data analyses

Discuss conclusions and implications

Contents of Quantitative Research Reports

The information within quantitative research reports is generally organized into sections with headings such as "Background" or "Literature Review"; "Purpose," "Questions," or "Hypotheses"; "Method," including "Subjects," "Instruments," and "Procedure"; "Results"; "Conclusions"; and "References."

The **background section** contains (*a*) an explanation of the researchers' chosen problem area, (*b*) its educational importance, (*c*) summaries of other researchers' results that are related to the problem (called a *literature review*), and (*d*) strengths from the related research that were used, and weaknesses or limitations that were changed. The background section is often preceded by an **abstract,** a complete overview of the report. Researchers usually omit the literature review from the abstract.

Refer to the example research report, "Effects of Classroom Structure on Student Achievement Goal Orientation," at the end of chapter 1, pages 19–26. This research report did not have an abstract. The information starting at [2] contains the introduction and background section, as well as a review of related research literature. The related research is discussed beginning at [4].

The **purpose section** contains the specific goal (or goals) of the research project. The purpose can be expressed as a statement, as questions, or as an hypothesis (or set of hypotheses). In the sample research report "Effects of Classroom Structure on Student Achievement Goal Orientation," the researcher has indicated some preliminary purposes at [3] and [5]. The full statement of purpose and the research hypotheses are at [7]—the last paragraph of the introduction.

The following is an example from a research report by Nist and Olejnik, in which both a purpose and specific questions are expressed.

General Purpose of the Study

The overall focus of this study, then, was to examine the role that varying levels of context and dictionary definitions play in college students' acquisition of new words, assessed under four different testing formats. The following two questions were posed:

Specific Questions of the Study

1. Are there significant differences in subjects' abilities to learn and remember new vocabulary words, depending on strength of context and adequacy of dictionary definitions?
2. Can significant differences in subjects' abilities to learn and remember new vocabulary words as a function of context and dictionary definitions be replicated across four levels of word knowledge? (Nist & Olejnik, 1995, p. 179)

From reading this purpose section, a consumer could easily identify and classify the type of research and the research variables (independent and dependent, when appropriate). In the example, the words *role, play,* and *acquisition* indicate that "something" is making "something else" change. From these words, the reader knows that the study used experimental research. In Nist and Olejnik's questions, the three independent variables were "strength of context," "adequacy of dictionary definitions," and "levels of word knowledge." The dependent variables were "ability to learn" and "ability to remember new vocabulary words."

Sometimes, researchers like Nist and Olejnik do not place their purpose, questions, or hypotheses in a section with a separate heading. In such cases, they include this information in a background section, *most often in the section's last paragraph.* The following is an example in which hypotheses are stated in a subheaded section. Notice how the researcher, Moustafa, predicted the direction of the expected results.

RESEARCH HYPOTHESES

The following hypotheses were made:

Directional Hypotheses

(a) The onset/rime analogy explanation is a more viable explanation than the phoneme blending explanation for how young children learn to recode unfamiliar graphophonological print phonologically;
(b) The more print words children recognize, the better they are able to make analogies between letter strings representing onsets and rimes in known and unknown words to recode unknown ones phonologically; and
(c) Young children's ability to recode unfamiliar print phonologically is constrained when they have difficulty reversing their perceptions of parts and wholes in print. (Moustafa, 1995, p. 468)

The **method section** of quantitative research reports usually contains several subsections. These are *subjects, instruments,* and *procedures.* In the report "Effects of Classroom Structure on Student Achievement Goal Orientation," the researcher uses some standard subheadings and some other subheadings. As you read the information from [8] through [12], follow the annotations we have provided in the margin to locate information about *subjects, instruments, materials,* and *procedures.*

The **subjects section** contains a description of the individuals included in the study, giving general information about such factors as age, sex, grade level, intellectual and academic abilities, and socioeconomic level. The section also contains the number of subjects and an account of how the subjects were selected and assigned to groups. The subjects section is sometimes labeled "Sample" or "Participants." Research can focus on subjects such as parents, teachers, administrators, instructional materials, or even learning environments. In the report "Effects of Classroom Structure on Student Achievement Goal Orientation"(pp. 27–51), the researcher uses the term *participants* to mean *subjects* [8].

The following is a typical subjects section:

> *Identification of Sample and Target Population*

The sample included 118 students from Grades 3 and 6 in three middle-class elementary schools in an urban area of inland southern California. All three schools were ethnically diverse, with approximately 60% White, 30% Hispanic (predominately Mexican-American), 5% Black, and 5% Asian-American students each. Three hundred fifteen students who were asked to participate in the study had, according to school records and teachers' reports, at least average proficiency in English. None was classified as being gifted, having learning or emotional problems, or being involved in special education. One hundred twenty-nine students returned parental consent forms and were included in the original sample. Data from 11 of the students—that is, 6 third graders and 5 sixth graders—were not usable because of problems with tape recording, student absence, and faulty procedure. The numbers and ages of the students who remained in the sample were 18 boys, 41 girls (mean age = 9.0 years, SD = 0.3) at Grade 3 and 29 boys, 30 girls (mean age = 12.1 years, SD = 0.4) at Grade 6. This sample represented 11 third-grade classrooms (3 to 9 students, median = 5, from each classroom) and 10 sixth-grade classrooms (2 to 9 students, median = 7, from each). (Newman & Schwager, 1995, p. 357)

The **instruments section** contains a description of the data collection instruments: observation forms, standardized and researcher-made tests, and surveys. When instruments are *published* standardized tests, researchers usually assume the readers' familiarity with them and do little more than name them. (In chapter 6, "Reading and Evaluating Instrument and Data Collection Sections," is an explanation of how readers can obtain information about unfamiliar standardized tests.) When instruments are less well known, researchers describe or give examples of the tools and give evidence of their effectiveness. If tests other than standardized tests were administered, researchers explain the testing circumstances (and the qualifications or training of the test givers) and provide information about the test and how it was constructed. If observations or surveys were used, researchers relate how these were done and how the observers or interviewers were trained.

The following is a typical instruments section, which explains in detail how the researchers developed one instrument, an attitude inventory. The example refers to another unexplained test called a cloze test. The researchers are assuming the readers will know the term *cloze test.*

> *First Instrument: Description*

INSTRUMENTS

The Student Attitude Inventory (SAI) was used as a pre- and post-test measure. Constructed by the researchers, the SAI contains 33 questions related to five areas: listening

(7 items), speaking (7 items), reading (8 items), writing (6 items), and self-perceptions as learners (5 items). The items contained in the SAI were generated from a compilation of statements made by elementary students over a period of four years, who were responding to learning activities presented by preservice teachers during language arts practicum assignments. The practicum assignments included integrated language arts activities and elementary students would spontaneously comment about how much they enjoyed or disliked specific kinds (i.e., listening, reading, speaking, or writing) of activities. Preservice teachers reported students' comments to the university instructors, who sorted the comments according to the area represented. The researchers (i.e., course instructors) pulled from the item groupings the most frequently occurring statements and edited them for content and clarity.

First Instrument: Administration and Content

The SAI may be administered individually or in a group setting, with respondents marking the face illustration that best represents their feelings. Five face illustrations are shown at the end of each question, ranging from a big smile to a big frown. Respondents are told that the face illustrations represent the following feelings: very happy, happy, neither happy nor sad, sad, and very sad. The SAI includes questions, such as:

(a) *Listening*: How do you feel when someone reads a story to you? How do you feel when your teacher tells you the steps to follow in an activity rather than having you read the steps?

(b) *Speaking*: How do you feel when someone asks you to tell about something that has happened to you or something that you have done? How do you feel when you are given the chance to tell someone about a story that you have read?

(c) *Reading*: How do you feel when you are asked to read written directions and the teacher does not explain them? How do you feel when you have the opportunity to read magazines?

(d) *Writing*: How do you feel when you are writing a note to a friend or parent and you do not know how to spell a word? How do you feel when your teacher asks you to write a story?

(e) *Self-Perceptions as Learners*: How do you feel when you are asked to complete an assignment alone? How do you feel when you are asked to be the leader of a group activity?

First Instrument: Scoring

A Likert scale, ranging from 5 to 1, is used to score the SAI, with 5 representing "very happy" and 1 representing "very sad." Area scores on the SAI are obtained by summing the item responses in each of the five areas. The possible scores for Listening, Speaking, Reading, Writing, and Self-Perceptions as Learners are 35, 35, 40, 30, and 25, respectively. Summing the area scores produces a possible total score of 165. The researchers examined the internal consistency of the SAI and found that alpha coefficients for the area scores were as follows: .74 (Listening), .74 (Speaking), .82 (Reading), .77 (Writing), and .74 (Self-Perceptions as Learners), with .93 being the alpha coefficient for the overall (total) score. The validity of the SAI was examined by correlating the total scores obtained by a sample of 47 elementary students on the SAI with their total scores on the Elementary Reading Attitude Survey (ERAS); the obtained Pearson Product Moment correlation coefficient was .44 (p, 0.002), which the authors considered to be adequate for research purposes.

Second Instrument: Description

An oral cloze test was administered at the beginning of the study to determine whether differences existed initially between the treatment and comparison groups in their abilities to meaningfully process oral language. The cloze test contained 9 sentences with deletions representing 3 categories: final, initial, and medial positions (i.e., 3 sentences per deletion category). (Thames & Reeves, 1994, pp. 296–298. Used with permission of the copyright holder, College Reading Association.)

In the report "Effects of Classroom Structure on Student Achievement Goal Orientation," the researcher did not use tests to collect data. In the "Procedure" section [11] on p. 22, the researcher indicated the data that was collected. For each of the three treatments (types of instruction), the researcher indicated what data was collected. In essence, the forms on which the data was collected comprised the "instruments" for this research project:

- The teachers' evaluation of students at [11]
- The students' writing of their mathematical goals at [11], [12], [13], and [14]
- The token currency at [12], and
- The gold stars and positive verbal feedback at [13]

The **procedure section,** a subsection of the methods section, contains a detailed explanation of how researchers conducted their study. In descriptive and comparative studies, researchers explain how data were collected and analyzed. In experimental studies, researchers also describe the treatments and how they were administered. If special instructional materials were prepared for the study, they are described; often sample portions are included.

In the report "Effects of Classroom Structure on Student Achievement Goal Orientation," the researcher has several subsections comprising the "procedures" of the study. At [9], the researcher discusses the materials used. At [10], the research design is discussed. Further, at [11], [12], [13], and [14], the researchers provide an explanation about how the classes were selected and the teachers' and students' activities.

The **results section** contains the outcomes of the researchers' data analyses. This section contains not only the numerical or statistical results (often presented in tables and charts) but also an explanation of the importance (or educational implications) of those results.

In the report "Effects of Classroom Structure on Student Achievement Goal Orientation," the researcher has provided at [15] the results of the statistical analyses of the collected data. The statistical procedures are identified ("ANOVA" and a "Tukey post hoc test") and two tables are included. For both of these statistical procedures, the researcher has interpreted the numbers into findings.

Many research consumers, find results sections confusing because of the statistics. The next subsection of this chapter, "A Plan for Reading Research Reports," explains how to tackle reading these sections. In chapter 8, "Reading and Interpreting

Qualitative Procedure and Findings Sections," are discussions about how to judge researchers' presentations of both qualitative and quantitative data analyses.

The **discussion** or **conclusion** section contains researchers' ideas about the educational implications of research results: how results can be used in school, or what additional research may be needed. Often this explanation is prefaced with a brief overview of research results. When researchers obtain unusual or unexpected results, they discuss possible reasons for such results.

In the report "Effects of Classroom Structure on Student Achievement Goal Orientation," the researcher has provided at [16] a summary of the findings, a discussion of those findings in relation to other research, some possible limitations of the study, and some implications of the classroom use of the findings.

The **reference section** contains an alphabetical listing of the books, journal articles, other research reports, instructional materials, and instruments cited in the report. Sometimes researchers follow the reference section with appendixes that contain examples of instruments or special materials.

Contents of Qualitative Research Reports

Writers of qualitative research reports generally do not use the traditional headings and subheadings (discussed previously) to identify the content of their reports. The information within qualitative research reports is often organized into sections containing information such as

- background
- related research literature
- purpose
- general questions to which answers are sought
- methodology, including participants, data collection methods, and activities
- findings and interpretations of the findings
- conclusions
- references

However, qualitative researchers will likely use headings and subheadings that are descriptive of the ideas within each section. So, in the sample research report "Images of America: What Youth Do Know About the United States," the headings do indicate the major content of the report.

In a qualitative research report introduction, there is discussion about the researchers' concern for the topic and its educational importance. Qualitative researchers may summarize other related researchers' findings (called a *literature review*). But such a literature review is not as extensive as it is in quantitative research reports and may only provide a theoretical basis for the qualitative researchers' work. The background section is often preceded by an abstract, which is an overview of the report.

Refer to the research report, "Images of America: What Youth Do Know About the United States," at the end of chapter 1, pages 27–51, The information starting at [3] through [8] contains the introductory and background information, as well as some relevant related research findings.

The information about the purpose of the research is found at [6] and [8] and this part contains the general questions addressed by the research project. Notice that these questions are expressed as a statement of purpose, but they are *not expressed* as specific research questions, or as hypotheses. At [7] the researcher includes a statement of her theoretical approach to research.

Information about **participants,** or subjects, is found at [9] and [10].

There is no specific section saying "methods" in this research report. But that information is found beginning at [11] and continuing through [20]. Because qualitative researchers are constantly questioning and interpreting the data they collect, the information about methods is presented together, rather than in separate sections.

In this report, the researcher does include a heading that specifically identifies conclusions [21].

The **reference section** [25] contains an alphabetical listing of the cited books, journal articles, other research reports, instructional materials, and instruments. In this report, the researcher has an appendix following the references [26]. She includes a section with "notes" [24].

A PLAN FOR READING RESEARCH REPORTS

In most research reports, researchers use common terms and organize their ideas similarly. Research consumers can thus follow most reports by knowing this basic three-part procedure: prereading, reading, and postreading. In other words, first a research consumer recalls what he or she knows about the topic. The research consumer then develops a purpose for reading the report. Second, the research consumer systematically reads parts of the report, according to his or her own purposes. Finally, the research consumer decides if the report has matched his or her purpose.

This three-part reading strategy is illustrated well by the sample quantitative and qualitative research reports, "Effects of Classroom Structure on Student Achievement Goal Orientation," (a quantitative study) and "Images of America: What Youth Do Know About the United States" (a qualitative study). The reading strategy is fully explained in the following sections, with reference to the reports' labeled areas.

Reading a Quantitative Research Report

First Phase: Previewing and Predicting the Research Report.   In the first phase, you consider why you will read the report, and what information it will present. You can think of this first phase as a reconnaissance mission; you will find out what you know about the topic and you will predict whether the report meets your intended purpose. You will determine whether the report is written as a standard research report.

To complete the first phase:

1. Review the research report "Effects of Classroom Structure on Student Achievement Goal Orientation." Answer the question "Why am I reading this report—to gain knowledge, to apply the knowledge, or to implement an instructional practice?" For this demonstration, we will assume that you desire additional information about helping students to set goals for their instruction and achievement.
2. Read the report's title [1] and its first paragraph [2].
3. Answer the question "Will reading this report meet my purpose?" The answer is yes, because the study looks at classroom learning and student goal orientation.
4. Answer the question "What do I know about the topic?" On a sheet of paper or in the margin next to the report, list what you already know about factors such as different classroom environments and learning. List what you know about setting student goals. Start with those ideas listed in the title and the study's first paragraph: *classroom learning, goal setting, classroom evaluation structure,* and *classroom strategies for goal setting.*
5. Read each of the major headings. Answer the question "Is the report organized using typical section content and headings?" The answer is yes. For example: Introduction, Background Information, and Related Research (unlabeled) at [2] through [6]; Method [7], with Subjects [8], Materials [9], Design [10], and Procedure [11] through [14]; Results [15]; and Discussion [16]. The researchers have used additional headings and subheadings. These clues are also important, especially in the Procedure section, because they help you identify what the researcher did during the study.

Second Phase: Reading the Research Report.   In the second phase, you will find information suggested by your purpose for reading. You will confirm or modify your list of known information. Your purpose will determine whether you read the entire report or only select sections. To complete the second phase:

1. You will be keeping a list of factors related to teachers' reading habits and the reading procedures they use in their classrooms. As you read the report, remember that your purpose is to obtain information about teachers who read, and what reading practices they recommend for their students. Recall that some factors will be added to your list, and some will modify or contradict items on your list.
2. Read the research report sections in the following order. (Note that several sections have been intentionally omitted from the list.)
   Introduction [2], first paragraph
   (If the report had an Abstract, you would have read that first.)
   Introduction [7], last paragraph (Purpose)
   Design [10]
   Discussion [16]
3. You will not read the remaining sections now, because the information to meet your reading purpose can be obtained in the previously listed sections.

Third Phase: Confirming Predictions and Knowledge.   In the third phase, you will verify that your purpose has been met and you will recall key information. You can now decide which information supports the proposed purpose and adds to your knowledge.

To complete the third phase:

1. Refer to the list you made during the first phase, "What do I know about the topic?" Revise the list by adding new information and deleting inappropriate information. Answer the questions "Were the students similar to those in my school? Were the teachers (those who applied the goal-orientation practices and provided students with feedback) similar to me and teachers at my school? Can the insights drawn from the results be applied at my school?"
2. Write a short (two- to three-sentence) statement that applies to the proposed purpose for reading the report and contains the report's key points.

Reading a Qualitative Research Report

Notice that in a qualitative research report, there are no traditional headings and sub-headings. The report "Images of America: What Youth Do Know About the United States" (pp. 27–51) is an example of a qualitative research report. To apply the three-step reading plan, first try to understand the type of information contained in a qualitative report. Doing so will help you to interpet the researcher's ideas.

First Phase: Previewing and Predicting the Research Report. In the first phase, you will determine why you wish to read the report. You will decide what kinds of information it presents. Find out what you know about the topic, and predict whether the report meets your intended purpose. You can also determine whether the report is written as a standard research report. To complete the first step:

1. Review the research report "Images of America: What Youth Do Know About the United States." Answer the question "Why am I reading this report—to gain knowledge, to apply the knowledge, or to implement an instructional practice?" For this demonstration, we will assume that you desire additional information about working with other teachers to modify or expand your school's American history syllabus, to more effectively present information about the United States.
2. Read the report title [1], the Abstract [2], the beginning of the Introductory section [3] and [4], and the last paragraph of the Introductory section [8].
3. Answer the question "Will reading this report meet my purpose?" The answer is yes, because the study looks at the knowledge and beliefs students have about the United States.
4. Answer the question "What do I know about the topic?" On a sheet of paper or in the margin next to the report, list what you believe about the United States in regard to topics such as *race, economy,* and *gender inequity; freedom* and *diversity.* Start with the ideas enumerated in the first sentence of the Abstract.
5. Read each of the major headings [9], [12], [13], [14], [15], [16], [17], [18], [19], [20], [21], [22], and [23]. Answer the question "How is the report organized?" The answer is Introduction, Background Information, and Related Research (un-labeled) at [3] through [8]; Subjects/Participants [9] through [11]; Data Collection [12]; Findings and Interpretation [13] through [20]; Conclusions and Implications [21] through [23].

Second Phase: Reading the Research Report. In the second phase, you will find information suggested by your purpose for reading. You will confirm or modify your list of known information. Your purpose will determine whether you read the entire report or only select sections. To complete the second phase:

1. You will be keeping a list of factors related to your beliefs and perceptions of the United States. As you read the report, remember that your purpose is to obtain information about students' perceptions and beliefs about the United States. Recall that some factors will be added to your list, and some will modify or contradict items on your list.
2. Read the entire research report in the following order:
   - Abstract [2]
   - Introduction [3] through [8]
   - Subjects/Participants [9] through [11]
   - Procedure [12]
   - Conclusions and Implications [21] through [23]
   - Findings and Interpretations [13] through [20]; read only the first one or two paragraphs of each of these sections
3. At this point you will not read all of the sections containing Findings, because the information to meet your reading purpose can be obtained in the previously listed sections.

Third Phase: Confirming Predictions and Knowledge. In the third phase, you will verify that your purpose has been met. You will recall key information. You can decide which information supports the researcher's proposed purpose and adds to your knowledge.

1. Refer to the list you made during the first phase, "What do I know about the topic?" Revise the list by adding new information and deleting inappropriate information. Answer the questions "Were the students similar to those in my school or school district? Were the students' ideas similar to those in my own teaching situation and those of others I know in my school? Can the findings of this research be applied to my school?"
2. Write a short (two- to three-sentence) statement that applies to the proposed purpose for reading the report and contains the report's key points.

EVALUATING REPORTS

Informed retail shoppers compare and buy products by using a set of criteria. In the same way, consumers of research can "shop" among research reports to identify well-written reports, of appropriate methodology. You have already begun to be an aware consumer by learning to read research reports like a research producer. Now you will learn how to use the questions in Figure 3.1 and Figure 3.2 to evaluate research reports. The questions in those figures are about each of the major aspects of research reports.

At this point in your learning, you should not be expected to answer all the questions appropriately. Because the content and length of research reports are often determined by the editors of the journals or books in which the reports appear, our determinations as research consumers about the appropriateness and adequacy of the information in a report will necessarily be subjective. Remember that these subjective decisions change as you gain increased understanding of research methods

Abstract

Organization
- Is information included about the major aspects of the research—purpose, subjects, instruments, procedures/treatment, results?
- Is the abstract brief and clearly written?

Introductory Section

Problem Area
- Are the problem area (and its educational importance) explained?
- Are the researchers' assumptions and theoretical perspectives about the topic explained?

Related Literature
- Are research studies presented that relate to the problem area?
- Has the related research been evaluated and critiqued?
- Does the intended research logically extend the understandings from the related research?

Hypothesis(es), Purpose(s), Question(s) in Quantitative Research
- Is there a purpose that can be studied in an unbiased manner?
- Are the research variables (independent and dependent, when appropriate) easily identified from the hypothesis, question, or purpose statement?
- Are key terms or variables operationally defined?

Method Section

Subjects
- Do the researchers clearly describe target populations and subjects, sampling and selection procedures, and group sizes?
- Are these subjects and procedures appropriate for the research design?

Standardized Instruments and Other Tools
- What instruments are used in the study?
- Are these appropriate for the design of the study?
- Are the instruments valid for collecting data on the variables in the study? Are reliability estimates given for each instrument?
- Are researcher-made instruments included (or at least samples of the instrument items)?
- Are the instruments appropriate for use with the target population and the research subjects?
- In the case of authentic (or performance-based) assessments, what evidence is presented that the devices reflect realistic samples of students' learning?

Design and Procedure in Quantitative Research
- Are the research design and data collection procedures clearly described?
- Is the research design appropriate to the researchers' purpose?
- Can the study be replicated from the information provided?
- In experimental designs, are treatments fully explained?
- Are examples of special materials included?

Results Section

Data Analysis in Quantitative Research
- Are the statistical procedures for data analysis clearly described? Are the procedures appropriate for the type of quantitative research design?

Research Validity in Quantitative Research
- Are the procedures free from the influence of extraneous variables?
- Does the study have any threats to its internal and external validity?

Significance in Quantitative Research
- Are statistical significance levels indicated? Does the research have practical significance?

Discussion Section

Discussion (Conclusions, Recommendations)
- Are conclusions related to answering the research question(s)? Are the conclusions appropriate to the results?
- Is the report free from inappropriate generalizations and implications?
- If inappropriate, are suggestions for additional research provided?

Figure 3.1
Evaluating Quantitative Research Reports

Abstract

Organization
- Is information included about the major aspects of the research—purpose, participants, data collection, procedures, and results?

Style
- Is the abstract brief and clearly written?

Introductory Section

Problem Area
- Is the problem area (and its educational importance) explained?
- Are the researchers' assumptions and theoretical perspectives about the topic explained?
- Is it clear from the discussion as to the type of qualitative research being undertaken?

Related Literature
- Are research studies presented that relate to the problem area?
- Has the related research been evaluated and critiqued?
- Does the intended research logically extend or challenge the understandings from the related research?

Purpose(s), Question(s) in Qualitative Research
- Is the relationship between the study and previous studies explicit?
- Is there a clear rationale for the use of qualitative procedures?
- Are researchers' assumptions and biases expressed?

"Method" or Procedure Section(s)

Participants/Subjects and Setting
- Are the setting and participants fully described?
- Are participants or subjects, and selection procedures, clearly described?
- Are these subjects and procedures appropriate for the research design?
- Is there evidence of close collaboration between researcher and participants?
- If focus groups are used, are the members well described? Is how they are selected clearly described?

Data collection devices
- What devices (questionaires, surveys, interview forms) are used in the study?
- Are these devices appropriate for the design of the study?
- Are the data collection devices appropriate for collecting data about the purpose(s) of the study?
- Are researcher-made devices included (or at least samples of them)?
- Are the data collection devices appropriate for use with the participants?

Design and Procedure in Qualitative Research
- Has the researcher obtained information from different sources and perspectives?
- Are research questions stated and additional questions generated?
- Is the method explained in detail?
- Has the researchers' presence influenced the behavior of the subjects?
- Is there abundant evidence, from multiple sources?

Findings Section(s)

Data Analysis in Qualitative Research
- Are the findings integrated with the collection and interpretation information?
- Are the processes clearly described for organizing data, identifying patterns, and synthesizing key ideas as theories and research questions?
- Has the researcher searched for disconfirming or negative evidence?
- Has the researcher reported personal beliefs, values, and biases?
- Have external authorities reviewed the data, data analysis, and data interpretations?

Research Verification and Authenticity in Qualitative Research
- Are there multiple procedures for corroborating research evidence and researchers' judgments?

Discussion Section

Discussion (Conclusions, Recommendations)
- Are there conclusions related to answering the research question(s)? Are the conclusions appropriate to the results?
- Is the report free from inappropriate generalizations and implications?
- If inappropriate, are suggestions for additional research provided?

Figure 3.2
Evaluating Qualitative Research Reports

and research reporting. Your skills will improve as you gain more experience in reading and evaluating research reports, and in writing about them. Your work with this text is a beginning step in acquiring understanding and experience.

The questions presented in Figure 3.1 provide an overview of the discussions in later chapters about quantitative research reports. The major headings within Figure 3.1 represent common major headings found in quantitative research reports published in professional journals. As you can see by reviewing the sample reports, researchers modify these major headings to fit their purposes and to highlight particular information. Research reports in other sources—books, encyclopedias, newspapers, and popular magazines—may have different organizations and formats. Some of these variations are discussed in later chapters.

ACTIVITY

Activity 1

Select two research reports (one quantitative and one qualitative). These reports may be of your own choosing or from the sources in Appendix A. With one or more partners (that is, other students in the class), read the research reports. Use both the peer-interacting procedure discussed in the Activities section of chapter 1 on page 18, and also the research report reading plan discussed in this chapter. You and your partner(s) should take turns explaining the reasons for selecting sections to be read and the location of key information. Discuss differences you may have about these choices.

FEEDBACK

Activity 1

Discuss your response with your partners, other partner teams, and the course instructor.

CHAPTER 4

Reading and Evaluating Introductory Sections: Abstract, Background, and Purpose

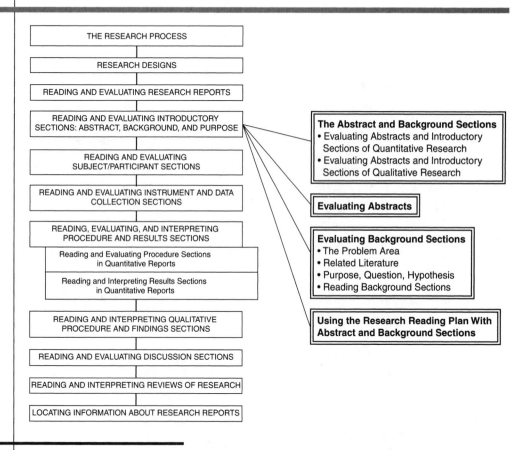

FOCUS QUESTIONS

1. What information should research consumers get from the abstract and background sections of quantitative and qualitative reports?
2. What criteria are used to evaluate abstracts?
3. What criteria are used to evaluate background sections?
4. What should research consumers know about research purposes and hypotheses?
5. What is the plan for reading abstracts and background sections?

In the background section, a researcher introduces readers to the problem area and its educational importance. Researchers also provide brief summaries of other researchers' results that are related to the problem area. The part with these summaries is called the *literature review*. In this review, researchers indicate strengths from the related research that were used in their study, and weaknesses or limitations that were changed. In many professional journals, the background section is preceded by an abstract, an overview of the report. Often researchers omit the literature review from their abstract.

THE ABSTRACT AND BACKGROUND SECTIONS

In the plan for reading research reports discussed in chapter 3, the abstract and background sections are read first. From these sections, research consumers should be able to answer the following questions:

- What are the researchers' issues and concerns?
- What have other researchers found out about these issues?
- What question(s) did the researchers try to answer?
- What kind of research was conducted by the researchers? What variables were being studied?
- Were there any independent and dependent variables?
- Are the researchers' issues and concerns relevant to me as a professional, or to my teaching situation?

The questions for evaluating abstract and background sections (taken from Figure 3.1 and Figure 3.2, pp. 86–87) follow.

Evaluating Abstracts and Introductory Sections of Quantitative Research

ABSTRACT

Organization
- Is information included about the major aspects of the research—purpose, subjects, instruments, procedures/treatment, results?
- Is the abstract brief and clearly written?

INTRODUCTORY SECTION

Problem Area
- Is the problem area (and its educational importance) explained?
- Are the researchers' assumptions and theoretical perspectives about the topic explained?

Related Literature
- Are research studies presented that relate to the problem area?
- Has the related research been evaluated and critiqued?
- Does the intended research logically extend the understandings from the related research?

Hypothesis(es), Purpose(s), Question(s) in Quantitative Research
- Is there a purpose that can be studied in an unbiased manner?
- Are the research variables (independent and dependent, when appropriate) easily identified from the hypothesis, question, or purpose statement?
- Are key terms or variables operationally defined?

Evaluating Abstracts and Introductory Sections of Qualitative Research

---

ABSTRACT

Organization
- Is information included about the major aspects of the research—purpose, participants, data collection, procedures, and results?

Style
- Is the abstract brief and clearly written?

INTRODUCTORY SECTION

Problem Area
- Is the problem area (and its educational importance) explained?
- Are the researchers' assumptions and theoretical perspectives about the topic explained?
- Is it clear from the discussion as to the type of qualitative research being undertaken?

Related Literature
- Are research studies presented that relate to the problem area?
- Has the related research been evaluated and critiqued?
- Does the intended research logically extend or challenge the understandings from the related research?

Purpose(s), Question(s) in Qualitative Research
- Is the relationship between the study and previous studies explicit?
- Is there a clear rationale for the use of qualitative procedures?
- Are researchers' assumptions and biases expressed?

EVALUATING ABSTRACTS

Abstracts are to be written in a particular style and manner that helps the reader to ascertain whether the research is appropriate for their purposes as consumers. Abstracts contain information about purpose, subjects, instruments, procedure (and treatment, when applicable), findings, and conclusions.

Abstracts are usually short, containing 100 to 200 words, and they are set in special type (or indented) to distinguish them from the main body of the research report. Some journals do not require abstracts; the decision is set by the journal editors and advisory boards. Some publications, such as *Psychological Abstracts* and *Current Index to Journals in Education (CIJE),* contain short abstracts that do not have the style and content of journal abstracts. Other publications, such as *Dissertation Abstracts International,* have abstracts 600 to 800 words long, obviously containing more information than journal abstracts. A discussion of these publications and samples of their abstract forms is found in chapter 11, "Locating Information About Research Reports."

The following abstract, from a report entitled "Differences in Teaching Between Six Primary and Five Intermediate Teachers in One School," illustrates the normal abstract style. The types of information are annotated in the margin. For this sample abstract, read the abstract for the purpose of finding out whether there is a difference between the two groups of teachers in their communications with their students.

Purpose

Subjects

Procedures

This study examined differences between primary and intermediate teachers concerning teacher behaviors, teacher communications, grouping control, and materials. Six primary classrooms (grades 1 and 2) and 5 intermediate classrooms (grades 4 and 5) were each observed for 4 45-minute periods. In addition, observers, teachers, and 5 students from each

*Data
Analysis*

Results

classroom responded to 2 vignettes depicting classroom situations and 1 vignette asking respondents to describe a lesson on nutrition. Responses were coded for teacher behaviors, goals, and instructional methods. Analyses of observational data showed that in comparison with teachers in intermediate grades, primary teachers used significantly more sanctions, procedural communications, and total teacher communications. Primary teachers also used a greater proportion of small-group instruction and manipulative materials than did intermediate teachers. Analysis of subjects' responses to vignettes clarified these findings and added further detail. (Van Scoy, 1994, p. 347)

Evaluative question: Is information included about the major aspects of the research—purpose, subjects, instruments, procedures/treatment, and results?   As shown by the margin annotations, the abstract contains information about the major aspects of research. What is *not* included is the statistical procedure used to code the subjects' responses.

Evaluative question: Is the abstract brief and clearly written?   In the example, the researcher has used only terms that any knowledgeable research consumer would be expected to know. The only technical term used in the abstract (which is explained in the example) is *significantly,* which is a clue that the researcher used quantitative data analysis procedures. The abstract presents the information about the research aspects without unnecessary information.

Researchers sometimes omit specific information and merely refer to the type of information included in the full research report. Such a tactic does not provide readers with a complete summary and might hinder their understanding of the research, because the specific details of the research report are omitted. In the sample abstract, the last statement illustrates this weakness. Other statements in abstracts that indicate incomplete information are "The study examined various instructional techniques," "The results are presented," and "The implications of the results are given."

EVALUATING BACKGROUND SECTIONS

Background sections contain three types of information:

1. Problem area and educational importance
2. Related literature
3. Research purpose, questions, or hypotheses

The Problem Area

In chapter 1, we discussed the five characteristics of a profession and its members. Briefly, professionals (*a*) verify existing ideas and practices, (*b*) discover new ideas and practices, (*c*) clarify and expand information about ideas and practices, (*d*) express ideas that complicate educational practice, and (*e*) discover ideas and practices that are counterintuitive. Researchers try to justify the importance of their research in light of these five aspects of professional activity. For example, in a causal-comparative study to determine if gifted and average-ability junior-high students differed in learning and study strategies, the researcher indicated that

*Importance
of Research
Area*

In general, we know that gifted students are able to achieve more in school than average-ability students (Scruggs & Cohn, 1983; Scruggs & Mastropieri, 1988). However, we also

<table>
<tr><td>

Need for Additional Research

Purpose of This Research
</td></tr>
</table>

know that not all gifted children do well in school, and not all are able to achieve to their predicted level. Further research is needed to examine learning and study strategies of gifted children as they compare to less able learners. More information is also needed to determine whether the study strategies of gifted learners are adequate. Therefore, two studies were undertaken to explore these issues. These studies were designed to determine if high-ability junior high students differed from their average-ability peers on learning and study strategies (Tallent-Runnels et al., 1994, p. 145)

Related Literature

Researchers also need to examine what others have found to be important. By reviewing relevant research, researchers gain insights about the problem area. These insights should then influence their research questions and methods. During this phase of research, research producers act as consumers. They critically analyze research using questions similar to those in Figures 3.1 and 3.2, pages 86–87. As a result of their evaluation, they can

1. Extend knowledge about a problem area. This task can be attempted because the researchers see a next step in answering questions about the problem. For example, after reviewing research about parents who read aloud to their children, one group of researchers realized that no one had described the views of those parents. So their research was concerned with identifying what parents thought about reading to their children (Manning, Manning, & Cody, 1988).
2. Change or revise knowledge about a problem area. This task can be attempted because the researchers see weaknesses or limitations in other researchers' attempts to answer questions about the problem area. For example, after reviewing research about oral-reading cue strategies of skilled and poor readers, a researcher identified several limitations with those studies and made modifications in materials that were used, the reading task assigned to the students, and the number and type of errors evaluated (Fleisher, 1988).
3. Replicate the study. Sometimes researchers wish to redo the research of others. **Replication** means repeating an investigation of a previous study's purpose, question, or hypothesis.

Researchers can replicate research in several ways. First, they can use the same method with different subjects. In this case, the researchers keep the original purpose, method, and data analysis procedure. The subjects have the same characteristics as the original subjects, but they are different people. For example, one team of researchers replicated a study looking at the effect on learning-disabled and slowly developing readers of two instructional programs designed to teach the students how to detect their own errors (Pascarella, Pflaum, Bryan, & Pearl, 1983). In the original study, conducted by two members of the same research team, the subjects were individual students. In the replication, data were analyzed for both individual students and groups because the researchers felt that working with individuals overlooked the "potential interdependencies among individual [student] observations within the same reading group" (p. 270).

Second, in a procedure known as **cross-validation,** the researchers use the same purpose, method, and data analysis procedure to investigate subjects from a different target population. For example, if the subjects in an original study were second and third graders, a different target population might be high school students.

Third, in a procedure known as **validity generalization,** the researchers use the same purpose, method, and data analysis procedure; but they use subjects from a unique population. For example, if the subjects in an original study were suburban students with hearing impairment, a different population might be rural students with vision impairment.

Fourth, researchers can reanalyze other researchers' data. In this case, no new study is undertaken. For example, after reviewing research about students' silent reading, a team of researchers (Wilkinson, Wardrop, & Anderson, 1988) indicated that the results of one study in particular did not warrant certain conclusions. So they reanalyzed the data presented by the original researchers.

Purpose, Question, Hypothesis

Most examples so far in this text have shown researchers stating their research aims as purposes or questions. This text has done so because current practice in research journals is to use this form. Journal editors as well as authorities on effective reading practice often feel that readers of research get a better mindset from purposes and questions than they do from hypotheses. Nevertheless, research reports are often written with traditional hypotheses.

A **hypothesis** is a conjecture about the relationship among the research variables in a quantitative study. This statement is created after researchers have examined the related literature, but *before* they undertake the study. The hypothesis is considered a tentative explanation for particular behaviors, phenomena, or events that have happened (or will happen). A hypothesis is a statement of researchers' expectations concerning the relationship among the variables in the research problem (Gay & Airasian, 2003).

One way to state a hypothesis is as a **nondirectional** (or two-tailed) **hypothesis,** which is a statement of the specific relationship or influence among variables. Researchers use this form when they have strong evidence from examining previous research that a relationship or influence exists, but when the evidence does not provide them with indications about the nature or direction (positive or negative) of the relationship or influence. The following examples, taken from a study about the connection between computer technology and reading comprehension, are illustrations of nondirectional research hypotheses stated to show that differences will exist between variables. Note that the researchers do not state how—positively or negatively—using a computer to mediate manipulations of the text (the independent variable) will influence reading comprehension (the dependent variable).

Non-directional Hypotheses

1. The comprehension of intermediate-grade readers reading expository texts will be affected by using a computer to mediate manipulations of the text.
2. Comprehension of expository text will be affected by varying control of textual manipulations from the reader to the computer program. (Reinking & Schreiner, 1985, p. 540)

If the researchers' evidence supports a statement of the specific way one variable will affect another, then the research hypothesis is stated as a **directional** (or one-tailed) **hypothesis.** The following example is from a study about the effects of teacher expectations and student behavior. It contains two directional research hypotheses.

Directional Hypotheses

The first hypothesis under investigation was that adults who are deliberate and more reserved would be more likely to adopt a task-oriented approach than would adults who are impulsive and highly sociable. Thus the reserved, deliberate adults would make more attempts to structure the task for the child, would more often redirect the child's attention to the task, and would make fewer task irrelevant comments to the child than would the sociable, impulsive adult. In addition [the second hypothesis], compared with inexperienced teachers, experienced teachers are more likely to be task oriented. (Osborne, 1985, p. 80)

In this example, the researcher predicted that teachers' temperament factors (the independent variable) would have a direct effect on how they structure children's tasks (the dependent variable). Not only was an effect predicted, but also the particular effect was predicted. The researcher predicted that teachers with reserved, deliberate temperaments would be more directive and offer fewer irrelevant comments. The second prediction was that teachers' experience (the independent variable) would affect task orientation (the dependent variable); and further, that experienced teachers would more likely be task oriented.

Another form of hypothesis is the null hypothesis. In contrast to the research hypothesis (directional and nondirectional), the null hypothesis is used exclusively as a basis for statistical analysis and rarely explicitly included in research reports.

Reading Background Sections

The following, a typical background section, is taken from a report entitled "The Effect of Instruction in Question-Answer Relationships and Metacognition on Social Studies Comprehension." Key information in this background section is annotated.

Background

Teachers expect students to be critical readers, comprehending most of the material read in the classroom; but Durkin's (1978–1979) classroom observation studies suggest that while comprehension is expected, it is never taught. Teachers do not 'teach' comprehension during social studies instruction; they merely assess it.

Questions are an integral part of school life. They are used routinely by teachers as a means of gauging student understanding of text. Teachers ask questions, but rarely do they do anything with the student responses—except acknowledge their correctness (Durkin, 1978–1979).

Early comprehension taxonomies first classified questions by type. Pearson and Johnson's (1978) more recent comprehension taxonomy, however, labels questions based upon the demands they make on the reader. In other words, the Pearson-Johnson taxonomy categorizes questions according to the relationship between the question and the answer generated. The Pearson-Johnson comprehension taxonomy recognizes three categories of questions: textually explicit, textually implicit, and scriptally implicit.

Related Literature

Recent research in metacognition has recognized that some children appear to be more capable of processing information efficiently when taught to monitor their own comprehension and to use reading strategies that take into account the variety of reading tasks assigned in school (Brown, 1981, p. 504). Raphael (1982) used the Pearson-Johnson comprehension taxonomy to develop a Question-Answer Relationship (QAR) model which could be used to teach students to successfully respond to four types of questions typically found in content area textbooks. The QAR model categorizes questions based upon the location of the answer generated by a query. The Question-Answer Relationship model considers the demands that questions make upon readers as they strive to arrive at correct responses.

Purpose

This research study was designed to teach students the QAR model and to provide additional metacognitive instruction in conjunction with the adopted social studies textbook. The social studies instruction provided was used in place of the basal reading instructional program typically employed for reading instruction. Three research questions were posed: Would students, as a result of the QAR and metacognitive instruction, complete the social studies textbook questioning tasks more successfully? How would students perform on the different types of QARs in the social studies text following the treatment? Would student scores on a global reading comprehension measure increase as a result of the social studies QAR-metacognitive instruction? (Benito, Foley, Lewis, & Prescott, 1993. Used by permission of the publisher, Blackwell Publishers, Inc.)

Evaluative question: Is the problem area (and its educational importance) explained? In the example, the researchers succinctly presents the importance of the problem area. Although the first paragraph is short, the researchers indicate the importance of questioning in the teaching of comprehension, and they substantiate this importance with references.

Evaluative questions: Are research studies related to the problem area presented? Has the related research been evaluated and critiqued? Does the intended research logically extend the understandings from the related research? In the third and fourth paragraphs, the researchers provide a summary of relevant research results. In the fifth paragraph, the researchers indicate their two major purposes. What research consumers need to determine is this: Do the purposes provide the means for extending the results of the previous research? This question can be answered in relation to the next evaluative question.

Evaluative questions: Is there a purpose that can be studied in an unbiased manner? Are the research variables (independent and dependent) easily identified from the hypothesis, question, or purpose statement? Are key terms or variables operationally defined? The first research purpose in the example was to determine if students complete the social studies textbook questioning tasks more successfully as a result of the QAR and metacognitive instruction. For this purpose, the researchers collected data to examine their claim that these strategies are more effective. The second research purpose was to determine how students would perform on different types of QARs in the social studies text following the treatment. It was possible to conduct this comparative and experimental study without bias; the only way research consumers can be confident that no bias was introduced would be to evaluate the method section (this evaluation is discussed in the next four chapters). No terms needed special definition.

USING THE RESEARCH READING PLAN WITH ABSTRACT AND BACKGROUND SECTIONS

By using the research reading plan presented in chapter 3 (see pp. 82–85) for the initial reading of abstracts and background sections, research consumers can efficiently seek out information in a particular order. The abstract and background sections of the reports for the model research reports at the end of chapter 1 contain annotations to facilitate the reading of the studies. For this demonstration, you should read the background sections of these two reports:

1. "The Effects of Classroom Structure on Student Achievement Goal Orientation," pp. 19–26, for the purpose of gaining knowledge about why researchers want to know how classroom structure and organization may be connected to students' achievement goals.
2. "Images of America: What Youth Do Know About the United States," pp. 27–51, for the purpose of gaining knowledge about why the researcher wants to know about students' knowledge about the United States.

You can read the abstract and background sections using the following steps:

1. Read the titles to gain a broad overview of the research topics.
2. Only the report "Images of America" has an abstract. In "Effects of Classroom Structure," there is no abstract.
3. In "Images of America," the first sentence of the abstract contains the researchers' research purposes.
4. Generally, researchers place information about their purposes at the end of the background section. In "Effects of Classroom Structure," the author places an indication of the purpose at the end of the first paragraph [3].
5. From reading [1] through [7] in "Effects of Classroom Structure," you can understand why the researcher arrived at her purpose. From reading [1] through [9] in "Images of America," you can determine the researcher's purpose and her reason for conducting this type of research.
6. Read the background sections to gain an understanding of the topics and the researchers' involvement in the research.

ACTIVITIES

Activity 1

Using the focus questions at the beginning of this chapter, create a summary of the key ideas of the chapter.

Activity 2

Using one quantitative research report and one qualitative research report of your own choosing (from those referred to in Appendix A), read and evaluate the abstracts and introductory sections of those reports.

FEEDBACK

Activity 1

What information should research consumers get from the abstract and background sections of quantitative and qualitative research reports? Abstracts contain information about the purpose, subjects, instruments, procedure (and treatment when applicable), findings, and conclusions.

The background section contains an introduction to the researchers' problem area and the educational importance they place on their study. Researchers also provide a brief literature review of other researchers' results that are related to their problem area. Researchers usually indicate strengths from the related research that were used in their study and weaknesses or limitations that were changed. Based upon an examination of the related literature, a researcher determines whether to develop a new study or replicate (repeat) a study. It is common to find the researchers' purposes at the end of this section.

What criteria are used to evaluate abstracts?   To evaluate the abstracts of quantitative research reports, ask "Is information included about the major aspects of the research—purpose, subjects, instruments, procedures/treatment, and results? Is the abstract brief and clearly written?"

To evaluate the abstracts of qualitative research reports, ask "Is information included about the major aspects of the research—purpose, participants, data collection, procedures, and results? Is the abstract brief and clearly written?"

What criteria are used to evaluate background sections?   To evaluate background sections of quantitative reports, ask these questions:

1. Is the problem area (and its educational importance) explained?
2. Are the researchers' assumptions and theoretical perspectives about the topic explained?
3. Are research studies presented that relate to the problem area?
4. Has the related research been evaluated and critiqued?
5. Does the intended research logically extend the understandings from the related research?
6. Is there a purpose that can be studied in an unbiased manner?
7. Are the research variables (independent and dependent, when appropriate) easily identified from the hypothesis, question, or purpose statement?
8. Are key terms or variables operationally defined?

To evaluate background sections of qualitative reports, ask the following:

1. Is the problem area (and its educational importance) explained?
2. Are the researchers' assumptions and theoretical perspectives about the topic explained?
3. Is it clear from the discussion as to the type of qualitative research being undertaken?
4. Are research studies presented that relate to the problem area?
5. Has the related research been evaluated and critiqued?
6. Does the intended research logically extend or challenge the understandings from the related research?
7. Is the relationship explicit between the study and previous studies?
8. Is there a clear rationale for the use of qualitative procedures?
9. Are researchers' assumptions and biases expressed?

What should research consumers know about research purposes and hypotheses?   Some research reports contain traditional hypotheses, often stated as directional or nondirectional research hypotheses. Nondirectional hypotheses are statements that a possible influence exists, but the researcher does not indicate whether it is a positive or negative influence. Directional hypotheses contain statements of the specific way one variable will affect another. In many professional journals, the background section is preceded by an abstract, an overview of the report.

What is the plan for reading abstracts and background sections?   Read the title to gain a broad overview of the research topic. Then read the abstract to understand the purpose, subjects, and general results. Scan the introductory section and locate the paragraph with the purpose or research questions. This paragraph is usually near the end of the introduction. Read that paragraph to gain a specific understanding of the research. Then, determine that your purpose (gaining knowledge) will be met by reading the report. In the margin of the text or on a piece of paper, note what you already know about the topic. Read the remainder of the background section to gain an understanding of the topic, and the related literature subsection read to understand what other researchers know about the topic.

Activity 2

Discuss your responses with one or more of your classmates and with the course instructor.

CHAPTER 5

Reading and Evaluating Subject/Participant Sections

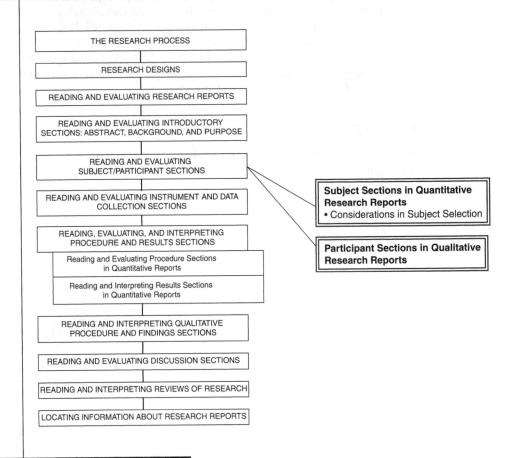

THE RESEARCH PROCESS

RESEARCH DESIGNS

READING AND EVALUATING RESEARCH REPORTS

READING AND EVALUATING INTRODUCTORY SECTIONS: ABSTRACT, BACKGROUND, AND PURPOSE

READING AND EVALUATING SUBJECT/PARTICIPANT SECTIONS

READING AND EVALUATING INSTRUMENT AND DATA COLLECTION SECTIONS

READING, EVALUATING, AND INTERPRETING PROCEDURE AND RESULTS SECTIONS

Reading and Evaluating Procedure Sections in Quantitative Reports

Reading and Interpreting Results Sections in Quantitative Reports

READING AND INTERPRETING QUALITATIVE PROCEDURE AND FINDINGS SECTIONS

READING AND EVALUATING DISCUSSION SECTIONS

READING AND INTERPRETING REVIEWS OF RESEARCH

LOCATING INFORMATION ABOUT RESEARCH REPORTS

Subject Sections in Quantitative Research Reports
• Considerations in Subject Selection

Participant Sections in Qualitative Research Reports

FOCUS QUESTIONS

1. What are populations and target populations?
2. What are subjects and samples?
3. What criteria should be used to evaluate subject sections in quantitative research reports?
4. What considerations do quantitative researches give to subject selection?
5. What considerations do quantitative researchers give to sample size?
6. What considerations do qualitative researchers give to participant selection?
7. What are focus groups and why are they used?

In both quantitative and qualitative research reports, information about the individuals or groups included in the study is provided in a separate section or subsection.

SUBJECT SECTIONS IN QUANTITATIVE RESEARCH REPORTS

In quantitative research reports, the subject section (which is a subsection within the larger *method section*) is where researchers describe the individuals, objects, or events used in their studies. Such researchers often wish to apply the answers to research questions to others, in addition to their subjects. In chapter 1 we discussed a hypothetical research team dealing with quantitative questions. They were concerned about the extent to which their results could be applied. They asked questions such as the following: "Are the answers applicable only to the students in one specific school, grade level, or class? Can the answers be used for the students in an entire district, state, region, or nation?"

Of course subjects can be others besides students; subjects can be teachers, principals, parents, non-school-age individuals (preschoolers or adults), or entire groups (classes, schools, or teams). Subjects can also be nonhuman. Subjects can be classrooms, or school instructional materials. For example, subjects can be groups of textbooks or groups of classrooms (the physical aspects of the rooms, without studying the people in them). In such cases, researchers may be interested in looking at the physical characteristics of the books or rooms. In this text, our discussion focuses on human subjects; nevertheless, the same principles of subject selection apply equally to human and nonhuman subjects. Research consumers can use the same criteria for judging the appropriateness of nonhuman subjects as they use for judging the appropriateness of human subjects.

Quantitative researchers usually want to use their results to make decisions about a larger group of subjects. That group constitutes the **population,** which is a group of individuals or objects having at least one characteristic that distinguishes them from other groups. Populations can be any size and can include subjects from any place in the world. For example, a population of human subjects could be "students with learning disabilities," or "fourth-grade students," or "beginning teachers." In these cases, the populations are large and include people with many additional characteristics, or variables. The existence of these other variables makes it unlikely that the population will be fully homogeneous and that the research answers will be equally applicable to all. An example of a nonhuman subject population is "seventh-grade social studies textbooks." Researchers, therefore, narrow the range of a population by including several distinguishing variables. This narrowing results in the defining of a **target population,** which is the specific group with which the researchers would like to use their findings for educational purposes. It is from the target population that researchers select the **sample,** which becomes the subject of their study. Figure 5.1 shows the relationship of the sample to the target population and to the population.

In the model quantitative research report, "Effects of Classroom Structure on Student Achievement Goal Orientation," the subject section (labeled *Participants*) is found at [8], p. 21.

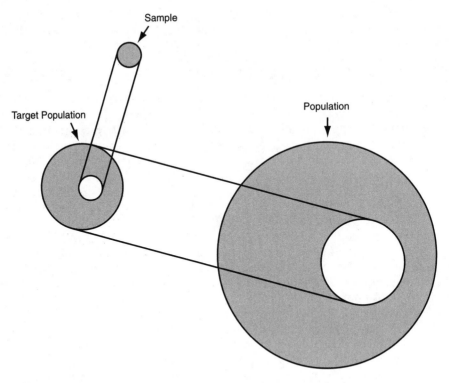

Figure 5.1
Relationship of Sample to Target Population

Subject sections contain relevant information about the sample and how it was selected. Subject information might include age, gender, ethnicity (for example, Black, Hispanic, or Native American), ability level (perhaps mental maturity or intelligence), academic performance (such as test scores), learning characteristics, affect (meaning emotional stability, attitudes, interests, or self-concept), and geographic location (for instance, New York state, Chicago, rural/suburban, or Australia). Subject selection information should include the number of subjects, procedures for identifying subjects, methods of actual subject selection, and, in the case of experimental research, steps for assigning subjects to groups or treatments. From a subject section, research consumers should be able to answer the following:

- What was the intended target population?
- Who were the subjects?
- How were the subjects selected, and did the researchers show bias in their sampling procedures?
- Were the subjects truly representative of the target population?
- How were the subjects assigned to groups (or treatments) in experimental research?
- Will the research results be applicable to my teaching situation and the students I teach?
- (Am I part of the target population? Are my students part of the target population?)

Subject sections of quantitative research reports should be evaluated using the following questions, which are from Figure 3.1, page 86.

Method Section

Subjects
- Do the researchers clearly describe target populations and subjects, sampling and selection procedures, and group sizes?
- Are these subjects and procedures appropriate for the research design?

Considerations in Subject Selection

In subject sections of quantitative research reports, researchers should provide information about (*a*) the target population, (*b*) the sampling process, and (*c*) the sample size.

Target Population.   Answers to quantitative researchers' questions should be applicable to individuals other than those included in the study. The group to which they wish to apply their results is the target population. When researchers can apply their results to the target population, the results are considered to be **generalizable.** An example of how a researcher identifies the target population within the larger population is found in the comparative study entitled "Concepts of Reading and Writing Among Low-Literate Adults" (Fagan, 1988). The researcher's purpose was to provide information about the perceptions of reading and writing held by low-functioning adults (the population). The subjects were selected from the target populations. In the following portion of the subject section, the number of subjects is indicated along with descriptions of the target populations. (Specific information about sampling procedures has been omitted from this example.)

<table>
<tr><td>

Subjects

</td><td>

A possible purpose for reading the study would be to gain information to help in planning an adult literacy program. Two groups of 26 adults each who were functioning below a grade 9 reading achievement level were selected—one designated as prison inmates and the other as living in mainstream society Prison inmates were defined as sentenced prisoners in a medium-minimum correctional institution housing approximately 300 prisoners. Adults living in mainstream society were defined as noninstitutionalized adults, that is, not living in prisons, mental, or old age institutions. They were considered "ordinary" people who had freedom of movement, and who could use such city facilities as transportation, recreation, and social interaction. (Fagan, 1988, p. 48)

</td></tr>
<tr><td>

Target
Population

</td><td></td></tr>
</table>

Because of practical considerations, researchers may not always have equal access to all members of the target population. For example, researchers might wish their target population to be urban, primary-grade students in cities where there are at least 500,000 people, having 20% or more Spanish-speaking students. An examination of the U.S. Department of Education census shows that there are at least ten such cities, including Los Angeles, Houston, Miami, and New York. The researchers might be able to use the entire target population as their subjects, or they might choose to select some subjects to represent the target population. More realistically, researchers work with **accessible populations,** which are groups that are convenient but are representative of the target population. Practical considerations that lead to the use of an accessible population include time, money, and physical accessibility.

Researchers should fully describe their accessible populations and their specific subjects so that research consumers can determine the generalizability of the findings. It is the research producers' responsibility to provide the necessary descriptive information about target populations and subjects. It is the research consumers' responsibility to make the judgments about the appropriateness of the subjects to their local situation. In evaluating subject sections, research consumers can be critical of the researchers only if the researchers have not provided complete subject information.

The Sampling Process.   If quantitative researchers' results are to be generalizable to target populations, the subjects must be **representative** of the population. A representative group of subjects, called the sample, is a miniature target population. Ideally, the sample would have the same distribution of relevant variables as found in the target population. Those relevant variables are described in subject sections. For example, one researcher (Swanson, 1985) felt it important to keep the same ratio of gender and ethnicity in the sample as found in the target population. She investigated whether socioeconomic status, reading ability, and student "self-report" reading attitude scores were differentiated by teacher judgments or reading enthusiasm.

Balanced Ratio

> The sample consisted of 117 first-grade students from seven classrooms in a school system located in northeastern Georgia. The rural county has a population of approximately 8,000, of which 37.3 percent is nonwhite. The racial and gender composition of the sample maintained a representative balance. Students repeating first grade, absent during initial testing, and/or not present during reading achievement assessment were deleted from the study. (Swanson, 1985, p. 42)

The most common procedure researchers use to ensure that samples are miniature target populations is **random sampling.** Random sampling works on the principle of **randomization,** whereby all members of the target population should have an equal chance of being selected for the sample (Gall, Gall, & Borg, 2002; Gay & Airasian, 2003; Kerlinger, 1973). Further, the subjects finally selected should reflect the distribution of relevant variables found in the target population. Any discrepancy between the sample and the target population is referred to as **sampling error.**

The following example does *not* illustrate a random sample, because it is not known whether all classes had an equal chance of being selected and whether the students in selected classes represented all the students in the grade level. The classes may have been heterogeneous, but researchers did not indicate whether the classes were equal. Although the school principals may have tried to be objective, they may have had an unconscious bias.

Non-random Sampling

> One self-contained, heterogeneous classroom of third-grade students (N = 22) and one self-contained, heterogeneous classroom of fifth-grade students (N = 23) from a rural school district in the Midwestern U.S. participated in the study. The third-grade classroom was one of three in a K–4 building, while the fifth-grade classroom was one of two in a 5–8 building. The participating classrooms were selected by the building principals. (Duffelmeyer & Adamson, 1986, p. 194)

The following is an example of random sampling, because each subject had an equal chance of selection from among the students at each grade level.

<table>
<tr><td>

Random Sampling

</td><td>

Thirty-two children were tested at each grade level; second, third, fourth, and sixth. An equal number was randomly chosen from each of three different elementary schools in a Midwestern city of 50,000. The city is a predominantly white, middle class community. Subjects were replaced by other randomly selected students if they failed a vocabulary reading test. (Richgels, 1986, p. 205)

</td></tr>
</table>

Random sampling is conceptually, or theoretically, accomplished by assigning a number to each member of the target population and then picking the subjects by chance. One way researchers used to accomplish this task was by placing everyone's name in a hat and drawing out as many as needed (Popham & Sirotnik, 1973). A simpler way (and one that is more commonly used in current research studies) is to assign numbers to each possible subject and then use a list of subjects' numbers randomly created by a computer program. The specific way researchers randomize is not important. The important consideration for research consumers is that a randomized sample has a better chance of being representative of the target population than does a nonrandomized one; and therefore, the researchers' results are more likely to be generalizable to the target population.

In addition to randomly selecting subjects, it is common in experimental studies for researchers to randomly assign the subjects to treatments. To illustrate this double randomization procedure, here is a sample: subject section. It is from a study about the occurrence of behaviors that reflect social competence components and informational-processing components of problem solving.

<table>
<tr><td>

Random Selection

Random Assignment

</td><td>

Subjects for the study were 48 children from a middle-class, midwestern school system who were participants in a larger Logo project. From a pool of all children who returned a parental permission form (more than 80% return rate), 24 first graders (10 girls, 14 boys; mean age 6 years, 6 months), and 24 third graders (13 girls, 11 boys; mean age, 8 years, 8 months) were randomly selected. Children were randomly assigned to either Logo or drill and practice treatment groups, so that 12 in each treatment group were from first grade and 12 were from third grade. (Clements & Nastasi, 1988, p. 93)

</td></tr>
</table>

An extension of random sampling involves stratification. In a **stratified random sample,** the subjects are randomly selected by relevant variables in the same proportion as those variables appear in the target population. One example of non-randomized stratified sampling is shown in the earlier extract with subjects from Georgia (Swanson, 1985). Although the sample was stratified, the researchers did not indicate whether the subjects were randomly selected. The National Assessment of Educational Progress (NAEP) uses a complex form of stratified random sampling. The NAEP is financially supported by the U.S. Department of Education and conducted by the Education Commission of the States.

<table>
<tr><td>

Stratified Random Sampling

</td><td>

As with all NAEP national assessments, the results for the national samples were based on a stratified, three-stage sampling plan. The first stage included defining geographic primary sampling units (PSUs), which are typically groups of contiguous counties, but sometimes a single county; classifying the PSUs into strata defined by region and community type; and randomly selecting schools both public and private, within each PSU selected at the first stage. The third stage involved randomly selecting students within a school for

</td></tr>
</table>

participation. Some students who were selected (about 7 to 8 percent) were excluded because of limited English proficiency or severe disability. (Langer et al., 1995, p. 172)

As indicated previously, subjects may be intact groups; for example, classes to which students have been preassigned. When intact groups are selected, the procedure is called **cluster sampling.** Intact groups are selected because of convenience or accessibility. This procedure is especially common in causal-comparative research. If a number of intact groups from a target population exist, researchers should randomly select entire groups as they would individuals.

The following subject description, which illustrates cluster sampling, is from a study that examined the instructional organization of classrooms and tried to explain why students achieved in some classes but not in others. Note that the researchers do not indicate whether their "preselected" classes were chosen through random procedures.

Cluster Sampling

This study was conducted during the math instruction of eight sixth-grade classes in four elementary schools in a school district in southwest Germany. These classrooms had been preselected out of a total population of 113 sixth-grade classes in this school district.... Altogether, 194 students and their 8 math teachers participated. (Schneider & Treiber, 1984, p. 200)

Regardless of the nature of researchers' sampling procedures, an important concern in all designs is the use of **volunteer subjects.** Volunteers, by nature, are different from nonvolunteers because of an inherent motivational factor or connection to the researcher.

The following subject section, from a study which examined mothers' deviations from printed text as they read to their children, is an example of using volunteer subjects. Notice, though, that from all volunteers, the researchers randomly selected those involved in the study.

Volunteer Sampling

From a pool of volunteers attending a large university in the Rocky Mountain region, 25 mother-child pairs were randomly selected. All of the mothers either were students or had spouses who were students at the university. Care was taken not to select students enrolled in the teacher education programs of the university, since teacher education students might have been taught specific early book reading methods, i.e., shared book experience. Mothers' ages ranged between 21 and 29 years, with the exception of three in their early 30's. Five comparison groups were formed according to the chronological ages of the children (6, 12, 18, and 24 months, plus or minus two months, and 4 years, plus or minus 4 months). (Martin & Reutzel, 1999)

Results from the use of volunteer subjects might not be directly generalizable to target populations containing seemingly similar, but nonvolunteer, individuals or groups. For example, in the previous study, the volunteers may have a distinctive point of view about parenting. The results, then, can be generalized only to a target population with a similar orientation. Or, researchers using volunteers to study the effect of a particular study-skill instruction on social studies achievement might be able to generalize their results only to students who are motivated to learn and use such a procedure in school. Nonvolunteers might need a different kind of instruction to be successful in that subject. Researchers, then, are faced with a seemingly unanswerable question: Can results from research with volunteer subjects be generalized to nonvolunteer subjects?

The issue has wide implications, especially when human subjects are used in experimental research. It has become uniform practice by researchers to require the prior permission of subjects. In cases where the subjects are minors (under the age of 18 years), permissions from parents or guardians are necessary. Granting of permission is a form of volunteering. Permission for including human subjects is not a problem in descriptive or correlational research because (*a*) confidentiality is maintained through the use of grouped rather than individual data collection procedures and (*b*) such research does not involve intrusive activities. For example, an ethical and legal concern might be raised by subjects when they are assigned to what becomes a less-effective treatment. They may say their educational progress was hindered rather than enhanced by the instructional activity.

Sample Size.   The size of samples is important to quantitative researchers for statistical and practical reasons. There are several practical issues researchers need to consider. In collecting data, researchers must consider factor such as the availability of research personnel, the cost involved in paying personnel and securing instruments and materials, the time available for collecting and analyzing data, and the accessibility of subjects.

More important, researchers who want to generalize from the sample (the smaller group) to the target population (the larger group) should do this generalization with as little statistical error as possible. Statistically, the size of the sample influences the likelihood that the sample's characteristics are truly representative of those of the target population (Gall et al., 1996; Gay & Airasian, 2000; Kerlinger, 1973). That is, the distribution of relevant variables found in the sample should not be significantly different from that of the target population. Any mismatch between the sample and the target population caused by an inadequate sample size will also contribute to sampling error. Clearly, errors associated with sampling are reduced with larger sample sizes. Statisticians frequently examine the *power* associated with sample size as an indication of this error.

PARTICIPANT SECTIONS IN QUALITATIVE RESEARCH REPORTS

Many researchers conducting qualitative research do their work from a constructivist perspective. They may not be as concerned about adhering to the same specific subject selection procedures as researchers working from an empiricist perspective.

> In the model qualitative research report, "Images of America: What Youth Do Know About the United States," information about the participants is found at [9] and [10] on p. 30.

Subject sections of qualitative research reports should be evaluated using the questions in Figure 3.2 on page 87.

"Method" or Procedure Section(s)

Participants/Subjects and Setting
- Are the setting and participants fully described?
- Are participants or subjects, and selection procedures, clearly described?
- Are these subjects and procedures appropriate for the research design?
- Is there evidence of close collaboration between researcher and participants?
- If focus groups are used, are the members (and how they are selected) clearly described?

As we indicated in previous chapters, researchers working from a constructivist perspective believe that research is a search for meaning. Therefore, information collection for them should start with the issues around which participants are actively trying to construct meaning. This idea is illustrated by Mehra (2003) in the following study. She attempts to understand some of the issues related to the educational experiences of Asian Indian children from their perspective, and that of their parents and teachers.

<table>
<tr>
<td>

Looking for Meaning in People's Lives

</td>
<td>

The researchers working in the naturalist paradigm believe that there is no single, objective reality "out there," and that people perceive and construct their own realities based upon their experiences and understanding of the world around them (Lincoln & Guba, 1985). My aim in this study was to understand the experiences of three Asian Indian children and their families, so the reality I was seeking was constructed. I was trying to make sense of people's experiences, and these experiences were constructions of my participants. They were telling me how they felt about certain aspects of their lives, and how they made sense of their experiences. I was making sense of their sense of reality. In this way, I was actually constructing reality based on the constructed realities of my participants. Furthermore, I was not dealing with a single construction of reality. Even though the aim was to understand the experiences of children, I thought it was important to get a sense of what their parents thought of their children's educational experiences, and also how the teachers of these children helped them adjust in the school setting, in addition to the teachers' own experiences with these and many other international students in their classrooms. Thus, I was working with multiple realities, or sometimes multiple constructions of the same reality. (Mehra, 2003, p. 381. Used by permission of *The Qualitative Report.*)

</td>
</tr>
<tr>
<td>

Multiple Meanings

</td>
<td></td>
</tr>
</table>

When researchers undertake qualitative research with a constructivist perspective, they may use a convenience or purposeful selection of participants (Guba & Lincoln, 1989; LeCompte, Preissle, & Tesch, 1993). Their selection procedure may even be considered to introduce bias. However, they are more interested in obtaining what they believe to be knowledgeable and insightful responses to their questions. So, they are interested in creating a sample that is representative of a particular target population. Nor will they be concerned about meeting any strict standards of randomization. The selection procedure may even be thought of as being recursive. That is, constructivist qualitative researchers may not stay with their original sample but may add or change participants as they redefine their target population, or as the scope of their study changes because of information gained through data collection procedures (LeCompte, Preissle, & Tesch, 1993).

The selection of participants for a qualitative study will have one or more of six different representations:

a. Typical participants
b. Extreme or deviant participants
c. Maximum variation of participants
d. Critical cases of participants
e. Politically important participants
f. Conveniently obtained participants (LeCompte, Preissle, & Tesch, 1993; Patton [1980] as cited by Guba & Lincoln, 1989)

Mehra (2003) explains in this example her three reasons for selecting the participants for her study.

GATHERING THE STORIES

The school, Jackson Elementary, where I did my study was selected partly based on some prior knowledge about the school's international student population, partly on its convenient location, and partly on its record in encouraging research on diversity related topics. I wanted to do the study at an elementary school, because I was interested to learn the experiences of the children who come to the U.S. with their parents at very young age, and are still not as "Americanized" as middle or high school aged children. Also the peer pressure is just starting to show its effect at the elementary level, which would allow me to understand the emerging conflicts in children's lives. (Mehra, 2003, p. 381. Used by permission of *The Qualitative Report*.)

Another researcher, Sommers (2003), was interested in understanding how effective middle-school teachers developed. She believed that such teachers are more than the sum total of their educational beliefs and practices. Thus, she sought a particular group of middle-school teachers—a unique sample that was based on the recommendation of others. As she indicated,

a major task was to find effective middle school teachers willing to give of their time and themselves to participate in my study. I wanted to work with teachers recognized by fellow educators as effective middle school teachers. This led me to follow Maxwell's (1996) suggestion of using purposeful sampling when persons are "selected deliberately in order to provide important information that [cannot] be gotten as well from other choices" (p. 70). I combined purposeful sampling with reputational selection, or participants "chosen on the recommendation of an 'expert' or 'key informant'" (Miles & Huberman, 1994, p. 28). This made sense because key informants, like the [teacher's name], have had experiences I have not been privy to. (Sommers, 2003, p. 531)

Another method for organizing participants is the use of **focus groups.** Focus groups involve the "explicit use of group interaction to produce data and insights that would be less accessible without the interaction found in a group" (Morgan, 1988, p. 12). There are no specific rules for the creation or use of focus groups, nor are there specific guidelines for determining group size, membership, or selection procedures. Most often, focus group membership is a purposeful sample—researchers create group membership to gain the greatest amount of information. A group usually has no more than ten representative people. The discussion, guided by a facilitator, is given focus by a series of topic- or task-related questions. The aim is to draw information from local experience and traditions and to provide understanding about the impact of the project on those involved (that is, the stakeholders) (Donnelly et al., 1997).

Focus group discussions provide some advantages over individual interviews. These advantages include

- the greater amounts of information that can be gathered in a shorter and more efficient period
- the group interaction that promotes thinking and analyzing and can result in a wider range of thought, ideas, and experiences
- the possibility to observe group interaction among participants that can provide additional insights about the topic of event under discussion (Nassar-McMillan & Borders, 2002)

An example of the use of a focus group is provided by Morris (2002) in a study aimed at providing research on teachers' perspectives about year-round schools.

FOCUS GROUP DISCUSSION

To interpret issues, Stringer (1999) suggested a group process. The focus group discussion is appropriate for this interpretation. A focus group provided me with an opportunity to observe group interactions. Since teachers were the primary professionals who implemented the year-round school on a daily basis, it is appropriate for focus groups to center on teachers. Morgan (1997) suggested that five to ten questions that are open-ended are an appropriate amount.

For the purposes of the study four teachers were involved in the focus group discussion. The four teachers were selected based on the grade level they taught, the level of participation in the implementation of the year-round school, and the number of years of teaching experience. Varying these factors provided a diverse group of teachers. (Morris, 2002)

ACTIVITIES

Activity 1

Using the Focus Questions at the beginning of this chapter as a guide, summarize the chapter's key ideas.

Activity 2

Read each of the following subject sections extracted from quantitative research reports. The researchers' research purposes have been included for your information. Using the questions and criteria on pages 102–103, evaluate the subject sections. For each, list questions and concerns you may have about

a. Characteristics of the subjects
b. Sampling procedures
c. Representativeness of the subjects, in relation to the target populations
d. Appropriateness of the subjects for the researchers' purposes

EXTRACT A

Purpose: The study examined children's views of the world after they personally experienced a natural disaster—specifically, Hurricane Andrew in South Florida during the summer of 1992.

PARTICIPANTS

Participants were 127 fourth- and fifth-grade students at the two school sites. From a pool of students who personally experienced Hurricane Andrew and whose parents gave written permission for their children to participate, 10 or 11 students were randomly selected from each of 12 groups in terms of ethnicity, SES, and gender. The three ethnic groups included African American, Hispanic of diverse national origins, and White non-Hispanic students. Student ethnicity was taken from official school records, as reported by parents. The status of lunch programs is a variable frequently used by education researchers to identify students by socioeconomic status (SES). The two socioeconomic levels were distinguished by including students on free or reduced-price lunch programs in the lower

SES group and those who paid for lunch or brought lunch to school in the higher SES group. (Lee, 1999, p. 192)

EXTRACT B

Purpose: The study examined the impact of an intervention targeting economically disadvantaged children in child care centers.

PARTICIPANTS AND SETTINGS

Systematic random sampling procedures were used to select a sample from the larger number of centers receiving the intervention. On the basis of economic need, the majority of centers (255) were from Philadelphia. To take into account the disproportionate number of child care centers in the city, a strategy was devised to oversample five counties (Bucks, Chester, Delaware, and Montgomery in Pennsylvania, and Camden in New Jersey, with a total of 82 centers), and slightly undersample Philadelphia. Philadelphia was partitioned in five separate regions considered to represent differing neighborhoods and economic areas and treated as if they were separate regions. Five centers in each of these 10 regional areas were then randomly selected: five counties and five areas within the metropolitan Philadelphia area for a total of 50 centers. Within each of these centers, four children (two girls and two boys) from two classrooms, one for 3- and one for 4-year-olds, were randomly selected to participate in the study. The initial sample, therefore, represented 50 centers (5 per region) and 100 classrooms (10 per region), for a total of 400 children (40 per region).

At the same time, regional directors were asked for names of comparable child-care centers that would not be involved (e.g., they might have already received a grant from the Foundation for another project or did not have nonprofit status), but shared similar demographic characteristics as those in the Books Aloud program. Ten of these child-care centers agreed to participate; 5 children were then randomly selected from two classrooms in each center, totaling 20 classrooms of 100 children in the designated control classrooms. Tables 2a (the pre- and posttest sample) and 2b (the posttest only sample) give the distribution of the sample by age, gender, and ethnicity, as well as by the percentage of children whose parents received subsidies from the government toward the cost of child care as a general measure of income level. (Neuman, 1999, p. 291)

Source: From Neuman, Susan B. (1999, July/Aug/Sept). Books make a difference: A study of access to literacy. *Reading Research Quarterly, 34*(3), 286–311. Reprinted with permission.

FEEDBACK

Activity 1

What are populations and target populations?   The larger group of people or objects to whom researchers wish to apply their results constitutes the population, which is a group having at least one characteristic that distinguishes it from other groups. A target population is the specific group to which the researchers would like to apply their findings.

What are subjects and samples?   Subjects are the individuals or groups included in the study. A representative group of potential subjects, called the *sample,* is a miniature target population. Ideally, the sample would have the same distribution of relevant variables as found in the target population.

What criteria should be used to evaluate subject sections in quantitative research reports? From reading the subject sections, research consumers should be able to answer these questions:

    What was the intended target population?

    Who were the subjects?

    How were the subjects selected, and did the researchers show bias in their sampling procedures?

    Were the subjects truly representative of the target population?

    How were the subjects assigned to groups (or treatments) in experimental research?

    Will the research results be applicable to my teaching situation and the students I teach?

    (Am I part of the target population? Are my students part of the target population?)

What considerations do quantitative researchers give to subject selection? Subjects should be representative of the large population so that results can be generalized from the subjects to the target population. Random sampling, or randomization, works on the principle that all members of the target population have an equal chance of being selected for the sample. The subjects finally selected should reflect the distribution of relevant variables found in the target population.

What considerations do quantitative researchers give to sample size? Research producers and consumers should be sensitive to any mismatch between the sample and the target population caused by an inadequate sample size. The mismatch is a source of error, called *sampling error.* The probability of making an error relative to sample size is unique to each data analysis procedure. Usually, the larger the sample, the smaller the chance the sampling error has been introduced.

What considerations do qualitative researchers give to participant selection? Many researchers conducting qualitative research do their work from a constructivist perspective. They may not be as concerned about adhering to the same specific subject selection procedures as researchers working from an empiricist perspective. Researchers working from a constructivist perspective believe that research is a search for meaning. Therefore, information collection for them should start with the issues around which participants are actively trying to construct meaning. They may use a convenience or purposeful selection of participants.

What are focus groups and why are they used? Focus groups involve the explicit use of group interaction to produce data and insights that would be less accessible without the interaction found in a group. There are no specific rules for the creation or use of focus groups, nor are there specific guidelines for determining group size, membership, or selection procedures. Most often, focus group membership is a purposeful sample—researchers create group membership to gain the greatest amount of information. Focus group discussions provide some advantages over individual interviews.

Activity 2

Extract A: From a very special target population—children who had experienced a natural disaster—the researcher randomly selected a stratified sample using three variables for the stratification. The categories of demographic information about the subjects was provided, but no information was provided as to the number of individuals within each group. It can be inferred that approximately 120 to 132 individuals took part in the study. A federal government edict requires parental permission to study children. But, because of the circumstances of the selection criteria (i.e., experience of a disaster), parental approval may be considered a form of volunteering. Although the target population is clear and the sample is a stratified random sample, the results of the study should only be generalized to other children who experienced a similar disaster.

Extract B: The researcher started with an accessible target population. Then, to offset obtaining a disproportionate sample (one with a high proportion of representation from Philadelphia), other regions contiguous to Philadelphia were included. To avoid bias in the portion of the sample procedure, the researcher used double-random selection to select the child care centers. First, the centers were randomly selected from those available in the region. Then, within each center, the subjects were randomly selected.

However, the alternate (comparison) sample was identified in a manner that might have introduced bias. That pool was identified by opinion with only the criterion of having "similar demographic characteristics." Because the identified centers "agreed" to participate, there was an element of volunteering in the sample. Also, the criteria for selecting the two classrooms in the centers were not provided. But, within those classrooms, no bias was shown in the selection of subjects because they were randomly selected.

What was not included in Extract B is the table summarizing the demographic information that accompanied the discussion of participants. That table shows the two groups were proportionately similar in characteristics.

CHAPTER 6

Reading and Evaluating Instrument and Data Collection Sections

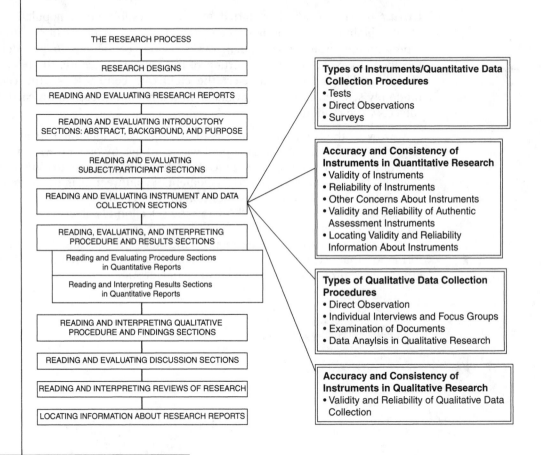

THE RESEARCH PROCESS

RESEARCH DESIGNS

READING AND EVALUATING RESEARCH REPORTS

READING AND EVALUATING INTRODUCTORY
SECTIONS: ABSTRACT, BACKGROUND, AND PURPOSE

READING AND EVALUATING
SUBJECT/PARTICIPANT SECTIONS

READING AND EVALUATING INSTRUMENT AND DATA
COLLECTION SECTIONS

READING, EVALUATING, AND INTERPRETING
PROCEDURE AND RESULTS SECTIONS

Reading and Evaluating Procedure Sections
in Quantitative Reports

Reading and Interpreting Results Sections
in Quantitative Reports

READING AND INTERPRETING QUALITATIVE
PROCEDURE AND FINDINGS SECTIONS

READING AND EVALUATING DISCUSSION SECTIONS

READING AND INTERPRETING REVIEWS OF RESEARCH

LOCATING INFORMATION ABOUT RESEARCH REPORTS

**Types of Instruments/Quantitative Data
Collection Procedures**
- Tests
- Direct Observations
- Surveys

**Accuracy and Consistency of
Instruments in Quantitative Research**
- Validity of Instruments
- Reliability of Instruments
- Other Concerns About Instruments
- Validity and Reliability of Authentic
  Assessment Instruments
- Locating Validity and Reliability
  Information About Instruments

**Types of Qualitative Data Collection
Procedures**
- Direct Observation
- Individual Interviews and Focus Groups
- Examination of Documents
- Data Anaylsis in Qualitative Research

**Accuracy and Consistency of
Instruments in Qualitative Research**
- Validity and Reliability of Qualitative Data
  Collection

FOCUS QUESTIONS

For reading and evaluating quantitative research reports:
1. What are the different types of instruments used in research projects?
2. How is information from different instruments reported?
3. What are instrument validity and reliability, and how are they determined?
4. What criteria should be used to determine whether instruments are appropriate for the research?

For reading and evaluating qualitative research reports:
1. What are the different ways data is collected in qualitative research projects?
2. What is the role of a participant observer in collecting data?
3. How is the collected information analyzed?
4. What does it mean to have accurate and consistent data collection?
5. How should data collection sections be read and evaluated?

Researchers use devices and procedures to collect data within all types of research designs. In quantitative research reports, the term **instruments** is used to denote a broad range of specific devices and procedures for collecting, sorting, and categorizing information about subjects and research questions. In qualitative research reports, the term *data collection procedures* is used to denote the use of many of the same specific devices and procedures for collecting, sorting, and categorizing information about participants and research questions as are used in quantitative research projects. However, especially for researchers with a constructivist perspective, these devices and procedures are usually not termed *instruments;* such researchers often prefer to use a term such as *information* rather than *data,* because the collected material is analyzed inductively, not quantitatively (Meyers, 1997). In the following discussion, these differences will be made apparent; we use *data* and *information* interchangeably in discussions of constructivist qualitative research.

Research consumers need to understand three main points about collection. First, readers should know what instruments and data collection procedures are available to educational researchers, how instruments and data collection procedures are used to categorize information, and how data from different instruments and data collection procedures are reported. Second, readers should understand what criteria should be used to determine whether instruments and data collection procedures accurately and truthfully present information. Third, readers should realize how instrument and data collection procedures sections in research reports should be read and interpreted.

From a section about instrument or data collection, consumers should be able to answer the following questions:

- What types of instruments or data collection procedures were used?
- If standardized instruments were used, were they valid and reliable for the research project?
- In quantitative and qualitative studies, were the instruments appropriate for use with the target populations and the research subjects or participants?
- In qualitative studies, were the data collection devices and procedures able to provide credible, dependable, confirmable, and transferable information?
- Will the research results or findings be applicable to my teaching situation and the students I teach, because the instruments or data collection procedures are appropriate for use with the students I teach?

Instrument sections in quantitative research reports describing standardized and other instruments should be evaluated using the following questions, which are from Figure 3.1, page 86.

Method Section (in Quantitative Research Reports)

Standardized and Other Instruments

- What instruments are used in the study?
- Are they appropriate for the design of the study?
- Are the instruments valid for collecting data on the variables in the study? Are reliability estimates given for each instrument?
- Are researcher-made instruments included (or at least samples of the instrument items)?
- Are the instruments appropriate for use with the target population and the research subjects?
- In the case of authentic, or performance-based, assessments, what evidence is presented that the devices reflect realistic samples of students' learning?

Data collection procedures in qualitative research reports should be evaluated using the following questions, which are from Figure 3.2, page 87.

"Method" or Procedure Section(s) (in Qualitative Research Reports)

Data Collection Devices

- What devices (questionnaires, surveys, interview forms) are used in the study?
- Are these devices appropriate for the design of the study?
- Are the data collection devices appropriate for collecting data about the purpose(s) of the study?
- Are researcher-made devices included (or at least samples of them)?
- Are the data collection devices appropriate for use with the participants?

TYPES OF INSTRUMENTS/QUANTITATIVE DATA COLLECTION PROCEDURES

The following discussion explains how quantitative researchers collect and organize data and what procedures are used to analyze the data.

Quantitative researchers collect data with tests, direct observation (including observation of student work products, known as *authentic assessments*), and surveys. In reports of all three kinds of quantitative research, these instruments provide data about subjects' characteristics (as reported in subject sections) and about subjects' responses in various situations (as reported in procedure sections). Information about instruments discussed in any section of a research report is usually given in an instrument section.

All researchers collect data. Data on its own has little or no meaning. It is when researchers organize and analyze data that they can attribute some meaning to the data. In the model quantitative research report, "Effects of Classroom Structure on Student Achievement Goal Orientation," the data collection devices are found at [11] on p. 22.

Tests

Test information includes scores or other data from individual or group standardized norm-referenced tests, standardized criterion-referenced tests, competency tests, and researcher-made tests. The following discussion of tests applies to all quantitatively collected data, and to work done by researchers with a positivist perspective about research.

A **standardized test** is one for which the tasks and procedures of administering, recording, scoring, and interpreting are specified so that other testers can make comparable measurements in different locations (Harris & Hodges, 1995). The test constructors use accepted procedures and research the test's (*a*) content, (*b*) procedures for administering, *(c)* system for recording and scoring answers, and (*d*) method of turning the results into a usable form. Everything about the test has been made uniform (standardized), so that if all its directions are correctly followed, the results can be interpreted in the same manner, regardless of where the test was administered.

Standardized tests are of two main types: norm-referenced and criterion-referenced. Norm-referenced tests compare individuals' scores to a standardization, or norming, group. A **norming group** consists of individuals used in researching the standardization of the test's administration and scoring. The section in this chapter called "Accuracy and Consistency of Instruments" contains a discussion about how to determine the appropriateness of a relationship between a norm group and a target population.

The scores from norm-referenced tests are reported as standard scores (e.g., SS = 53), grade equivalents (e.g., GE = 4.6), percentiles (e.g., 67th percentile, or percentile rank = 67), stanines (e.g., fifth stanine, or stanine 5), scale scores (e.g., scale score = 450), or normal curve equivalents (e.g., NCE = 72). Each of these scores can be used to describe subjects' characteristics or subjects' relative performance. Additional information about the different types of scores is in chapter 8, "Reading and Interpreting Qualitative Procedure and Findings Sections."

In the following example from a subject section, percentile scores are used to describe the subjects.

| Sample |

Purpose of the study: To determine if subject matter text could be rewritten such that students' comprehension of unfamiliar topic words could be enhanced.

| Percentile Scores |

    Subjects were 55 eighth grade students enrolled in two state history classes at a university laboratory school. They first were stratified by standardized achievement test (Stanford Achievement Test, 1981), and then grouped by high and average ability levels. The high ability group, with 28 subjects, had scores ranging from 75–99, with a mean score of 89.28 (SD = 7.14). The average ability group, with 27 subjects, had scores ranging from 12–68, with a mean score of 47.80 (SD = 12.59). (Konopak, 1988, p. 4)

On **criterion-referenced tests,** or measurements, students' performance is tested in terms of the expected learner behaviors or to specified expected levels of performance (Harris & Hodges, 1995). Scores on these tests show students' abilities and performance in relation to sets of goals, or to what a student is able to do. The tests do not show subjects' ranking compared with others, as norm-referenced tests do. A standardized criterion-referenced test is one for which the administration and scoring procedures are uniform but the scoring is in relation to the established goals (or standards), not to a norm group. In many states there are proficiency tests for students; these tests are forms of criterion-referenced tests.

The assessment of students' work and the products of their learning, commonly referred to as *authentic assessment,* has increasingly replaced or supplemented other test data in research. This form of data, similar to criterion-referenced tests, is used to compare students' levels of performance and products (for example, oral reading, writing samples, art or other creative output, and curriculum-related projects) to specified levels of performance. In authentic assessment, researchers use materials and instruction that are true representations of "the actual learning and activities of the classroom and out-of-school worlds" of the children (Hiebert, Valencia, & Afflerback, 1994, p. 11).

Through using authentic assessment, teachers are expected to provide students with meaningful educational experiences that facilitate learning and skill development as well as greater understanding of what is needed for good performance (Messick, 1994). Specifically,

> authentic assessments aim to capture a richer array of student knowledge and skill than is possible with multiple-choice tests; to depict the processes and strategies by which students produce their work; to align the assessment more directly with the ultimate goals of schooling; and to provide realistic contexts for the production of student work by having the tasks and processes, as well as the time and resources, parallel those in the real world. (pp. 17–18)

Direct Observation

When collecting data from direct observation, researchers from both quantitative and qualitative research perspectives take extensive field notes or use observation forms to record the information. They may categorize information on forms in response to questions about subjects' actions or categories of actions. These are considered open-ended responses. Or, researchers may tally subjects' actions within some predetermined categories during a specified time period (e.g., on a check list), which are considered closed-ended responses. It is how the collected data is collected and analyzed that distinguishes quantitative and qualitative researchers.

Field notes consist of written narrative describing subjects' behavior or performance during an instructional activity. These notes are then analyzed, and the information is categorized for reporting. The analysis can start with predetermined categories, and information from the notes is recorded accordingly. Or, the analysis can be open-ended, in that the researchers cluster similar information and then create a label for each cluster.

The following description of an observational assessment and the information in Figure 6.1 are from an empirical naturalistic investigation (Clements & Nastasi, 1988). Notice how the researchers explain their instrument and provide examples of the behaviors to be categorized.

Purpose of the study: To study the occurrence of first- and third-grade students' behaviors that reflect social competence components, and information-processing components of problem solving while using computers in school.

> *Use of an Observational Assessment*

INSTRUMENTS

Observational Assessment of Social Behaviors

The observation scheme was adapted from a more comprehensive instrument (covering six components of social competence) developed by the second author to assess social behaviors (Nastasi & Clements, 1985). Behavioral indicators of social problem solving included cooperative work, conflict, and resolution of conflict. Indicators of effective motivation included self-directed work, persistence, rule determination, and showing

Observation Scheme for Social Behaviors

Behavior	Definition
Social problem solving	
Cooperative work	Child works with another child on an academic task (i.e., jointly engages in computer activity) without conflict (as opposed to cooperative play—engagement in nonacademic activities or conversation not related to the task at hand).
Conflict	Child engages in verbal or physical conflict with another child.
Resolution of conflict	Child reaches successful resolution of conflict, without adult intervention.
Effectance motivation	
Self-directed work	Child initiates or engages in an independent work activity without teacher's coaxing or direction: including constructive solitary or parallel work.
Persistence	Child persists on a task after encountering difficulty or failure without teacher's coaxing or encouragement.
Rule determination	Child engages in self-determination of rules, for example, making plans or establishing parameters of a problem situation. Includes use of verbal heuristic for solving problems.
Showing pleasure	Child shows signs of pleasure at solving a problem or at discovery of new information (e.g., child cheers after reaching a solution).

Observation Scheme for Information-Processing Components

Component	Definition	Examples
Metacomponents		
Deciding on nature of the problem	Determining what the task is and what it requires	"What do we make here?" "We gotto go over here, then put lines around it like our drawing."
Selecting performance components	Determining how to solve the problem: choosing lower order components	"Read the list [of directions] again, but change all the LEFTs to RIGHTs for this side." "How are we gonna make this thing go over this way? We did RIGHT 20. What's 90 – 70 . . . 20, right? We need not RIGHT 90, but 70!" "We got to add these three numbers."
Combining performance components	Sequencing the components selected	"First, you have to get it over that way a little . . . LEFT 45, then FORWARD 30." "We'll make the turtle go up this way about 10, then RIGHT 90 and 10 down, then FORWARD halfway—5—and we're done."
Selecting a mental representation	Choosing an effective form or organization for representing relevant information	No verbalizations recorded
Allocating resources	Deciding how much time to spend on various components	"That's enough time talking. We should draw it." "We go it." Let's think and make sure."
Monitoring solution processes	Keeping track of progress and recognizing need to change strategy	"Put 70." "70? We already did 50 . . . type FORWARD 20." "You're gonna go off the screen, I'm telling you."
Being sensitive to external feedback	Understanding and acting upon feedback	"I know—if it's wrong it goes 'blub, blub, blub' and sinks down."
Performance components	Executing the task; includes encoding and responding	"5 times 7 is 35." "Type R-I-G-H-T-4-5." "It says, 'What is 305 – 78?'"
Other	Miscellaneous; includes off-task and uninterpretable verbalizations	"They're recording us, you know." "I'm tired of this; can we do another game?"

Figure 6.1
Sample Information From an Observational Assessment
Source: From Clements, D. H., & Nastasi, B. K. (1988). Social and cognitive interactions in educational computer environments. *American Educational Research Journal, 25,* 87–106. Adapted with permission of the publisher.

pleasure at discovery. [Figure 6.1 top] lists the behaviors observed and provides an operational definition of each. Reliability of the instrument was assessed in previous research; interrater agreement, established through simultaneous coding of behaviors by two observers, was 98% (Nastasi & Clements).

Observational assessment of information-processing components. As stated, initial analysis of the data on social behaviors revealed that (a) one of the most striking differences between the experimental (Logo) and control (drill and practice) groups was in determining rules and (b) as defined, the construct of rule determination was too general. The rule-determination category involved planning, establishing parameters for problem solving, and use of verbal heuristics. A more detailed framework was needed to differentiate among such metacognitive behaviors. Therefore, a scheme for categorizing information-processing components of problem solving was constructed based on the componential theory of Sternberg (1985). The following metacomponents were delineated in the present study: deciding on the nature of the problems; selecting performance components relevant for the solution of the problem; selecting a strategy for combining performance components; selecting a mental representation; allocating resources for problem solution; monitoring solution processes; and being sensitive to external feedback. Frequencies of behaviors indicative of each metacomponent were recorded. Performance components, used in the actual execution of a task, included such behaviors as encoding, applying, and reporting. These behaviors were relevant to problem solution, but not reflective of metacognitive processing. Because the investigation focused on metacomponential processes, behaviors were not defined more specifically than the "performance" category level. A final category of "other" included off-task behaviors. [Figure 6.1, bottom] presents the definitions and examples of behaviors for each category. Interrater agreement was 87%. (Clements & Nastasi, 1988, p. 95. Copyright 1988 by the American Education Research Association. Reprinted by permission of the publisher.)

In the previous example, the researchers indicate that the material shown in Figure 6.1 provides an operational definition of each behavior. For example, for the behavior *social problem solving, cooperative work,* they specify the particular subjects' activities that would be counted as an instance of the behavior. An **operational definition** is a definition of a variable that gives the precise way an occurrence of that variable can be seen. In the Clements and Nastasi study, the operational definitions were verbal. Operational definitions can also be test scores. In the Konopak (1988) study discussed earlier, high- and average-ability students were operationally defined by percentile ranges on the Stanford Achievement Test. (To aid research consumers in understanding technical vocabulary and determining the appropriateness of operational definitions, there are specialized professional directionaries. Chapter 11, "Locating Information About Research Reports," contains information about locating and using these dictionaries.)

Surveys

Surveys include questionnaires, interviews including focus groups, scales, inventories, and check lists.

Questionnaires require the respondent to either write or orally provide answers to questions about a topic. The answer form may be structured in that there are fixed choices, or the form may be open-ended in that respondents can use their own words. Fixed-choice questionnaires may be called **inventories.** They may require subjects to simply respond to statements, questions, or category labels with a

1. Approximate number of students in your department:
   undergraduate _____ graduate _____

2. What is your department's emphasis?
   ( ) categorical ( ) cross-categorical

3. Does your department offer a course on *working with parents of exceptional students?*
   ( ) yes ( ) no

   a. Is *working with parents of exceptional students* included as a component of another course?
      ( ) yes ( ) no

   b. Is working with parents of exceptional students offered by another department?
      ( ) yes ( ) no

   c. Is the course required by your department?
      ( ) yes ( ) no

      At what level? (mark each that applies)
      ( ) graduate ( ) undergraduate

   d. Is the course required for certification by your state's Department of Education?
      ( ) yes ( ) no

Figure 6.2
Sample Information From a Questionnaire
(From Hughes, Ruhl, & Gorman, 1987)

"yes" no "no," or they may ask subjects to check off appropriate information within a category.

Questionnaires also are used to collect information from files such as subjects' permanent school records. When the respondent answers orally and the researcher records the answers, the instrument is considered an **interview.** Interviews are used to obtain structured or open-ended responses. They differ from questionnaires in that the researcher can modify the data collection situation to fit the respondent's responses. For example, additional information can be solicited, or a question can be rephrased.

The following explanation of a fixed-response questionnaire is from a descriptive study, and sample questions from that questionnaire are presented in Figure 6.2.

Purpose of the study: To determine the nature, extent, and impact of preservice training for special educators working with parents.

INSTRUMENT

Survey I questionnaire is displayed as [Figure 6.2]. Questions on the survey form included demographic information and series of questions designed to ascertain whether content on working with parents was offered [in college courses preparing special-education teachers] and, if so, to what extent. Respondents whose departments [of special education] offered a course on this topic were asked to provide a course syllabus, which became permanent product data. (Hughes, Ruhl, & Gorman, 1987, p. 82. Copyright 1987 by Teacher Education and Special Education. Reprinted with permission.)

Use of Fixed-Response Questionnaire

The following explanation of an inventory is from a study to develop a way to measure student achievement in terms of a school's local curriculum. Sample items

Consequences Teacher, target learner, and peer responses to learner behavior (c)

C1   Teacher response to correct answer:

meaningful immediate reinforcement _____
meaningful delayed reinforcement _____
no reinforcement _____

C2   Target learner response to success:

positive _____ negative _____ no response _____

C3   Peer response to target learner's correct answer:

positive _____ negative _____ no response _____

C4   Teacher response to incorrect answer:

immediate feedback _____ delayed feedback _____
modeled correct responses _____
required learner to imitate correct response _____
no corrective feedback _____
punishment or sarcasm _____

C5   Target learner response to incorrect response or failure:

guessed _____
corrected self _____
gave up and said "I don't know" _____
made another response _____ (please describe) _____
sat and said nothing _____
became negative and refused to work _____
became hostile (i.e., engaged in verbally and/or physically aggressive behavior) _____

C6   Peer responses to target learner's incorrect answer:

positive _____ negative _____ no response _____

Figure 6.3
Sample Information From an Inventory

from the inventory are presented in Figure 6.3. Notice that although the instrument was labeled an inventory, its items could easily be restructured as questions.

> *Purpose of the study: To describe a model for a schoolwide curriculum-based system of identifying and programming for students with learning disabilities.*
>
> The final measure used in the [Curriculum-Based Assessment and Instructional Design] (C-BAID) process is the environmental inventory. Its purpose is to assist teachers in identifying factors that may facilitate or impede instruction in the classroom. It is used to provide information once a particular student is determined to be significantly discrepant from peers either academically, in work habits, or both. The checklist used in C-BAID is an adaptation of ones previously developed [by other researchers]. The inventory is based on the ABC model of instruction and thus focuses on the Antecedents, or events taking place prior to or during instruction; the Behavior, or how learners perform; and the Consequences, or events taking place after learners have performed. Many of the variables selected for inclusion in the environmental inventory have been shown to be positively correlated with academic achievement [by other researchers]. The environmental inventory can be conducted by the school psychologist or principal. Classroom teachers may also complete the inventory after a lesson has ended. A portion of the inventory is shown in [Figure 6.3]. (Bursuck & Lesson, 1987, pp. 23, 26)

Use of an Inventory

Scales commonly measure variables related to attitudes, interests, and personality and social adjustment. Usually, data are quantified in predetermined categories representing subdivisions of the variable. Subjects respond to a series of statements or questions showing the degree or intensity of their responses. Unlike data from tests, which are measured in continuous measurements (e.g., stanines 1 through 9, or percentiles 1 through 99), data from scales are discrete measurements, forcing respondents to indicate their level of reaction; common forced choices are "Always," "Sometimes," or "Never." This type of data quantification is called a **Likert-type scale.** Each response is assigned a value; a value of 1 usually represents the least positive response.

The following explanation of a scale is from a study to assess parent attitudes toward employment and services for their mentally retarded adult offspring. Although the report does not include sample items from the survey, the presentation of the results, as shown in Figure 6.4, clearly states that a Likert-type scale was used in the original form.

Purpose of the study: To assess parent/guardian attitudes toward employment opportunities and adult services for their own mentally retarded adult sons or daughters who are currently receiving services from adult community mental retardation systems.

Use of a Likert-Type Scale

The format of the survey for the attitude section was a Likert-type scale. In this section [of the survey], parents were asked to indicate the degree to which they perceived that their sons or daughters were currently exposed to the six qualitative conditions already listed and their opinions regarding the optimal amount of exposure to each practice. Therefore, attitude questions were presented in pairs. The first of the pairs asked for the parents' attitude toward the current situation as they perceived it and the second of the pair asked the parents for the preferred situation on each issue. The first item of the pairs permitted responding on a four-point Likert scale ranging from "never" (1) to "frequently" (4); a "don't know" response was (5). The responses on the second of the paired items regarding preferences employed a five-point continuum, which ranged from "much less than now" (1) to much more than now" (5) [see Figure 6.4]. (Hill, Seyfarth, Banks, Wehman, & Orelove, 1987, p. 12. Copyright © 1987 by The Council for Exceptional Children. Reprinted with permission.)

ACCURACY AND CONSISTENCY OF INSTRUMENTS IN QUANTITATIVE RESEARCH

Quantitative researchers are concerned that data they collect with various instruments are accurate and consistent. They wish to be sure they have positive answers to questions such as "Do the data represent real aspects of the variable being measured?" and "Will the data be similar if the instrument is administered a second or third time?" These questions refer to an instrument's validity and reliability. **Validity** refers to the extent to which an instrument measures what it is intended to measure. **Reliability** refers to the extent to which an instrument measures a variable consistently.

Additional information about the validity and reliability of instruments, including that concerning observations, is found in chapter 7.

Validity of Instruments

Instruments have validity when they are appropriate for a specific purpose and a particular population. To use an instrument with confidence, researchers must be able

Parental Attitudes Toward Working Conditions

Perceptions of Current Working Conditions		Preferred Working Conditions	
Condition	**Percent**	**Condition**	**Percent**
Average current wages		*Preferred wages*	
No pay	41%	No pay	5%
Less than $1/hour	23%	Less than now	.4%
$1.01 to $2.50/hour	10%	Same as now	49%
$2.52 to $3.34/hour	.3%	More than now	25%
Above $3.35/hour	3%	Much more	12%
Don't know	21%	Not sure	9%
Current interaction with nonhandicapped		*Preferred interactions*	
Never	7%	Less than now	2%
Rarely	13%	Somewhat less	4%
Sometimes	22%	Same as now	54%
Frequently	46%	Somewhat more	30%
Don't know	11%	Much more	10%
Currently responsibility and advancement opportunities		*Preferred responsibility and advancement opportunities*	
Never	36%	Less than now	0%
Rarely	13%	Somewhat less	.4%
Sometimes	28%	Same as now	59%
Frequently	25%	Somewhat more	28%
Don't know	17%	Much more	12%
Current level of work without supervision		*Preferred level of work without supervision*	
Never	17%	Less than now	0%
Rarely	13%	Somewhat less	2%
Sometimes	28%	Same as now	52%
Frequently	25%	Somewhat more	29%
Don't know	17%	Much more	17%
Requirements to exhibit "normal" behavior during work		*Preferred level of requirement to exhibit "normal" behavior during work*	
Never	14%	Less than now	3%
Rarely	7%	Somewhat less	5%
Sometimes	16%	Same as now	66%
Frequently	25%	Somewhat more	20%
Don't know	38%	Much more	7%
Current performance of same tasks as nonhandicapped workers		*Preferred level of performance of same tasks as nonhandicapped workers*	
Never	19%	Less than now	9%
Rarely	14%	Somewhat less	3%
Sometimes	19%	Same as now	61%
Frequently	21%	Somewhat more	28%
Don't know	26%	Much more	7%

Vocational Placement

Current placement		*Preferred placement*	
Institution	10.4%	Institution	5.6%
Home (no program)	17.2%	Home (no program)	4,0%
Activities center	23.3%	Activities center	25.6%
Sheltered workshop	43.7%	Sheltered workshop	52.0%
Competitive employment	5%	Competitive employment	12.8%

Attitudes Toward Work
Work should be a normal part of life for my son or daughter.

Strongly Disagree	Mildly Disagree	Not Sure	Mildly Agree	Strongly Agree
4%	2%	18%	18%	60%

Figure 6.4

Sample Information From a Likert-Type Scale

Source: From Hill, J. W., Seyfarth, J., Banks, P. D., Wehman, P., & Orelove, F. (1987). Parent attitudes about working conditions of their adult mentally retarded sons and daughters. *Exceptional Children, 54,* 9–23. Reprinted with permission of the publisher.

to answer yes to "Does the instrument measure what it is intended to measure at the time it is being used?" and "Are the results generalizable to the intended target population?" These questions imply that instruments are not universally valid. Instruments are considered valid only for clearly identified situations and populations.

The creators of instruments (tests, observation procedures, and surveys) are responsible for establishing the validity of their instruments. When researchers use others' instruments, they must present evidence that the instrument is valid for the research project. When researchers create new instruments for their projects, they must detail how they established the instrument's validity. Research consumers want to know "Does the instrument provide a real picture?" An instrument's validity is investigated using one or more of several generally accepted procedures. Even though each procedure can be used to determine an instrument's validity, research consumers need assurance that the particular way an instrument was validated makes it appropriate for a particular research project.

One validation procedure establishes that an instrument has been developed according to a supportable educational, sociological, or psychological theory. The theory can relate to any human characteristic or to any aspect of society. A theory is based on supportable research and tries to explain the nature of human behavior (such as intelligence or learning) and action (such as teaching). A theory's usefulness depends on how clearly it explains those behaviors and actions. A theory should not be considered as complete; it should be considered adequate only for describing a particular set of conditions, but not all conditions. Any theory must be modified or even discarded as new evidence is encountered, and every theory should (*a*) explain a complex phenomenon (such as reading ability, the nature of learning disabilities, mathematics aptitude, or the social interaction within a classroom), (*b*) describe how the phenomenon operates, and (*c*) provide a basis for predicting changes that will occur in one aspect of the phenomenon when changes are made in other aspects. When an instrument's creator demonstrates the instrument as representing a supportable theory, it is said to have **construct validity.** Consumers should expect every instrument to have construct validity. It is the researcher producers' responsibility to select an instrument with a construct validity appropriate for the research question, purpose, or hypothesis.

In the example that follows, the developers of a reading test [the "Information Reading-Thinking Inventory" (IR-TI)] explain their theoretical frame of reference.

Explanation of Test Construction to Establish Its "Construct Validity"

Three principal facts encourage us to believe that a new kind of Informal Reading Inventory [IRI] can address a number of [the technical measurement problems of existing IRIs] and other emerging assessment issues the and, more importantly, can result in better decisions in planning instruction. First, the IR-TI was constructed from the start to address some of the technical psychometric issues that have plagued IRIs for five decades. For example, you will see later how we were able to solve the problem of intermixing passage dependent and independent questions rather easily with a design modification that essentially separates the two question types. A second related point is that the IR-TI attempts to be responsive to the new issues that have arisen from recent theories of comprehension and from philosophies of instruction. Chief among these new concerns is the distinction between reconstructing an author's intended meaning (the usual view of comprehension) and the "constructivist" concept of constructing a reasonable interpretation of what one reads. The IR-TI is designed to assess both of these dimensions of comprehension in a manner that grounds it in current theory by acknowledging the "constructivist" ideal of promoting higher-order literacy or literate responses. Third, the movement toward alternative forms of assessment entails reduced emphasis on product measures, such as standardized tests, and greater focus on "process" measures, or performance-based and diagnostic evaluation of the student's thinking, reflection, and strategy choices. Instead of teachers continuing the practice of not assessing at all what cannot be assessed easily and definitively, we urge teachers to use the IR-TI to become more expert in continuing to informally assess critical/creative reading and thinking in a variety of settings and classroom situations. This again, is the basis of "performance-based" assessment. (From *Informal Reading-Thinking Inventory,* 1st Edition, by MANZO/MANZO. © 1995, Reprinted with permission of Wadsworth, a division of Thomson Learning: www.thomsonrights.com Fax 800 730-2215.

A second validation procedure establishes that the instrument is measuring a specific body of information. This consideration is important, especially when the instrument is an achievement or performance test. An instrument that is intended to measure science achievement should contain test items about the specific information the users (subjects or students) had the opportunity to learn in science classes. For example, achievement tests appropriate for use at the elementary level should contain items that test facts, concepts, and generalizations normally found in typical elementary-school science curricula. When an instrument's creators demonstrate that the specific items or questions represent an accurate sampling of specific bodies of knowledge (i.e., curricula or courses of study), it is said to have **content validity.** Instruments' creators establish content validity by submitting the instruments' items to groups of authorities in the content areas. It is their expert opinions that determine whether the instruments have content validity. Before research consumers can generalize research results, it must be determined that any instruments' content is appropriate (valid) for their educational situation and student population.

In the following example (from a study to assess the perceptions and opinions of students who completed teacher-education programs), the researchers explain the source of their questionnaire's content. (The "Dean's Grant" to which they refer was a federally funded grant competition for the development and implementation of preservice teacher preparation models that would prepare regular and special-education teachers for the mainstreaming of special-education students.)

> *Purpose of the study: To assess the perceptions and opinions of students who completed the teacher education program at a large Midwestern university.*
>
> A questionnaire comprising four parts was used to survey students. In part 1, respondents rated 34 competency statements related to mainstreaming of handicapped students on two scales. On the first scale, the Coverage Scale, respondents rated the extent to which they thought mainstream content had been covered in their teacher education program. On the second scale, the Knowledge Scale, they rated their knowledge of the mainstream curriculum content. The 34 statements were adapted from competency statements developed during the early years of the Dean's Grant that were still being used as guidelines for infusing mainstream curriculum throughout the undergraduate program. (Aksamit & Alcorn, 1988, p. 54)

Content of the Test

A first-level aspect of content validity is face validity. **Face validity** refers only to the extent to which an instrument appears to measure a specify body of information. In other words, "Does the instrument look as if it would measure what it intends to measure?" "Does a mathematics test look like actual mathematical tasks?" Instruments' users, or other subject-area experts, usually establish face validity by examining the test without comparing it to a course of study (curriculum).

A third validation procedure establishes the extent to which an instrument measures something to the same degree as does another instrument. The second instrument must previously have had its validity established by one or more accepted pro-cedures. To establish validity for a new instrument, the instrument's creator administers both instruments to the same group of individuals. The extent to which the results show that the individuals correlated, or scored similarly on both instruments, is an indication of **concurrent validity.** This procedure is common for establishing a new instrument's validity, but research producers and consumers must interpret the new instrument's results with some caution. They must be sure of the older instrument's construct and content validity. If the older instrument has questionable construct or content validity, the new instrument may not be appropriate even though there is high concurrent validity with the older instrument. Research consumers should expect evidence about the comparison instrument's validity. Research producers should indicate the instrument used to establish concurrent validity, and data about the level of correlation.

Information about an instrument's concurrent validity is usually found in studies whose purpose is to develop or assess an instrument. The following example is taken from such a study. It should be noted that the reported negative correlations were a desired result, because the two instruments are meant to measure students' behavior in inverse ways.

Purpose of the study: To revise and standardize a checklist of adaptive functioning designed for school use at the kindergarten level.

CONCURRENT VALIDITY WITH WALKER PROBLEM BEHAVIOR IDENTIFICATION CHECKLIST

[Twenty] students from grade levels kindergarten, 2, 4, and 6 were also used to examine the concurrent validity of the revised [Classroom Adaptive Behavior Checklist].

The teachers of these selected students were asked to complete both the revised checklist and the Walker Problem Behavior Identification Checklist (Walker, 1976), with a return rate of 70%.

The overall Pearson correlation between the total scores on the revised checklist (where higher scores indicate more adaptive behavior) and on the Walker (where higher scores indicate more problem behavior) was 2.78 (df = 54, p < .001) The correlation for kindergarten, grades 2, 4, and 6 were, respectively, 2.77, 2.84, 2.86, and 2.95. (Hunsucker, Nelson, & Clark, 1986, p. 70)

> *Estimate of Validity (concurrent)*

A fourth validation procedure establishes the extent to which an instrument can predict a target population's performance after some future situation. This **predictive validity** is determined by comparing a sample's results on the instrument to their results after some other activity. An example of predictive validity is the ability of college admissions officers to predict college students' first-year grade-point average from their scores on the Scholastic Aptitude Test (SAT).

Reliability of Instruments

Instruments are said to have reliability when they are consistent in producing their results. That is, there will be consistency in the instrument scores when the instrument is repeatedly administered to the same individuals, and there is an absence of possible random error when the instrument is administered (Rudner & Shafer, 2001). To use an instrument with confidence, researchers must be able to answer yes to "Does the instrument measure what it is intended to measure in a consistent manner?" and "Are the results going to be similar each time the instrument is used?" The implication of these questions for research producers and consumers has to do with dependability and the degree to which the results can be trusted. Reliability is not an either-or phenomenon; reliability is a statistical estimate of the extent to which the results can be considered dependable.1

The creators of instruments (tests, observation procedures, and surveys) are responsible for establishing the reliability of their instruments. When researchers use others' instruments, they must present evidence of the instruments' reliability. When researchers create new instruments for their projects, they must detail how they established the instruments' reliability. Research consumers want to know, "Does the instrument give a dependable picture of data?"

Evidence of an instrument's reliability is demonstrated with one or more of several generally accepted procedures. Even though each procedure gives only an estimate of an instrument's reliability, research consumers need assurance that the particular way an instrument's reliability was determined deems it appropriate for a particular research project. Whatever procedure is used, the reliability of an instrument is given in a numerical form called **reliability coefficient.** The coefficient is expressed in decimal form, ranging from .00 to 1.00. The higher the coefficient, the higher the instrument's reliability; that is, the higher the chance that the subject's observed score and true score can be considered similar.

The common procedures for establishing an instrument's reliability are (*a*) test-retest reliability, (*b*) equivalent forms (parallel, or alternate) reliability, (*c*) internal consistency reliability, and (*d*) scorer or rater reliability.

Test-retest reliability, also referred to as *test stability,* is determined by administering the same instrument again to the same subjects after time. When subjects' results are statistically compared, researchers gain evidence of the instrument's reliability over time, or its stability. It is considered the lowest level of reliability.

Equivalent forms reliability (sometimes called *parallel forms reliability*) is determined by creating two forms of an instrument, differing only in the specific nature of the items; the same subjects are given both forms, and their results are statistically compared. This method results in a much more consequential estimate of reliability than test-retest reliability.

Internal consistency reliability, sometimes called *rationale equivalence reliability,* is determined by statistically comparing the subjects' scores on individual items to their scores on each of the other items, and to their scores on the instrument as a whole. Split-half reliability, a commonly used form of internal consistency, is determined by dividing the instrument in half and statistically comparing the subjects' results on both parts. The most common way to split a test is into odd- and even-numbered items. Most often, this method is used when the test designers want to avoid the additional costs associated with developing a parallel (equivalent or alternate) form of a test. Statistical adjustment to split-half reliability estimates must be conducted to account for the seemingly reduced number of items (half) used in the procedure.

---

[1] There are some test experts (psychometricians) who believe that a test does not have reliability per se. Rather, they believe that reliability is an indication of the consistency of the test results for a particular instance of a test's use.

Scorer or rater reliability, sometimes called *interrater* or *interjudge reliability,* is determined by comparing the results of two or more scorers, raters, or judges. Scorer reliability may be presented as a percentage of agreement and not as a co-efficient. In the following example, which is taken from a previously cited study about the standardization of a behavior check list (Hunsucker et al., 1986), two methods of establishing the instrument's reliability are used. Both methods, test-retest and interteacher (or interrater), involve the use of the Pearson correlation formula.

Purpose of the study: To revise and standardize a check list of adaptive functioning designed for school use at the kindergarten level.

TEST-RETEST RELIABILITY

Test-Retest Method of Showing Instrument's Reliability

Subgroups of 20 subjects from grades kindergarten, 2, 4, and 6 were randomly selected from the normative group to examine the test-retest reliability of the revised checklist. The teachers of these students were asked to complete the checklist twice over a 4-week period (x elapsed days = 31.3), with a return rate of 66.2%.

Using the Pearson correlation coefficient on total checklist scores, test-retest reliability was .72 for kindergarten (n = 11), .95 for grade 2 (n = 11), .89 for grade 4 (n = 15), and .67 for grade 6 (n = 26). Using the exact agreement method for specific checklist items (agreements on both occurrence and nonoccurrence divided by total number of items), test-retest reliability was .90 for kindergarten, .92 for grade 2, .90 for grade 4, and .89 for grade 6.

INTERTEACHER AGREEMENT

Subgroups of 15 subjects from grade levels 1, 3, and 5 who were in team-taught classrooms were selected from the normative group to examine interteacher agreement for the revised checklist. Both teachers in the teaching team completed checklists for 68.8% of these selected students.

Interrater Method of Showing Instrument's Reliability

Using the Pearson correlation coefficient on total checklist scores, interteacher agreement was .92 for grade 1 (n = 11) .86 for grade 3 (n = 10), and .89 for grade 5 (n = 10). Using the exact agreement method for specific checklist items, interteacher agreement was .92 for grade 1, .93 for grade 3, and .86 for grade 5.

From Hill, J. W., Seyfarth, J., Banks, P. D., Wehman, P., & Orelove, F. (1987). Parent attitudes about working conditions of their adult mentally retarded sons and daughters. *Exceptional Children 54:* 9–23. Copyright © 1987 by the Council for Exceptional Children. Reprinted with permission.

In the following example, from a study involving the use of various phonemic awareness tests, the researcher uses an internal consistency reliability procedure. Note that although the type of reliability procedure is not indicated, the researcher reports a commonly used statistical formula—the Cronbach *alpha.* Another commonly used formula for establishing internal consistency reliability is the Kuder-Richardson formula 20.

Purpose of the study: To determine the reliability and validity of tests that have been used to operationalize the concept of phonemic awareness.

*Internal Con-
sistency Proce-
dure for
Showing In-
strument's
Reliability*

The reliability of each test was determined using Cronbach's *alpha*. Seven of the tests had high internal consistency, with *alpha* = .83. The Roswell-Chall (1959) phoneme blending test showed the greatest reliability (*alpha* = .96) followed closely by the Yopp-Singer phoneme segmentation test (*alpha* = .95). Two tests showed moderate to high reliability: Rosner's (1975) phoneme deletion test (*alpha* = .78) and the Yopp rhyme test (*alpha* = .76). The Yopp modification of Wallach's (1976) word-to-word matching test had the lowest reliability (*alpha* = .58) for this sample. (Yopp, 1988, p. 168)

Other Concerns About Instruments

The standardization (or norm) group is a key attribute of a standardized test. It is the research consumer's responsibility to ensure that this group, on which the norms of the test have been developed, is comparable to the group to which the consumer wishes to generalize the findings. Most often, major test publishers ensure generalization by creating a stratified-sample standardization group. That process usually results in norm groups that are representative of all regions of the country, and various ethnic groups in proportion to their population statistics.

A common concern about instruments deals with how and by whom instruments are administered. An instrument may have validity and reliability, but the person using it must be competent and must use it in appropriate settings. For example, certain standardized tests must be administered by fully trained and qualified examiners. Standardized tests requiring special training and certified personnel include the Wechsler Intelligence Scale for Children–Revised and the Stanford-Binet Intelligence Scale, 4th edition. All instruments, whether they are tests, observations, or surveys, should be administered by appropriately trained personnel.

The following three passages illustrate how researchers indicate instrument users' proficiencies.

Purpose of the study: To investigate differences in parent-provided written language experiences of intellectually superior nonreaders and accelerated readers.

*User
Proficiency*

Test Administration. All 125 potentially gifted children were administered the Stanford-Binet Intelligence Test and Letter-Word Identification subtest from the Woodcock-Johnson Psycho-Educational Battery by certified examiners. (Burns & Collins, 1987, p. 243)

Purpose of the study: To compare students' instructional placements as predicted by a standardized test and an informal reading inventory.

*User
Proficiency*

All of the tests were administered over a period of about six weeks (three per grade) by a research assistant trained in the use of both the [Degrees of Reading Power] and the [informal reading inventory]. (Duffelmeyer & Adamson, 1986, p. 195)

Purpose of the study: To determine the effects of education, occupation, and setting on reading practices.

Procedures.   A guided interview was constructed based on a review of previous research in measuring reading practice (Guthrie & Seifert, 1984). Two enumerators were recruited who were paid for their services. They had considerable experience in conducting surveys but were not experienced with reading activity inventories. In a 4-hour training session, they were informed about the purpose of the survey, taken step by step through the inventory, and given a demonstration of its administration. The enumerators individually interviewed an adult wage earner in each designated household. (Guthrie et al., 1986, p. 152)

A factor that may be important in test administration is the familiarity of the examiner to the subjects. Research evidence seems to show that some subjects' scores increase when they are tested by familiar examiners (Fuchs & Fuchs, 1986, 1989). Because researchers cannot always establish examiner-subject familiarity (because of time constraints or expense), research consumers need to be aware of the possible effect on results of subjects' unfamiliarity with examiners.

A second concern is when, in descriptive research, surveys or questionnaires are mailed to potential respondents. A major concern to researchers is the representativeness of the returned surveys or questionnaires. A return rate of about 70% is considered adequate to ensure that the obtained responses represent those of the entire target population (Gay & Airasian, 2000). When the percentage of returns is lower, researchers should conduct follow-up activities to get additional questionnaires. Also, when the return rate is the minimum acceptable, research consumers should be concerned whether there is a difference in traits between individuals who respond to the questionnaires and those who do not.

Validity and Reliability of Authentic Assessment Instruments

Authentic, or performance-based, assessment systems are often criticized for not having rigorous measures of validity and reliability. The major criticisms of authentic assessment deal with issues of the nature of the standards against which student performance is judged (validity) and the ability of educators at different times to apply those standards uniformly (reliability). For example, some educators advocate the use of portfolio assessment, one form of authentic assessment. However, there is no consensus, at this time, as to what constitutes an appropriate portfolio: What should a portfolio contain as samples of a student's work? Who should determine what student work is placed in the portfolio? At what point in the instructional process and how frequently should materials be placed in a portfolio? Further, what criteria should be used to determine the quality of a student's work?

Extensive research is being undertaken to answer these and related questions about authentic, or performance-based, assessment (Linn, 1994; Messick, 1994; Swanson, Norman, & Linn, 1995). For there to be validity and reliability in the authentic measurements, these researchers postulate that authentic assessment must be used with the following considerations:

1. Student performances or products used in an assessment should be based on the purposes of the testing, the nature of the subject area being tested, and the instructional theories about the skills and knowledge being tested.
2. Educators should indicate whether the focus of the assessment is the students' products, or performances, or the knowledge and skills needed to create the products or performances.
3. The selection of tasks to be assessed and the ways they are tested should reflect as much as possible actual school and life situations of the students. That is, the knowledge and performance tasks should be selected from the context

of students' learning and should be given in situations that simulate real-life situations.

4. There should be clarity about the outcomes of the assessments in regard to generalizability: Is the assessment being used to generalize to the performance of individuals, or large groups? Care should be taken that generalizations are related to, and do not exceed, the intended purpose of the assessment (see first item in list).

5. The method of scoring students' knowledge, products, and performances should be clear. There should be criteria for determining appropriate outcomes and consistency in the application of those criteria.

Locating Validity and Reliability Information About Instruments

Researchers do not always report the available information about instruments' validity and reliability. One reason for omitting validity and reliability information is the extensive reporting of it elsewhere. In such a case, researchers will refer readers to the appropriate research report. In the two examples that follow, the researchers use instruments whose validity information is reported elsewhere. Note that in both examples, the researchers report reliability data established in their research.

> *Purpose of the study: To improve understanding of the relationships between types of in-service training activities and changes in teaching behavior.*
>
> The Stallings Secondary Observation Instrument (SSOI) was used to measure teaching behavior. The validity measures obtained with this instrument in relation to student achievement and attitude has been established in previous studies (e.g., Stallings, Needels, & Stayrook, 1979). High interrater reliability (85% agreement or better) was established for the observers in this study. (Sparks, 1986, p. 218)

Validity and Reliability Information

> *Purpose of the study: To investigate the planning and debugging strategies and group processes that predicted learning of computer programming in small groups with students aged 11 to 14.*
>
> Six aptitude and cognitive style measures were administered at the beginning of the workshop. These were a test of mathematical computation and reasoning; a test of verbal inference; a short form of the Raven's Progressive matrices (Raven, 1958) to measure nonverbal reasoning ability; and three tests from the Educational Testing Service (ETS) kit of cognitive factor reference tests (French, Ekstrom, & Price, 1963): Surface Development (spatial ability), Gestalt Completion (holistic vs. analytic processing), and Hidden Figures (field independence). Internal consistency alpha for these tests ranged from .64 to .92 in this sample. (Webb, Ender, & Lewis, 1986, p. 246)

Validity and Reliability Information

Another reason for not including validity and reliability information is the instrument's extensive use in educational and psychological projects. It is assumed that its validity and reliability information is known by most of the research report's readers. This case is especially true when researchers use standardized tests such as the Wechsler Intelligence Scale for Children–Revised, the Metropolitan Achievement Tests, or the Woodcock Reading Mastery Tests. Research consumers can refer to several readily available sources to locate information about instruments' validity and reliability. When the instrument is a standardized test, research consumers can refer to the administration and technical information manuals provided by an instrument's publisher.

Research consumers may find it helpful to rely on reviews of standardized instruments. These reviews can be found in special yearbooks and handbooks, professional journals, and professional textbooks. Chapter 11, "Locating Information About Research Reports," contains information about how to locate and obtain authoritative reviews about instruments' validity, reliability, and appropriateness for target populations.

TYPES OF QUALITATIVE DATA COLLECTION PROCEDURES

Qualitative researchers collect information with many of the same devices and procedures as do quantitative researchers (Mahoney, 1997). Qualitative information, or data, consists of narrative information, observations, opinions, and beliefs about the research topic, event, and participants. Qualitative information "brings out the voices and viewpoints of individuals to explain what [quantitative data] alone cannot" (Annie E. Casey Foundation, 2002, p. 112). Unlike quantitative researchers, constructivist qualitative researchers believe that they should be involved as much as possible in the research event (Golafshani, 2003).

In the model qualitative research report, "Images of America: What Youth Do Know About the United States," pp. 27–51, the procedures for collecting information are found in more than one place. Often in reports of qualitative research, researchers present data collection procedures intermixed with information about general procedures and findings. In the research report "Images of America," data collection information is included in the same section as participant information, at [9] and in the section at [12].

Qualitative researchers may collect information through observations, surveys, interviews, and questionnaires. Information about qualitative researcher data collection procedures may be in a section so labeled, or in a general section about procedure.

During observations, researchers use a planned set of steps and information-gathering protocols, which may include checklists and rating scales. The information they seek about an situation includes (*a*) the setting, (*b*) the social environment, (*c*) the project implementation activities, (*d*) the native language of the project, (*e*) the use of nonverbal communication, and (*f*) any notable nonoccurrence, such as the absence of anything that might have been expected (Mahoney, 1997).

Methods for collecting qualitative information include

- Direct observation
- Individual interviews and focus groups (see chapter 5)
- Examination of documents

Note that in all of these instances of collecting information, the researcher is primary; that is, the researcher is a participant in the study itself.

Direct Observation

In qualitative research, information is obtained during direct observation through the use of **participant observers.** In qualitative research, the feature of *participant observer* distinguishes the study from quantitative research in the manner in which information is collected and analyzed during direct observations. The extent to which a researcher participates is along a continuum. The continuum ranges from complete involvement in the research context to complete separation from the context as on outside observer. While conducting observations, the qualitative researcher may

- Engage directly in the activities or event with participants
- Observe the setting and participants with limited participation in the activities or event
- Be a passive observer, present only to observe the activities or event

Participant observers must try to obtain a full sense of the experience as they try to understand the event and the participants' behaviors. They do this through direct personal experience, observation, and discussion with the other participants (while trying to be nonintrusive). The researcher's effectiveness will often depend on "the nature of the project and its participants, the political and social context, the nature of the evaluation questions being asked, and the resources available" (Mahoney, 1997).

Individual Interviews and Focus Groups

Interviews and focus group discussions may be either structured or unstructured. In structured interviews and discussions, the researcher works from a previously prepared questionnaire or set of questions. The idea is to obtain responses to these questions so there is some uniformity to the data gathering procedure. However, most qualitative researchers, especially those with a constructivist perspective, believe that some discussion-provoking questions should be used. Yet, they believe the specific direction taken during the interviews and focus group discussions should be determined by the participants and their responses.

Many qualitative researchers do not use interviews to get answers to questions or to test specific research questions or hypotheses. Rather, intensive interviews are seen as a means for understanding the experience of others and the meaning the interviews make of that experience (Seidman, 1998). Many constructivist qualitative researchers will change their questions in subsequent interviews because of responses obtained during earlier ones. As a result, some interviews will be entirely different in scope and content than others. This feature is not thought of negative, but as positive. During focus group discussions, researchers will often abandon the topic guide questions they have prepared, to allow participants to express their views and feelings without distraction.

Examination of Documents

There are numerous types of documents that qualitative researchers can examine to collect information about the topic, event, or participants being studied (Annie E. Casey Foundation, 2002; Hancock, 2002). These documents include written items, such as published public documents about policy, procedure, financial conditions, minutes of meetings, codes of conduct, school records, photographs, and information and curriculum bulletins. They can also include unpublished materials found in individuals' notes or journals, or instructional plans and students' portfolios. Although these materials may be included in the data collection of quantitative researchers, it is the inductive analysis of the material (rather than a specific coding and statistical analysis of the information) that distinguishes constructivist qualitative researchers.

Data Analysis in Qualitative Research

Just because the primary approach to qualitative data collection and analysis is inductive, qualitative research is not devoid of measurement (Berkowitz, 1997; Mays & Pope, 2000). Qualitative researchers are usually concerned with the classification (that is, the creation of a taxonomy) of information. It is concerned with the meanings the participants give to their experiences, behaviors, feelings, and knowledge, in an attempt to make sense of their world. Because of this concern, qualitative analysis is often referred to as *interpretive* research or analysis.

Good qualitative information collection is systematic and highly controlled. As we previously mentioned, quantitative data collection is usually presented in discrete aspects: instrumentation development, data collection, and data analysis. Information collection and analysis during qualitative research are usually intermixed in practice and reporting. What distinguishes qualitative analysis is "a loop-like pattern of multiple rounds of revisiting the data as additional questions emerge, new connections are unearthed, and more complex formulations develop along with a deepening understanding of the material. Qualitative analysis is fundamentally an *iterative* set of processes" (Berkowitz, 1997).

Qualitative researchers often do not make a distinction between information collection and analysis. As they collect information, they are creating meaning through these procedures:

- Analysis—using specific and detailed analysis schemes (for example, the use of open and axial coding systems within a Grounded Theory approach)
- Meaning—looking for meaning of textual material by an analysis of the material as a whole and of its parts
- Relationships—making sense of an entire organization and the relationships between and among its members, the organizational structure, and the organization's internal and external communication systems
- Interpretation—interpreting the metaphors and symbols used within the situation being studied.

Qualitative researchers with a constructivist perspective are concerned with using the results of their information analysis to make changes; that is, to "contribute to solutions to real problems" through these ways:

- An increase in understanding about the conditions of the setting
- An identification of needs
- A recognition of trends
- The encouragement of dialogue
- The engaging, mobilizing, and organizing of the participants and stakeholders
- A broadening of the participants' and stakeholders' agendas
- The support of further strategic planning
- A change in the way services are delivered, financed, and governed
- The development of partnerships
- An increase in resources (Annie E. Casey Foundation, 2002, chapter 5).

ACCURACY AND CONSISTENCY OF INSTRUMENTS IN QUALITATIVE RESEARCH

Information collection procedures in qualitative research done from a constructivist perspective do not have *validity* and *reliability* in the same sense as do instruments in quantitative research or qualitative research done from a positivist perspective. However, constructivist qualitative research information collection does have a precision that can be documented in ways to show the information obtained is both consistent with the purpose and goals of the research and accurate in its reporting and the information and analysis procedures (Anfara, Brown, & Mangione, 2002, Creswell & Miller, 2002; Golafshani, 2003; and Lacey & Luff, 2001). It is the consumer's responsibility to determine whether or not the researchers' findings and conclusions do represent the situation and stakeholders being studied.

Qualitative data analysis generally has several phases:

- Transcription of all orally obtained information
- Organization of information
- Familiarization with all the information
- Coding and categorizing information
- Identification of themes

To ensure that the qualitative information has the qualities of **consistency** and **accuracy,** qualitative researchers aim to establish these qualities as they gather and analyze their information. In regard to what quantitative researchers call *reliability*, qualitative researchers are concerned with

- Describing how information was collected and analyzed
- Justifying the reason(s) that this information is appropriate within the setting of the study
- Documenting extensively the process of generating themes, concepts, or theories from the information
- Providing references to other evidence, including previous research, against which the researcher's conclusions can be judged (Lacey & Luff, 2001)

Instead of considering the collection of their information as *reliable*, constructivist qualitative researchers would consider the essential criteria for quality of their information in terms of *credibility, neutrality* or *confirmability, consistency* or *dependability*, and

---

In the qualitative research report "Images of America," on pp. 27–51, the researcher provided information about her research perspective and beliefs, as well as the means she took to ensure the worthiness of her conclusions. These items are found at

[4], "Explanation of Personal Position on the Topic,"
[6], "Statement of Research Belief,"
[7], "Personal Orientation Toward Research,"
[9], "Participants and Researcher's Relationship With Participants,"
[11], "Research Methodology,"

and in extensive supporting examples throughout the report.

Research Type	Terms	Strategies Used
Quantitative	Reliability	• Reliability quotient • Test-retest • Equivalent forms • Internal consistency • Interrater reliability
	Validity	• Construct validity • Construct validity • Content validity • Face validity • Concurrent validity • Predictive validity

Qualitative	Credibility
	Dependability
	Confirmability
	Transferability
		• Triangulation
		• Disconfirming negative
		  evidence
		• Multiple data sources
		• Multiple data collection
		  points
		• Multiple researchers
		• Research reflexivity
		• Participant checking
		• Audit trail

Figure 6.5
Terms Used for Assessing Data/Information Collection Quality and Rigor

applicability or *transferability* (Anfara, Brown, & Mangione, 2002; Golafshani, 2003; Lincoln & Guba, 1985). Figure 6.5 summarizes the differences in critical terms used by quantitative and qualitative researchers in discussing the essential qualities of their data or information.

In regard to what quantitative researchers call *validity*, qualitative researchers stress the idea of how the information and its interpretation consistently, fairly, and accurately represents the ideas, feelings, behaviors, and activities of the participants.

Because constructivist qualitative researchers may modify some of their participant selection and information collection procedures during their study, their research may not be readily replicable. Therefore, guidelines for qualitative research have developed over time, and these rules are generally accepted by the research community. By adhering to these guidelines, researchers can demonstrate the **trustworthiness** (that is, the accuracy and consistency) of their research. The qualitative researchers' aim is to provide enough supporting evidence that the consumer of the research has *confidence* in the researchers' findings (Lincoln & Guba, 1985). Through the use of these guidelines, consumers can make judgments about the research.

Validity and Reliability of Qualitative Data Collection

In many qualitative research studies, the data gathering "instrument" is often a participant observer. The question can be raised about the validity and reliability of the data collected by these individuals. In chapter 8, there is extensive discussion about understanding the procedures and results of qualitative research. In that discussion, additional issues of data collection validity and reliability are addressed.

Qualitative researchers use several techniques and provide particular evidence to ensure that others will accept the trustworthiness of their information and conclusions. These include three factors, according to Anfra, Brown, and Mangione, 2002; Creswell and Miller, 2000; and Golafshani, 2003:

- Researcher Efforts
  - Triangulation—the collection of information from different participant perspectives about the setting, activities, and behaviors being observed (additional information is found in chapter 8). It should be noted that quantitative researchers also use triangulation; however, it is the manner in which the collected information is interpreted that is most important. Constructivist qualitative researchers have the perspective that multiple realities and beliefs exist, and that it is important to account for all ideas about what is occurring during the research activities.
  - Disconfirming Negative Evidence—the searching for information that differs from (or discredits) the evolving themes being developed during information collection and analysis
  - Multiple Data Sources—the collection of information from different sources other than just direct observations
  - Multiple Data Collection Points—the collection of information at different times; sometimes this collection is referred to as *prolonged engagement in the field,* a time when the researchers engage in repeated site visits to establish rapport with the participants
  - Multiple Researchers—the collection of information by other researchers, either simultaneously or at different times
  - Researcher Reflexivity—the researchers' self-disclosure about their assumptions, beliefs, and biases
- Participant Involvement
  - Participant Checking—the examination of the collected information and its interpretations by the participants themselves for their confirmation about how the material represents their perspectives, beliefs, feelings, and understanding of the researched situation
- Stakeholders and Other External Persons
  - The Audit Trail—the researchers' extensive documenting of all activities, information gathering and analysis procedures, and sources of information

ACTIVITIES

Activity 1

Using the Focus Questions at the beginning of the chapter, create a summary of the key ideas presented in the chapter.

Activity 2

Read each of the following two instrument sections of quantitative research reports. The researchers' purposes have been included for your information. Using the questions and criteria on page 116 for quantitative research, evaluate the researchers' instrumentation. For each, list questions and concerns you may have about

a. The validity of the instruments
b. The reliability of the instruments
c. The appropriateness of the instruments for the target population and research subjects
d. The appropriateness of the instruments for the researcher's purposes

Extract A: Parenting and School Achievement

Purpose: An examination of the relations between parenting and the school performance of fourth- and fifth-grade children in Asian American, Latino, and European American families.

PARENT QUESTIONNAIRE

A questionnaire was adapted from previous research (Okagaki et al., 1995; Okagaki & Sternberg, 1993, Schaefer & Edgerton, 1985; Small & Luster, 1990) to assess parents' beliefs about education, school achievement, and self-reported parental behaviors. Questionnaires were translated into Spanish and then backtranslated into English by a second translator. Discrepancies were resolved through discussion. The questionnaire consisted of seven sections: (a) educational attainment, (b) grade expectations, (c) childrearing beliefs, (d) self-reported parental behaviors; (e) parental efficacy, (f) perception of child's ability, and (g) demographic information.

Educational Attainment. Parents were asked to indicate (a) what the ideal amount of education they would like their child to attain would be (a single item, from 1 = complete some high school education to 6 = get a graduate of professional degree), (b) how much education they expect their child to obtain (a single item), and (c) what the very least amount of schooling they would allow their child to attain would be (a single item).

Grade Expectations. Parents indicated on a 4-point scale (1 = very happy: my child did a great job; 4 = upset: I want my child to do better) how they would feel if their child hypothetically brought home certain grades (a separate item for each letter grade from A to F).

Childrearing Beliefs. Three subscales were developed to assess the importance parents place on developing autonomous behaviors and attitudes in their children (8 items were adapted from Schaefer and Edgerton, 1985—e.g., How important do I think it is for my child to work through problems on his/her own? and How important do I think it is for my child to think and make decisions on his/her own?), the importance parents place on developing conformity to external standards (8 items adapted from Schaefer and Edgerton, 1985—e.g., How important do I think it is for my child to do what the teacher tells him/her to do? and How important do I think it is for my child to respect adults and people in authority?), and the importance parents place on parental monitoring of children's activities (16 items adapted from Small and Luster, 1990—e.g., How important do I think it is for me, as a parent, to know what my child does in school? and How important do I think it is for me, as a parent, to know how my child is treated by others at school?). The interitem reliabilities for these subscales were strong (as 5 ranging from .78 to .89).

Parental Behaviors. The parental behaviors section was divided into two subscales. For each scale, parents indicated on a 6-point scale (0 = rarely; 6 = daily) how frequently they did a specific activity. The first scale consisted of 10 items about activities the parent does to help the child with schoolwork (e.g., How often do you remind your child to study for a test? and How often do you help your child study for a test?). The second scale was composed of eight items related to general activities parents might do with children that would encourage them to read or think about issues or would provide opportunities to observe their parents reading (e.g., How often do you read a magazine at home? and How often do you have your child read a nonschool book at home?). Interitem reliabilities for these scales were strong (both αs =. 77).

Parental Efficacy Beliefs. Six items asked parents to rate the extent to which they agreed or disagreed with statements related to the confidence they felt about their ability to help their child succeed in school (e.g., There are times when I do not understand my child's math homework and there are times when I do not understand my child's reading homework). Items were rated on a 6-point Likert scale (0 = strongly disagree; 6 = strongly agree). The interitem reliability for his scale was satisfactory (α =. 72).

Perception of Child's Ability. Parents were presented six items related to their perception of their child's ability to do well in school (e.g., My child usually gets good grades in school and My child usually does not need help with homework). Items were rated on a 6-point Likert scale (1 = strongly disagree; 6 = strongly agree). The interitem reliability for this scale was strong (α = 81).

Source: From Okagaki, L., & Frensch, P.A. (1998). Parenting and children's school achievement: A multiethnic perspective. *American Educational Research Journal, 35*(1), 123–144. Reprinted with permission of the publisher.

Extract B: University and Urban School Collaboration

Purpose: The study focused on the collaboration component, which involved preservice teachers' interaction in the preschool. The researchers specifically wanted to determine if the field placement enhanced their understanding of the emerging literacy process. In addition, they wanted to investigate the varying roles of the preservice teacher, and the effect these roles had on these teachers' knowledge of preschoolers.

INSTRUMENTS

A questionnaire was given to the preservice teachers at the end of the semester to determine their perceptions of the experience. Twenty-three items were rated on the following scale:

1. not at all
2. somewhat
3. pretty much
4. a lot
5. very much

One item assessed the participants' overall enjoyment in the project (I enjoyed participating in the Long Branch preschool project during this semester.). Other more specific aspects of this collaborative venture were explored. Three questions were posed about their participation in the shared book experience (I felt that my participation in the preschool project gave me experience with the shared book reading. I enjoyed reading the children's literature that was utilized in the preschool.). Six questions focused on attitudes involving the Literacy Play Centers. (Participating in the Literacy Play Centers gave me insight into the natural and pretend play of three-, four- and five-year-olds. It was a valuable experience to participate in a Literacy Play Center rather than to read about one.) Additional questions were designed to ascertain if the preservice teachers observed developing language patterns, motor skill acquisition, and early attempts at reading and writing. (I felt that participating in the Long Branch project gave me a first-hand glimpse at early literacy development. I felt that my participation in the preschool project gave me exposure to the developing motor skill patterns of preschoolers: cutting, pasting, coloring.)

Two open-ended questions were also posed regarding the aspects of the project that were viewed as most advantageous for their professional growth as preservice teachers. Their perceptions on the strengths and weaknesses of the preschool program were assessed as well as their comments regarding future program improvement. Open coding was utilized to analyze this data (Strauss & Corbin, 1990). The complete questionnaire appears in [the] Appendix. . . .

Source: From Young, S. A., & Romeo, L. (1999). University and urban school district collaboration: Preschoolers and preservice teachers gain literacy skills. *Reading Research and Instruction, 38*(2), 101–114. Reprinted with permission of the publisher.

FEEDBACK

Activity 1

For Reading and Evaluating Quantitative Research Reports

What are the different types of instruments used in research projects?   How is information from different instruments reported? Instruments are used to denote a broad range of specific devices and procedures for collecting, sorting, and categorizing information about subjects and research questions. Three types of instruments are used in research: tests, observations, and surveys. A standardized test is one for which the tasks and procedures of administering, recording, scoring, and interpreting are specified so that other testers can make comparable measurements in different locations. Standardized tests are of two main types: norm-referenced and criterion-referenced. Norm-referenced tests compare individuals' scores with a standardization, or norming, group. Criterion-referenced tests and various forms of authentic assessment compare students' responses to specified expected learner behaviors or to specified expected levels of performance. Test information includes scores from individual or group standardized norm-referenced tests, standardized criterion-referenced tests, competency tests, and researcher- or teacher-made tests. When collecting data from direct observation, researchers take extensive field notes or use an observation form to categorize the information. They record information on forms in response to questions about subjects' actions or categories of actions. Surveys include a broad range of devices for data collecting, such as questionnaires, individual interviews and focus groups, scales, inventories, and check lists.

What are instrument validity and reliability, and how are they determined?   Validity refers to the extent that an instrument measures what it is intended to measure. Reliability refers to the extent that an instrument measures a variable consistently. When an instrument's creator demonstrates the instrument as representing a supportable educational theory, the tool is said to have construct validity. When an instrument's creator demonstrates the instrument as representing an accurate sampling of a specific body of knowledge, the tool is said to have content validity. An instrument's creator establishes content validity by submitting the instrument's items to a group of authorities in the content area. They determine whether the instrument has content validity. When the subjects' results on one instrument correlate (or result in a similar rank order of scores) with those on another instrument, the new instrument is said to have concurrent validity. A fourth validation procedure establishes the extent to which an instrument can predict a target population's performance after some future situation. This process is predictive validity.

The common procedures for establishing an instrument's reliability are (*a*) test-retest reliability, a measure of the test's stability; (*b*) equivalent forms reliability; (*c*) internal consistency reliability; and (*d*) scorer or rater reliability. Test-retest reliability is determined by administering the same instrument again to the same subjects after time. When the subjects' results are compared, researchers gain evidence of the instrument's reliability over time, or its stability. Equivalent forms reliability is determined by creating two forms of an instrument. The instrument should be the same in every aspect, except for the specific items. The same subjects are given both forms, and their results are compared. Internal consistency reliability, which is sometimes called *rationale equivalence reliability,* is determined by comparing the subjects' scores on individual items to their scores on each of the other items, and to their scores on the instrument as a whole. Split-half reliability, a common type of internal-consistency reliability, is determined by dividing the instrument in half and comparing the subjects' results on both parts. The most common way to split a test is into odd- and even-numbered items. Scorer or rater reliability, which is sometimes called *interrater* or *interjudge* reliability, is determined by comparing the results from two or more scores, raters, or judges. Sometimes scorer reliability is presented as a percentage of agreement and not as a coefficient.

What criteria should be used to determine whether instruments are appropriate for the research?   Consumers should consider the following: What instruments are used in the study? Are they appropriate for the design of the study? Are the instruments valid for collecting data on the variables in the study? Are reliability estimates given for each instrument? Are researcher-made instruments included (or at least samples of the instrument items)? Are the instruments appropriate for use with the target population and the research subject?

For Reading and Evaluating Qualitative Research Reports

What are the different ways data is collected in qualitative research projects?   Qualitative researchers collect information with many of the same devices and procedures as do quantitative researchers. They use observations, surveys, interviews, and questionnaires. Information about qualitative researcher data collection procedures may be in a section so labeled, or in a general section about procedure.

What is the role of a participant observer in collecting data?   The extent to which a researcher participates is along a continuum that ranges from complete involvement in the research context, to complete separation from the context as an outside observer. Participant observers must try to obtain a full sense of the experience, while trying to understand the event and the participants' behaviors through personal experience, observation, and discussion with the other participants. This process must be done while trying to be noninstrusive.

How is the collected information analyzed?   Information collection and analysis during qualitative research are usually intermixed in practice and reporting. What distinguishes qualitative analysis is a loop-like pattern of multiple rounds of revisiting the data as additional questions emerge, new connections are unearthed, and more complex formulations develop along with a deepening understanding of the material. Qualitative analysis is fundamentally an *iterative* set of processes. Qualitative researchers often do not make a distinction between information collection and analysis. As they collect information, they are creating meaning. Qualitative data analysis generally has several phases: transcription of all orally obtained information, organization of information, familiarization with all the information, coding and categorizing information, and identification of themes.

What does it mean to have accurate and consistent data collection?   Constructivist qualitative researchers consider the essential qualitative criteria for quality of their information in terms of *credibility, neutrality* or *confirmability, consistency* or *dependability,* and *applicability* or *transferability.* In regard to what quantitative researchers call "validity," qualitative researchers stress the idea of how well the information and its interpretation consistently, fairly, and accurately represents the ideas, feelings, behaviors, and activities of the participants.

How should data collection sections be read and evaluated? Research consumers should consider the following: What devices (questionnaires, surveys, interview forms) are used in the study? Are they appropriate for the design of the study? Are the data collection devices appropriate for collecting data about the purpose(s) of the study? Are researcher-made devices included (or at least samples of them)? Are the data collection devices appropriate for use with the participants?

Activity 2

Extract A: Parenting and School Achievement. The questionnaire is not a standardized instrument. However, it was used in several previously published studies, so its content and construct validity have undergone scrutiny and review. The form of the questionnaire used in the present study was adapted from these earlier versions. The authors indicated how conformity in language was determined. The specific questionnaire was not included, but the content of each subsection was detailed, including examples of the specific questions. Also, for each subsection, the manner in which the parents' responses were coded was explained. The data in the subsections were quantified using a Likert-type scale.

For two sections, educational attainment and grade expectations, the parents' responses dealt with basic demographic information and beliefs. Statistical determination of reliability was not a consideration for those sections.

In four sections (childrearing beliefs, parental behaviors, parental efficacy beliefs, and perception of child's ability), there was a need to ensure that the parents responded in a consistent manner. For those sections, then, researchers determined coefficients of reliability. The symbol α (the Greek letter alpha) is used to show estimates of a test's reliability (see chapter 7, section I, "Reading and Evaluating Procedure Sections," and section II, "Reading and Interpreting Results Sections"). The researchers provided information to show the level of reliability for these sections of the questionnaire. In each case, they indicated the results for interitem or internal consistency reliability.

Extract B: University and Urban School Collaboration. The questionnaire is not a standardized instrument. The content of the device was explained and a copy of the full instrument was included in an appendix. Except for two open-ended questions, the responses were coded using a Likert-type scale. "Open coding," used for the last two questions, is a coding procedure used with analyzing qualitative data.

The researchers did not indicate how the construct and content validity of the instrument were established. It is up to the research consumer, then, to refer to the actual instrument and make such decisions. Also, the researchers did not indicate how reliability was established for the responses to the questions requiring a scaled response. The research consumer does not have assurance that the questionnaire had internal consistency and, therefore, may not be able to trust the results.

CHAPTER 7

Reading, Evaluating, Interpreting Procedure and Results Sections

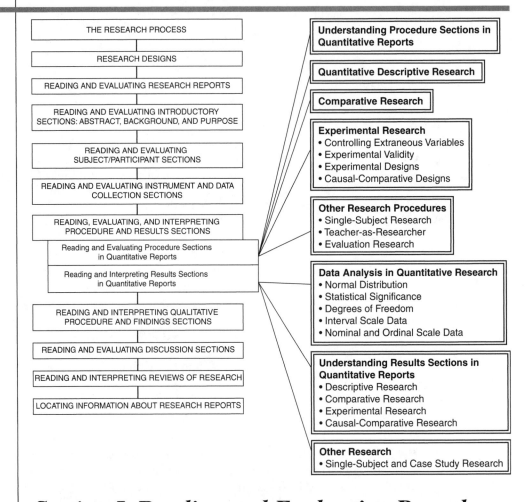

THE RESEARCH PROCESS

RESEARCH DESIGNS

READING AND EVALUATING RESEARCH REPORTS

READING AND EVALUATING INTRODUCTORY SECTIONS: ABSTRACT, BACKGROUND, AND PURPOSE

READING AND EVALUATING SUBJECT/PARTICIPANT SECTIONS

READING AND EVALUATING INSTRUMENT AND DATA COLLECTION SECTIONS

READING, EVALUATING, AND INTERPRETING PROCEDURE AND RESULTS SECTIONS

> Reading and Evaluating Procedure Sections in Quantitative Reports

> Reading and Interpreting Results Sections in Quantitative Reports

READING AND INTERPRETING QUALITATIVE PROCEDURE AND FINDINGS SECTIONS

READING AND EVALUATING DISCUSSION SECTIONS

READING AND INTERPRETING REVIEWS OF RESEARCH

LOCATING INFORMATION ABOUT RESEARCH REPORTS

Understanding Procedure Sections in Quantitative Reports

Quantitative Descriptive Research

Comparative Research

Experimental Research
- Controlling Extraneous Variables
- Experimental Validity
- Experimental Designs
- Causal-Comparative Designs

Other Research Procedures
- Single-Subject Research
- Teacher-as-Researcher
- Evaluation Research

Data Analysis in Quantitative Research
- Normal Distribution
- Statistical Significance
- Degrees of Freedom
- Interval Scale Data
- Nominal and Ordinal Scale Data

Understanding Results Sections in Quantitative Reports
- Descriptive Research
- Comparative Research
- Experimental Research
- Causal-Comparative Research

Other Research
- Single-Subject and Case Study Research

Section I: Reading and Evaluating Procedure Sections in Quantitative Reports

FOCUS QUESTIONS

1. What concerns should research consumers have about research procedures that are common to all research designs?
2. What concerns should research consumers have about research procedures that are specific to quantitative descriptive research designs?

3. What concerns should research consumers have about research procedures that are specific to quantitative comparative research designs?
4. What concerns should research consumers have about research procedures that are specific to experimental research designs?
5. How are extraneous variables controlled in experimental research?
6. What distinguishes simple and complex experimental research designs?
7. What concerns should research consumers have about research procedures that are specific to causal-comparative research designs?
8. What concerns should research consumers have about research procedures that are specific to single-subject, action, and evaluation research designs?
9. What questions should be used to evaluate procedure sections?

In procedure sections, researchers explain the specific way they conducted their research. In quantitative research reports, procedure sections are subsections of method sections. In qualitative research reports, procedures information is often provided in data analysis sections. Regardless of the type of research, if the researchers detail their procedures completely, other researchers can replicate the study. From a clear explanation of research procedures, research consumers can evaluate whether the study is free from bias and the influence of extraneous (or unaccounted for) variables. Research consumers need to understand how different types of research designs are implemented as studies (see chapter 2), what information should be included in procedure sections for the different types of research, and what questions are used for determining whether procedure sections are complete.

UNDERSTANDING PROCEDURE SECTIONS IN QUANTITATIVE REPORTS

Besides understanding principles of subject selection (chapter 5) and instrumentation (chapter 6), research consumers need to understand the steps taken by research producers to collect data, devise special materials, and carry out the specific aspects of the research. Although there are unique procedures for some types of research, several procedures are common to all types of educational research, both quantitative and qualitative.

First, research reports should have clear and complete explanations about every step of the research, so that other researchers can undertake similar studies. In all types of studies, there should be clear explanations about the settings from which data or information are collected, or in which other aspects of the study were undertaken. Research producers should indicate not only what was done but also where and when data collection or other procedures were carried out. Research consumers will recognize vague procedure sections when there is inadequate information for answering the previous questions.

Another procedure deals with the use of instructional materials. Researchers often study how subjects react to specific materials such as textbooks, stories, maps, graphs, and charts. These items may be commercially produced or specially devised by researchers for the study. Research consumers need to be able to judge the appropriateness of the materials for the research situation and for use with the target population. Therefore, researchers should provide citations of published materials and samples of unpublished, specially devised materials.

A third common procedure deals with trying out the research procedures in a pilot study. A **pilot study** is a limited research project with a few subjects, that follows the original research plan in every respect. By analyzing the results, research producers can identify potential problems. For example, in quantitative descriptive, comparative, and experimental studies, researchers can see whether the data collection instruments (questionnaires, interviews, or observations) pose any problems to the researchers or subjects. Researchers also have the opportunity to examine the need for modifying specially devised materials. Researchers should indicate that pilot studies were conducted. They need to include information about modifications to instruments, materials, procedures, and treatments that came from analyses of the pilot study results.

From reading a quantitative procedure section, research consumers should be able to answer the following:

What research design was used in the study?

What special procedures were used to collect data or conduct treatments?

What special materials were used?

Was the research free from researcher bias?

Can the study be replicated from the given information?

Procedure sections in quantitative research reports should be evaluated using the following questions, which are from Figure 3.1 on page 86.

Design and Procedure in Quantitative Research
- Are the research design and data collection procedures clearly described?
- Is the research design appropriate to the researchers' purpose?
- Can the study be replicated from the information provided?
- In experimental designs, are treatments fully explained?
- Are examples of special materials included?

QUANTITATIVE DESCRIPTIVE RESEARCH

Quantitative descriptive research designs statistically explain the status or condition of one or more variables or events. Consumers should be concerned that the information is valid, objective, and reliable, and that variables or events are portrayed accurately.

In observational research, researchers need to be concerned about factors that might affect the replicability of their studies (LeCompte & Goetz, 1982). They need to be sure that the data represent a true picture of what occurred and can be generalized to other situations. This replicability refers to the validity of the research. Researchers also need to be sure that they are consistent in identifying aspects of a behavior or event, so that others working in the same or similar situations could get similar results. This aspect pertains to the reliability of the research.

Several questions can help research consumers determine whether the results from quantitative observational studies are valid.

1. Could the researchers actually have seen what they reported observing?
2. Do the researchers' instruments limit or bias the type and extent of data that are collected?
3. Were the data collection instruments used unobtrusively?
4. Are their conclusions applicable to other situations and groups?

5. Could the observers' presence possibly have influenced the collected data (for example, influenced the way subjects responded or events occurred)?
6. Could the observers have collected only unique or exotic information (data not representative of usual responses or events)?
7. *Was there a major change in the make up of the group being observed during the research period?*
8. What status did the researchers seem to have in the group being studied?
9. Did the researchers seem to select informed subjects from whom to obtain information?
10. Were multiple observers used, and was interrater reliability established?

Purpose
Subjects

The following partial abstract is from a quantitative descriptive study. Note that the researchers are only interested in finding out about the students' perceptions. (In chapter 7, section II, we present the results, or findings, for each of the studies abstracted in this section.)

Instrument:
Name
Field Testing
Criteria for
Coding
Interrater
Reliability

The study (Vaughn, Schumm, Klingner, & Saumell, 1995) was conducted through individualized interviews with a stratified sample of LD and non-LD middle- and high-school students to better understand their perceptions of teachers' adaptations to meet the special learning needs of students in general education classrooms using the *Students' Perceptions of Textbook Adaptations Interview* (SPTAI), an adaptation of two previously developed and evaluated instruments. After field testing, the instrument was individually administered by trained interviewers. Interviews were tape-recorded. After establishing codes for the interview data and establishing interrater reliability in coding, the transcribed responses to all the questions were coded.

COMPARATIVE RESEARCH

In quantitative comparative research, researchers examine the descriptions of two or more variables so that they can make decisions about the differences or relationships. Research consumers should use the questions listed for procedures in descriptive research to determine whether the results from comparative research are valid and reliable.

The following abbreviated methods section is from a quantitative study comparing teachers' anxiety levels to their computer network use.

Research question.   Are educators' anxiety levels or demographics related to their voluntary use of networked resources?

Subjects.   The participants in this study were drawn from a group of approximately 8,000 educators on Tenet (Texas Educational Network), who had previously agreed, while updating account information online, to consider participation in future network-related research. A simple random sample of 300 network users was chosen from system records to form the mailing list of educators who received paper-based surveys by surface mail.

Variables
Compared

Methods.   The study investigated statistical correlations between subject attribute and network use variables. Subject attribute variables consisted of three apprehension or anxiety measures and three measures of experience. Various subgroup analyses were also completed using nominal level demographic information—such as gender, professional specialty, and teaching level—to investigate any relevant patterns related to network use.

Instruments

Writing apprehension was measured using the Daly-Miller Writing Apprehension Scale. The scale consists of 26 statements that reflect apprehension toward the writing process and asks respondents to mark their level of agreement with each statement on a five–point Likert scale.

Oral communication apprehension was measured using the *Personal Report of Communication Apprehension*, which consists of 23 statements related to a person's oral communication apprehension, such as "I'm afraid to speak up in conversations." Respondents indicate their level of agreement or disagreement on a five-point Likert scale.

Computer anxiety was measured using the *Computer Opinion Survey*. Respondents indicate on a six-point Likert scale their level of agreement or disagreement with 26 statements that reflect their personal levels of anxiety about the use of computers.

Source: Harris & Grandgenett, 1996. Reprinted with permission from the *Journal of Research on Computing in Education*, vol. 25, no. 3, copyright © 1993, ISTE (International Society for Technology in Education), 800.336.5191 (U.S. & Canada) or 541.302.3777 (International), iste@iste.org, www.iste.org. All rights reserved.

EXPERIMENTAL RESEARCH

In experimental research, researchers set out to answer questions about causation (Gall, Gall, & Borg, 1999; Gay & Airasian, 2000; Kerlinger, 1973). They wish to attribute any change in one variable to the effect or influence of one or more other variables. The influencing variable—the one that researchers expect to cause change in subjects' responses—is called the **independent variable.** The variable researchers try to change is called the **dependent variable.** Research consumers should be concerned about whether variables other than the independent variables influenced the observed changes in the dependent variable. To evaluate a study's results, consumers need to understand

1. How quantitative researchers control possible influences of variables other than those under systematic study
2. How research producers design quantitative studies to ensure the validity of the results

Controlling Extraneous Variables

Variables that might have an unwanted influence on dependent variables (or might change them) are called **extraneous variables.** Researchers can restrict the influence of extraneous variables by controlling *subject* variables and *situational* variables. Subject variables are variables on which humans are naturally different and that might influence their responses in regard to the dependent variable. Situational variables are variables related to the experimental condition (variables outside the subjects) that might cause changes in their responses relating to the dependent variable.

For example, let's consider a study investigating how the learning of syntactic context clues affects students' vocabulary acquisition in science. Variables that might influence the results are students' general learning ability (IQ), their reading abilities, and their prior knowledge of the science topic. In this example, researchers can control the possible influence of subject and situational variables by selecting subjects of the same general learning ability and reading ability. The researchers can select a science topic and materials unfamiliar to all subjects. Another way researchers can account for the influence of these variables is by including the variables as independent variables. They can do this (*a*) by selecting students of different general learning and reading abilities and then measuring the difference between (and among) the ability levels, or (*b*) by testing subjects' knowledge of the topic before the treatment and adjusting the after-treatment results to account for the subjects' prior knowledge.

Obviously, researchers can only use as independent variables those variables that (*a*) they are aware of and (*b*) they think might influence the dependent variable. Probably randomization is the best way to control subject variables, because it accounts for all subject variables, even those not known or suspected by the researchers to influence the dependent variable. Chapter 5 contains a detailed explanation and specific examples of randomization.

Other attempts at controlling extraneous subject variables include creating groups that are homogeneous on one or more variables, and the matching of subjects on several variables. These procedures, however, do not ensure that other (and possibly influencing) variables have an equally distributed effect on all groups. When subjects cannot be randomly selected or assigned to groups, researchers can equate them statistically. The procedure, known as **analysis of covariance (ANCOVA),** is used to equate subjects on selected variables when known differences exist. The differences, as measured by pretests, must be related to the dependent variables. (ANCOVA is explained further in chapter 7, section II, "Reading and Interpreting Results Sections.") In the prior example, differences in subjects' previous knowledge of a science topic could be used to adjust posttest outcomes statistically.

Experimental Validity

Extraneous variables can invalidate the results of experimental studies in two ways (Campbell & Stanley, 1971; Gay & Airasian, 2000). The first way occurs when researchers and consumers cannot attribute their results exclusively to the independent variable(s). The second source of invalidity occurs when the results cannot be used with other subjects and in other educational settings.

When researchers lack assurance that changes to dependent variables can be attributed to independent variables, then we say that the research lacks **internal validity.** Several factors can affect the internal validity of research. These factors include the following:

- *Current Events.* Current events include any historical occurrence during the experimental period. For example, a joint U.S. and Russian spacelab project, during a study about changing students' attitudes toward science careers, might influence the study's outcome. Research consumers may not be aware of the coincidence of such an event during the study, but research producers should strive for awareness, and they should report it.
- *Subject Growth and Development.* Subject growth and development includes the physical, emotional, and cognitive maturational changes occurring in subjects and the periodic fluctuations that occur in human responses because of fatigue, boredom, hunger, illness, or excitement. For example, in a study about the influence of daily periods of silent reading on subjects' overall reading performance, changes in reading performance might occur because the subjects matured even without the special reading periods.
- *Subject Selection.* Subject selection refers to the influence that improper or biased subject selection has on results. This phenomenon was discussed previously and in chapter 5.
- *Attrition.* Attrition is the loss of subjects during experimental research. The reason for subject loss may be important and may unduly influence the results. For example, consider a study about the effects on subjects with differing ethnic backgrounds of using calculators for learning of arithmetic number concepts. A major

loss of subjects from any group might influence the results. A loss, say, from an ethnic group with a school dropout rate known to be high may result in a small sample with low achievement scores. That result could cause an erroneous conclusion that individuals from that group do not benefit from using calculators. When attrition occurs, researchers need to determine why the loss occurred.

- *Testing.* In this context, *testing* refers to the possible positive and negative influences of pretests on results. For example, subjects' final test scores might be improved because they learned something from taking a pretest. Or, an initial interview might give subjects an inkling about what researchers are studying, thereby influencing their performance on subsequent tasks.
- *Instrumentation.* In this context, *instrumentation* refers to the influence of unreliable instruments on results. This phenomenon is discussed extensively in chapter 6.
- *Statistical Regression.* Statistical regression refers to the tendency of extreme high and low standardized test scores to regress (or move) toward the group mean. That is, very high and very low subjects' scores on pretests seem to come closer to middle scores on posttests—higher scores become lower and lower scores become higher. Research consumers need to understand that this phenomenon may occur "when, in fact, no real change has taken place in the dependent variable" (Kerlinger, 1973, p. 320).
- *Interaction.* Interaction refers to the effect of several factors on each other. For example, attrition might result because of testing (subjects become threatened by the information they are asked on a pretest), or current events may influence certain subjects because of selection bias (subjects have an advantage because they experienced some event).

When researchers lack assurance that results can be generalized to other persons and other educational settings, we say the research lacks **external validity.** Several factors can affect the external validity of research. These factors include the following:

- *Subject-Treatment Interaction.* Subject-treatment interaction occurs when subjects do not represent a target population, and selection procedures produce a sample that is either positively or negatively biased toward a treatment. For example, when researchers use paid subjects, these individuals may undertake the activities solely for the money involved. Volunteer subjects, on the other hand, may have certain personal characteristics (which influence them to be volunteers) that are not present in the target population.
- *Reactive Effects.* Reactive effects refer to special situations that make subjects in a treatment group feel special. One reactive effect occurs when they know they are part of an experiment, or they sense that something special is happening to them. This phenomenon is called the *Hawthorne effect.* Another reactive effect occurs when subjects in a comparison or control group know or sense they are in competition with the treatment group, and they produce results above their normal behavior. This phenomenon is called the *John Henry effect,* after the legendary railroad builder.
- *Multiple-Treatment Interaction.* This phenomenon might occur when researchers include more than one treatment in a study. For example, in a study to determine which study skills program might be more effective, subjects are given three content-area study strategies: the SQRRR, ReQuest, and Overview methods. If each subject receives instruction about all three, the learning of one might help or hinder the learning of the others. In this

case, the order in which subjects learned the strategies might influence the results.

- *Researcher Effects.* Research (or experimenter) effects refer to the influences imposed on treatments by researchers themselves. For example, when researchers use an experimental instructional program that they developed, they may exert undue (although not conscious) influence on the subjects to use the program successfully. Also, instructional techniques may be complex, and only those with the researchers' knowledge and dedication could effectively implement them.

Research producers cannot control for the effect of all possible extraneous variables. If they were to do this, much research would be difficult to undertake, if not impossible. So researchers do two things. They limit or manipulate pertinent factors affecting their studies' validity, and they identify as possible influences other factors that were not controllable or could not be manipulated. Research consumers need to judge whether researchers have missed or underestimated factors that might affect research validity. To make this judgment, consumers need to understand the experimental designs that researchers use to reduce possible effects of extraneous variables.

Experimental Designs

Experimental designs are the blueprints that researchers use in making decisions about the causative effect of one or more variables on other variables. The plans provide researchers with structures for studying one or more independent variables with one or more groups of subjects. Researchers select designs that best fit their purposes, answer questions about causation, and efficiently control extraneous variables.

In studying educational and psychological research, some authorities divide experimental designs into several groups, such as "true experimental," "quasi-experimental," "preexperimental," and "action" research (Campbell & Stanley, 1971; Gall, Gall, & Borg, 1999; Gay & Airasian, 2003; Wiersma, 1995). The criterion for inclusion, or exclusion, from a group is the strictness with which a design controls for the effect of extraneous variables. The continuum goes from "true experimental," representing the strictest control; to "action," representing the least strict control. Other authorities consider all designs used to answer questions of causation as experimental (Kamil, Langer, & Shanahan, 1985). These researchers do not identify designs by the previously discussed criteria but by other factors. The factors are (*a*) the number of independent or treatment variables and (*b*) the extent to which results can be generalized from the immediate subjects to a larger target population.

In our discussion, experimental designs are presented as a continuum from simple to complex plans. Simple experimental plans deal with a single independent variable, and complex experimental plans deal with multiple independent variables. In reading and evaluating both sets of plans, research consumers are concerned with the question "How generalizable are the results from the research subjects to other individuals and groups?"

Simple experimental designs deal with one independent variable or have subject selection procedures that limit the generalizability of their results. In chapter 2, single-variable studies were shown to provide limited insight about educational questions. In chapter 5, subject selection techniques that produced samples unrepresentative of target populations were discussed. Simple designs are presented here so that research consumers can recognize them and understand their limitations.

Randomized group 1 (experimental group)		
Pretest	Treatment	Posttest

Randomized group 2 (control or comparison groups)		
Pretest	Alternate treatment(s)	Posttest

Randomized group *n* (other control or comparison groups)		
Pretest	Alternate treatment(s)	Posttest

Figure 7.1
Pretest-Posttest Control Group Design

In some simple experimental designs, two or more groups of subjects are studied with a single independent variable. Subjects are randomly selected and randomly assigned to a group, but each group differs in the experimental condition. An experimental condition refers to how the independent variable is manipulated, varied, or subcategorized. When treatments are involved, one or more groups are randomly designated as **treatments** or **experimental groups** and the other(s) as **control** (or comparison) **group(s).** In educational and psychological research, a control group is one that has received alternative activities, not the one(s) under study. All groups are given the same pretest and posttest (survey, observation, or test). This simple experimental design is called the **pretest-posttest control group design,** diagrammed in Figure 7.1.

The following excerpt is from the method section of a pretest-posttest control group design that has a single independent variable. The independent variable is an instructional method, so it is called the *experimental condition.* Note that there are three dependent variables; but the researchers are trying to determine whether the change in each is attributable to the single *independent* variable.

Purpose of the study: To assess the effects of learning strategy instruction on the completion by learning-disabled students of job applications.

SUBJECTS

Thirty-three students (20 boys and 13 girls) with LD served as participants in the study. All were receiving special education services in a public high school in a city in the Northwest.

DEPENDENT MEASURES

Dependent Variables

Student Performance

Three measures were employed to assess the effects of the learning strategy instruction on the completion of job applications by students: information omissions, information location errors, and a holistic rating of overall neatness of the job application.

Independent Variable

Design

A pretest-posttest control group design was employed. Students were randomly assigned by age and gender to one of two experimental conditions: learning strategy instruction or traditional instruction. This resulted in 16 students (10 boys and 6 girls) being assigned under the learning strategy instruction condition and 17 students (10 boys and 7 girls) under the traditional instruction condition. The results of a preliminary analysis revealed that there were statistically nonsignificant differences in characteristics (i.e., intelligence, achievement, age, years in special education, and percentage of each school day spent in special education) between the two groups.

Source: From "The Effects of Learning Strategy Instruction on the Completion of Job Applications by Students with Learning Disabilities" by J. R. Nelson, D. J. Smith, and J. M. Dodd, 1994, *Journal of Learning Disabilities, 27*(2), pp. 104–110, 122. Copyright 1994 by PRO-ED, Inc. Reprinted by permission.

There are some other less-used, simple experimental designs. One is the **posttest-only control group design,** in which the experimental and control groups are not pretested. An example of this design is an instance in which researchers have two or more randomized groups engaged in alternative activities, but they do not give a pretest. The groups are assumed to be similar because of randomization; but the differences in group results are determined only by the posttest. This procedure's weakness is that there is no assurance that the groups were equal at the start on the dependent measure (such as a reading test). Also, researchers cannot account for the effect of any subject attrition in each group.

A second simple design is the **nonequivalent control group design.** In it, the groups are not randomly selected or assigned, and no effort is made to equate them statistically. Obviously, when comparison groups are known to be unequal, the research results can occur from many possible causes.

A third simple design is the **matched groups design.** In it, the experimental and control subjects are selected or assigned to groups on the basis of a single-subject variable, such as reading ability, grade level, ethnicity, or special disabling condition. A major limitation of this design is the possibility that one or more variables, unknown to and unaccounted for by the researchers, might influence the dependent variable.

For all simple experimental designs, extraneous variables affect the internal and external validity of the research. Research consumers should be wary of generalizing the results of simple design research to other educational settings and populations.

More complex experimental designs deal with multiple experimental and subject variables. Some complex designs are built on the pretest-posttest control group design and are expansions of it. In these complex designs, researchers not only study the effect of one variable on one or more other variables, but also they study the interaction of these variables on the dependent variable. Previously, subject-treatment interaction and multiple-treatment interaction were noted as threats to research validity. Nevertheless, researchers can use complex designs to account for the effect of these interactions.

Not all complex designs use random selection or assignment of subjects. When randomization is not used, statistical procedures are employed to account for the possible influence of the differences between and among subjects. Chapter 7, section II contains a discussion of these statistical procedures.

Two important threats to research validity are subject growth and development and testing. These threats can be accounted for in a design called the **Solomon four-group design.** Using random selection and random assignment, four groups are formed. All four groups are posttested. However, only two groups are pretested. One pretested group and one nonpretested group are then given the experimental condition.

The Solomon four-group experimental design is diagrammed in Figure 7.2. In addition to the effect of the experimental variable, the possible effects of pretesting can be measured by comparing the posttest results of groups 1 and 3, to groups 2 and 4. If the pretest had an effect, the results of groups 1 and 2 would be higher respectively than those of groups 3 and 4. The possible effect of subjects' growth and

Randomized group 1 Pretest	Experimental condition	Posttest
Randomized group 2 Pretest	Alternate condition	Posttest
Randomized group 3	Experimental condition	Posttest
Randomized group 4	Alternate condition	Posttest

Figure 7.2
Solomon Four-Group Experimental Design

development and current events has been controlled because both would have an equal effect on all groups.

The Solomon four-group experimental design is not often used in educational and psychological research, however, because of several limitations. The first limitation is that a large number of subjects is required. In a study employing one independent variable with no factors, approximately 100 subjects (four groups of 25 subjects) would be needed. Each additional independent variable requires another 100 subjects. Therefore, researchers often use other experimental designs to control for the effect of pretesting and subjects' growth and development.

Another complex design built on the pretest-posttest control group design is called the **counterbalanced design.** In counterbalanced designs, two or more groups get the same treatments; however, the order of the treatments for each group is different and is usually randomly determined. For this type of design to work, the number of treatments and groups must match. Although the groups may be randomly selected and assigned, researchers often use this design with already existing groups of subjects—for example, when researchers use all classes in a grade level. A major problem with this design is the possibility of multiple-treatment interaction. Research consumers need to determine that the individual treatments are unique, and that one treatment could not directly increase or decrease the effectiveness of another. Figure 7.3 shows a counterbalanced design for a three-treatment, three-group design.

Educational and psychological researchers are often concerned about questions involving multiple variables. Although the Solomon four-group design accounts for the possible influence of some extraneous variables, its use does not allow researchers to easily study two or more independent variables. In the sample diagram in Figure 7.2, one independent variable is used with two subcategories: experimental condition and alternate condition. This variable could represent an experimental science program versus the previously used science program. Many questions are left unanswered in this design type. For example, "Does the experimental science program or the existing program produce greater learning with girls? With students with learning disabilities? Does the experimental science program lead to greater learning after shorter periods of instruction?" These are questions of interaction. Questions about the interaction of human variables and instructional and environmental situations are important to educators. Teaching and learning involve the interplay of many variables, and variables do not occur in isolation. Rarely does one educational treatment work equally well with all students.

Group 1	Group 2 (randomized or unrandomized)	Group 3
	Pretest (all groups)	
Treatment C	Treatment B	Treatment A
	Interim Test 1 (all groups)	
Treatment B	Treatment A	Treatment C
	Interim Test 2 (all groups)	
Treatment A	Treatment C	Treatment B
	Posttest (all groups)	

Figure 7.3
Counterbalanced Experiment Design

Questions of interaction are examined in complex experimental designs called **factorial designs,** in which there are multiple variables and each variable is subcategorized into two or more levels, or factors. The simplest factorial design involves two independent variables, each of which has two factors. This is called a 2×2 factorial design. Factorial designs can have any combination of variables and factors. The practical consideration for research producers is having an adequate number of subjects in each subdivision. Generally, 15 subjects per group is considered the minimum, although group size in factorial designs can be as small as 5 subjects.

Figure 7.4 shows three common factorial designs. Notice how the number of groups increases as independent variables and factors increase. Although multivariable designs can provide educators with valuable insights about teaching and learning, research consumers should be wary of research studies containing what seem to be unnecessary factors. When there are too many possible interactions (because there are many groups), the meaning of the interactions could become confusing. Research consumers need to consider whether the number of variables and factors is appropriate. As a general rule, factorial designs in experimental research larger than $2 \times 2 \times 2$ become unwieldy.

Causal-Comparative Designs

Causal-comparative experimental research is ex post facto, or after-the-fact. Researchers use it in trying to establish one or more causal effects between or among existing conditions. The researchers want answers to questions but they cannot manipulate the independent variable(s) for practical or ethical reasons. They realize a condition exists and are unsure about what might have been its cause. Causal-comparative designs are built on the posttest-only control group design.

A major concern for researchers doing causal-comparative research is that the causal effect should be one-way. The distinguishing variables must precede and be the cause of the differences. For example, chapter 2 presents a representative causal-comparative study about the effect of Black students' figurative language on their school language. The existence of out-of-school language experiences preceded their school language experiences; thus, the causal effect can be only one-way.

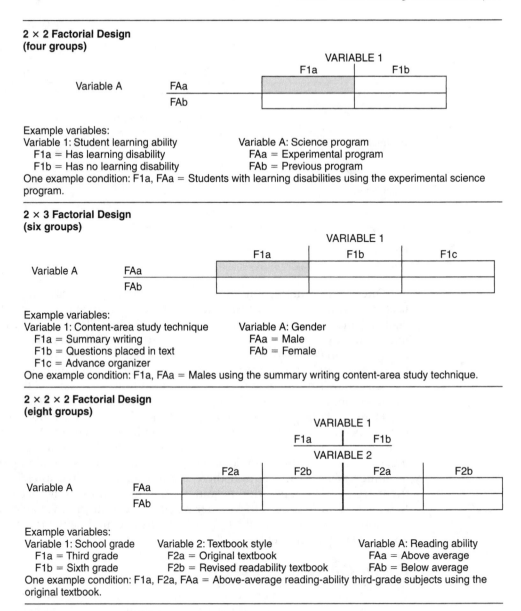

Figure 7.4
Common Factorial Designs

In using the causal-comparative design, researchers can randomly select subjects from target populations that differ in respect to one or more variables. Because there are no manipulated, or treated, independent variables, the subjects cannot be randomly assigned to groups. The subjects should be similar except for the variables being studied. For example, selection procedures can ensure that subjects are similar in such characteristics as age, socioeconomic status, or intellectual ability, so long as these are not variables that might cause the difference between groups. If it is not possible to select comparable groups, the differences between them can be equated statistically.

> The study in the research report "Effects of Classroom Structure on Student Achieve-
> ment Goal Orientation," on pp. 19–26, is an example of a 2 × 3 factorial analysis design.
> (Refer to Figure 7.4 for a graphic representation of this research design.) At [10] in that
> study, "Design," the independent and dependent variables are identified. There are three
> levels of the independent variable, *classroom structure*, and two levels of the depend-
> ent variable, *goal type*. The section "Procedure," at [11], [12], [13], and [14], explains
> how the three types of treatment were conducted in the two types of classrooms.

For research consumers to generalize the results from causal-comparative
studies to other populations and educational situations, they need to be sure that
any differences between groups cannot be attributed to one or more important
variables that were not accounted for by the researchers. There is always the possibility that these outside variables may be the true causes of the observed differences. Also, research consumers should be sure that researchers' description of the
subjects is clear, and that operational definitions are used to identify and distinguish the comparison groups. Therefore, research consumers should cautiously interpret the results of causal-comparative research; and whenever feasible, they
should expect researchers to follow up tentative results with additional experimental research.

The following partial abstract of a research report contains an example of a
causal-comparative design. The researchers sought to determine the effect of a preexisting condition (the independent variable) on how children learned, in what was
supposed to be a typical homework assignment. It should be remembered that researchers using the causal-comparative design are trying to find causal relationships
or predictions about already existing conditions. There is one independent variable
and three dependent variables.

Purpose

Independent Variable

The purpose of the study was to examine the teaching strategies used by mothers of
sons with learning disabilities and normally achieving sons. The subjects, with normal
IQ's ranging in age from 8–11 years in two groups matched for socioeconomic status,
were 30 boys, with learning disabilities (LD as defined by the National Joint Committee on Learning Disabilities and confirmed by a series of standardized tests), 30 boys
without any reported learning problems (NLD), and their mothers drawn from schools
in the province of Central Finland; all spoke Finnish as their native language. The interactions of the mother-child dyads were videotaped in a laboratory setting while the
dyads worked on four structured, interactive tasks. The mother was asked to teach her
son a set of five Finnish pseudowords and the meanings that were attached to them.
The pseudowords were phonologically acceptable letter strings in Finnish, and were
easily pronounced. The mother was requested to take the teacher's role, and she was
encouraged to do her best in assisting her son in memorizing the new words. The experimenter reminded the pair of the similarity of the situation to times when the child
is at home, learning words of a foreign language as homework. Two coders who were
blind with respect to the child's group status (LD/NLD) were trained to code the data
of the maternal strategies during the teaching session in ten categories which represented two main categories for different levels of distancing strategies. A distinction
was made between perceptually based strategies, which relied on information from the
ongoing present, and nonperceptually based, or conceptual, strategies, which evoked

Dependent Variables One and Two

Dependent Variable Three

mental representations of the words to be learned. The coding consisted of recording the time that the mother used in each of the teaching strategy classes specified above. Percentages were formed by proportioning these times with the total duration of the task. A measure of the child's performance on the task was reached by summing the number of the words he learned correctly. The quality of each mother-child interaction was rated on a Likert-type (5-point) scale. Interobserver reliability was assessed on 25% of the data by having two assistants independently code the same randomly selected cases.

Source: From Lyytinen, P., Rasku-Puttonen, H., Poikkeus, A. M., Laakso, A. L., & Ahonen, T. (1994). Mother-child teaching strategies and learning disabilities, *Journal of Learning Disabilities* 27: 186–192.

OTHER RESEARCH PROCEDURES

Single-subject research, action research, and evaluation research are other ways researchers describe, compare, and draw causative conclusions about educational problems and questions.

Single-Subject Research

Single-subject research is any research in which there is only one subject or one group that is treated as a single entity (e.g., when an entire school is studied without regard to individual students' performances). Single-subject research may be descriptive or experimental. A case study is a form of single-subject research. Case studies are undertaken on the premise that someone who is typical of a target population can be located and studied. In case studies, the individual's (*a*) history within an educational setting can be traced, (*b*) growth pattern(s) over time can be shown, (*c*) functioning in one or more situations can be examined, and (*d*) response(s) to one or more treatments can be measured.

Many insights gained from single-subject and case study research have greatly influenced educational and psychological practice. Classic examples of single-subject and case study research that have produced significant hypotheses are those of Jean Piaget and Sigmund Freud. Case study research often follows qualitative research procedures, and it can often be combined with single-subject research (Bisesi & Raphael, 1995). Single-subject experimental designs are variations of pretest-posttest counterbalanced designs. The basic aim of single-subject experimental research is to "establish the effects of an intervention (i.e., an independent variable) on a single individual" (McCormick, 1995, p. 1). Figure 7.5 shows three forms of single-subject experimental designs. In single-subject research, the pretest is called a *baseline measure* and can sometimes take the form of several measurements. Also, each posttest can consist of several measurements, because they become the baseline for subsequent treatments. Baselines are the results to which posttest results are compared to determine the effect of each treatment.

Because of the unique relationship that can develop between researcher and subject, and because of the possible effect of multiple testing and treatment, single-subject research can have its external and internal validity threatened in several ways. Single-subject research and case study research should have clear, precise descriptions of the subject. This factor is most important. The results of research with a single subject are not directly generalizable to a target population without replica-

Pretest-Posttest Two-Treatment
 A–B Design
  Pretest
   Treatment A
    Posttest 1
     Treatment B
      Posttest 2

Pretest-Posttest Counterbalanced Two-Treatment
 A–B–A Design
  Pretest
   Treatment A
    Posttest 1
     Treatment B
      Posttest 2
       Treatment A
        Posttest 3

A–B–A–B Design
 Pretest
  Treatment A
   Posttest 1
    Treatment B
     Posttest 2
      Treatment A
       Posttest 3
        Treatment B
         Posttest 4

Figure 7.5
Single-Subject Experimental Designs

tions with other individuals, or without follow-up descriptive, comparative, or experimental research with larger samples. The threats to the internal validity of single-subject research include testing, instrumentation, subject-treatment interaction, reactive effects, and research effects. Research consumers should anticipate that research producers will follow the same guidelines as would be used for conducting descriptive and experimental research.

The following method section is from research with a single subject in a pretest-posttest, two-treatment design (referred to as an A-B design in Figure 7.5). The subsections have clarifying headings.

Purpose of the study: To determine the effects of a peer-tutoring procedure on the spelling behavior of a mainstreamed elementary-school student with a learning disability.

METHOD

Subjects and Setting

[A]n 11-year-old learning disabled male student in a regular grade six classroom in a large urban school with a demonstrated four-year deficiency in at least two academic areas. The tutor was an 11 year old male student from the same classroom as the above-mentioned subject who excelled in all academic areas. The classroom was self-contained with 27 students and one certified teacher.

Response Definition

[T]wo dependent variables were employed in the study.

Percent Correct.   Data were collected from biweekly spelling tests. . . . A response was defined as correct if it matched the spelling in the word list. The percent correct was calculated by dividing the number of correct responses by the total number of possible words for each test.

Clinical Significance.   [The] subject . . . [wrote] . . . self-reports . . . [in which they indicated] whether they liked the program, worked harder in it, and/or performed better than in the regular classroom lesson. In addition, the subject rated how well [he] felt . . . [he was] learning by marking two pluses (11) for very good, one plus (1) for satisfactory (same as in the regular class), and one minus (2) for unsatisfactory. . . .

Design Elements and Experimental Conditions

An AB design was employed to examine the effects of peer tutoring (Hersen & Barlow, 1976). A description of the experimental condition follows. . . . (etc.)

Source: From Mandoli, M., Mandoli, P., & McLaughlin, T. F. (1982). Effects of same-age peer tutoring on the spelling performance of a mainstreamed elementary LD student. *Learning Disability Quarterly, 5,* 185–189. Reprinted with permission of the publisher.

Teacher-as-Researcher

Teachers doing research in their classroom or school can use both quantitative and qualitative research methods and either single-subject or case study research (see "Teachers as Researchers" in chapter 1). The results and implications of this type of research are not usually generalized beyond the study's specific subjects/participants and educational setting. It is the type of research that exemplifies the work done by teachers in conjunction with other researchers, for example, university or college professors. Teacher-as-researcher projects seek answers or solutions to specific questions or problems related to their teaching or school programs. The goal is to create immediate change.

For quantitative method studies, teachers-as-researchers use the same general plans and procedures as used in more controlled research. However, there are differences in how they select and assign subjects. Also, they do not apply strict procedures to control for the possible influence of extraneous variables. They do complete many steps; they identify a problem area and seek out what others have done, create operational definitions, select appropriate instruments, identify possible influencing variables and factors, select appropriate designs for collecting data, and analyze data either qualitatively or quantitatively. Most often, teachers-as-researchers use convenience samples. Because students are usually assigned to classes before the research begins, random selection and assignment are not possible. Experimental teacher-as-researcher studies are usually done with a simple design, such as a pretest-posttest control group(s) design with one or two independent and dependent variables. If the groups are known to differ on important variables, the groups can be equated statistically.

Evaluation Research

Educational evaluation research has developed to a great extent because of federal and state mandates to assess the impact (influence) of funded compensatory programs for students who are educationally disadvantaged, have limited English proficiency, or have special educational needs. Educational evaluation is the systematic study of existing curriculums and instructional programs (treatments). Evaluation researchers wish to know whether a particular instructional program or teaching technique results in improved student performance or achievement. Researchers can use both quantitative and qualitative research methods.

Evaluation research differs from other research in several ways:

- In the level of complexity of the research design
- In the degree to which the possible effects of extraneous variables are controlled
- In the extent to which the results can be generalized to other educational settings

Research consumers can use the following questions to help them judge the appropriateness of the evaluation researchers' statement of the problem, identification of subjects, selection of instruments, collection of data, and analysis of data. Standards for educational evaluation have been established by educational researchers and by a consortium of educational associations, including the American Educational Research Association and the American Evaluation Association (Bogdan & Biklen, 1998; Charles, 1995; Sanders & the Joint Committee on Standards for Educational Evaluation, 1994; see Appendix B). The standards are grouped as (*a*) utility standards, in which an evaluation serves the information needs of intended users; (*b*) feasibility standards, in which an evaluation is realistic, prudent, diplomatic, and frugal; (*c*) propriety standards, in which an evaluation is conducted legally, ethically, and with due regard for the welfare of those involved in the evaluation, as well as those affected by its results; and (*d*) accuracy standards, in which an evaluation reveals and conveys technically adequate information about the features that determine worth or merit of the program being evaluated. The following program evaluation questions are based on these standards.

- In evaluation research using quantitative methods, could the research be useful to the school or agency conducting the study, in that its results answer a clearly defined question or problem?
- In evaluation research using qualitative methods, could the research be useful to the school or agency conducting the study, in that its results provide meanings for and understanding about the processes occurring during teaching and learning?
- In both quantitative and qualitative designs, was the evaluation research appropriate to the educational setting, in that it was minimally disruptive to the subjects (administrators, teachers, students, and other school personnel)?
- Were the rights and well-being of the participating administrators, teachers, and students protected? Was information about individuals obtained and stored in such a way that confidentiality was maintained?
- Was the evaluation research report clearly written so that the reliability and validity of the collected data and the internal and external validity of the study could be determined?

ACTIVITIES

Do not read the Feedback section until you have completed each of the activities.

Activity 1

Using the Focus Questions at the beginning of the chapter as a guide, summarize the chapter's key ideas.

Activity 2

Using quantitative studies of your own choosing (or located through the resources in Appendix A), locate one experimental and one other type of quantitative research. You can team with fellow students and do the activity collaboratively. Or, each of you may want to do the activity independently and compare your answers.

Then,

- Identify the researchers' purposes.
- Read the sections containing research procedures for the studies.
- Using the questions and criteria on page 146, evaluate the studies.
- List questions and concerns you may have about the following:
  - The appropriateness of the research design to the researchers' purposes
  - The research design and data collection procedures
  - The replicability of the study
  - For experimental research, the study's internal and external validity

---

FEEDBACK

Activity 1

What concerns should research consumers have about research procedures that are common to all research designs?   All research reports should have clear and complete explanations of every step of the research. All instruments should be valid and reliable, and administered by trained examiners. Research procedures should be tested in pilot studies.

What concerns should research consumers have about research procedures that are specific to quantitative descriptive research designs?   Consumers need to be sure the data represent a true picture of what occurred and can be generalized to other situations. This process refers to the validity of the research results. Researchers also need to be sure that they are consistent in identifying aspects of a behavior or event and that others working in the same or similar situations would get similar results. This process refers to the reliability of the research results.

What concerns should research consumers have about research procedures that are specific to quantitative comparative research designs?   Research consumers should use the questions for procedures in descriptive research to determine whether the results from comparative research are valid and reliable.

What concerns should research consumers have about research procedures that are specific to experimental research designs?   Research consumers should be concerned about whether variables other than the independent variables caused the observed changes in the dependent variable. Variables that might have an unwanted influence on, or might change, dependent variables are called *extraneous variables*. One of the best ways to control subject variables is through randomization. When subjects cannot be randomly selected or assigned to groups, researchers can equate them statistically.

How are extraneous variables controlled in experimental research?   Variables that need to be controlled to maintain the internal validity of experimental research are current events, subject growth and development, subject selection, attrition, testing, instrumentation, statistical regression, and interaction. Variables that need to be controlled to maintain the external validity of experimental research are subject-treatment interaction, reactive effects, multiple-treatment interaction, and research effects.

What distinguishes simple and complex experimental research designs?   Simple and complex experimental research designs are distinguished by (*a*) the number of independent or treatment variables and (*b*) the extent to which results can be generalized from the immediate subjects to a larger target population. Experimental designs are a continuum from simple to complex plans. Simple experimental plans deal with single independent variables, and complex experimental plans deal with multiple independent variables. Simple experimental designs deal with one independent variable or have subject selection procedures that limit the generalizability of their results. More complex experimental designs deal with two or more experimental and subject variables.

What concerns should research consumers have about research procedures that are specific to causal-comparative research designs?   A major concern for researchers doing causal-comparative research is that the causal effects should be one-way. Because there are no manipulated, or treated, independent variables, the subjects cannot be randomly assigned to groups. For research consumers to be able to generalize the results from causal-comparative studies to other populations and educational situations, they need to be sure that any differences between groups cannot be attributed to one or more important variables that were not accounted for by the researchers. There is always the possibility that these outside variables may be the true causes of the observed differences. Also, consumers should be sure that the researchers' description of the subjects is clear, and that operational definitions are used to identify and distinguish the comparison groups.

What concerns should research consumers have about research procedures that are specific to single-subject, action, and evaluation research designs?   Single-subject research is any research in which there is only one subject or one group that is treated as a single entity. Single-subject research may be descriptive or experimental. Action research is directed to studying existing educational practice and to producing practical, immediately applicable findings. The questions or problems studied are local in nature. Evaluation research is applying the rigors of experimental research to the judging of the worth or value of educational programs, projects, and instruction.

Threats to the internal validity of single-subject research include testing, instrumentation, subject-treatment interaction, reactive effects, and researcher effects. Research consumers should expect research producers to adhere to the same guidelines as used for conducting descriptive and experimental research. Research consumers should expect published action research reports to have the same specificity in detail as other research reports. Research consumers can use several questions to help them judge the appropriateness of the evaluation researchers' statement of the problem, identification of subjects, selection of instruments, and collection and analysis of data.

What questions should be used to evaluate procedure sections?   Are the research design and data collection procedures clearly described? Is the research design appropriate to the researchers' purpose? Can the study be replicated from the information provided? To evaluate qualitative experimental research, the question is, "Has the researchers' presence influenced the behavior of the subjects?" In studies with treatments, "Are experimental procedures fully explained? Are examples of special materials included?" To determine research validity, "Are the procedures free from the influence of extraneous variables? Does the study contain any threats to its internal and external validity?"

Activity 2

Compare your answers with those of fellow students and discuss them with your instructor.

Section II: Reading and Interpreting Results Sections in Quantitative Reports

FOCUS QUESTIONS

1. What are the different ways quantitative data are recorded?
2. What is a normal distribution curve?
3. What statistical procedures are used in educational and other behavioral science research?
4. What are statistical significance and effect size?
5. What criteria should be used to read and evaluate results sections?

After collecting data, researchers use several methods to describe, synthesize, analyze, and interpret the information. In contrast, in all types of quantitative research, statistical procedures facilitate understanding of a vast amount of numerical data. These procedures are the techniques by which researchers summarize and explain quantitative data and determine the existence of relationships and causal effects. In qualitative research, the outcomes of research are the generation of hypotheses and research questions, not the verification of predicted relationships or outcomes. Therefore, qualitative researchers use verbal rather than statistical procedures to analyze data. These inductive analytic procedures involve organizing data, identifying patterns, and synthesizing key ideas as research questions and hypotheses.

By reading a quantitative results section, research consumers should be able to understand

- The way researchers match data analysis procedures to research designs
- The different statistical analyses available to educational and other behavioral and social science researchers
- The assumptions researchers make about those analyses to use them effectively
- The concept of statistical significance and the criteria generally used to set the point at which results can be considered reliable
- The assumptions researchers make about qualitative data analyses
- The way to read and interpret results sections in quantitative and qualitative research reports

DATA ANALYSIS IN QUANTITATIVE RESEARCH

Data analyses in quantitative research involve the use of statistics. Statistics are precise numerical ways to describe, analyze, summarize, and interpret data in a manner that conserves time and space. Researchers select statistical procedures after they have determined what research designs and types of data will be appropriate for answering their research questions. For example, in answering descriptive research questions, researchers use statistics to show the data's central tendencies and variability. In answering comparative and experimental research questions, researchers use other statistics to draw inferences and to make generalizations about target populations. In all three types of research, the specific statistical procedures are determined by the research design and by the type of data that are collected. Further, in comparative and experimental research, researchers use statistics to gain two other insights: (*a*) an estimate of the sampling error, the error (or difference) between the research sample and the target population, and (*b*) the confidence with which research producers and consumers can accept the results.

The way quantitative data are recorded depends on the instruments (measuring devices). Data are recorded as (*a*) intervals, (*b*) rankings, (*c*) categories, and (*d*) ratios. Each means of recording data requires the use of different statistics. **Interval scales** present data according to preset, equal spans. They are the most common form of data reporting in education and the social sciences. They are identified by continuous measurement scales: raw scores and derived scores such as IQ scores, standard scores, and normal curve equivalents. They are the way data from most tests are recorded.

Rankings, or **ordinal scales,** show the order, from highest to lowest, for a variable. There are no indications about the value (or size of differences) among items in a list; the indications refer only to the relative order of the scores. For instance, subjects can be ranked according to their performance on a set of athletic tasks. In this case, what will be reported is the order in which they scored (such as first, second, or third), not their actual accumulation of points. Olympic medal winners are reported using ordinal scales. Data from surveys and observations are sometimes recorded in this manner.

Categories separate data into two or more discrete aspects, such as male-female, red-white-blue, or always-frequently-infrequently-never. The data can be reported as numbers of items or as percentages of a total. Data recorded this way are considered **nominal scales.** Data from surveys and observations are sometimes recorded in this way.

Ratio scales, rarely used in educational and other behavioral and social science research, show relative relationships among scores, such as half-as-large or three-times-as-tall. In dealing with educational variables, researchers usually do not use these presentations.

Normal Distribution

Chapter 2 contains an explanation of central tendency and variability. The most common forms of each of these statistics for interval scale data are the mean and the standard deviation. To reiterate, the **mean** is the arithmetical average score, and the **standard deviation (SD** or σ**)** shows how the scores were distributed around the mean. The SD is based on the concept that given a large enough set of scores, the scores will produce a graph in the shape of a bell. This graph is called the **normal distribution curve** and shows a normal distribution of scores. In a normal distribution, the scores, or measures, are distributed symmetrically around the mean. In a normal distribution, the mean, median, and mode are identical.

The normal distribution graph, shown in Figure 7.6, represents a theoretical statistical picture of how most human and nonhuman variables are distributed. Let us use as an example a human variable, such as ability to draw human figures as measured by a test. In this case, the curve would show that few people have scores indicating little of the trait (the extreme left end of the graph); that is, an inability to draw

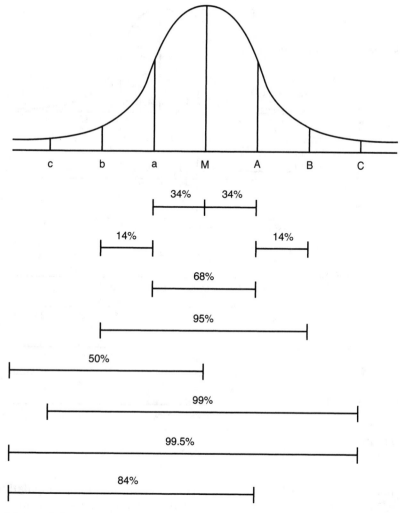

Figure 7.6
The Normal Distribution Curve

human figures. Few people have scores showing a great deal of the trait (the extreme right end of the graph); that is, a great ability to draw human figures. The center of the graph shows that most people have scores indicating some ability to draw human figures. This distribution is commonly called the **norm.**

There is a direct relationship between the SD and the normal distribution curve. Starting at the center, or mean, of the distributed variable, each SD represents a fixed, specific proportion of the population (indicated in Figure 7.6 by the vertical lines). For example, the range between the mean and either extreme end of the graph (left or right) equals 50% of the population represented by the graph. The ranges between the mean and +1 SD (the area M ← → A), and the mean and −1 SD (the area a ← → M) each equal a little more than one-third (34%) of the distributed population. The ranges between +1 SD and +2 SDs (A ← → B), and −1 SD and −2 SDs (b ← → a) each equal about 14% of the population. Therefore, the range of scores included

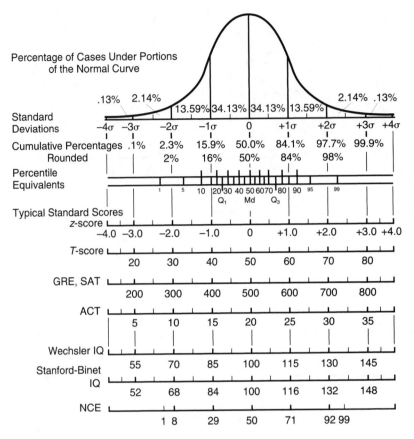

Figure 7.7
Common Derived Scores

between −1 and +1 SD (a ←→ A) equals about 68% of the population; and between −2 and +2 SDs (b ←→ B) equals slightly over 95%. Most statistical procedures are based on the assumption that data approximate the normal distribution curve. In reality, the graphs produced from the data of many research studies are not as symmetrical as the normal distribution curve.

Frequently, scores used in research are derived from raw standardized test scores (the number of items correct). **Derived,** or converted, **scores** are changed to other scores such as *grade equivalents, age equivalents, percentiles, normal curve equivalents, stanines, scale scores,* or other *standard scores.* Figure 7.7 illustrates the more common of these derived scores and relates them to the normal distribution curve.

Each of these derived scores is used to describe test performance, and their relation to the normal curve allows the user to compare performance on several measures of performance. The research consumer should note the different derived scores that fall at the mean and the SD points on the normal curve illustrated in Figure 7.6.

Statistical Significance

The normal distribution curve is also called the *normal probability curve* because it is used to estimate the likelihood of an interval score or set of interval scores happening by chance. In comparative and experimental research, researchers want to be sure that the observed differences between the means of two or more groups of subjects, or two or more variables are truly different. That is, they want to know if the difference is a reliable one. If these means differ, researchers need to know the extent to which the difference could have happened by chance. When the observed difference between these means is large enough to be beyond a predetermined chance level, the difference is considered as significant. **Statistical significance** occurs when the difference between the means of two sets of results exceeds a predetermined chance level. Researchers can thus know how confident they can be about the conclusions that they make from their findings.

Three interrelated factors are usually considered in a statistical analysis:

- The difference between group means
- The variability of the groups
- The number of subjects in each group

All other things being equal, there is an increased likelihood that difference(s) between the means of two or more sets of scores is statistically significant when

- The difference between the means becomes larger
- The variability of each set of scores becomes smaller
- The size of the sample increases

These three relationships can be seen in Figure 7.8.

When researchers statistically conclude if a difference or relationship exists, then there is the possibility of error. Two kinds of error can occur:

- Researchers accept the results as true when the results are not true (specified as a Type I error)
- Researchers do not accept the results as true when the results actually are true (specified as a Type II error)

For example, in the first error (Type I), researchers find what appears to be a statistically significant difference in student performance (over previous performance) when using a new instructional program. However, because of imperfections in sampling procedures (subject selection error) and the measuring instruments (reliability estimates), there may not be a true difference in student performance after using the new program, even though it appears as if a difference does exist. In such a case, the researchers will have concluded that the new instructional program is better than the old one when in fact that conclusion is not true. In the second error (Type II), researchers do not find a significant difference in student learning when

The possibility of statistical significance **increases** as

differences between means		variability		sample size
	or		or	
↓		↓		↓
get larger		gets smaller		gets larger

Figure 7.8
Factors Affecting Statistical Significance

actually there is a difference. In this case, there is a change resulting from teachers' use of an instructional technique, but the researchers do not observe it; that is, the change is not large enough to be seen. The second error may also result from imperfections in the sample and instrumentation.

In educational and other behavioral and social science research, researchers try to avoid making the first type of error; but to do this, they increase the possibility of making the second type of error. Relative to the discussion of the normal probability curve, researchers have commonly used certain probability levels. These conventional levels correspond to the extreme ends of the curve and designate a very small chance of the first type of error. It is important to realize that research producers and consumers never know whether either of these two error types is being made. Researchers use a decimal to report the probability that the first type of error has occurred. The probability level is shown in research reports as $p = .05$. This figure means that the chances of concluding that differences or relationships exist (when they truly do not exist) are no more than 5 chances out of 100.

Sometimes researchers report the probability level as $p < .05$, which is read as "the probability is less than 5 chances out of 100," or as $p \leq .05$, which is read as "the probability is equal to, or less, than 5 chances out of 100." Of course, when researchers realize that the probability is even less than $p = .05$, they may report it as $p = .01$, or even as $p = .001$.

Research consumers need to be wary of accepting any results (even if they are statistically significant) without considering whether the results are practical or meaningful in educational settings. What is of prime importance to research consumers is the usefulness of the results in terms of improving teacher effectiveness, student learning, and efficient uses of instructional resources. To determine whether research results have **practical significance,** research consumers need to answer the following: In my teaching situation, how effectively can the results be used?

In recent years, researchers have begun to add to their findings an indication of the **effect size** of their statistical analyses. Effect size gives the consumer of research an indication of the magnitude (meaningfulness or importance) of the results by providing an additional measure to the significance level, without regard to sample size. Also, reporting effect size is useful in interpreting results of studies with large samples, which might show statistical significance for very small (not practical) differences. It is also recommended that researchers include with the numerical indication of effect size some comments that place those effect sizes in a practical and theoretical context (Wilkinson & APA Task Force on Statistical Inference, 2000). Researchers may use one of several techniques; however, they most often show effect size in relation to the standard deviation of the data gathering instrument. Effect size is reported in several ways; but, most commonly, it is reported as a decimal fraction. Effect sizes of .20 are usually considered small; .50, medium; and .80, large.

One group of researchers reported their results in the following way.

Means

The means and standard deviations for the elementary schools showing increasing and decreasing computer use are presented in a table, as are the effect sizes for the differences between means. The largest effect size [d] was evident for differences in assault/battery/robbery. For the decreasing schools, the mean number of incidents was 3.23, while for the increasing schools, the mean was 0.99, a difference of approximately 2/3 of a standard deviation ($d = -0.67$). Similarly, negative effect sizes were evident for disorderly conduct/fighting/harassment ($d = -0.09$) and total conduct violations ($d = -0.14$), but these were much smaller in magnitude. Similarly, increasing schools showed reduced

Effect Sizes

rates of disciplinary action with *d* values of −.10 and −.13 for in-school and out-of-school suspensions, respectively. Finally, daily attendance was higher in the increasing schools (*d* = 0.25), while both staff turnover (*d* = −0.09) and dropout prevention enrollment (*d* = −0.18) were lower. (Barron, Hogarty, Kromery, & Lenkway, 1999)

Degrees of Freedom

Frequently, tables reporting the results of statistical analyses show an entry that identifies the **degrees of freedom** (*df*) used in the analysis. For the purposes of this text, degrees of freedom can be best understood as the number of ways data are free to vary in a statistical problem (Gay & Airasian, 2000; Kerlinger, 1973; Wiersma, 1995). In practice, degrees of freedom ordinarily are a function of the number of subjects and groups being analyzed. Usually, degrees of freedom are the total number of subjects or groups, minus one. After the frequency of scores has been identified, then the variation remaining equals the number of subjects or groups, minus one.

Interval Scale Data

Statistical procedures used with interval scales are based on certain assumptions, all of which are related to the concept of a normal distribution curve. These statistical procedures are called *parametric statistics*. In using parametric statistics, researchers are trying to draw some conclusion from the differences between the means of sample groups or sets of scores.

The assumptions for using parametric statistics are as follows:

- The variables are measured in interval scales.
- The score of any subject is not influenced by those of any other subjects; that is, each is an independent phenomenon.
- The subjects are selected from (and represent) a normally distributed population.
- When the research involves two or more groups of subjects, each of which represents different populations, the variables that distinguish each population are similarly distributed between or among each population.

A common parametric statistic is the *t test*. It is used when there are two sets of scores to determine whether the difference between the means of the two sets of scores is significant. It is reported as numbers such as *t* = 1.6 or *t* = 3.1. After determining the value of *t*, researchers consult a statistical table to determine whether the value is significant at a certain probability level. A *t* test can be used, for example, to examine the mean scores in reading and mathematics for one group of subjects, or it can be used to examine mean scores in reading for two different groups of subjects. The *t* test is used frequently in single-variable comparative and experimental research, and its use is limited by the same factors that limit single-variable research.

Another parametric statistic used with interval data in comparative research is the **product-moment correlation,** which refers to the quantified relationship between two sets of scores for the same group of subjects. The result of the arithmetic computation is a correlation coefficient, which is expressed as *r*, a decimal between −1.0 and +1.0. The most common interval scale correlation coefficient is the **Pearson product-moment correlation.** Correlations show whether two or more variables have a systematic relationship of occurrence; that is, whether high scores for one variable occur with high scores of another (a positive relationship), or whether they occur with low scores of that other variable (a negative relationship). The occurrence of low scores for one variable, with low scores for another, is also an example of a positive relationship. A correlation coefficient of zero indicates that the two variables have no relationship with each other; that is, they are independent of each other.

Correlations can also be used to establish predictions. When a strong relationship has been established between two variables, a correlation can be used to predict the possible occurrence of either variable. The predictive use of correlation is important for such educational endeavors as early intervention programs for students with special needs. For example, certain tests, including tests of basic concepts and cognitive abilities, are appropriate for young children and are highly predictive of students' later school performance.

Table 2.4 (chapter 2, p. 59) shows how correlation coefficients are reported in table format, from a study about the relationships between topic-specific background knowledge and measures of overall writing quality. When correlation coefficients are statistically significant, they indicate that the variables are probably systematically related beyond a certain level of chance. In other words, the two variables go together; significant correlations do not indicate that there are any causal effects of one variable on the other. In Table 2.4, the relationship between the holistic scoring method and teachers' marks is positive and significant—high coherence scores were given to the same students' work that also received high teacher marks. On the other hand, the relationship between coherence and the number of words and clauses, which is negative, was not significant; and therefore, the two scoring methods can be said to be unrelated. Again, no causality is implied, nor should it be assumed.

When research designs call for examining differences among the means of two or more groups of subjects, or two or more variables, researchers frequently use the **analysis of variance** (ANOVA), which is reported in *F* ratios. The advantage in using an ANOVA is that several independent variables, as well as several factors, can be examined. In its simplest form, ANOVA can be thought of as a multiple *t* test. The ANOVA is appropriate for use with numerous comparative research designs and with experimental research designs, such as the pretest-posttest with multiple control groups, the Solomon four-group design, counterbalanced designs, common factorial designs, and causal-comparative designs. The ANOVA procedure can be used when more than one independent variable is involved. Table 2.5 (chapter 2, p. 64) shows the ANOVA results for a two-way factorial design from a study using two independent variables: the effect of two levels of reading potential (disabled reader versus slow learner) and two levels of reading placement (*at* instructional level versus *above* instructional level). Notice that the researchers indicated two significance levels: $p < .05$ and $p < .01$. The results show that there were differences in results (on the dependent variable: vocabulary achievement) based on the subjects' reading potential and for their reading placement. There was no difference in vocabulary achievement when potential and placement were considered (Potential X Placement). On comprehension tests, only Potential showed significant differences ($p < .01$).

An important feature of ANOVA is that it can show the **interaction effects** between and among variables. The negative consequence of treatment interaction is discussed here as well as the possibility of measuring the interaction in factorial designs. Interactions are also expressed as *F* ratios within an ANOVA table, and often the interaction is illustrated in a graph. For research consumers, treatment interactions permit instructional modifications for particular groups of learners. For example, referring again to Table 2.5, there were no significant two-way interactions (Potential X Placement) for achievement in either vocabulary or comprehension. That result can be interpreted as indicating important information about how this group of subjects learns. How they will achieve in vocabulary and comprehension will not be influenced by the combination of their potential and instructional placement. In this case, there is no interaction effect. Obviously, in other situations an interaction effect may exist. In such situations, an interaction effect may indicate that the two independent variables *do* affect the dependent variable differently.

In previous chapters, reference was made to situations in which two or more groups of subjects differ on one or more variables, thereby limiting the generalizability of the studies' findings. The differences might have occurred because researchers used preexisting groups of subjects, instead of randomly selecting and assigning groups of subjects. Sometimes research producers think that these variables might influence the dependent variables under study (and the variables are not features that are used to distinguish between groups, e.g., distinguishing between male and female, or high and low mathematical performance). To mitigate the influence, researchers use a statistical procedure to equate the groups on these independent variable factors.

One frequently used procedure is known as **analysis of covariance** (ANCOVA). It allows researchers to examine differences among the means of groups of subjects, as if the means were equal from the start. They do this by adjusting the differences in the pretest means, to make them hypothetically equal. The equalizing variable is known as the *covariate*. The procedure is similar to the use of a "handicap" in bowling or golf leagues to balance out differences among players and teams. In all other ways, ANCOVAs are interpreted like ANOVAs.

When researchers wish to examine the relationships among more than two variables, they can use a multiple correlation technique. The procedure is interpreted similarly to a single correlation coefficient. Multiple correlations can also be used to make predictions. Prediction scores are reported as a multiple correlation coefficient, or *R*, and have the same range as single correlations. Multiple regression is used frequently in causal-comparative experimental research because it combines ANOVA and correlational techniques. Research consumers need to keep in mind that the causality in causal-comparative research is assumed because of a strong, highly predictive relationship. This assumed causality needs to be reconfirmed by researchers, by further experimental studies.

One technique related to multiple correlation technique is based on **hierarchical linear models (HLM).** HLM is based on the premise that many subjects within a group are more similar to each other than they are to subjects randomly sampled from the entire population. For example, an entire school is similar when broken down by classroom, because students are not usually randomly assigned to classrooms. The students in a particular class have many experiences in common, for example, the same teacher, physical environment, and similar experiences. These factors can lead to an increased in commonality, or homogeneity. Thus, the data collected on subjects within a group may not be fully independent and discrete. Because most statistical analyses are based on the premise that data on subjects is independent for each subject, the HLM technique was devised to be able to separate the effect of the independent variable on individual subjects from that on the entire group, or the effect from multiple variables on each subject (Osborne, 2000).

Following is information from a study about the effect of small classes on students' performance. Here, the HLM is used because of the possible effect on students of other variables than just small class size.

*Purpose and
Research
Questions*

*Researchers'
Expectations*

Data Analysis

*Reason for
Using HLM*

The purpose of this investigation (Finn, Gerber, Achilles, & Boyd-Zaharias, 2001) was to extend our knowledge of the effects of small classes in the primary grades on pupils' academic achievement. Three questions were addressed that have not been answered in previous research: (1) How large are the effects of small classes relative to the number of years students participate in those classes? (2) How much does any participation in small classes in K–3 affect performance in later grades when all classes are full-size? (3) How much does the duration of participation in small classes in K–3 affect the magnitude of the benefits in later grades (4, 6, and 8)? Rationales for expecting the continuing impacts of small classes were derived in the context of other educational interventions (for example, Head Start, Perry Preschool Project). The questions were answered using data from Tennessee's Project STAR, a statewide controlled experiment in which pupils were assigned at random to small classes, full-size classes, or classes with a full-time teaching assistant. Hierarchical linear models (HLMs) were employed because of the multilevel nature of the data; the magnitude of the small-class effect was expressed on several scales including "months of schooling."

Nominal and Ordinal Scale Data

When researchers collect data that are measured in nominal and ordinal scales, they must use different types of statistics. These statistics, called *nonparametric statistics*, work on different assumptions. Nonparametric statistics are used when:

- The populations do not have the characteristics of the normal distribution curve
- Symbols or numbers are used as labels on categories (nominal scales)
- An expected or rank order is apparent, but the order is not necessarily equally spaced, as is the case with interval data

For each parametric statistical procedure, there are corresponding nonparametric statistical procedures. In general, nonparametric statistics are less frequently used in educational and other behavioral and social science research than are parametric statistics. Table 7.1 shows corresponding parametric and nonparametric statistics.

One popular nonparametric statistical procedure is the **chi-square test** (χ^2). It is used to test the significance of group differences between observed and expected outcomes when data are reported as frequencies or percentages of a total or as nominal scales. Table 2.3 (chapter 2, p. 58) shows an example of chi-square reporting from a study that examined how teachers responded when students made miscues (deviant oral reading responses). In their analysis, the researchers found that teachers who dealt with unattempted miscues supplied words more often than they used all other responses combined. Indications of statistical significance are interpreted the same for nonparametric statistics as they are for parametric statistics.

Table 7.1
Corresponding Parametric and Nonparametric Statistics

Parametric	Nonparametric
t test	Mann-Whitney *U* Test
ANOVA	Friedman two-way analysis of variance
	Kruskal-Wallis one-way analysis of variance
Pearson product-moment correlation	Spearman rank-order correlation

UNDERSTANDING RESULTS SECTIONS IN QUANTITATIVE REPORTS

The results sections of quantitative research reports are usually the most difficult for research consumers to read and interpret. Often research consumers are intimidated by the statistical procedures and the presentation of numerical data in charts and tables. However, these sections can be read systematically by following the reading plan outlined in chapter 3. By the time research consumers read the results sections, they should already know the researchers' purpose, questions, and research design; major results and conclusions; target population and subject selection technique; instrumentation; and research method. What is left for the reader to understand are the specific results relative to the research questions.

Results sections are read during the third phase of the reading plan, when the research consumer is confirming predictions and knowledge. The goal of this phase for research consumers is to verify that their purposes (not the research producers') have been met. In this phase, research consumers can decide what information supports the researchers' purpose and adds to their (the consumers') knowledge.

In reports of quantitative research, the results of statistical procedures (such as the *t* test, correlation, and ANOVA) are not always put into table format; the numerical information may be part of the general discourse of the report because of space limitations. Research consumers should expect, however, that the reports' authors give an explanation of the numerical information, whether it is within the text or in the tables.

The results sections are presented for each of the studies whose method sections were abstracted and discussed in the first section of chapter 7. From reading results sections, research consumers should be able to answer the following:

- What types of data analysis were used?
- What statistical analyses did the researchers use?
- Were the statistical analyses appropriate for the researchers' questions, purposes, or hypotheses, and for the research design?
- What were the research results?
- Were the results of quantitative research statistically significant?
- Were the qualitative analyses appropriate and logical? Were they meaningful?
- Were the results of practical use and importance?
- Will the results be applicable to other educational settings, especially the one in which I teach?

Results sections should be evaluated using the following questions, which are from Figure 3.1, page 86.

Results Section

Data Analysis in Quantitative Research
- Are the statistical procedures for data analysis clearly described? Are they appropriate for the type of quantitative research design?

Research Validity in Quantitative Research
- Are the procedures free from the influence of extraneous variables?
- Does the study have any threats to its internal and external validity?

Significance in Quantitative Research
- Are statistical significance levels indicated? Does the research have practical significance?

Descriptive Research

The following partial results section is from a quantitative descriptive study (see section I of chapter 7, to review the purpose and method information for this study). The researchers present their results as percentages because they are only interested in providing information about the status of students' perceptions. Note that the researchers present a general conclusion about each result before they provide specific data. When they do note differences in students' responses, these differences are not interpreted statistically. (In the full report, the researchers provide tables with the numerical frequencies of responses.)

RESULTS

Textbook Adaptations vs. *No Adaptations (Questions 1–5)*

> *Explanation*
> *of Findings*

Students in both grade groupings (middle and high school) overwhelmingly agreed that textbook adaptations help them understand difficult content material. However, students differed somewhat on their rationales for selecting adaptations. In general, middle-school students preferred adaptations to promote interest whereas high-school students, in general, preferred adaptations to promote learning.

> *Numerical*
> *Data But No*
> *Analysis*

Of the textbook adaptations, students were most enthusiastic about learning strategies, with 100% of the sample favoring strategy instruction. Students of all groups commented that strategies make learning more effective. Also highly favored were purpose statements (preferred by 95% of the students). . . . Study guides or outlines (preferred by 83%) "tell you what to focus on" and "help you understand better." Seventy-five percent of the same preferred projects and experiments to textbook reading . . . [and] fourteen students (15%) advocated the combined use of text and direct experiences. . . . Although the majority of students felt they learned by writing summaries or answering questions (74% of the total sample, and 65% of the ESOL and AA students), this was not a well-liked learning procedure. . . . (Vaughn et al., 1995)

Comparative Research

In quantitative comparative research, researchers examine the descriptions of two or more variables and make decisions about the variables' differences or relationships. They can also make predictions about one variable based on information about another. Research consumers should be concerned that only appropriate generalizations are made from comparative and predictive quantitative data.

The following abbreviated results section is from a quantitative study comparing teachers' anxiety levels and their computer network use. (See chapter 7, section I, pp. 147–148, to review the research question and method section of this study.) Only a portion of the statistical results are given here. Note that the researchers clearly indicate which of their statistical analyses are significant (or are not) and they provide an interpretation of their quantitative findings.

RESULTS

> *Explanation*
> *of Statistical*
> *Procedure*

The 189-subject sample participating in this study showed relatively high levels of network use, with means of 186 logins and 2,528 min for the year. The variance within each use category was also large, with a standard deviation of 360.3 for network logins and 4,844 min for online time.

Results of Correlations with Significance Levels

The analysis of statistical correlations between network use and subject attribute variables was conducted using an eight variable matrix of correlation coefficients (Pearson's Product Moment correlation). This matrix consisted of pairwise correlations for all eight interval level variables, including the two network variables of total logins and online time; the three apprehension variables of writing apprehension, oral communication apprehension, and computer anxiety; and the three experience-related variables of teaching experience, age, and telecomputing experience.

Correlations with the three apprehension variables indicated that only writing apprehension was significantly related to total network logins, $r = -.19$, $p < .009$, and total online time, $r = -.15$, $p < .046$. Both correlations were negative, meaning that higher apprehension scores were associated with lower login frequency and online times. Writing apprehension was also significantly correlated with oral communication apprehension, $r = .52$, $p < .001$, and computer anxiety, $r = .17$, $p < .023$. As would be expected, total network logins and total network online time were strongly correlated with each other, $r = .78$, $p < .001$.

Statistical Results and Interpretation of Results

The general experience level indicated by this sample was 51% of the sample having more than 15 years of teaching experience. Seventy percent of the sample had two or more years of telecomputing experience. However, telecomputing experience was the only experience-related variable to be correlated with a network use variable (total online time: $r = .16$, $p < .034$). As might be expected, a significant pairwise correlation was also found between teaching experience and age, $r = .45$, $p < .001$, indicating that more years of teaching experience were generally associated with older subjects. (Harris & Grandgenett, 1996)

Experimental Research

Researchers use experimental designs when conducting research about the causative effect of one or more variables on other variables. The plans provide researchers with structures for studying one or more independent variables with one or more groups of subjects. Researchers select designs that best fit their purposes, answer questions about causation, and control extraneous variables.

The common experimental designs are discussed in section I and illustrated in Figures 7.1 (p. 152), 7.2 (p. 154), 7.3 (p. 155), and 7.4 (p. 156).

The following results section is taken from a pretest-posttest control group design that has one independent variable and three dependent variables. In this section, the results of an analysis of variance (ANOVA) are presented. The subjects did not differ at the start on pretest measures so no analysis of covariance (ANCOVA) was needed. The table shows only the groups' means and standard deviations. (The method section of this report is in section I, pp. 152–153.)

Purpose of the study: To assess the effects of learning strategy instruction on the completion of job applications by learning-disabled students.

RESULTS

Preliminary analyses indicated that there were nonsignificant differences between the groups on the pretest measures. Posttest measures were analyzed in condition (traditional, strategy) by gender (male, female) analyses of variance (ANOVAs). For every dependent measure, only a significant main effect for condition was obtained. The F values for these effects, along with the means and standard deviations for each of the dependent measures, are presented. . . . (etc.) (Nelson, Smith, & Dodd, 1994)

The study in the research report "Effects of Classroom Structure on Student Achievement Goal Orientation", on pages 19–26, is an example of a 2 × 3 factorial analysis design (Refer to Figure 7.4 for a graphic representation of this research design and refer to chapter 7, section I, for information about the Design and Procedure of the study.) At [15], "Results," the findings of the study are presented. Note that two specific findings are given and the reader is referred to two tables.

Causal-Comparative Research

Causal-comparative research is ex post facto, or after-the-fact, research, because researchers are trying to establish a causal effect between existing conditions. Researchers want answers to questions but cannot manipulate the independent variable(s) for practical or ethical reasons. They realize a condition exists and sometimes are unsure about what might have been its cause. Causal-comparative designs are built on the posttest-only control group design.

The following results section contains an example of a causal-comparative design (see section I for the method section of this study). The researchers sought to determine the effect of a preexisting condition (amount of previous mathematics instruction) on mathematics achievement. Remember that researchers using the causal-comparative design are trying to find causal relationships or predictions.

Purpose of the study: To examine the teaching strategies used by mothers of sons with learning disabilities and normally achieving sons.

RESULTS

Mothers' Teaching Strategies

Differences between the LD and NLD groups were tested by using a one-way ANOVA. The mean proportion of the low- and medium-level teaching strategies used by the mothers did not significantly differ between the groups. However, the mothers of NLD children (M = 19.90 vs. M = 9.13) used more high-level strategies, $F(1,58) = 4.06$, $p < .05$, and the total time they used in teaching (M = 76.5 vs. M = 66.1) was higher, $F(1,58) = 4.63$, $p < .05$, than that of the mothers of children with LD. No differences between the groups were found in the amount of speech produced by both mothers and children during the task. . . . (etc.)

From Lyytinen, P., Rasku-Puttonen, H., Poikkeus, A. M., Laakso, A. L., & Ahonen, T. (1994). Mother-child teaching strategies and learning disabilities. *Journal of Learning Disabilities* 27:186–192.

OTHER RESEARCH

Single-subject research, action research, and evaluation research are other ways researchers describe, compare, and draw causative conclusions about educational problems and questions.

Single-Subject and Case Study Research

The following results section is from research done with a single subject in an A-B design. Note that although data were collected and presented in graph form, no tests of statistical significance were performed. Therefore, the research consumer does not know whether the subject's increased spelling scores after tutoring differed significantly from those before tutoring, or whether the difference might be attributed to chance or error variations. (See chapter 7, section I, pp. 159–160, to review the method section of this study.)

Purpose of the study: To determine the effects of a peer-tutoring procedure on the spelling behavior of a mainstreamed elementary school student with a learning disability.

RESULTS

Percent Correct

The overall results indicated that the tutee obtained a greater percent of accuracy on the spelling tests during the peer-tutoring condition than during the baseline condition. As shown in Figure 1, the student increased his mean percent correct from 61.25 percent in baseline to 77.5 percent in the peer-tutoring condition, that is, an improvement of 16.25 percent. The spelling performance of the peer tutor (S-B) did not decrease during either of the experimental conditions; it was 100 percent.

Clinical Significance: Student Self-Reports and Ratings

Both the tutee and the tutor rated the peer-tutoring procedure favorably. . . . The program was rated as very good five times, satisfactory on four occasions, and unsatisfactory once. Subject A rated the program as unsatisfactory on the day when he scored 45% on his spelling test. (Mandoli et al., 1982, pp. 187–188)

ACTIVITIES

Do not read the Feedback section until you have completed each of the activities.

Activity 1

Using the Focus Questions at the beginning of the chapter as a guide, summarize the chapter's key ideas.

Activity 2

Using quantitative studies of your own choosing or located through the resources in Appendix A, locate one experimental and one other type of quantitative research. You may team with one or more fellow students and do the activity collaboratively. Or, each of you may do the activity independently and compare your answers. You may want to use the studies that you used for the activity in chapter 7, section I.

Read the results of those studies. Using the questions and criteria discussed in this chapter, evaluate the studies. For each, list questions and concerns you may have about

1. The appropriateness of the statistical procedures to the researchers' purposes and designs
2. The indicated statistical significance levels
3. The practical significance of the research

FEEDBACK

Activity 1

What are the different ways quantitative data are recorded?   Statistics are numerical ways to describe, analyze, summarize, and interpret data in a manner that conserves time and space. Researchers select statistical procedures after they have determined what research designs and types of data will be appropriate for answering their research questions.

In answering descriptive research questions, statistics let researchers show the data's central tendencies and variability. In answering comparative and experimental research questions, other statistics allow researchers to draw inferences from samples and to make generalizations about target populations. In all three types of research, the specific statistical procedures are determined by the research design and the type of data that are collected. Further, in comparative and experimental research, statistics are tools that let researchers gain two other insights: (*a*) an estimate of the error (or difference) between the research sample and the target population and (*b*) the confidence with which research producers and consumers can accept the results.

Data are recorded as (*a*) categories, (*b*) rankings, (*c*) intervals, and (*d*) ratios. Each requires the use of different statistics. Interval scales present data according to preset, equal spans. They are the most common form of data reporting in education and social science. They are identified by continuous measurement scales: raw scores and derived scores such as IQ scores, standard scores, scaled scores, and normal curve equivalents. Interval scores are the form in which data from most tests are recorded. Rankings, or ordinal scales, show the order, from highest to lowest, for a variable. There are no indications as to the value or size of differences between or among items in a list; the indications refer only to the relative order of the scores. Subjects can be ranked according to their performance on a set of athletic tasks, and what will be reported is the order in which they scored (such as first, second, or third), not their actual accumulation of points. Data from surveys and observations are often recorded in this manner. Categories separate data into two or more discrete aspects, such as male-female, red-white-blue, or always-frequently-infrequently-never. The data can be reported as numbers of items, or as percentages of a total. Data recorded in that way, often from surveys and observations, are considered nominal scales. Ratio scales, less frequently used in educational and other behavioral and social science research, show relative relationships among scores, such as half-as-large or three-times-as-tall.

What is a normal distribution curve?   Parametric statistics are based on the concept that if a set of scores is large enough, the scores will be distributed systematically and predictably. They will produce a graph in the shape of a bell, which is called the *normal distribution curve*. There is a direct relationship between the standard deviation (SD) and the normal distribution curve. Starting at the center, or mean, of the distributed variable, each SD represents a fixed, specific proportion of the population.

What statistical procedures are used in educational and other behavioral science research?   A common parametric statistic is the *t* test. It is used when the difference between two sets of scores is being tested. It is reported as numbers such as $t = 1.6$ or $t = 3.1$. Another parametric statistic used with interval data in comparative research is the product-moment correlation, which refers to the quantified relationship between two sets of scores for the same groups of subjects. The result of the arithmetic computation is a coefficient of correlation, which is expressed as r, a decimal between -1.0 and $+1.0$. When research designs call for examining differences among the means of two or more groups of subjects or two or more variables, they frequently use the analysis of variance (ANOVA), which is reported in F ratios. The advantage in using an ANOVA is that two or more variables (as well as two or more factors) can be examined. In its simplest form, ANOVA can be thought of as a multiple t test. The ANOVA is appropriate for use with some comparative research designs and with experimental research designs, such as the pretest-posttest with multiple control groups, the Solomon four-group design, counterbalanced designs, common factorial designs, and causal-comparative designs. Analysis of covariance (ANCOVA) allows researchers to examine differences among the pretest means of groups of subjects, as if the means were statistically equal from the start. Researchers accomplish this task by adjusting the differences in the pretest means to make them hypothetically equal. In all other ways, ANCOVAs are interpreted like ANOVAs. When researchers wish to examine the relationships among more than two variables, they can use multiple or partial correlation techniques. These procedures are interpreted similarly to a single correlation coefficient.

For each parametric statistical procedure, there are corresponding nonparametric procedures. In general, nonparametric statistics, which use nominal or ordinal data, are less frequently employed in educational and other behavioral and social science research than are parametric statistics.

What are statistical significance and effect size?   In comparative and experimental research, researchers want to be sure that the differences between the means of two or more groups of subjects, or two or more variables, are truly different. If the means differ, researchers need to know whether the difference happened by chance. When the difference between the means is large enough that it cannot be attributed to chance, the difference is considered as significant and, therefore, reliable. Statistical significance occurs when results exceed a particular p (probability or chance level) and researchers are confident about the conclusions they make from their findings. When researchers determine whether a difference or relationship exists, there is the possibility of error. Two kinds of error can occur: (*a*) researchers accept the results as true when the results are not true and (*b*) researchers do not accept the results as true when the results actually are true.

The effect size gives the consumer of research an indication of the *meaningfulness* or *importance* of the results by providing an additional measure to the significance level. Researchers may use one of several techniques; however, they most often show effect size in relation to the standard deviation of the data gathering instrument. Effect size is reported in several ways, but, most commonly, it is reported as a decimal fraction of the standard deviation.

What criteria should be used to read and evaluate results sections?   Consumers need to be able to answer these questions about research reports: What types of data analyses were used? What statistical analyses did the researchers use? Were the statistical analyses appropriate for the researchers' questions, purposes, or hypotheses, and for the research design? What were the research results? Were the results of quantitative research statistically significant? Were the qualitative analyses appropriate and logical? Were the results of practical use and importance, and educationally meaningful? Will the results be applicable to other educational settings, especially the one in which I teach?

Activity 2

Compare your answers with those of fellow students and discuss them with your instructor.

Reading and Interpreting Qualitative Procedure and Findings Sections

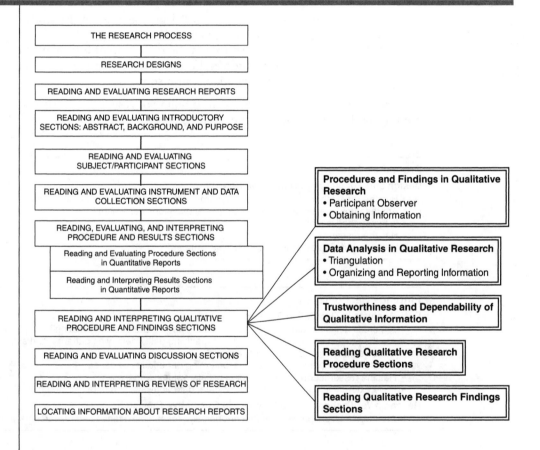

FOCUS QUESTIONS

1. What concerns should research consumers have about research procedures that are specific to qualitative research designs?
2. What are some ways that information is analyzed in qualitative research?
3. What questions and criteria should be used to read and evaluate qualitative research procedure and findings sections?

In chapter 2, the basic nature, types, and characteristics of qualitative research were presented. Chapter 6 contains a discussion of the main instrument for qualitative information collection—the researcher—and various ways that information is collected in qualitative research reports. The discussion here in chapter 8 focuses on the specific activities qualitative researchers use to record and analyze the information. Basically, the information-gathering activities are observing people and events, interviewing people, and examining documents (Wolcott, 1992). The information-analyzing activities are primarily coding the information and developing themes.

From reading procedure and findings information in qualitative reports, research consumers should be able to answer the following:

- What type of qualitative research design was used in the study?
- What procedures were used to collect information?
- What was the researchers' role in the collection of information?
- Were the details of the researchers' activities complete so that the research seemed trustworthy, dependable, and confirmable?

Procedure and finding sections in qualitative research reports should be evaluated using the following questions, which are from Figure 3.2 on page 87.

Procedure Sections

Design and Procedure in Qualitative Research
- Has the researcher obtained information from different sources and perspectives?
- Are research questions stated and additional questions generated?
- Is the method explained in detail?
- Has the researchers' presence influenced the behavior of the subjects?
- Is there abundant evidence, from multiple sources?

Findings Section(s)

Data Analysis in Qualitative Research
- Are the findings integrated with the collection and interpretation information?
- Are the processes clearly described for organizing data, identifying patterns, and synthesizing key ideas as theories and research questions?
- Has the researcher searched for disconfirming or negative evidence?
- Has the researcher reported personal beliefs, values, and biases?
- Have external authorities reviewed the data, data analysis, and data interpretations?

Research Verification and Authenticity in Qualitative Research
- Are there multiple procedures for corroborating research evidence and researchers' judgments?

PROCEDURES AND FINDINGS IN QUALITATIVE RESEARCH

Information in qualitative studies is collected in particular contexts, that is, educational and related settings. The act of collecting contextualized information is commonly called **fieldwork.** Important issues include why a particular site was selected and how permission was obtained for researchers to access the site. Before entering the site, researchers need to think about questions such as "What will be done at the site?" and "How will the researcher keep from disrupting the normal routine at the site?"

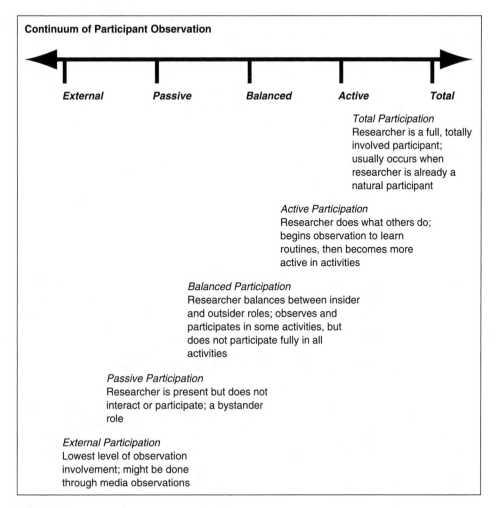

Figure 8.1
Continuum of Participant Observation

Participant Observer

While doing fieldwork, researchers need to determine where to be on a continuum of being a **participant observer.** (See Figure 8.1.) The continuum runs from being completely divorced from the research setting, to being totally involved in it. Sometimes which role to assume is determined by constraints within the fieldwork site; sometimes by the researchers themselves (Bogdan & Biklen, 2003; Maxwell, 1998). They need to decide whether to collect their information in the following ways:

- Through a means such as video recording that allows them to be external to the research situation
- By observing from within the setting, but remaining a passive onlooker
- By participating in some activities, but not others, to have a balance between active and passive participation

- By fully participating in all activities within the research setting
- As an insider; that is, as a member of the research setting who is also researching the situation

When researchers are participating in some way, they need to determine whether to act like a teacher, or to do what the children are doing. Their relationship to students might be influenced by factors such as gender, age, personality, and the way they are perceived by students and teachers under observation. Researchers need to be discreet while being efficient recorders of data. For example, if they openly take notes during class time, students may become curious about what is being written. In the sample illustrative qualitative research study given in chapter 2, the researcher took his field notes under the guise of taking class notes as a student.

There are several advantages of assuming the role of total insider participant observer, as well as several disadvantages (Edwards, 2002). As an insider, advantages include more chance that the researcher

- Is strongly grounded in long-standing relationships and knowledge of the research context
- Can identify charades and "cover stories" more readily
- Knows better the group agendas and histories
- Knows individual agendas and histories
- Knows organizational cultures
- Is aware of subcultures

Some disadvantages include that the researcher

- Might overlook the familiar
- Not know *how* or *which way* to respond to other participants
- Might have the relationships with others change because of the new researcher role
- Be in a quandary about *how much* and *how* to disclose in the written report

The question of duration and frequency of observations is critical (Bogdan & Biklen, 2003; Spindler & Spindler, 1992). Valuable qualitative data cannot be obtained without rapport between the subjects and researchers, so there needs to be preliminary visits so that all participants are comfortable, even in the case of an external collection of information. Researchers want to collect as much information as possible, and that process takes time. If they are concerned about the influence of direct note taking during observations, then they should not observe longer than their memory span. Further, they must spend sufficient time at the site so that they see events and relationships happening repeatedly.

Obtaining Information

To ensure that qualitative researchers obtain meaningful information, they often use a purposeful sampling technique (Creswell, 1998; Gay & Airasian, 2003; Maxwell, 1998), in which they deliberately select particular settings, persons, and events for the important information they provide. (See chapter 5.) The selection can be (*a*) random when the sample is large, (*b*) stratified when the sample consists of subgroups, (*c*) typical when a normal situation is to be shown, or (*d*) extreme when differences from the typical are to be shown.

While observing people and events, researchers create **field notes.** These notes are written descriptions of people, objects, places, events, activities, and conversations. These notes supplement information from official documents and interviews. An important part of these notes is the researchers' reactions, reflections, and tentative assumptions or hypotheses. Field notes can have two basic aspects, descriptive and reflective (Bogdan & Biklen, 2003). The descriptive aspect might include (*a*) verbal portraits of individuals, (*b*) reconstructions of dialogues between the researchers and others, (*c*) complete descriptions of physical settings, (*d*) accounts of particular events—who was involved, how, and what was done, (*e*) details about activities, and (*f*) the researchers' (observers') behavior. The reflective aspect of field notes might include (*a*) speculations about the data analysis—emerging themes and patterns, (*b*) comments on the research method—accomplishments, problems, and decisions, (*c*) records of ethical dilemmas and conflicts, (*d*) analysis of the researchers' frames of mind, and (*e*) points of clarification.

Throughout the course of qualitative analysis, the researcher should be asking (and re-asking) the following questions (Berkowitz, 1997):

- What patterns and common themes emerge in responses dealing with specific items? How do these patterns (or lack thereof) help to illuminate the broader study question(s)?
- Are there any deviations from these patterns? If yes, are there any factors that might explain these atypical responses?
- What interesting stories emerge from the responses? How can these stories help to illuminate the broader study question(s)?
- Do any of these patterns or findings suggest that additional data may need to be collected? Do any of the study questions need to be revised?
- Do the patterns that emerge corroborate the findings of any corresponding qualitative analyses that have been conducted? If not, what might explain these discrepancies?

In recent years, the concept of field notes has been expanded to include the use of photography, audio, and video. Such media can be used to provide records of the physical layout of the setting, artifacts, or details that would be difficult to document verbally. However, use of that equipment can be unproductive if it creates distractions among the subjects.

Field notes are not objective data in the strictest sense of the term; their form and content fully reveal that qualitative research is a subjective process. However, subjectivity should not be considered undesirable or negative. Currently, there is a shift in thinking about the concept and definition of subjectivity (Jansen & Peshkin, 1992). It no longer is thought of as distortion or bias, but rather as a unique, useful, personal quality of research. "When subjectivity is seen as distortion and bias, the [research] literature offers more or less prescriptive advice; when seen as an interactional quality, we learn about personal or reflexive, or political and theoretical stands" (p. 682).

Interviewing in qualitative research is used to obtain data in the subjects' own words. The purpose is to gather information from which insights on how the subjects interpret the situation being observed can be obtained (Bogdan & Biklen, 2003; Eisner, 1991). How interviews are conducted and the type of data gathered often depend upon whether the researcher is fulfilling a role as a full, active participant or as a non- or partial participant. In the latter cases, the nature of the data is partly determined by the trust the subject has in the interviewer. In qualitative research, researchers generally use open-ended, informal interview techniques. They do not use fixed-response questionnaires or surveys to guide the talks. The researchers encourage the subjects to talk about their perceptions about what is happening, what they believe about the event, and how they are feeling. Most important, qualitative researchers need to be good listeners. During interviews, researchers may use audio or video recorders and later transcribe the dialogues for analysis.

Other sources of information include documents and artifacts (Bogdan & Biklen, 2003; Eisner, 1991). These sources include materials produced by the subjects (such as samples from students' writing portfolios), students' and teachers' personal documents (diaries or letters), school records (memoranda, students' files, minutes of school board meetings, or newsletters), school memorabilia (newspapers, yearbooks, or scrapbooks), and documents and photographs from school and historical society archives. In certain situations, qualitative researchers may include official statistics as data. Such quantitative data can be useful for examining who collected the information, and how and why it has been quantified. Quantitative data are not always objective; that is, data are often collected and quantified for social or political reasons; and, as was explained in greater detail in the section "Data Analysis in Quantitative Research" in chapter 7, section II, there are inherent errors in all statistical analyses.

DATA ANALYSIS IN QUALITATIVE RESEARCH

In qualitative studies, researchers verbally analyze data. This process involves examining and organizing notes from interviews and observations. Researchers reduce the information into smaller segments from which they can see patterns, trends, and themes. In addition, researchers interpret the meanings of these patterns, trends, and themes and create research hypotheses and questions for verification in further research. Qualitative researchers begin their analyses while still in the research setting and finish it after all the information has been collected. An important point about qualitative research is that qualitative researchers often *do* measure and count; in other words, they quantify some data. However, they do not use statistical analyses to verify or support their results and conclusion, nor do they consider statistical probabilities.

Research consumers should expect qualitative researchers to fully explain their analysis methods so that the logic of their decisions can be followed and evaluated. In chapter 2, there is a discussion of the features of qualitative research methods, and earlier in this chapter are questions that can be used to determine the consistency of observational research. Research consumers may wish to review those sections before continuing the discussion here, which is a synthesis of the ideas of several scholars who use qualitative research methods (Bogdan & Biklen, 2003; Creswell, 1998; Eisner, 1991; Firestone, 1987; Gay & Airasian, 2003; Guthrie & Hall, 1984; Jacob, 1987, 1988; Lancy, 1993; Lincoln & Guba, 1985; Maxwell, 1998; Putney et al., 1999; Smith, 1987; Smith & Heshusius, 1986; Van Maanen et al., 1982; Wilson, 1977).

In the research setting, commonly called the *field*, qualitative researchers continually make decisions that narrow their study. They may start out with broad questions and begin looking at an entire educational setting, but as their study proceeds, they concentrate on smaller issues and create more specific, analytical questions. Data collection is an additive process. New information is looked for and collected on the basis of previous data, because the qualitative researchers are interpreting as they assemble additional information. This process does not mean they discard or selectively omit information. On the contrary, they maintain extensive on-site field notes. It is the influence of the events in the field and their ongoing interpretation of those events that guide qualitative researchers in their search for additional information. For example, while observing middle-school science lessons to study teachers' use of graphic organizers, a qualitative researcher takes notes in one class about students' collaborative activities in examining and recording the mealworm's life cycle. What the researcher notes is a combination of formalized small-group behaviors and seemingly unstructured, random student interaction. Noting this finding, the researcher later seeks out information leading to a hypothesis about a possible interrelationship among teachers' teaching style, their development of student collaborations, and students' use of graphic organizers.

Triangulation

One procedure used by qualitative researchers to support their interpretations is **triangulation.** (See Figure 8.2.) This procedure cross-validates information. Triangulation is collecting information from several sources about the same event or behavior. For example, in studying parents' attitudes about their involvement in their children's homework activities, data would be collected from interviews with parents, students, siblings, teachers, and from observations of parent-student behaviors during homework activities.

Organizing and Reporting Information

The information, or data, of qualitative researchers are verbal statements, oral and written. These researchers are trying to make meaning of the material they have collected. That information only can be analyzed to the extent that it has been made a part of their "meaning-world" (Lemke, 1998). Remember, researchers with a constructivist perspective believe there are multiple meanings in any social context, including schools and classrooms. Their aim is to understand and interpret some or all of these meanings.

Because verbal information is not analyzed directly, after collecting information in the field, qualitative researchers first must transcribe the information they have obtained from interviews, observations, videotaped surveys, and documents into a common written form. They then organize that written information by sifting through it and clustering seemingly similar ideas. As they do this, they begin to see commonalities among several ideas. These findings become the basis of their categories. These categories of information are labeled, or coded, for ease of use and cross-referencing. The sorting and grouping of the information can be accomplished through manual or automated techniques.

Qualitative researchers start with broad categories or themes:

- Settings—*where* teaching and learning occur
- Situations—*when* an activity or behavior occurs
- Activities—*what* teachers and students do

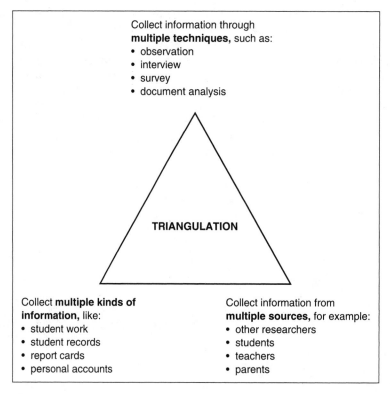

Figure 8.2
Triangulation

- Behaviors—*how* teachers and students act and respond
- Communications—*how* teachers and students express opinions and ideas, both verbally and nonverbally
- Techniques or methods—*how* and *why* teachers and students respond to an event
- Socializations—*with whom* teachers and students regularly interact
- Notable nonoccurrences—*what* is not occurring that might be expected

Depending on the nature of the information collected, these categories may be expanded, subdivided, eliminated, or renamed. Some notes may be cross-referenced because they contain information relevant to more than one category.

Consumers need to know the researchers' coding categories and how the classification systems were developed and revised. Because qualitative analyses are subjective, producers should be explicit about their theoretical formulations and their conceptual positions regarding the topic being investigated. When these factors are not explicitly stated in research reports, research consumers need to be aware that these formulations and positions usually are reflected in researchers' purpose questions and classification systems.

The qualitative research procedure **grounded theory** has an extensive system of coding information (Corbin & Strauss, 1990; Dick, 2002; Glazer & Strauss, 1967). The coding procedure consists of three interrelated codings: *open, axial,* and *selective.*

Open coding, the initial process in grounded theory, consists of identifying important categories. It involves breaking down, analyzing, comparing, and categorizing information. In open coding, information from all sources are labeled and grouped together by continuous comparison, to form categories and properties.

Axial coding is usually undertaken when categories are more advanced in their development. Axial coding is the setting down of hypothetical relationships between categories and subcategories. In this process, researchers relate codes (categories and properties) to each other through inductive and deductive thinking. To simplify this process, researchers using grounded theory often begin with the use of a basic frame of generic relationships: *subject of the event or action, events or actions leading to the subject, context, purposeful action stategies of participants,* and *consequences of the action strategies.*

Selective coding is used when a *core category* is identified; that is, when a central or general category shows a relationship among all other categories in the developing theory. In this process, researchers relate categories to the core category, eventually forming the basis for the grounded theory.

Grounded theory is a detailed and systematic procedure for information collection, analysis, and theorizing. The theory is concerned with the quality of developing theory. It offers many advantages. However, because it is such a specific method of research, it requires high levels of both experience and insight on the part of the researcher. Thus, it is generally recommended that beginning or inexperienced researchers avoid using grounded theory research until they have developed the skills needed to use the coding system effectively.

In all qualitative research there is the possibility that there will be missing or missed information (Singh & Richards, 2003). For example, one type of information that often is missing from transcribed field notes is nonverbal communications (that is, body language, facial expressions, hand movements). Little is really known about how nonverbal language integrates with verbal language to modulate meaning (Lemke, 1998). Missing data are important for understanding the way individuals create meaning in different social and cultural contexts. Information might be missing because there are some questions that participants do not want to answer. Participants may evade questions. Most significantly, there can be aspects of the situation that they take for granted, so they do not report them. In qualitative studies, theory development can always benefit from additional information. As noted previously, at the end of the study, questions often differ from those questions that initiated the study. Missing information can lead to new research questions.

TRUSTWORTHINESS AND DEPENDABILITY OF QUALITATIVE INFORMATION

A concern of all researchers, quantitative and qualitative, is the representativeness of the collected data. In chapter 6, the reliability and validity of instruments was discussed. In qualitative research, because the major instrument is the researcher, it is difficult to establish the reliability of the observer. However, the reliability, or dependability, of researchers' information can be ensured through appropriate research procedures in which researchers fully explain their procedures, verify their observations, and cross-check their sources (Bogdan & Biklen, 2003; Creswell, 1998; Eisner, 1991; Hillocks, 1992; Lincoln & Guba, 1985; Marshall & Rossman, 1995; Pitman & Maxwell, 1992).

There is a relationship between terms referring to the quality of quantitative research and that of qualitative research. Depending on the perspective of the researcher, different terms are often used (Lincoln & Guba, 1985).

Quantitative Research	Qualitative Research
internal validity	credibility or trustworthiness
external validity (generalizability)	transferability
reliability (replicability)	dependability
objectivity	confirmability

Qualitative researchers expect that different researchers will collect different information. In part, that situation results from different theoretical perspectives and beliefs about the nature and goals of qualitative research (see chapter 2). Because qualitative researchers' backgrounds and interests may differ, the researchers may collect different information and arrive at different interpretations. However, in all cases, the reliability or dependability of the information collected can be seen as a "fit between what they record as data and what actually occurs in the setting under study" (Bogdan & Biklen, 2003, p. 48).

The issue of consistency, or dependability, is also related to the possible replication of a study. Even though qualitative researchers are not usually concerned with replicating a study in the strict sense of the term because of the belief that "the real world changes" (Marshall & Rossman, 1995, p. 146), there are procedures they can follow to ensure the trustworthiness of their data. They can keep thorough notes and records of their activities, and they can keep their data in a well-organized and retrievable form.

Research consumers should look for the following specific evidence of the dependability of information (Marshall & Rossman, 1995):

- The researchers' method is detailed so its adequacy and logic can be determined, and there is an abundance of evidence.
- The researchers provide evidence of their qualifications as participant observers.
- The researchers' assumptions are clear.
- The researchers' questions are stated, and the study seeks to answer those questions and generate further questions.
- The researchers used preliminary days of the study to generate a focus for the study.
- The researchers were present in the research context for an adequate period of time, and the researchers observed a full range of activities over a full cycle of those activities.
- The data were collected from multiple sources.
- The researchers saved their data for reanalysis.

An important aspect of quantitative research is its generalizability. In qualitative research, the arguments for generalizability are not particularly strong; that is, qualitative researchers do not presume to be able to generalize from one classroom to another (Erickson, 1986; Firestone, 1993; Maxwell, 1998; Nielsen, 1995).

However, that fact does not mean that a qualitative study should not have a quality similar to that of the internal and external validity of quantitative research (Creswell, 1998; Maxwell, 1998; Spindler & Spindler, 1992). Nor are qualitative researchers usually concerned with the replicability of their studies, or with a broad generalizability of their results. Research consumers need to be able to identify the trustworthiness and dependability of the inferences that qualitative researchers draw from their data, to determine whether or not the researchers' findings are transferable to other situations.

Research consumers do not need to ask, "Does the research apply to all individuals within a target population?" Rather, consumers might try to determine whether other researchers have made similar or different conclusions about the instructional implications of the research topic. More important, research consumers should determine whether the qualitative researchers' conclusions and instructional implications have meaning for the students in their own classes, being fully aware that there might be more than one interpretation of the researchers' analyses.

Research consumers should understand that trustworthiness, or validity, in qualitative research is relative to the researchers' purpose and the circumstances under which the information was collected. Qualitative researchers analyze information differently depending upon their conceptual perspectives, views that should be stated explicitly. Research consumers can look for the following specific evidence of the trustworthiness of information in qualitative research reports (Biklen, 1993; Marshall & Rossman, 1995; Maxwell, 1992, 1998; Pretty, 1994):

- The researchers acknowledge, show sensitivity about, and maintain an ethical stance toward the individuals being researched.
- The researchers' work and their analyses "in-field" are fully documented, the logic of their data categorizations are evident, and the relationships among those concepts seem accurate within an identified theory of learning and instruction.
- The researchers' descriptions are factual, and they provide evidence of minimal distortion from possible errors of omission and commission; they include cases or situations that might challenge their emerging hypotheses or conclusions.
- The data were collected from more than one source (triangulation), and there is evidence confirming the accuracy of the respondents' accounts.
- The researchers are tolerant of ambiguity; they have searched out alternative explanations through multiple sources of data and have devised ways for checking the quality of their data.
- The researchers show evidence of formulating and reformulating their interpretations and analyses of data; there are comparisons of data and checks of hypotheses against new data.
- The researchers are self-analytical and recognize the limits of their subjectivity, they show evidence of guarding against value judgments in their analyses.
- The researchers' results are presented in a manner such that others might be able to use them (if deemed appropriate).
- The study is linked to the larger educational context in which the data were collected.
- The researchers acknowledge the limitations of their study as far as generalizing to other educational settings.
- The researchers show that their study has had an impact on stakeholders' capacity to know and act.

Research within a constructivist perspective can also be judged by a set of criteria known as **authenticity criteria** (Schwandt, 1997). These criteria are:

- *Fairness*—the extent to which the respondents' different constructions and their underlying values are solicited and represented in a balanced, even-handed way by the inquirer.
- *Ontological authenticity*—the extent to which respondents' own constructions are enhanced or made more informed and sophisticated as a result of their having participated in the inquiry.
- *Educative authenticity*—the extent to which participants in an inquiry develop greater understanding and appreciation of the constructions of others.
- *Catalytic authenticity*—the extent to which action is stimulated and facilitated by the inquiry process.
- *Tactical authenticity*—the extent to which participants in the inquiry are empowered to act. (p. 7)

READING QUALITATIVE RESEARCH PROCEDURE SECTIONS

> In the report "Images of America: What Youth Do Know About the United States," on pages 27–51, the researcher has presented how the information was collected at [9] to [11]. The researcher clearly indicates her total participatory role as researcher, [9], that of an insider. At [12], the researcher presented the research questions and broad findings (themes).

Other researchers, too, clearly identify their role as researcher. For example, following is an abridged excerpt from a study to understand the experiences of Asian Indian children in an elementary school. The researcher wanted to understand how these children made sense of their schooling experiences in the United States (Mehra, 2003). You can note in the sample how the author clearly identifies her role as researcher.

> *Researcher's Background*

[A]n important part of the study was my own perspective that I brought as an Asian Indian graduate student at the same university. At the time of the study, I was living in the U.S. for two years with my husband, who was also a graduate student. Being an Asian Indian, and living in the same university housing complex as my participants, did make me an insider in many ways to the culture and ways of life of my participants, giving me an advantage in understanding their perspectives. But at the same time, at many points of the study I had to struggle with my own biases and subjectivity creeping into the data collection and analysis. I was also an outsider to the setting in two important ways. First, I was not a mother. . . . Secondly, being a foreigner, I was an outsider to the American public school system, which was an important part of the study. . . . Doing this study gave me an opportunity to reflect on some of my own biases and beliefs about living in a foreign country as immigrants.

> *Relationship of Researcher to Participants*

It is important to mention that while I lived in the same neighborhood as my research participants, prior to this study I had not communicated with Ajay's family, and the only contact I ever had with Veena and Rohit's family was at a social event in the neighborhood.

> *Obtaining Information*

The study was conducted in multiple naturalistic settings. I observed the children in their classrooms, and also rode the school bus with them a few times. I interviewed the

*Information
from Multiple
Points of View*

*Balanced Role
as Participant
Observer*

*Multiple
Sources of
Information*

teachers at the school during their free time. . . . For my interviewes with parents, I switched the setting from their homes to my home, depending upon the convenience of my participants and mine. I interviewed children in different settings too. . . . This variety of settings widened my focus and enabled me to understand their experiences from multiple perspectives. All these natural settings allowed my participants to feel "at home" and did not restrain them in any perceivable manner. . . .

In the children's classrooms, my role was of a participant-observer. At times I read some of the books with the students in the classes, and at other times I was more of an observer sitting at the back of the room, taking notes. I also assisted one teacher with some project activity . . . and . . . I helped some [other] students in the class . . . with their work. All the field notes from the observations were word processed and coded.

In order to understand the school context better, I interviewed the school principal, the administrator of the "multicultural program," the librarian, and four teachers that teach the children in my study. These interviews were semi-structured, and ranged from 20 minutes to an hour long, and often conducted more than once. In addition, some of the casual conversation with the teachers and other people in the school proved to be very useful. I also collected some useful information about the school in the form of written documents about the school's multicultural program. In the case of parents and children, the interviews were again semi-structured, and often open-ended, ranging from a 10-minute casual talk to 45-minute-long interviews conducted at different times. First, I interviewed the parents together, and later mother and father separately to get multiple perspectives on the issues. I gave the choice to parents to talk either in Hindi or English . . . and most . . . chose Hindi. This in itself indicated their intent to maintain Indian identity, which they also emphasized for their children. All the interviews were tape-recorded, and later transcribed and coded.

Open-ended conversations with the children were more useful than semi-structured interviews. . . . Most of the data collected through these conversations was highly relevant, and even if it did not directly fit with my research agenda, it helped me understand the children better and get a feel for the things that interested them. This gave me a chance to use those topics to get them to answer some of the questions I had. With children, as well as their parents, I found that they were also curious to know about my family. Two children even wanted to see the pictures of my parents and siblings (which I did show them). Ajay, the five-year-old kindergartner, who was very fond of drawing and painting, was very interested to know about my sister who is an artist, and thus art or pictures gave us a topic to talk about. In the process I was able to hear his views not just about art, but also on issues such as his ambitions, his parents' expectations of him, and his relation with his brother.

*Assuming an
Insider Role
as Researcher*

*Triangulation
of Information*

Insider Role

To better understand the school context—the diverse nature of its population, the multicultural program, and the services provided to international students in the school—I triangulated the data by asking similar questions from different data sources. The written documents about the history of the multicultural program, and its philosophy were also useful. I also used classroom observations and interviews . . . for understanding the children's interaction patterns, behavior, and experiences at school. During the course of this study, I attended several Indian social gatherings and celebrations in the town and reflected upon my experiences to understand my socialization and acculturation in order to explore the feelings and experiences of my participants. At two of these gatherings, I got an opportunity to talk to one of the three children informally and get some valuable information. (Mehra, 2003. Used by permission of *The Qualitative Report*.)

READING QUALITATIVE RESEARCH FINDINGS SECTIONS

In the report "Images of America: What Youth Do Know About the United States," on pages 27–51, the researcher has presented findings at [13] to [20]. Each of the identified themes is supported with examples from students' statements. The researcher explained at [11] how the themes were identified. Many qualitative researchers use a coding system that allows them to categorize information. From those categories, themes or trends can emerge.

In the study about Asian Indian students, the researcher explained how she arrived at the general themes (Mehra, 2003).

*Data Analy-
sis and Cre-
ation of
Categories*

Data analysis involved various steps. After a first reading of all the transcripts and field notes, I made a tentative list of the issues reflected in the data. This list underwent a lot of additions and subtractions with subsequent readings of the data. The grouping and re-grouping of these issues in categories was followed by cutting and pasting sessions. As a result, I developed a broad scheme of organizing the different sub-categories in more comprehensive and inclusive categories. My analysis was more holistic and inductive in nature, as I was trying to paint a comprehensive picture of the experiences of these children. . . . I was looking at the wider scenario of the adjustment of these children in a new educational and cultural setting, rather than their specific classrooms. Thus, during the data analysis stage, I was more interested in the general patterns emerging from the data, rather than the individual teacher-level factors, which may or may not facilitate the student's adjustment. (Mehra, 2003. Used by permission of *The Qualitative Report.*)

In addition, the researcher was concerned about the trustworthiness of her information and reporting (Mehra, 2003). She took several steps to maintain as objective a position as possible.

*Maintaining
Objectivity*

*Triangulation
of Information*

*Sharing
With
Participants*

*Examining
Personal
Biases*

As I tried to look for patterns and themes in the data, my personal construction of my reality as an Asian Indian, as an international student, and as a potential immigrant often surfaced and interacted with the constructed realities of my research participants. While minimizing the *distance* and *objective separateness* . . . between myself and my research participants, I still found it necessary to monitor my subjectivity by recording my reactions and opinions in a journal as I went about the data analysis. . . . The length of the time spent on the research setting, doing observations, and conducting interviews was an important factor in establishing a trusting relationship between myself and the research. . . . Observations, interviews, and casual conversations were used to triangulate the data. . . . I also maintained a research log where I kept a record of the interview and observation schedules. I also maintained a subjectivity journal through which I regularly evaluated my bias in seeing and interpreting things and people in and around the research setting. I regularly discussed portions of data with colleagues, friends, and faculty. . . . This method of peer-debriefing . . . also served as a tool for triangulating the findings of the study. I also shared the interpretive process with research participants, by obtaining their reactions to the working drafts of the interview transcripts and field notes, and also by sharing with them the progress of study. . . . The participants were also asked to make me aware of the sections of the data that, if made public, could have been problematic for either personal or other reasons. (Mehra, 2003. Used by permission of *The Qualitative Report.*)

ACTIVITIES

Activity 1

Using the Focus Questions at the beginning of the chapter as a guide, summarize the chapter's key ideas.

Activity 2

In 1970, Kuhn confronted the research communities and challenged existing beliefs about positivist notions of *scientific research*. Some of these statements seem relevant today. Here are a few of his key points:

- Science has emotional, political, as well as cognitive elements.
- Scientific knowledge is not objective or neutral.
- All paradigms, or conceptions of the world, are replete with unconscious assumptions about reality.
- Language is never neutral.
- In modern science there are conflicting assumptions that underlie our reasoning.
- It is not important to argue the superiority of any particular paradigm, but rather to be able to consider multiple perspectives and their underlying assumptions.

Select one or more of these points and discuss them from the perspective of a constructivist qualitative researcher. In addition to the discussions in this chapter, you may find it helpful to refer to discussions in chapters 1 and 2.

FEEDBACK

Activity 1

What concerns should research consumers have about research procedures that are specific to qualitative research designs?   Qualitative research reports should show how the researchers' method is detailed so that its adequacy and logic can be determined, and there should be an abundance of evidence. Research consumers should be sure that the researchers provide evidence of their qualifications as participant observers. Consumers should be sure that the researchers' assumptions are clear, that the researchers' questions are stated, and that the study sought to answer those questions and generate further questions.

The research report should indicate that the researchers used the preliminary days of the study to generate a focus for the study, that the researchers were present in the research context for an adequate period of time, and that the researchers' observations are of a full range of activities over a full cycle of those activities. The research consumer should ascertain that the data were collected from multiple sources. The researchers should have saved their data for reanalysis.

What are some ways that information is analyzed in qualitative research?   In qualitative studies, researchers verbally analyze data. This involves examining and organizing notes from interviews and observations, and reducing the information into smaller segments from which they can see patterns, trends, and themes. In addition, researchers interpret the meanings of these patterns, trends, and themes to create research hypotheses and questions for verification in further research. Qualitative researchers begin their analyses while still in the research setting and finish it after all the information has been collected. An important point about qualitative research is that qualitative researchers often *do* measure and count; in other words, they quantify some data. However, they do not use statistical analyses to verify or support their results and conclusion, nor do they consider statistical probabilities.

What questions and criteria should be used to read and evaluate qualitative research procedure and finding sections?   From reading procedure and findings information in qualitative reports, research consumers should be able to answer the following:

What type of qualitative research design was used in the study?

What procedures were used to collect the information?

What was the researchers' role in the collection of information?

Were the details of the researchers' activities complete, so that the research seemed trustworthy, dependable, and confirmable?

Has the researcher obtained information from different sources and perspectives?

Are research questions stated and additional questions generated?

Is the method explained in detail?

Has the researchers' presence influenced the behavior of the subjects?

Is there abundant evidence from multiple sources?

Are the findings integrated with information collection and interpretation?

Are there clearly described processes for organizing data, identifying patterns, and synthesizing key ideas as theories and research questions?

Has the researcher searched for disconfirming or negative evidence?

Has the researcher reported personal beliefs, values, and biases?

Have external authorities reviewed the data, data analysis, and data interpretations?

Are there multiple procedures for corroborating research evidence and researchers' judgments?

Activity 2

Discuss your response(s) with your instructor and others in your class.

CHAPTER 9

Reading and Evaluating Discussion Sections

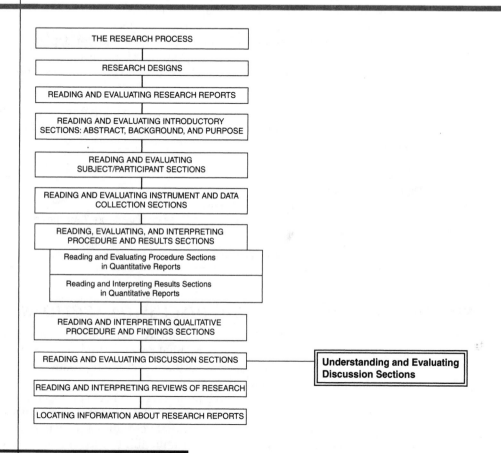

| THE RESEARCH PROCESS |
| RESEARCH DESIGNS |
| READING AND EVALUATING RESEARCH REPORTS |
| READING AND EVALUATING INTRODUCTORY SECTIONS: ABSTRACT, BACKGROUND, AND PURPOSE |
| READING AND EVALUATING SUBJECT/PARTICIPANT SECTIONS |
| READING AND EVALUATING INSTRUMENT AND DATA COLLECTION SECTIONS |
| READING, EVALUATING, AND INTERPRETING PROCEDURE AND RESULTS SECTIONS |
| Reading and Evaluating Procedure Sections in Quantitative Reports |
| Reading and Interpreting Results Sections in Quantitative Reports |
| READING AND INTERPRETING QUALITATIVE PROCEDURE AND FINDINGS SECTIONS |
| READING AND EVALUATING DISCUSSION SECTIONS |
| READING AND INTERPRETING REVIEWS OF RESEARCH |
| LOCATING INFORMATION ABOUT RESEARCH REPORTS |

Understanding and Evaluating Discussion Sections

FOCUS QUESTIONS

1. What information should research consumers get from discussion sections of research reports?
2. What criteria should be used to evaluate discussion sections?
3. What is the plan for reading discussion sections?

In chapter 3, a plan was provided for reading research reports. The plan calls for the reading of the discussion section as part of the second stage of the plan. The demonstrations of the plan show that discussion sections usually contain several types of information: (*a*) a restatement of the researchers' purposes (or research questions or hypotheses), (*b*) a summary of the results, (*c*) a discussion or interpretation of those results, and (*d*) recommendations based on those results. By reading the discussion section together with the abstract, research consumers will have an overview of the research project.

From reading discussion sections, research consumers should be able to answer the following:

- What were the researchers' purposes for the study?
- What were the researchers' major results?
- How did the researchers interpret their results?
- What recommendations did the researchers make for applying the results to instructional situations, or for future research projects?
- Are the researchers' issues and concerns relevant to me as a professional, or to my teaching situation?

Discussion sections of both quantitative and qualitative research reports should be evaluated using the following questions, which are from Figure 3.1 and Figure 3.2, pages 86 and 87.

Discussion Section

Discussion (Conclusions, Recommendations)
- Are there conclusions related to answering the research question(s)? Are the conclusions appropriate to the results?
- Is the report free from inappropriate generalizations and implications?
- If inappropriate, are suggestions for additional research provided?

UNDERSTANDING AND EVALUATING DISCUSSION SECTIONS

Some researchers label the discussion sections as *conclusions, summary,* or *implications,* and they may subdivide the section to highlight specific information. As a consumer, you will have determined the specific format of research producers' discussion sections during the first step of the reading plan.

A common procedure for research producers is to begin discussion sections with a statement of the research purpose and then to follow that statement with an overview of their results. Further, in the case of quantitative studies, they will state whether the results were statistically significant and meaningful. In the remainder of the section, the researchers usually explain (*a*) whether the results answered their research questions, (*b*) how their results relate to related literature presented in the introduction, and (*c*) what implications the results have for practitioners and other researchers.

These elements can be seen in the model research reports presented at the end of chapter 1. In the quantitative research report, "Effects of Classroom Structure on Student Achievement Goal Orientation" (pp. 19–26), the Conclusion and Discussion begins at [16]. In the qualitative research report, "Images of America: What Youth Do Know About the United States" (pp. 27–51), the conclusions and discussions are not in a single section. These elements of the qualitative research report begin at [21] and continue through [23].

The following section, called *Conclusions* by the researchers, has all the elements of a discussion section in a quantitative research report.

Purpose of the study: To investigate a broad-based program to foster children's social development that includes supportive teacher-student relationships and opportunities for students to interact and collaborate in cooperative groups.

CONCLUSIONS

Purpose

General
Results

The goal of the present project was to devise, implement, and assess the effectiveness of a comprehensive school-based program designed to enhance children's prosocial orientations. In this paper we have demonstrated, through quasi-experimental analyses, that the program was implemented by classroom teachers and that it had substantial positive effects on children's interpersonal behavior in the classroom (without impeding their achievement).

Specific
Results

Children in the first-cohort classrooms participating in the program over 5 years of program implementation were observed to be more supportive, friendly, and helpful, and to display more spontaneous prosocial behavior toward one another than children in a group of comparison classrooms. A replication with a second cohort, in kindergarten and grade 1, produced similar results. Outcomes such as these have not often been investigated in classroom observational studies, despite a growing concern with problems relating to students' interpersonal behavior in classrooms and recent calls for schools to renew their emphasis on preparing students for responsible roles in our democratic society (e.g., Bastian, 1985; Honig, 1985). If social development is a legitimate goal of elementary education, then research identifying factors that can serve to promote it is essential. The project described in this paper is one such effort.

When the program developed in this project is being fully implemented, students exercise considerable autonomy and self control: they help make decisions about their classrooms, participate in rule-development and revision, discuss and help solve classroom problems, and in general develop a shared sense of membership in, and responsibility for, their community. It is our expectation, as Dewey (1916) suggested long ago and others have more recently (e.g., Wood, 1986), that engaged participation in activities such as the ones used should help to prepare students for adult democratic responsibilities.

Relation to
Other
Research

The approach to classroom organization and activity embodied in this program, particularly its attempt to minimize the use of extrinsic incentives, represents a fairly radical departure from some of the classroom management systems currently in vogue (e.g., Canter's 1976, "assertive discipline"). It is however, quite consistent with the ideas and findings of much recent research concerning the conditions that enhance intrinsic motivation. Several researchers (see Lepper, 1983) have investigated the deleterious effect on intrinsic motivation of the use of external incentives (rewards in particular), often from an attributional perspective. Ryan, Connell, and Deci (1985), in a discussion of classroom factors that influence the development of students' self-regulation and intrinsic motivation for learning, emphasize teachers' provision of autonomy and decision-making opportunities, and the minimization of external control "in a context of adequate structure and guidance" (p. 44). The present findings suggest that these factors may also play a role in enhancing students' social orientations and behavior.

Significance

The two general aspects of classroom life that have been found to be related to children's social development in prior research—establishment of supportive teacher-student relationships and provision of opportunities for collaborative interstudent interaction—are incorporated in our Positive Discipline and Cooperative Activities program components, respectively. These aspects have previously been investigated separately. Our approach has been to combine these, along with other consistent elements (providing experiences in helping and understanding others; exposure to and discussion of examples of prosocial behavior, motives, and attitudes) into a general, pervasive, and coherent whole. We believe that the data reported in this paper indicate that the total program has had clear and strong effects on children's classroom behavior. We do not know whether these results could have been obtained with less than the total program (for example, with Developmental Discipline alone, or Developmental Discipline combined with Cooperative Activities). Because these elements are designed to be mutually supportive and interrelated (and are in fact intercorrelated), it is somewhat arbitrary and perhaps somewhat misleading to describe them as separate "components." We do intend, however, to conduct a series of natural variation analyses to try to assess the relative influence on student social behavior of various combinations of teacher behavior and classroom activity measures.

It is our hope and expectation that through participating in an environment in which certain central values of the society are both discussed and exemplified (e.g., mutual concern and respect, responsibility, helpfulness), such values and behaviors consistent with them will become more deeply ingrained in the children. While the present data, indicating substantial effects on students' behavior in the classroom, reflect only some surface aspects of the kinds of change we hope to engender, including a long-range commitment to democratic values, they do suggest that such changes may result from participating in this program. In other papers, we will be describing effects outside the classroom and on other areas of children's functioning. (Solomon, Watson, Delucchi, Schaps, & Battistich, 1988, pp. 545–546. Used with permission of the copyright holder, American Educational Research Association.)

Research consumers need to evaluate research producers' interpretations of results carefully for unwarranted or overgeneralized conclusions. They need to examine four aspects of the research producers' conclusions: (*a*) predicted results (in the case of quantitative research), (*b*) unpredicted results, (*c*) statistical and practical significance, and (*d*) further research or replications of the studies.

Researchers should explain whether results logically answer their research purposes or questions. Also, they need to indicate whether results are consistent with results of other researchers. As stated in chapter 4, background sections provide three major kinds of information: problem areas and their educational importance, related literature, and research purposes. Research consumers need to compare research producers' conclusions about anticipated or predicted results with the information provided in background sections. Also, research consumers need to determine whether research producers have drawn appropriate conclusions from the research designs and statistical procedures they used. For example, quantitative research producers should not conclude causality from descriptive or comparative research, and they should not generalize beyond the target population in any category of research.

Because comparative studies provide information about the existence of relationships (similarities and differences), it is not appropriate for research producers and consumers to infer a causal effect among variables. Most research producers avoid making this error, as did the researchers of a spelling program who found the existence of strong relationships and appropriately indicated that "the results support the idea of a common conceptual base for varying aspects of word knowledge" (Zutell & Rasinski, 1986, p. 111). This statement is not one of causation, but of coexistence.

Nevertheless, the error of inferring causality from relationship studies is common. A newspaper reporter, writing about educational television and young children, included statements that imply causation, an inappropriate conclusion based on correlation data.

In the article, the reporter indicated that in the years the preschool television program *Sesame Street* has been on the air, assorted research studies have shown that the program helps teach numbers and the alphabet to preschool children, and thus helps prepare them for school. He then wrote about a newer study, reporting that preschoolers in low-income areas around Kansas City who had watched educational television programs such as *Sesame Street* not only were better prepared for school, but also had performed better on verbal and math tests (up to age 7) than would otherwise have been expected. Further, the study found that preschoolers who had watched primarily adult programming and entertainment cartoons performed worse on those tests than would have been expected. The reporter quoted a then-visiting scholar at Harvard University's School of Education who also helped found the now-inactive advocacy group Action for Children's Television. After reading the new study, she was reported to have said,

Inappropriate Conclusion of Causation

> "This study shows that terrific television causes kids to be more receptive to learning, more receptive to reading, more receptive in school" (Mifflin, 1995).

A different newspaper reporter discussing the results of several studies about the relationship between television viewing and school achievement made a more appropriate statement about those results. The studies under discussion reported that children who watched certain popular television programs were those most likely to have low scores on standardized achievement tests. In other words, there was a specific relationship between the television shows viewed by students and their achievement levels. In this case, the reporter did not attribute causality to the relationships, but concluded that

Appropriate Statement About Causation

> "It is widely believed that children who spend more time watching the popular programs on commercial television tend to be lower achievers in school, but researchers have yet to show that television causes that poor performance" (Maeroff, 1982).

Researchers sometimes need to explain results that they did not expect. For example, one research team found that one of their treatments in an experimental study produced an unusual outcome. The following discussion section shows how those researchers put forth a possible reason for the unexpected finding.

Purpose of the study: To examine the effects on students' comprehension of voiced versions (i.e., prose that invites reading) of more and less coherent texts.

DISCUSSION

General Findings and Conclusions

In this study, students were presented with one of four versions of a passage, either its original form taken directly from a textbook, a version of the textbook passage with features of voice added, a more coherent version of the original textbook passage, or a version that exhibited both coherence and voice. Given that the present study worked with four versions of one base text, the study should be viewed as an initial exploration of whether text that appears to be more engaging can provide advantage for readers. There has been a long-standing assumption that more lively text language will lead to better reader outcomes, but heretofore there was no empirical evidence to back up those intuitions. Thus we felt that it was important to delve into the area of the value of "vivid language," "liveliness," and other such qualities of text that are attributed to tradebooks and tend to be lacking in textbooks. Given the findings, further research is now warranted for fleshing out the effects of these more elusive text qualities.

Specific Findings

The results showed the strongest advantage for the passage that exhibited both coherence and voice, with the coherent passage showing advantage over the other two in performance on questions, and over the original textbook version in recall. These results pertained to students' responses on recall and questions immediately after reading. The same results were obtained on the questions after a week's delay, yet differences in recall after delay did not reach significance.

Problem With the Results

As mentioned earlier, the study unfortunately provided for a somewhat flawed test of how much text content was retained after delay. A problem apparently arose because some of the students in the study were given a tradebook to read that was about the Revolutionary War period. The book is a lively and interestingly written one, and it seemed to have left an impression on at least some of the students. We saw this effect, particularly in recalls of students who read the textbook and voiced textbook versions, because some of their recalls included information that was accurate about the period, but had not been contained in the passages they read for this study. Additionally, some of the students in both textbook conditions improved in the quality of recall after a week's delay.

Explanation of Possible Reasons for Unusual Findings

The effect of the tradebook was not noticed in the coherent and voiced coherent conditions, probably for two reasons. First, fewer students in these conditions had read the tradebook (8 vs. 12). But more importantly, it seems that these students were less in a position to benefit from additional information or another exposure to engaging text, since they had already developed higher quality representations of the events portrayed in the texts. Thus the same potential for enhancing comprehension did not exist for readers of the coherent passages as for readers of the textbook passages.

Modified Conclusions

Interestingly, exposure to the tradebook did not have the same effect on question performance. Perhaps that is because, although students who had read the tradebook account were able to add some of that information to their retelling, they seemed unable to enhance their responses to the questions that required them to understand the role of certain information within the chain of events (i.e., the three issue questions). Thus, although we cannot be as definitive as we would like about the retention effects from a coherent text with features of voice, there is a suggestion that positive potential exists for lasting effects. This suggestion is based on the results of the question measure and the trend in the recall data.

Further Discussion of Findings

The present study focused on the understanding that students can get from working independently with texts that exhibit various characteristics. Yet when texts are used in classrooms, instructional and social factors mediate the text interaction. For example, teachers may provide background, add explanations, or question students about their understanding. Additionally, other students may question or comment on the text and provide responses to teacher questions. The ways in which these influences may interact with text features is an issue for further study. The results of this study do not speak directly to that issue, but consideration of the pattern of results may provide some basis for pursuing the interaction of classroom factors with text characteristics.

Relationship of This Study to Other Research

The overall pattern of results in this study indicates that comprehension is promoted when text is written to exhibit some of the features of oral language, to communicate the immediacy of events and emotional reactions of agents, and to vitalize relationships among agents. The pattern of results adds to our understanding of the relationship between interesting or engaging features of text and comprehension. Previous research pointed out problems in adding isolated pieces of engaging information to text, finding that such information was well remembered, but to the detriment of central information in a text (Britton et al., 1989; Duffy et al., 1989; Garner et al., 1989; Graves et al., 1991; Hidi & Baird, 1988; Wade & Adams, 1990). The present study indicates that, when engaging features are used to enhance central information, comprehension of that central material can be improved.

The present findings also extend caveats about the role of interesting or engaging text features, however. That is, the results of this study suggest that such features may not have effect when added to a text that lacks coherence. The voiced version of the textbook passage did not enhance comprehension. This finding highlights our notion that the role of voice is to engage students in a text. Potential for engagement, however, is not productive if the content of the text is not accessible. In the case of the textbook versions, the information provided seems just too far beyond the reach for most young students to make sense of it on their own, even when the language of the text promotes engagement.

Implications of the Findings for Instruction

Potential for increasing comprehension through voice may be better realized under certain text circumstances. One such circumstance involves situations that are pivotal to making sense of a text. That is, students who received the voiced coherent passage were better able to recall the concepts of representation and the colonists' protests, which were central to the conflict between Britain and the colonies. On the other hand, voice features did not improve recall of Britain's reaction of removing the taxes. The role of this information was made less crucial to comprehension of the passage because another, simpler and more general, statement of resolution existed—that "things quieted down." Students were apparently able to substitute this information to satisfy the need for closure to the events, rather than using the more specified information about Britain's action. Thus students seemed to fill in the needed information in the most accessible way.

Another circumstance that may optimize the potential for the effects of voice is situations that can portray emotion and active response. These qualities characterized the segments of text that showed a difference in recall between the coherent and voiced coherent passages. However, the better remembered concepts—representation and protest—were also central to the situation portrayed in the text, so it cannot be determined whether the enhancement was due to the voicing of those specific concepts or to a general effect of voicing that interacted with their role in the text.

A more general consideration of the circumstances under which features of voice enhance understanding is the extent to which the concept of voicing texts can be implemented. One direction to explore is whether voicing is appropriate for text content other than history. Our results allow us to speculate that voicing may be more widely applicable. Consider the three voicing themes used here—orality, activity, and connectivity. Certainly, features of oral language can be brought to bear on text presentations of a wide range of phenomena and need not be restricted to sequences of human action. The theme of activity was used here in relation to human events in a causal sequence. Yet, one component of activity, the notion of immediacy of events, could apply to sequences of events in the natural world as well. Connectivity pertains to relationships both among text agents and between the text and the reader. Although the first type may be limited for some content, features of text that provide for relationship between reader and text, such as directly addressing the reader, have wide applicability.

The essential concept is that, for understanding to be developed from encounters with text, readers need to engage with the text. Engagement should be possible for an almost endless assortment of text types and topics. The key is to discover elements through which engagement can be promoted. Creating texts so that they exhibit features of voice is certainly one of those elements, and the extent of its applicability is an interesting question for further study.

In the meantime, how can insights about engaging texts be applied to classroom instruction? A ready resource of engaging material exists in tradebooks. Tradebooks on historical topics can bring the past alive for young readers, and may help to reinforce the motivations and principles that drove people to action.

In focusing on bringing engagement to encounters with text, however, one must not lose sight of other text aspects that may need to be present to promote understanding. Our results suggest that engaging features can contribute to understanding when such features coincide with a coherent presentation of ideas. Engaging text might invite a reader's participation, focus attention within a text, and place emphasis on certain ideas. But once a reader's engagement and attention are activated, the text ideas that are attended to must have adequate connection and explanation to allow the building of meaning.

Source: From Beck, Isabel L., McKeown, Margaret G., & Worthy, Jo. (1995, Apr/May/Jun). Giving a text voice can improve students' understanding. *Reading Research Quarterly, 30* (2), 220–238.

> *Restatement of General Conclusion*

For some reason, quantitative research reports published in journals all seem to have statistically significant results. Less-often published are studies with nonsignificant results. Reports of this kind sometimes occur when one set of researchers attempts to show that particular treatments do not produce results that other researchers have previously produced. It is important that professionals examine each others' work and that researchers be able to replicate their work. In fact, many journals will ask for "responses" from researchers when publishing studies that seem to refute their position. Research consumers need to examine both sets of reports for biases, and they need to determine the practical significance of all research. For example, the July/August/September 1994 issue of *Reading Research Quarterly* contains an exchange of ideas:

> McCarthy, S.J. Authors, text, and talk: The internalization of dialogue from social interaction during writing.
> Bloome, D. Response to McCarthy: On the nature of language in classroom literacy research.
> Rowe, D.W. Response to McCarthy: The limitations of eclecticism in research.
> McCarthy, S.J. Response to Bloome: Violence, risk, and the indeterminacy of language.
> McCarthy, S.J. Response to Rowe: Aligning methods to assumptions.

Consumers need to be concerned with the applicability of researchers' results to their own educational situation: "Are the results generalizable to my local educational setting? Can the treatment, when there is one, be implemented with practical considerations given to time, effort, money, and personnel?"

Researchers often cite questions that their research has left unanswered. These questions can, and often do, become the research purposes in future studies by the researchers themselves or by others. The questions might be about research design, research procedures, subject selection, instrumentation, data analysis, or research results. Research consumers need to examine the logic of these recommendations.

ACTIVITIES

Activity 1

Using the Focus Questions at the beginning of the chapter, write a summary of the key ideas found in the chapter.

Activity 2

Using one quantitative and one qualitative study of your own choosing (or located through the resources in Appendix A), read and evaluate their Conclusion sections. Use the criteria for evaluation conclusion found in this chapter. You may team with fellow students and do the activity collaboratively. Or, each of you may do the activity independently and compare your answers.

FEEDBACK

Activity 1

What information should research consumers get from discussion sections of research reports? Research producers often begin discussion sections with a statement of the research purpose and then follow with a statement of their results and, in the case of quantitative studies, whether the results were statistically significant and meaningful. In the remainder of the section, the researchers usually explain (*a*) whether the results answered their research questions, (*b*) how their results relate to related literature presented in the introduction, and (*c*) what implications the results have for practitioners and other researchers.

What criteria should be used to evaluate discussion sections?   From reading discussion sections, research consumers should be able to answer questions such as:

What were the researchers' purposes for the study?

What were the researchers' major results?

How did the researchers interpret their results?

What recommendations did the researchers make for applying the results to instructional situations or for future research projects?

Are the researchers' issues and concerns relevant to me as a professional, or to my teaching situation?

Are conclusions related to answering the research question(s), and are they appropriate to the results?

Is the report free from inappropriate generalizations and implications?

If inappropriate, are suggestions for additional research provided?

What is the plan for reading discussion sections?   By reading the discussion section together with the abstract, research consumers have an overview of the research project.

Activity 2

Compare your answers with those of fellow students and discuss them with your instructor.

Reading and Interpreting Reviews of Research

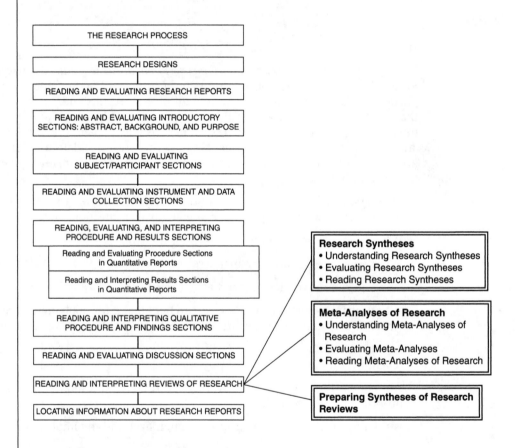

THE RESEARCH PROCESS

RESEARCH DESIGNS

READING AND EVALUATING RESEARCH REPORTS

READING AND EVALUATING INTRODUCTORY SECTIONS: ABSTRACT, BACKGROUND, AND PURPOSE

READING AND EVALUATING SUBJECT/PARTICIPANT SECTIONS

READING AND EVALUATING INSTRUMENT AND DATA COLLECTION SECTIONS

READING, EVALUATING, AND INTERPRETING PROCEDURE AND RESULTS SECTIONS

Reading and Evaluating Procedure Sections in Quantitative Reports

Reading and Interpreting Results Sections in Quantitative Reports

READING AND INTERPRETING QUALITATIVE PROCEDURE AND FINDINGS SECTIONS

READING AND EVALUATING DISCUSSION SECTIONS

READING AND INTERPRETING REVIEWS OF RESEARCH

LOCATING INFORMATION ABOUT RESEARCH REPORTS

Research Syntheses
- Understanding Research Syntheses
- Evaluating Research Syntheses
- Reading Research Syntheses

Meta-Analyses of Research
- Understanding Meta-Analyses of Research
- Evaluating Meta-Analyses
- Reading Meta-Analyses of Research

Preparing Syntheses of Research Reviews

FOCUS QUESTIONS

1. What are research syntheses?
2. What criteria are used to evaluate research syntheses?
3. What are meta-analyses?
4. What criteria are used to evaluate meta-analyses?
5. How are teacher-as-researcher research syntheses prepared?

In chapter 4, part of the discussion about introductory sections dealt with researchers' brief summaries of other researchers' results that were related to the same area. In these limited reviews, called *literature reviews,* researchers indicate strengths from reviewed research, which they used in their own research; and weaknesses or limitations in the reviewed research, which they changed. A set of questions was given in chapter 4 so that research consumers could evaluate how critically researchers analyzed related research. These limited literature searches, however, are not intended to be comprehensive, in-depth reports of research related to a problem area. When researchers report comprehensive reviews of research related to problem areas, they do so in research syntheses or in meta-analyses of research.

Comprehensive reviews of research are important to educators—both to research producers and research consumers. First, preparers of research reviews provide overviews of the research related to a particular problem area. They explain why the problem area is important as a research concern and also report the extent to which the problem area has been researched. Second, research reviewers provide information about the types of research designs used to study the problem, and they may show methodological changes over time in how research producers approach the problem. Third, they identify and define key terms related to the problem area, and they may discover differences in the operational definitions researchers used. Fourth, research reviewers can provide insights about the appropriateness of research producers' methodology. These insights are important for consumers when consumers wish to determine the generalizability of results from various research situations to other teaching and learning situations. Fifth (and possibly the most important reason for these reviews), reviewers join together and interpret the results from a group of research studies dealing with a research problem area. Through their interpretation of the collective results and their general commentary, research reviewers in education indicate trends in the development of concepts about learning and instruction. These ideas help research producers understand possible areas for future research and help research consumers gain insight about education-related issues.

Research consumers need to understand (*a*) researchers' reason(s) for preparing reviews of research, (*b*) the way research reviewers prepare research syntheses, (*c*) the rationale underlying meta-analyses of research and the procedures for doing meta-analyses, and (*d*) how to read and interpret syntheses and meta-analyses of research.

From reading a synthesis or meta-analysis of research, research consumers should be able to answer the following questions:

- How did the research reviewer define the problem area?
- What questions did the reviewer seek to answer, and why did he or she think the answers would be important for educators?
- How did the reviewer locate relevant research reports?
- How did the reviewer determine what studies to include in the review?
- What procedures did the reviewer use to analyze and interpret the results of the research?
- What conclusions did the reviewer make from the research?

Research consumers should keep in mind that research related to any educational problem can be summarized, interpreted, and reported for different purposes and for different consumers (Ladas, 1980). Here are some examples. Research can be summarized in order to provide educators with an overview of the type of research being conducted and the results of that research. Research can be reviewed in order to point out weaknesses or limitations in instruction and to make recommendations for improvement in teaching practices. It can be reviewed to establish the improvement of research practices. It can be reviewed to influence broad educational policy and to provide conclusions for applied use. The reviews can be directed at audiences such as those in powerful or influential positions, researchers, practitioners, or the public at large. Research consumers, then, need to identify the intended audience(s) of research syntheses and meta-analytic reviews of educational research.

RESEARCH SYNTHESES

A research synthesis is undertaken as a research project in which the sources of data are the primary research reports of other researchers. These reviews are more than summaries of research; **research syntheses** are critical examinations of research producers' methods and conclusions, and of the generalizability of their combined results.

What are now considered *research syntheses* have in the past been called *integrative reviews of research*. The terms *research syntheses, integrative reviews of research,* and *research integration* can be considered synonyms. The newer term is used because it is felt that *synthesis* more clearly describes how the results of primary research are combined so that the knowledge constructed from those results is applied to issues of instructional practice and policymaking (Shanahan, 2000). The discussion will cover the aspects of problem formulation, data collection, data evaluation, analysis and interpretation, and public presentation.

Understanding Research Syntheses

Research syntheses consist of five stages (Cooper, 1982; Cooper & Lindsay, 1998; Jackson, 1980). These stages are (1) problem formation, (2) data collection, (3) evaluation of data quality, (4) data analysis and interpretation, and (5) presentation of results.

The stages of research synthesis are summarized in Table 10.1. The table includes the characteristics of each stage of the review process and the issues research reviewers need to address. For each stage, these characteristics include (*a*) a research question that needs to be asked, (*b*) the activities that need to be done, (*c*) the sources of differences among reviewers that can cause variations in their conclusions, and (*d*) the possible sources of threats to the validity of the review. The discussion that follows is based on ideas expressed in several sources (Abrami, Cohen, & d'Apollonia, 1988; Cooper, 1982; Cooper & Lindsay, 1998; Eisenhart, 1999; Jackson, 1980; Schwandt, 1999; Shanahan, 2000).

Problem Formulation.   The first stage of research synthesis begins with a search of existing research syntheses for ideas about questions or hypotheses. Ideas are sought for questions about the phenomenon being researched and variations in methods that might account for variations in results. In addition, questions might be formulated from available theory and the reviewers' own insights. Research reviewers then set out operational definitions for key concepts within the problem area. These definitions may reflect those used by primary researchers or may be created for the research review. Research reviewers use the operational definitions to identify relevant primary research studies for inclusion in the research synthesis. For example, the following is how one team of research reviewers operationally defined key concepts

Table 10.1
Research Synthesis Conceptualized as a Research Process

			Stages of Research		
Stage Characteristics	Problem Formulation	Data Collection	Data Evaluation	Analysis and Interpretation	Public Presentation
Research question asked	What evidence should be included in the review?	What procedures should be used to find relevant evidence?	What retrieved evidence should be included in the review?	What procedures should be used to make inferences about the literature as a whole?	What information should be included in the review report?
Primary function in review	Constructing definitions that distinguish relevant from irrelevant studies	Determining which of potentially relevant studies to examine	Applying criteria to separate "valid" from "invalid" studies	Synthesizing valid retrieved studies	Applying editorial criteria to separate important from unimportant information
Procedural differences that create variation in review conclusions	1. Differences in included operational definitions 2. Differences in operational detail	Differences in the research contained in sources of information	1. Differences in quality criteria 2. Differences in the influence of nonquality criteria	Differences in rules of inference	Differences in guidelines for editorial judgment
Sources of potential invalidity in review conclusions	1. Narrow concepts might make review conclusions less definitive and robust 2. Superficial operational detail might obscure interacting variables	1. Accessed studies might be qualitatively different from the target population of studies 2. People sample in accessible studies might be different from target population	1. Nonquality factors might cause improper weighting of study 2. Omissions in study reports might make conclusions unreliable	1. Rules for distinguishing patterns from noise might be inappropriate 2. Review-based evidence might be used to infer causality	1. Omission of review procedures might make conclusions irreproducible 2. Omissions of review findings and study procedures might make conclusions obsolete

Source: Cooper, H. M., & Lindsay, J. J., "Research Synthesis and Meta-Analysis." In L. Bickman & D. J. Rog (Eds.), Handbook of Applied Social Research Methods, pp. 315–341. Copyright © 1998 by Sage Publications, Thousand Oaks, CA. Reprinted by permission of Sage Publications.

such as linear and nonlinear texts. Note that the reviewers indicate the references upon which they based their operational definitions.

> *Purpose of the review: To examine empirical investigations that relate to subject-matter information and interest and that involve connected discourse presented either in traditional written form or on computer.*
>
> We use the term *linear text* to designate connected discourse presented in written form where decisions relative to processing are left solely to the reader. Defined in this manner, linear text is text of a more traditional nature—that is, the writings students are apt to encounter in textbooks, journals, and magazines. Nonlinear text is also connected discourse; however, it is discourse accompanied by some type of data base management system. This system guides or prompts readers to reaccess or extend the main text through associative computer-based links to other informational screens (see Gillingham, Young, & Kulikowich, in press, for an extensive discussion of the nature of nonlinear text). One category of nonlinear texts that we will inspect in this review, for example, is hypertext. With the evolution of situated theories of learning that emphasize rich and unique learning environments (e.g., Brown, Collins, & Duguid, 1989; Greeno, 1989; Resinick, Levine, & Teasley, 1991), nonlinear texts, such as hypertext, have gained in popularity. Many of these hypertexts are part of extensive multimedia systems that include not only nonlinear texts but also supporting videos, maps, and commercial movie clips (Christense, Giamo, & Jones, 1993; Trumbull, Gay, & Mazur, 1992). Therefore, it is important to consider the impact of these more nontraditional texts on the acquisition of subject-matter knowledge (Bolter 1991b). (Alexander, Kulikowich, & Jetton, 1994, pp. 202–203)

Operational Definition

Operational Definition

Sources of Definition

Sources of Definition

Sources of Definition

In some cases, researchers synthesize the research that has been reviewed or synthesized in other researchers' studies. Such syntheses might be considered syntheses of syntheses!

Data Collection.   In collecting, organizing, and summarizing data, research reviewers try to use as many information sources as possible. An important responsibility of research reviewers is to identify the target population, accessible population, and sample population of primary research reports. The target population of primary research resports is the total body of research reports about which generalizations can be made. Therefore, accessible populations of research reports may be determined by the availability to researchers of library holdings and electronic databases. The sample population of research reports is the specific research reports the reviewers select for review. Practical considerations for reviewers about selection relate to the resources for locating primary research reports (see chapter 11, "Locating Information About Research Reports") and the time period(s) to be covered (such as only research published between 1995 and 2005). Also, research reviewers cluster research reports by research designs, because each type of research must be judged by separate criteria.

Data Evaluation.   In evaluating data quality, research reviewers set up evaluation criteria before they search the literature. As a rule, research reviewers ask critical questions about research that are similar to those that this text describes for primary research. (See Figures 3.1 and 3.2, pages 86–87, and chapters 4 to 9).

Analysis and Interpretation.   In analyzing and interpreting data, the research reviewers should explicitly state how they made inferences. They should distinguish between inferences they made on the basis of individual studies, and those they made as a result of their review of a group of studies.

Public Presentation. In presenting their results, authors of research syntheses try to avoid omitting details and evidence. In other words, in making a research synthesis comprehensible, they attend to the same factors that make a primary research report understandable.

The article "English-as-a-Second-Language Learners' Cognitive Reading Processes," in this chapter's appendix, pages 227–245, is taken from a research synthesis about the cognitive processes used by English-as-a-second-language learners. It includes a general background and introduction, the procedures for locating and selecting research reports, the categorization of the studies and the general findings of the primary researchers, and a summary and discussion of the combined findings. The report is annotated with these stages. What has not been included here, for reasons of space, is the example's table containing brief summaries of the primary reports and the references.

Before reading the article you may want to refer to the upcoming section, "Reading Research Syntheses," on page 215. When reading the article, note that in "Methods," the researcher details how the studies were located and selected, and in "Limitations of the Studies," she critically evaluates the research methodology of the studies. Compare the limitations she notes with the criteria for evaluating research in Figure 3.1 and Figure 3.2, pages 86–87.

Evaluating Research Syntheses

Research consumers need to determine whether research reviewers have critically analyzed and interpreted the data that the reviewers present. The information in Table 10.1 and the following discussion indicate characteristics in reviews that may lead the reviews' conclusions to be invalid. Consumers need to identify whether reviewers controlled variables that could threaten the internal and external validity of their reviews. If the researcher has synthesized information from other researchers' syntheses, research consumers can use the information in Table 10.1 to determine the effectiveness of the synthesis of research syntheses.

Procedural Differences That Create Variation in Review Conclusions, and Sources of Potential Invalidity in Review Conclusions.
In the problem formulation stage, research reviewers should identify differences that exist among their operational definitions, those of other reviewers, and those found in the sampled research. Reviewers should indicate how the specific details of the reviewed studies differ. Research consumers should be able to distinguish precisely between aspects of primary researchers' methods that reviewers believe are relevant to their review critique, and those that are not.

In the data collection stage, reviewers should identify differences that exist between the target population of available studies, their sample of studies, and studies used in other reviews. The target population of research studies consists of all published research reports related to the problem area. The studies selected for analysis constitute the review sample. Consumers need an understanding of the target population of studies and the representativeness of the reviewers' sample of studies. Also, because reviewers determine their own criteria for including or excluding primary research reports from their reviews, it is possible for reviewers to select different samples of studies for analysis. (This limitation is similar to the one discussed in chapter 5 about the need for consumers to be sensitive to primary researchers' identification of their target populations and subject selection techniques.) Reviewers should explain the time span covered by the research and the type of research designs used. Also, research consumers need assurance that there was no selection bias. Differences in conclusions by different research reviewers can result from differences in their samples.

Also, consumers need to understand subject sampling procedures used by primary researchers. It is possible for several primary researchers to use similar labels for their subjects while actually dealing with different target populations. Research consumers should expect research reviewers to delineate the operational definitions used in the primary researchers' subject selection.

In the data evaluation stage, reviewers should indicate what differences exist between the criteria they used for evaluating the research and those criteria used by other reviewers. Reviewers should indicate whether their critical evaluations were limited by the absence of information in the primary studies. Also, if more than one evaluator is used in reviewing the primary studies, reviewers should report inter-evaluator agreements.

In the analysis and interpretation stage, research reviewers should indicate how their method of interpretation and their conclusions differ from those of other research reviewers. They need to indicate how they distinguished between relevant information (patterns of results) and extraneous information (noise). Research consumers need to identify whether reviewers effectively synthesized results and noted trends, or whether reviewers made inaccurate inferences (such as basing causality on relationship results) or came to conclusions not directly related to their purpose questions, or extended beyond the data.

In the public presentation stage, research reviewers might not be responsible for differences in editorial guidelines; however, research consumers should be critical of research review reports that are not complete. Omissions restrict the replicability of a research synthesis, thereby limiting the effective use of the reviewers' results and conclusions.

Research consumers can use these questions when evaluating research syntheses:

- Are there differences in operational definitions among the synthesis reviewers, other reviewers, and the primary researchers? Are those differences explained?
- Has the target population of research been identified? Are there differences between the samples of studies in the review and other reviews? What is the nature of those differences?
- Are there explicit evaluation criteria? Do these criteria differ from those of other reviewers? Have the synthesis researchers cited studies with methodological limitations? Have those limitations been explained?
- Have the reviewers drawn conclusions that are different from those of other reviewers? Are those differences discussed?
- Does the review report present information in a standard research format? Is the report complete?

Reading Research Syntheses

Research syntheses can be read using the plan for reading research reports discussed in chapter 3, with some slight modifications. The idea is to understand the purposes and conclusions of the research reviewers before reading their data collection and data analyses. As you read, keep in mind the evaluative questions.

- You will be looking at the article "English-as-a-Second-Language Learners' Cognitive Reading Processes: A Review of Research in the United States," on pages 227–245. Your first reading step is to read the title [1] and predict.
    - Briefly, list answers to these questions: "What do I know about the topic? What do I know about the authors? What information would I expect to gain from this review?"
    - Read the abstract [2] for an overview of the report and its findings.
    - Then, read the major headings and subheadings [9] through [31] and answer, "Is the review organized logically, and is the location of information clearly identified?"
- The second phase, reading the research synthesis, is to find information suggested by your expectations and to confirm or modify the information you know about the topic.
    - Reread the report title [1] and abstract [2]. Read the background section [3], the method section [9], the theoretical frameworks section [12], and the summary and discussion section [28].
    - Note as you read: (*a*) the identification of a target population, (*b*) the discussion of reliability of data interpretations, and (*c*) the operational definitions presented in paragraph 3.
    - Read any of the remaining sections that might help you better understand the reviewers' methodology and conclusions.
- The third phase, confirming predictions and knowledge, is to verify that the purpose has been met and to immediately recall key information. You should decide which information supports the reviewers' purpose and adds to your knowledge.
    - Answer the question "Can the instructional implications presented in this review be used in my teaching situation?"
    - Read all other sections to obtain information to satisfy your purpose questions.
    - Write a short (two- to three-sentence) statement that applies to the purpose for reading the review and that contains the review's key points.

META-ANALYSES OF RESEARCH

Meta-analyses of research are ways of critically examining primary research studies that use quantitative data analyses. Research reviewers use meta-analysis as "analysis of analyses" (Glass, 1976, p. 3); that is, statistical data analysis of already completed statistical data analyses. In meta-analyses, reviewers convert the statistical results of the individual studies into a common measurement so that they can obtain an overall, combined result. Research reviewers convert primary researchers' statistical results into standard numerical forms, and then they analyze those measures by traditional statistical procedures. A key assumption of this analysis is that by putting together results from various studies, a more accurate representation of the target population is provided than by the individual studies.

The following discussions about understanding and evaluating meta-analyses are synthesized from several sources (Abrami et al., 1988; Bangert-Drowns & Rudner, 1991; Boston, 2004; Carlberg et al., 1984; Cooper & Lindsay, 1998; Glass, 1976, 2000; Joyce, 1987; MacColl & White, 1998; Moore, 1999; Slavin, 1984a, 1984b, 1986, 1987b; Stock et al., 1982; Thompson, 1999).

Understanding Meta-Analyses of Research

The meta-analysis approach was devised as an attempt to eliminate reviewer biases in synthesizing results from primary quantitative research reports. Some researchers wished to reduce the possible influence of reviewers' biases in the selection and interpretation of research reports. To accomplish this task, they designed several quantitative procedures for tabulating and comparing research results from a large number of primary research reports, especially experimental research. A simple quantitative tabulation for estimating the effectiveness of a treatment is called *vote counting*. Vote counting consists of tabulating the number of positive significant results (1), the number of negative significant results—those in which the control results exceed the treatment (2), and the number of studies without significant results (0). Vote counting, however, can provide misleading ideas about the effectiveness of a treatment or the relationship among variables because vote counting does not take into account the magnitude of the effect or relationship. Magnitude can be thought of as the size of the difference between two or more variables.

Meta-analysis is a quantitative procedure that research reviewers use to account for the magnitude of an effect or relationship. The meta-analysis procedure has become increasingly popular with research reviewers because it is systematic and easily replicable. Given the same set of research reports (selected by the same set of criteria) and using the same statistical procedures, all research reviewers should get the same results. Also, its users say meta-analysis can be used with the results of research projects with varying methodological quality, with similar but not exactly the same statistical procedures, and with different sample sizes. Further, it allows research reviewers to examine concurrently the degree of influence or relationship among the methods, subjects, treatments, duration of treatments, and results of primary research (regardless of whether results are significant).

Meta-analyses have stages similar to those of research syntheses. In meta-analyses, (1) problems are formed, (2) research studies are collected, (3) pertinent data are identified, (4) analyses and interpretations are made of the data, and (5) results and conclusions are presented to the public. Meta-analyses begin with reviewers doing an exhaustive, complete search to locate previous research syntheses and meta-analyses, and all primary research studies relating to the education questions or problems under review. We will next examine problem formulation, data collection and coding of studies, reporting results, and public presentation.

Problem Formulation.   The first stage of a meta-analysis is the same as that in a research synthesis. The reviewers set the purpose and scope of the review and identify key concepts. They discuss the theoretical framework of the problem area, present operational definitions, and pose specific research questions.

Data Collection and Coding of Studies.   In the second stage, the meta-analysts survey the existing primary research and indicate how they located and selected the studies for review. Meta-analysts usually indicate the procedures used (*a*) to obtain studies, (*b*) to identify those for inclusion in the review, and (*c*) to select the variables for analysis. These procedures are similar to those used in research syntheses. To ensure accurate coding, meta-analysis researchers use multiple raters and report inter-rater reliability. Summaries of the coding are sometimes, but not always, reported in tables that list characteristics of the research studies and the computed effect size of each study (see the next paragraph for an explanation of effect size).

Reporting Results.   In the third stage, the reviewers describe the results of their analyses. After coding, meta-analysis reviewers use statistical procedures to examine the combined research results. They group the research according to research designs. Most often, meta-analyses are done with research using experimental designs. Meta-analysts create an effect size for each experimental study. Effect sizes are standard scores, created from a ratio derived from the mean scores of the experimental and control groups and the standard deviation of the control group. Effect size scores are based on the number of subjects in the primary studies. The scores show the extent of the difference between the mean scores of the experimental and control groups in relation to the standard deviation. For example, an effect size of +.50 would mean that the experimental group scored about .5 SD (half a standard deviation) above the control group. An effect size of −.50 would mean that the experimental group scored about .5 SD below the control group.

These effect sizes can be averaged, and significant differences (e.g., *t* or *F* ratios, or *r*–correlations) can be determined between treatment and control groups, or among several other independent variables. The following excerpt is from the results section of a meta-analysis of a school drug-prevention program.

> *Purpose: To provide an updated meta-analysis on the effectiveness of Project D.A.R.E. in preventing alcohol, tobacco, and illicit drug use among school-aged youths.*
>
> The average weighted effect size (*r*) for all studies was 0.011 (*d* = 0.023; 95% Confidence Interval = −0.04, 0.08), indicating marginally better outcomes for individuals participating in D.A.R.E. relative to participants in control conditions. The fact that the associated CI included a negative value indicates that the average effect size was not significantly greater than zero at *p* < .05. According to the guidelines developed by Cohen (Note 13), both of the effect sizes obtained were below the level normally considered small. Four of the included studies noted no effect of D.A.R.E. relative to control conditions, and 1 study noted that D.A.R.E. was less effective than the control condition.
>
> Furthermore, the 6 reports indicating that D.A.R.E. had more positive effects were, for the most part, small (Figure 1). The largest effect size was found in a report (Note 14) in which the only outcome examined was smoking. Finally, we conducted a test of cumulative significance to determine whether differences existed between D.A.R.E. participants and non-D.A.R.E. participants. This test produced nonsignificant results (*z* = 0.73, N[ot] S[ignificant]).

Effective Size as a Correlation

Analysis of Results

Comparison With Control Groups

Source: From West, S. L. & O'Neal, K. K. (2004). Project D.A.R.E. outcome effectiveness revisited. *American Journal of Public Health*, *94* (6), 1027–1030. Reprinted by permission of American Public Health Association.

Public Presentation.   In presenting their results, authors of meta-analyses try to avoid omitting details and evidence. Their approach to reporting is no less stringent than that of primary researchers and synthesis reviewers in making their analyses understandable.

The article in this chapter's appendix, "The Effects of Instruction in Solving Mathematical Word Problems for Students With Learning Problems: A Meta-Analysis," pages 245–266, is taken from a meta-analysis about the effects of students' cooperative and competitive learning on their problem-solving achievement. All sections are included except the reference section and the tables.

Evaluating Meta-Analyses of Research

Consumers need to determine whether research reviewers using meta-analytic techniques have critically analyzed and interpreted the data that they present. Consumers need to know how research reviewers using meta-analyses controlled variables that could threaten the internal and external validity of their reviews.

Although meta-analyses are systematic and their results may be replicable, several major limitations affect the usability and generalizability of their results. Some of these limitations are common to both synthesis and meta-analytic research reviews. Consumers need to understand what these limitations are and how to critically evaluate meta-analytic reviews of research.

In evaluating meta-analyses, research consumers need to have the same understanding about the various stages (problem formulation, data collection, data evaluation, analysis and interpretation, and public presentation) as they have about these stages in research syntheses.

A limitation specific to evaluating meta-analyses in the data evaluation stage is the possible lack of appropriate data in the primary studies. Meta-analysis reviewers must have the means, standard deviations, and sample sizes for all subject groups. When data are insufficient, primary studies are excluded; therefore, meta-analyses are only effective in examining the results of well-reported research.

Further, meta-analyses involve the specific coding of primary research reports on several factors. The coding procedures involve judgments that are rational or subjective (not statistical or objective). Therefore, meta-analysis reviewers should use more than one coder; and they need to report the factors of consistency or reliability among coders.

Another limitation of meta-analyses is that reviewers can examine only primary research with direct quantitative evidence. Direct evidence comes from the examination of explicit variables and specific defined subjects. However, one benefit of a research synthesis is that reviewers can provide indications of indirect evidence that might give research producers and consumers insight about possible effects or relationships. And, research synthesizers can analyze and combine results from qualitative research.

Also, meta-analyses include only primary research studies with complete data in the analyses. Primary research studies that have major methodological weaknesses or problems are not excluded. Consequently, poorly designed and implemented research studies are given equal status with well-designed and implemented studies. Thus, important qualitative information may be hidden by the statistical averaging of simple numerical data.

Additionally, meta-analyses may seem to indicate a greater precision or accuracy than syntheses of research because they may appear more scientific. If the researchers have demonstrated that their selection of studies is representative of the research in the area, then consumers of research can have more confidence in accepting the results. Also, in interpreting effect sizes, researchers undertaking meta-analyses need to interpret for research consumers the meaning of the relative magnitude of those effect sizes. What constitutes a small, average, or large effect size seems to be different in different educational and psychological disciplines (Cooper & Lindsay, 1998).

An issue related to the previous one is that most of the published quantitative research studies are those with significant findings. Research studies without significant findings are often not submitted for publication for various reasons. So, the population of research to be analyzed through a meta-analysis may be biased.

These problems have been highlighted by some researchers who reviewed meta-analyses of research. One review team did a synthesis critique and comparison of six meta-analyses of research concerning the validity of college students' rating of instruction (Abrami et al., 1988). These reviewers found that all six meta-analyses resulted in different conclusions about students' rating of instruction. The reviewers concluded that they

> found differences at each of five steps in the quantitative syntheses which contributed to the discrepant conclusions reached by the [six meta-analytic] reviewers. The [six] reviewers had dissimilar inclusion criteria; thus the operational definitions of the problems were not the same, making the questions addressed somewhat incomparable. . . . Only one reviewer coded study features. This suggests an undue emphasis on single summary judgments of the literature without attempts to analyze thoroughly factors contributing to variability in the main relationship[s]. Agreement among the reviewers in reported effect magnitudes were low . . . [so] extracting data from reports and then calculating individual study outcomes appears more difficult than was initially envisioned. Finally, methods of analysis differed, most noticeably with regard to variability in effect magnitudes where opposite conclusions about the importance of outcome variability were reached.
>
> Overall, the differences uncovered [by the reviewers of the meta-analyses] were in both conception and execution, not limited to technical details of quantification. Clearly, computing effect magnitudes or sizes provided no assurance of an objective review. Thus the enterprise of quantitative synthesis must be conceived broadly by reviewers to include both statistical and substantive [or problem-related] issues. Attention must be paid to the procedures used and decisions reached at each step in a quantitative synthesis. (pp. 162–163)

Consumers can use these questions when evaluating meta-analytic reviews of research:

- Are there differences in operational definitions among the meta-analysis reviewers, other reviewers (synthesis and meta-analysis), and the primary researchers? Are those differences explained?
- Have the target populations of studies been identified? Are there differences between the samples of studies in the meta-analysis and other reviews?
- Are there explicit coding and evaluation criteria? Do these criteria differ from those of other meta-analysis reviewers? Have the meta-analysis reviewers produced separate results for methodologically strong and weak studies? Has more than one coder been used, and are interrater reliability coefficients provided?

- Have the meta-analysis reviewers drawn conclusions that differ from those of other reviewers? Are those differences discussed?
- Do the meta-analysis reports present information in a standard research format? Are the reports complete?

Reading Meta-Analyses of Research

Meta-analyses of research can be read using a plan similar to that used for reading research syntheses. Again, the idea for the reader is to understand the purposes and conclusions of the meta-analysts before reading their data collection and analyses. As you read, keep in mind the evaluative questions given previously.

- You will be reading the meta-analysis in this chapter's appendix, "The Effects of Instruction in Solving Mathematical Word Problems for Students With Learning Problems: A Meta-Analysis," pages 245–266. The first step is to read the title [1] and predict.
  - Briefly, list answers to these questions: "What do I know about the topic (for example, mathematical work problems and students with learning problems)? What do I know about the authors? What information would I expect to gain from this meta-analysis (i.e., how might the results help me in developing effective classroom instruction)?"
  - Read the abstract [2] for an overview of the report and its findings.
  - Then, read the major headings and subheadings [5] through [22] and answer, "Is the meta-analysis organized logically, and is the location of information clearly identified?" Note that the researchers have included sections about locating the studies, computing the statistical analysis, coding the studies for "features" and "characteristics," determining the rater reliability, and presenting the results.
- The second phase, reading the meta-analysis report, is to find information suggested by your expectations and to confirm or modify the information you know about the topic.
  - Reread the report title [1], the abstract [2], the introductory section [3] with the theoretical frameworks and specific research questions [4], the results sections [10] through [15], and the discussion and implications sections [16] to [21].
  - As you read, note the discussion about the problems the meta-analysts believe their analysis will solve. Be aware of the operational definitions used. Examine the discussion of why their results may be different than other researchers'.
  - Read any of the remaining sections that might help you better understand the authors' methodology and conclusions.
- The third phase, confirming predictions and knowledge, is to verify that the purpose has been met and to immediately recall key information. You should decide which information supports the authors' purpose and adds to your knowledge.
  - Answer the question "Can the instructional implications presented in this meta-analysis be used in my teaching situation?"
  - Finally, write a short (two- to three-sentence) statement that applies to the purpose for reading the meta-analysis and contains the authors' key points.

PREPARING SYNTHESES OF RESEARCH REVIEWS

Research consumers may need to synthesize, or bring together, the results of research concerning a school-related organizational, learning, or instructional issue. Following are some examples. Teachers and supervisors in a middle school may wish to examine the research relating to alternative ways to integrate or include special education students into general education classes. The members of a high school English department may wish to examine research related to the holistic scoring of students' writing. The staff of an early childhood center may wish to gain additional insights about the development of children's self-concept during structured and spontaneous play.

Research syntheses are prepared by going through stages similar to those shown in Table 10.1. However, research reviews produced for local use can be considered **teacher-as-researcher syntheses** rather than full synthesis reviews. Teacher-as-researcher reviews are to synthesis reviews, what teacher-as-researcher research is to quantitative and qualitative research (see chapter 7 and chapter 8).

To prepare teacher-as-researcher synthesis reviews, research consumers can use the concept of best evidence (Slavin, 1986, 1987a). To conduct these syntheses, teachers-as-researchers should select and review only studies that

- Have purposes specifically related to an immediate issue or concern
- Are methodologically adequate
- Are generalizable to the local situation

In selecting studies specifically related to an immediate issue, research consumers would include only quantitative studies that have explicit descriptions of independent and dependent variables, and qualitative studies that have clear explanations of the researchers' perspectives and approach to research. An early childhood staff, for example, would only select studies that clearly define "self-concept," "structured play," and "spontaneous play."

Because no research project is without some methodological limitation, research consumers need to determine what aspects in the primary quantitative research they would expect to have been rigidly controlled, and for what aspects they could tolerate less rigorous controls. That is, reviewers might include quantitative studies without complete information about instrument reliability or subject selection procedures, but not include studies without full documentation of structured play as a treatment. And, reviewers might exclude primary quantitative studies in which the subjects are not representative of local students, and those studies containing apparent research biases or influences. Primary qualitative studies selected should contain clear explanations of the setting, participants, and the researchers' involvement in the study.

To conduct a teacher-as-researcher research synthesis, a teacher will first locate, summarize, and interpret the most recent syntheses and meta-analytic reviews of research. (Chapter 11 contains discussion about locating primary research reports and research reviews.) Then, using the principle of best evidence, the teacher should locate, summarize, and interpret the most recent primary research, working back to studies published in the previous five to eight years.

As an aid to organizing information from these two steps, teachers can use forms such as those in Figures 10.1, 10.2, and 10.3. Figure 10.1 contains a form for summarizing information from synthesis reviews of research and meta-analyses. Figure 10.2 contains a form for summarizing information from primary

Authors: _____
Date: _____
Title: _____
Journal: _____
Volume: _____ Pages: _____
Location: _____

Type of review: _____ Synthesis _____ Meta-analysis

Purpose(s): _____
_____
_____

Operational definitions: _____
_____
_____

Conclusions: _____
_____
_____

Generalizability of conclusions to local issue: _____
_____
_____

Evaluation:
    Appropriateness of reviewers' evaluation criteria: _____
_____
_____

    Appropriateness of reviewers' explanation of differences in definitions or selection criteria/coding with other reviewers: ___
_____
_____

    Appropriateness of reviewers' explanation of differences in conclusions with other reviewers: _____
_____
_____
_____

Figure 10.1
Summarizing Information From Research Syntheses and Meta-Analyses

research. Figure 10.3 contains a form for synthesizing the major results from the reviews and primary research reports. These three forms should be used in conjunction with the evaluation questions in Figure 3.1 and Figure 3.2, pages 86–87, and those questions in this chapter for evaluating synthesis reviews and meta-analyses.

To complete Figure 10.1:

- Enter the appropriate information in the heading. On the Location line, indicate the place (such as the specific library) where the original research review is located—in case it has to be reexamined.
- Summarize the pertinent information about the type of review and the stated purposes, definitions, and conclusions of the reviewers.
- Enter your decisions about the generalizability of the reviewers' conclusions to your local situation.
- Enter your evaluative comments about the appropriateness of the reviewers' evaluation criteria, definitions, coding procedures, and conclusions.

Authors: _____

Date: _____

Title: _____

Journal: _____

Volume: _____ Pages: _____

Location: _____

Type of research: _____ Descriptive   _____ Comparative   _____ Experimental
                             _____ Quantitative   _____ Qualitative

Purpose(s): _____
_____
_____

Instruments: _____
_____

Operational definitions:
    Subjects: _____
    Treatments: _____
    Special materials: _____

Results and conclusions: _____
_____
_____

Generalizability of results and conclusions to local issue: _____
_____
_____

Evaluation:
    Validity and reliability and appropriateness of instruments: _____
_____

    Possible influence of extraneous variables: _____

    Possible threats to internal and external validity:
_____
_____

Figure 10.2
Summarizing Information From Primary Research

To complete Figure 10.2:

- Enter the appropriate information in the heading. On the Location line, indicate the place (such as the specific library) where the primary research report is located.
- Summarize pertinent information about the primary research.
- Indicate the generalizability of the primary researchers' results and conclusions to your local situation.
- Enter your evaluative comments about the appropriateness of the primary researchers' methodology.

Figure 10.3 is a prototype of a form for synthesizing information from several primary research reports. It is shown shortened and should be drawn wider to accommodate the number of primary research studies obtained. The last right column, Synthesis, should remain the same.

	Citation:	Citation:	Citation:	Synthesis
Purpose				
Design				
Subjects				
Instruments				
Procedures Treatment Materials				
Results				
Generalizability				
Weaknesses				

Figure 10.3
Synthesizing Information About Primary Research
Note: The user may add more citation columns.

To complete Figure 10.3:

- List the citations for the selected research reviews in the spaces along the top of the form; use the authors' last names and the dates of publication. For example, the research synthesis about the cognitive reading processes of ESL readers would be listed as "Fitzgerald (1995)" and the primary research study about whether boys and girls equally share in performing science-related activities (discussed in chapter 4) would be listed as "Jovanovic & King (1998)."
- Place pertinent information about each synthesis review, meta-analysis, and primary study in the appropriate box for each of the evaluative topics; your comments should be taken from the information you entered on the summary forms shown in Figures 10.1 and 10.2.

- Synthesize the results, generalizability to your local situation, and weaknesses of the reviews and primary research; appropriate synthesizing comments should reflect a conclusion you have drawn about the research result as a whole, not just a repeat of individual results. These sentences would become key or main ideas when preparing action reports; each could be used as a main idea for paragraphs or subsections.

ACTIVITIES

Activity 1

Using the Focus Questions at the beginning of the chapter, summarize the key ideas of the chapter.

Activity 2

Select a research synthesis of your own choosing or one cited in Appendix A. Then, with a partner from your class, evaluate the synthesis using the criteria included in this chapter.

FEEDBACK

Activity 1

What are research syntheses?   Research syntheses are undertaken as research projects in which the sources of data are the primary research reports of other researchers. Synthesis are critical examinations of research producers' methods and conclusions, and of the generalizability of the producers' combined results. Syntheses consist of five stages: (1) problem formulation, (2) data collection, (3) evaluation of data quality, (4) data analysis and interpretation, and (5) presentation of results.

What criteria are used to evaluate research syntheses?   These questions can be used to evaluate research syntheses:

Are there differences in operational definitions among the synthesis reviewers, other reviewers, and the primary researchers? Are those differences explained?

Has the target population of research been identified? Are there differences between the samples of studies in the review and other reviews? What is the nature of those differences?

Are there explicit evaluation criteria? Do the criteria differ from those of other reviewers? Have the synthesis reviewers cited studies with methodological limitations? Have those limitations been explained?

Have the reviewers drawn conclusions that are different from those of other reviewers? Are those differences discussed?

Does the review report present information in a standard research format? Is the report complete?

What are meta-analyses?   Meta-analyses of research are ways to critically examine primary research studies that use quantitative data analysis. Research reviewers use meta-analyses as "analyses of analyses" (data analyses of previously accomplished data analyses). In meta-analyses, reviewers convert the statistical results of the individual studies into a common measurement so that they can obtain an overall, combined result. Meta-analyses have stages similar to those of synthesis research reviews. In meta-analyses, (1) problems are formulated and research studies are collected, (2) pertinent data are identified, (3) analyses and interpretations are made of the data, (4) results are presented to the public. Meta-analyses begin with reviewers doing an exhaustive, complete search to locate previous synthesis research reviews, meta-analyses, and all primary research studies relating to the education question or problem under review.

What criteria are used to evaluate meta-analyses?   In addition to the questions for evaluating synthesis research reviews, these questions can be used:
    Are there differences in operational definitions among the meta-analysis reviewers, other reviewers (synthesis and meta-analysis), and the primary researchers? Are those differences explained?
    Have the target populations of studies been identified? Are there differences between the samples of studies in the meta-analysis and other reviews?
    Are there explicit coding and evaluation criteria? Do they differ from those of other meta-analysis reviewers? Have the meta-analysis reviewers produced separate results for methodologically strong and weak studies? Has more than one coder been used, and are interrater reliability coefficients provided?
    Have the meta-analysis reviewers drawn conclusions that differ from those of other reviewers? Are those differences discussed?
    Do the meta-analysis reports present information in a standard research format? Are the reports complete?

How are teacher-as-researcher research syntheses prepared?   Teacher-as-researcher research syntheses are prepared by going through stages similar to those for preparing research syntheses. Research reviews produced for local consumption can be considered teacher-as-researcher research reviews rather than full synthesis reviews. To prepare these research reviews, consumers can use the concept of best evidence. Best evidence is an idea about selecting and reviewing studies that (*a*) have purposes specifically related to an immediate issue or concern, (*b*) are methodologically adequate, and (*c*) are generalizable to the local situation.

Activity 2

Discuss and compare your responses with others in your class and with your course instructor.

Chapter 10 Appendix A

(1)   **English-as-a-Second-Language Learners' Cognitive Reading Processes: A Review of Research in the United States**

Jill Fitzgerald

The University of North Carolina at Chapel Hill

(2)   An integrative review of United States research on English-as-a-second-language (ESL) learners' cognitive reading processes suggested that, on the whole, ESL readers recognized cognate vocabulary fairly well, monitored their comprehension and used many metacognitive strategies, used schema and prior knowledge to affect comprehension and recall, and were affected differently by different types of text structures. In the main, where United States ESL readers' processes appeared to be used differently from those of native English readers, the differences were in speed and depressed activation of selected processes. Significantly, overall, the findings from the studies suggested a relatively good fit to preexisting reading theories and views generally thought to describe native-language readers. However, the quantitative differences between processes of ESL readers and those of native English readers indicated that the preexisting theories and views might need to be revisited and elaborated to address a subset of factors special to ESL learners.

Problem Formation   (3)

Ethnic and racial diversification in the United States is growing, particularly among school-age children. In our schools there are currently about 2.3 million students identified as having "limited English proficiency" (United States Department of Education, 1992). About 50% of all Californian students speak a language other than English as their primary, or only, language, and it is predicted that by 2030 that percentage will increase to about 70% (E. Garcia, 1992a). As non-White Hispanic and Asian/Pacific Islander presence in schools increased considerably from 1976 to 1986 (by 6% and 116%, respectively), Caucasian and non-Hispanic enrollment decreased (by 13%) (E. Garcia, 1992a). However, the educational achievement, including reading achievement, of language minorities has not kept pace with that of English-speaking Caucasians. For example, among Hispanics there is a 40% high school dropout rate, a 35% grade (4) retention rate, and a two- to four-grade-level achievement gap (E. Garcia, 1992b).

As our population has become more diverse, educators' concerns about English-as-a-second-language (ESL) literacy have also increased. Perhaps as an outgrowth of such concerns, more and more research has been conducted on ESL reading issues over the last decade or so. Many facets of ESL reading have been studied, ranging from instructional evaluations to sociocultural issues to cognitive processes. The purpose of this article is to characterize United (5) States research and integrate findings in one area of ESL reading, namely, cognitive processes.

For the purposes of this review, ESL learners in the United States were considered to be individuals living in the United States who meet the federal government's definition of "limited English proficient" (Public Law 100–297 [1988]). These individuals (a) were not born in the United States, (b) have native languages other than English, (c) come from environments where English is not dominant, or (d) are American Indians or Alaskan natives from environments where languages other than English impact their English proficiency levels. The term ESL learner is used as a special case of the more general term language minority, which refers to individuals who are living in a place where they do not speak the majority's language. Cognitive reading processes refers to any internal or mental aspects of reading—that is, aspects of the brain's activity during reading (q.v. Bernhardt, 1991; Just & Carpenter, 1987).

Source: From Fitzgerald, J. (1995). English-as-a-second-language learners' cognitive reading processes: A review of research in the United States. *Review of Educational Research, 65*(2), 145–190. Copyright 1995 by the American Educational Research Association. Reprinted by permission of the publisher.

(6)   By focusing solely on cognitive reading processes, I do not in any way wish to imply that other aspects of ESL reading are unimportant. To the contrary, some other aspects, such as the social setting in which students learn to read English, the classroom instructional method, and congruence between learners' native-language culture and the target-language culture, may be as important, if not more important, than ESL readers' cognitive processes. Further, there may be interactions of cognitive processes with other aspects of ESL reading. Notably, researchers investigating cognition in ESL reading have tended not to explore such complex interrelations, highlighting instead isolated cognitive features.

Also, I do not want to imply that this article reflects an English-only position. It does not. Research suggests that many benefits may accrue from the development and maintenance of bilingualism, and some long-term benefits of bilingual education might outweigh those gained from English-only approaches (Hakuta, 1986; Hakuta & Gould, 1987; Snow, 1987; Wong, Fillmore, & Valadez, 1986).

(7)   There are several reasons why an in-depth integration of research findings on United States ESL learners' cognitive reading processes is needed. First, there are currently countless situations in our country where ESL programs are offered in lieu of bilingual education programs (Hakuta & Gould, 1987; U.S. Department of Education, 1991, 1992). Also, ESL reading is a significant component of bilingual education programs. Further, there are situations where ESL learners do not have the benefit of teachers trained in ESL issues. More ESL students are served by Chapter I reading programs (about 1.2 million) than by Title VII programs (about 251,000), which are specially designed for ESL learners (U.S. Department of Education, 1992). It is highly likely that many Chapter I reading teachers have little background in ESL issues. Equally important, many ESL learners spend the majority of their school hours in regular classroom settings with teachers who also often have little background in ESL issues. A better understanding of the reading processes used by ESL learners could benefit virtually all teachers—ESL, bilingual, reading, and regular classroom teachers alike—as well as their students.

Second, to my knowledge no prior in-depth synthesis of reading-process research done solely with ESL learners either in the United States or in general has been conducted. A few selective reviews (e.g., Grabe, 1991; Hatch, 1974; Swaffar, 1988) and at least one comprehensive review (Bernhardt, 1991) of research in the broad area of second-language reading have been done. Both selective and comprehensive broad-based reviews of second-language reading research can certainly make significant contributions to our understanding of second-language reading processes. For example, Bernhardt used her review to begin to build a model of second-language reading.

However, it is not clear to what extent selective or broad-based reviews of second-language reading research deeply inform on specific issues such as cognitive processes, or to what extent conclusions drawn from such reviews apply to specific second languages and/or to specific settings in which a second language is learned. Indeed, authors of selective reviews generally do not intend to reveal details about a wide array of specific issues (and sometimes about any specific issues), and authors of broad-based reviews may not intend to imply that any generalizations drawn hold for any and all specific target languages. At the very least, drawing both general and specific conclusions from selective or sweeping reviews of second-language reading research is arduous. For example, after reviewing second-language data-based studies dating back to 1974, ranging from text analyses and reader factors to instruction and assessment, Bernhardt (1991) concluded that it was "extremely difficult" (p. 20) and "tantamount to impossible" (p. 68) to synthesize the information, largely due to "the wide array of subject groups studied [later referring to wide variability in language groups and language-proficiency levels], experimental tasks, and methodologies employed" (p. 20).

At least two factors might critically affect second-language reading processes (q.v. Grabe, 1991) and therefore impede generalizations about selected second-language cognitions across certain target languages and certain language-learning settings. A first factor is the target language to be learned. For example, there is some evidence that the target language may be relevant to any conclusion about the difficulty of various genres in second-language reading (Allen, Bernhardt, Berry, & Demel, 1988) and that the magnitudes of correlations between first- and second-language reading achievement may be different depending upon the languages involved (Bernhardt & Kamil, 1993; Bossers, 1991; Brisbois, 1992; Carrell, 1991).

A second factor which might potentially affect second-language learners' reading is the sociopolitical context in which the second language is learned. For example, elective bilinguals, such as students in their home cultures who are learning a foreign language, can be distinguished from circumstantial bilinguals, such as immigrants to a new country who more or less must learn a new language (Valdes, 1991). These groups are often quite different, not only in motivations for learning English, but also in educational background and socioeconomic status (Krashen, 1985a; Valdes, 1991). Any of these variables could impact how individual learners approach texts in the target language, how rapidly they advance, and ultimately, how well and how much they read.

Because the target language to be learned and the sociopolitical context in which second-language learning occurs may affect language minorities' learning about reading, reading development, reading achievement, and reading processes, it may be important to control for, or consider, these contexts when reviewing studies of second-language reading. One way (though not the only way) to do this is to select a particular target language in a particular type of setting and to review research done under those circumstances in order to see if an in-depth characterization would emerge for each particular group. This could be done for different languages and types of setting, and ultimately, comparisons could be made across the successive, highly detailed, particular characterizations. The comparative benefits and problems associated with such an approach as compared to sweeping reviews remain to be detailed.

⑧   The present review is a modest first step in such a programmatic approach; it scrutinizes research done on one target language group in one particular setting. Specifically, it attempts an in-depth integration of findings from research on cognitive reading processes of ESL learners in the United States. A characterization of this research might inform us on several issues, such as the particular strengths and/or weaknesses of United States ESL readers, the extent to which their cognitive reading processes are similar to those of native English speakers, and helpful directions for future research.

METHOD

| Data Collection |

⑨To locate research, a broad search was initially done with few limiting criteria. The following computer searches were done to locate studies for this review: ERIC documents back to 1980, using the limiters (a) literacy (reading and writing) and ESL, (b) literacy and ESL students, (c) literacy and bilingual education, (d) literacy and language-minority learners, and (e) literacy and limited-English proficiency; *Dissertation Abstracts International* back to 1989 with the limiters (a) literacy (reading and writing) and language-minority learners, (b) literacy and limited-English proficiency, (c) literacy and ESL, and (d) literacy and bilingual education; and *Linguistics and Language Behavior Abstracts* with the limiters (a) English as a foreign language, (b) English as a second language, and (c) bilingualism. Additionally, indexes from the following journals were searched back to 1980: *Reading Research Quarterly, JRB: A Journal of Literacy,* and *TESOL Quarterly*. The sections on "Teaching Bilingual and Other Learners" in the *Annual Summary of Investigations in Reading* were searched back to 1980. Further, program books for the following annual conferences were scanned for the years 1991 to date, and papers were requested from authors: International Reading Association, National Reading Conference, Teachers of English to Speakers of Other Languages, National Association of Bilingual Education, and American Educational Research Association. Finally, a "network" approach was used. That is, all reference lists of retrieved documents were checked for additional research pieces, and an effort was made to obtain those pieces.

Later, after much of the research had been read, the review was restricted to all published, data-based research (with no date restriction) and all recent data-based conference papers, technical reports, and dissertations dating back to 1989 which dealt with ESL reading processes in studies conducted in the United States. Unpublished reports of work prior to 1989 were excluded on the grounds that such reports had not undergone rigorous peer review. Additionally, for inclusion, reports had to be complete enough to determine important factors, such as what the outcome measures were, where the study was conducted, and what the study's procedures were. In a handful of cases, studies were excluded due to incompleteness with regard to one or more of these factors.

(10)   I analyzed studies reviewed for this project using a systematic interpretive procedure (similar to a constant-comparative method often used in qualitative research [Glaser, 1978]). The following steps were taken. First, I tried to detail all the data available to me. All studies were read and reviewed, and for each study notes were taken to reflect the number of, and any identifying information about, participants; procedures; instruments, and their reliabilities, if given; and main outcomes. Sometimes key words were written along with the notes to describe the main topics investigated. Second, I perused all of the notes on the studies to see if there were patterns and themes in research issues that were addressed. As these emerged, labels were given to tentative topic clusters. Third, I again perused the notes and sorted studies into the tentative clusters. Some studies fell into more than one cluster. Fourth, I worked within each cluster, one at a time, to discern themes by looking for similarities and differences in studies and their results. This pass through the data was highly detailed, and I often returned to the original pieces to reread for clarification, confirmation, or disconfirmation of emerging hypotheses. During this period, charts and lists were made to sort studies according to developing hypotheses. For example, a list was made of all schema studies—and their salient features, including results—done with younger participants and then with older participants. In this way, patterns and themes could be compared across ages. When hypotheses were confirmed (e.g., all studies with older participants suggested "x," while all studies with younger participants suggested "y"), at least one counterexplanation was entertained (e.g., is there a feature "z" correlated with age which is likely to be a mediating variable?). Also, at this stage, I further refined the clusters by moving some studies from one cluster to another and collapsing one to two others. As I worked through this process within each cluster, I also made separate notes about general problems with methods as they seemed to emerge. Fifth, as themes from a given section solidified, I wrote about that section. Sixth, after all clusters of studies had been analyzed, I read what had been written about each, considered the results as a whole, and, when any discrepancies occurred, reread original pieces. Seventh, to summarize across clusters, a chart was made of the main themes from each cluster of studies.

(11)   The issue of reliability of my interpretations centered on the extent to which the themes and images drawn from the review were fairly generalizable from the available data (q.v. Moss, 1994, p. 7). Reliability was clearly an aspect of validity defined as "consonance among multiple lines of evidence supporting the intended interpretation[s] over alternative interpretations" (Moss, 1994, p. 7). The criteria for reliability for this interpretive review were not quantitative. Rather, reliability should be assessed by the extent to which my interpretations were warranted using criteria such as these, given by Moss (1994, p. 7): the extent of my knowledge of the range of existing work on the topic (called "context" by Moss), the existence of "multiple and varied sources of evidence" (i.e., in this case, studies, and data and method contained in the studies), and the "transparency of the trail of evidence leading to the interpretations . . . [allowing others] to evaluate the conclusions for themselves." I worked to meet each of these criteria to the fullest extent possible. A further possible criterion suggested by Moss (1994, p. 7), the application of which I invite as response to this article, is that there might be an "ethic of disciplined, collaborative inquiry that encourages challenges and revisions to initial interpretations."

(12)   **THE STUDIES**

Theoretical Frameworks Used to Study ESL Readers' Processes in the United States

How researchers in the United States have situated investigations in ESL reading processes is in itself informative. Some reports did not provide a theoretical basis for the investigations, and in some of those instances, a theoretical basis was not easily inferred. (These reports were still included in the review because they might provide informative evidence to corroborate or to call into question conclusions drawn from other studies.) However, in general, the studies were seated in two sets of theories or views: (a) native-language reading theories, models, or views widely known and accepted in the reading research community at large; and (b) theories or views related to second-language acquisition and widely known in the second-language acquisition research community.

In particular, four preexisting theories, models, or views of reading, originally formed for readers in general and presumably for individuals reading in their native languages, were relied on: (a) a psycholinguistic view of reading, (b) schema theory, (c) an interactive view of reading, and (d) views of metacognition in reading. In some studies, investigators were specifically "testing" the applicability of aspects of a preexisting reading theory, model, or view in ESL reading situations. Occasionally they hypothesized easy applicability; sometimes they hypothesized how the theory, model, or view would need to be modified for ESL learners.

In brief, a psycholinguistic view of reading holds that reading is not a linear process, but that readers sample texts and make and test hypotheses and predictions, relying on their own background knowledge of the text's content as well as background knowledge about how language works (Goodman, 1970). In the sampling process, readers use three cueing systems: graphophonics, syntax, and semantics.

Schema theory postulates that knowledge is systematically organized (Rumelhart, 1980). A schema can be defined as having elements or components which can be delineated and which are ordered in specific ways. Readers are thought to use schemata to anticipate text content and structures, to guide understanding during reading, and to aid recall after reading. An interactive view of reading holds that reading is both "top-down" and "bottom-up" (Rumelhart, 1985). That is, stated in a very oversimplified way, part of the reading process entails interpreting graphic information from the page (bottom-up), and part involves using knowledge already present in the mind (top-down). The term interactive also refers to the interactions that can occur between and among "higher-level" and "lower-level" information, such as the influence of surrounding context (higher-level) on perception of individual letters or words (lower-level).

Finally, in reading, metacognition refers to awareness of one's own reading processes (Brown, 1980). Principally, it entails awareness of one's own understanding and nonunderstanding, of reading strategies, and of monitoring comprehension during reading.

The investigators' use of these reading views and theories is interesting because they were designed to explain reading processes in general, and presumably of individuals reading in their native languages. Some scholars have begun to detail why certain preexisting reading theories are particularly applicable to second-language learners (e.g., see Carrell, Devine, & Eskey, 1988, on interactive models of reading for second-language learners). It might also be argued, however, that by working from preexisting theories of reading, research on ESL reading might be limited. That is, questions that need to be asked about specific aspects of second-language reading might not be addressed, and therefore, advances in knowledge might be slowed (q.v. Bernhardt, 1991). Because the investigators relied heavily on preexisting views of reading, it was possible, in a broad sense, to assess in the present review the extent to which findings from the studies, taken collectively, were good fits to those preexisting views. Such an assessment will be made in the discussion section of this article.

Some ESL reading-process researchers situated their work in one or more theoretical positions predominant in the field of second-language acquisition. One position was that significant components of orality and literacy transfer from one language to another. This position was generally used as a foundation for studies which investigated various aspects of individuals' transfer of knowledge and skills from native-language orality or literacy to ESL literacy (or which investigated similarities in reading processes across languages). The Common Underlying Proficiency (CUP) model of how two languages are related is perhaps the most widely known model espousing this position (Cummins, 1981). Basically, it holds that a common set of proficiencies underlies both the first and second languages. What is learned in one language will transfer to another language. Also, using a skill or strategy in one language will transfer to another language. Also, using a skill or strategy in one language is pretty much the same process as in another. A significant feature of the CUP model is that major literacy skills thought to be the same in both languages have been identified, including conceptual knowledge, subject-matter knowledge, higher-order thinking skills, and reading strategies. A related refinement of the basic notion of CUP is Cummins's (1979) developmental interdependence hypothesis, which states that the development of second-language competence is partially a function of the competence already developed in the native language at the time when intensive exposure to the second language begins.

The other position was that second-language literacy and second-language orality are highly related. ESL reading-process researchers in the United States sometimes used this position to ground correlational studies of the relationship between ESL reading and ESL oral proficiency. This position has at least two forms in the second-language literature. In one form, the relationship is directional; second-language reading is dependent upon second-language oral proficiency (q.v. Clarke & Silberstein, 1977). That is, second-language orality must precede second-language literacy. In the other form, not only is the relationship directional, but there is a "threshhold of linguistic competence" necessary for successful second-language reading (Clarke, 1980; Cummins, 1979). As originally discussed by Cummins (1979), the threshold hypothesis referred to the need for optimal competence—presumably oral proficiency, though this was not specified—in both the native language and the second language in order for higher-level cognitive growth to occur. However, the threshold hypothesis has also been interpreted to mean that unless second-language orality is developed to some optimal level, second-language reading-process development and, consequently, reading and other academic achievement will be stunted. The most significant reading-instructional implication of the threshold hypothesis as originally presented was that students who have not developed native-language reading abilities to some optimal level should initially be taught to read in their native language. With respect to English learning, a significant instructional implication that has been extracted from these views is that second-language learners should develop their English oral abilities first, and then later, when oral proficiency is more developed, second-language reading should be introduced (see, for example, Krashen, 1985b, Wong, Fillmore, & Valadez, 1986).

Because some have interpreted positions such as the "threshold of linguistic competence" position as having dramatic implications for when and how reading should be introduced to ESL learners in the United States, a global assessment will be made in the summary of this article regarding the fit of the findings from the ESL reading-process studies reviewed to views such as the CUP model and the "threshold of linguistic competence" position.

(13) *Limitations of the Studies*

Some limitations posed difficulties and/or constraints on the interpretation of the studies and their results. It may be helpful to readers to keep these limitations in mind as the following sections are read. First, many authors failed to report what might have been salient features of participants—most importantly, the participants' extent of literacy in their native language and their ESL oral proficiency level. Such features may affect ESL learners' reading (McLaughlin, 1987). Also, inadequate information about participants sometimes made it difficult to determine whether participants met the required criteria for being ESL learners as defined in this review. Occasionally, studies were excluded because it could not be determined whether participants did meet the criteria. Second, in many instances, even when authors reported important related participant characteristics, such as native language background or ESL oral proficiency level, participants were not sorted by those variables for analyses. If such characteristics interact with ESL reading, then failure to account for them could lead to confounded results. Third, even when ESL proficiency level was mentioned, there was a widespread lack of clarity as to what authors meant by that phrase. For example, the phrase could refer to ESL oral, ESL reading, or ESL writing proficiency. As another example of difficulties in interpreting what authors meant by ESL proficiency, some authors referred to particular test scores as representing an intermediate ESL proficiency level, while at least one investigator said the same test scores meant that the participants could read college-level materials about as well as their average college-level native-English-speaking counterparts. A further problem was that some authors mentioned standardized tests, but did not provide complete references for them.

Fourth, measures were not always given in conjunction with authors' labels of ESL proficiency level, and evidence given at times did not clarify. In these cases, interpretation of participants' actual ESL oral and/or reading proficiency was impossible. For example, some authors stated the length of time participants had lived in the United States as evidence of proficiency level, but because individuals acquire English at differing rates, it would be helpful to have more clearly defined evidence. Fifth, a widespread lack of attention to reporting reliability and validity estimates of measures used in the quantitative studies considerably weakened interpretations of results at times.

(14) *What Has Been Asked and What Has Been Learned?*

The final sources of data were 67 research reports. A summary of key aspects of the studies reported is shown in Table 1. Six clusters were formed according to the main areas addressed in the studies: (a) vocabulary knowledge, (b) strategies (psycholinguistic and metacognitive), (c) schema and prior-knowledge utilization (reader-based and text-based), (d) the relationship between ESL reading and ESL oral proficiency, (e) the relationship between ESL reading proficiency and variables other than ESL oral proficiency, and (f) issues about similarities in cognitive reading processes across United States ESL learners and native English learners, as well as across United States ESL learners' native language and English. There was also a seventh cluster for miscellaneous studies. The two most researched areas (as gauged by the number of studies conducted) were strategies and schema use.

In each of the following sections, (a) typical paradigms are explained (where there were typical ones), (b) participants' ages, grade levels, ESL proficiency levels (as given by authors), and native language backgrounds are described, and (c) themes are presented. For some clusters, special issues are also discussed.

(15)   *ESL Readers' Vocabulary Knowledge.*   Paradigms varied in the eight reports of studies on vocabulary. For example, in one, participants took a standardized reading test and were interviewed, and then test items were analyzed. In another, participants read silently, circling all cognates (English-Spanish look-alike words with similar meanings), and also took vocabulary tests. Most participants were young (second through seventh grade), though there were 4 college students in one study and 12 in another. ESL proficiency levels, where reported, ranged from beginning to advanced. Participants were mainly Hispanic, though other ethnicities were represented.

One of the most important themes in this cluster was that vocabulary knowledge may be a highly significant variable in United States ESL readers' success. Unknown vocabulary in questions and answer choices on tests was a main linguistic factor adversely affecting the reading test performance of beginning-level and relatively proficient Hispanic and Cantonese third, fifth, and sixth graders (Ammon, 1987; G. E. Garcia, 1991). In one study, oral vocabulary production was a very strong correlate, and the only oral proficiency correlate, of English reading achievement (Saville-Troike, 1984). In another, vocabulary knowledge was even more important for test performance than was prior knowledge of content (G. E. Garcia, 1991).

Other studies looked at fourth- through seventh-grade Hispanic United States ESL learners' ability to recognize and use cognate relationships. Although cognates were fairly well recognized on the whole, the ability to recognize cognates was not fully developed; that is, there was substantial variability in cognate recognition (G. E. Garcia & Nagy, 1993; Jimenez, Garcia, & Pearson, 1991; Nagy, Garcia, Durgunoglu, & Hancin-Bhatt, 1992).

An additional finding was that there was considerable individual variability in approaches to learning English vocabulary for four United States ESL college students (Parry, 1991). Also, advanced ESL college students in the United States used first-language vocabulary knowledge to read idioms, with idioms that were identical in Spanish and English being easiest, similar idioms being almost as easy (but showing the most native-language interference), and different idioms being most difficult (Irujo, 1986).

(16)   *ESL Readers' Strategies.*   Two sorts of ESL readers' strategies have been studied in the United States. In one group of studies, here called psycholinguistic-strategy studies, researchers

investigated the psycholinguistic cueing systems (graphophonics, syntax, and semantics) that readers used to recognize and comprehend words. In another, here called metacognitive-strategy studies, researchers tried to determine the systematic ways in which readers approached texts, and how readers tried to repair miscomprehension.

(17)   *Psycholinguistic Strategies.*   In 12 of the 13 psycholinguistic-strategy studies, participants read orally and then retold the text without looking back. Either an examiner listened to the oral reading and simultaneously made marks on a copy of the text to record all deviations the participant made from the printed words, or the oral readings were tape recorded so the examiner could later listen and mark a protocol. In the 13th study, participants read (apparently silently), told what they understood, identified words they had found difficult, and guessed orally what the words might mean. In some studies only one text was read, and in others multiple texts were read. At least some participants in every study read in English, but some also read at least one passage in their native language. Twelve sets of investigators used miscue analysis. Basically, this means that each text deviation was assessed for whether it (a) looked and/or sounded like the text word (was graphophonically similar), (b) was syntactically acceptable, and (c) was semantically acceptable. Other details were also assessed, such as reader regressions and self-corrections. The main purpose of the analysis was to determine how readers approach text. For example, when readers made many graphophonic substitutions, made few syntactically and semantically acceptable substitutions, and rarely self-corrected, their strategies might have been characterized as overreliant on the graphic aspects of text, with little attention to text meaning.

Most of the studies in this group were done with children in elementary school grades, as low as second grade, but a few were done with participants covering the range from seventh grade to adult. Many authors identified English oral and/or reading proficiency level, and these levels covered the full range from beginner to advanced. By and large, in the studies dealing with psycholinguistic strategies, native language groups were not as mixed as in some other research clusters in this review. When there were individuals of diverse native languages within studies, several authors sorted results accordingly.

It was very difficult to arrive at pointed and highly meaningful themes across this group of studies. On the whole, the studies did not shed much light on the psycholinguistic strategies of ESL readers in the United States, at least not for ESL readers as a group. Even sorting studies by participants' English oral and/or reading proficiency, age, and whether or not investigators mixed native language groups did not reveal clear patterns leading to grand generalizations for subgroups of readers.

Following are statements about findings from the studies; most of these are either about mixed findings or supported by only one or two studies. First, the most pointed statement that can be made is that there was no single pattern in the use of psycholinguistic strategies across ESL readers. That is, there was no general reliance on a particular cue system, such as graphophonics, nor was there a general balanced reliance across the cueing systems. To the contrary, there was variability in ESL readers' psycholinguistic strategies. For example, some studies (covering participants from elementary school to high school and from beginning to intermediate English proficiency) showed that ESL readers' substitutions tended to be graphically similar (Rigg, 1976; Romatowski, 1981) and syntactically (Rigg, 1976; Romatowski, 1981) and semantically acceptable (Rigg, 1977, 1988; Romatowski, 1981). Also, adult ESL readers used graphophonic, syntactic, and semantic cueing systems to guess at word meanings after reading passages (Haynes, 1984). These results would suggest that ESL readers had a balanced set of psycholinguistic strategies; that is, it would seem that they did focus on meaning while reading English, but that they also took into account the graphic aspects of print. However, opposite results also emerged, sometimes with participants at the same age and proficiency level and/or with the same native language background. For example, Rigg's (1986) beginning ESL readers and McLeod and McLaughlin's (1986) beginning and advanced ESL readers tended to overrely on graphophonics. Participants in Haddad's (1981) study made many syntactically unacceptable miscues, and participants in Connor's (1981) and McLeod and McLaughlin's (1986) studies made many semantically unacceptable miscues.

Second, it was not clear whether language dominance and/or native language background affected ESL readers' psycholinguistic strategies. On the one hand, in at least three studies, strategies differed according to language dominance (Barrera, Valdes, & Cardenes, 1986; Miramontes, 1987, 1990); in another, participants' miscues reflected negative transfer from their native language (Romatowski, 1981). For example, Miramontes (1990) found complex and significant differences between three groups of Mexican American readers in numbers of miscues in various categories. The three groups were (a) good English readers (whose first language was considered English), (b) good Spanish (ESL) readers, and (c) mixed-dominant ESL readers who spoke only Spanish at home and only English at school. One major conclusion of the study was that, on the whole, the mixed-dominant group seemed to focus less on meaning than did the good Spanish readers. On the other hand, however, at least two investigators found more variation in miscue patterns within language groups than between them (Connor, 1981; Rigg, 1977).

Finally, there was some evidence that the number and/or rate of miscues, and of meaning-change miscues in particular, was negatively associated with retelling scores (Connor, 1981; Devine, 1988). That is, making fewer miscues (most notably, fewer meaning-change miscues) was aligned with better comprehension. But in one study, the pattern was reversed (Romatowski, 1981).

One set of possible reasons why more pointed thematic statements cannot be garnered from the psycholinguistic studies is related to the way the studies were conducted. First, in many studies, the research issues did not always seem precise. I often had a vague sense that a study was meant to reveal something about ESL readers' miscue patterns, but specific research questions were elusive.

Second, the analyses and/or interpretations of data sometimes tended to meander, probably because research issues regarding the use of strategies were not clearly specified. Authors infrequently moved past descriptions of the actual percentages of various types of miscues made to make inferences about readers' strategies or ways of thinking about comprehending while reading.

Third, two major methodological drawbacks in this group of studies may have contributed to the inability to infer pointed themes. In many cases, reports did not provide information about the match between readers' English reading levels and the texts' readability levels. A basic principle of miscue analysis is that participants should be reading texts which are slightly difficult for them so that there is enough contextual information to build on but also some opportunity to apply strategies in hard spots. Lack of information about the extent of adherence to that principle strained the interpretation of results.

Another methodological difficulty was that in ESL research, it may be difficult to characterize how closely miscues match text because the readers' oral pronunciations may be in transition from their native language to English (Bernhardt, 1987; Brown & Haynes, 1985). It is impossible to know how different researchers handled this problem.

Another reason for the inability to draw very pointed statements simply may have been that individual differences among ESL readers in the use of psycholinguistic strategies obviate overall statements. While factors such as native language background, extent of native language literacy, extent of homeland schooling, and age of entry into the United States may mediate ESL readers' strategies, individuals' own particular ways of using psycholinguistic text cues may outweigh, or interact with, any such factors.

(18)   *Metacognitive Strategies.*   The paradigm used in the 10 studies (in 11 reports) on United States ESL readers' metacognitive strategies was usually some variation on a typical paradigm used in studies with native English speakers. Participants read texts, always in English and sometimes additionally in Spanish, generally stopping at selected points to "think aloud," telling whatever was on their minds. Sometimes the texts had catalysts to miscomprehension, such as incoherent sentences. In at least one study, participants could do the "think aloud" in Spanish. The "think aloud" sessions were taped and later analyzed primarily to determine readers' metacognitive strategies and/or methods of monitoring their own comprehension.

All but three of the studies were done with individuals at the high school level or higher; the remaining three were done with third through fifth graders. Investigators rarely explored metacognitive strategies of individuals at beginning English proficiency levels; they favored instead intermediate or advanced learners. Two studies incorporated beginners, and a few authors did not report proficiency levels. All studies but one were done with Hispanic individuals; the remaining one was done with Chinese as well as Hispanic individuals.

Three main themes emerged. First, ESL readers in the United States did tend to monitor their comprehension (Block, 1992; Mikulecky, 1991; Padron, Knight, & Waxman, 1986; Pritchard, 1990). The monitoring process was described by one author as "evaluate, act, and check" (Block, 1992). That is, readers recognized problems and identified problem sources, they established strategic plans and attempted to solve the problems, and they checked and revised throughout problem recognition and solution.

Second, a myriad (probably over 50) of ESL readers' metacognitive strategies was commonly reported across seven studies (in eight reports). The following nine strategies all appeared in at least three of the seven studies: asking questions, rereading, imaging, using a dictionary, anticipating or predicting, reading fast or changing speed, thinking about something else while reading or associating, skipping, and summarizing or paraphrasing (Anderson, 1991; Anderson, Bachman, Perkins, & Cohen, 1991; Block, 1986a, 1986b; Knight, Padron, & Waxman, 1985; Padron et al., 1986; Padron & Waxman, 1988; Walker, 1983).

Third, at least one study supported the belief that language background did not influence the types of strategies used by ESL readers (Block, 1986a, 1986b).

(19)   *Schema and Prior Knowledge Utilization.*   Studies on the use of schemata by ESL readers in the United States tended to fall into two subtly different groups. Although in all instances the investigators were interested in the interaction of readers' schemata or prior knowledge with text content and/or structure, some researchers focused more on readers' schemata or prior knowledge, whereas others tended to emphasize the schemata or structures embodied in texts.

(20)   *Studies Emphasizing Readers' Schemata or Prior Knowledge.*   The methodologies of studies which emphasized readers' schemata or prior knowledge were typically patterned after what may now be termed classic reading studies in schema theory with native English speakers. Though exceptions can be identified, the methodologies used in the 10 reports of studies in this group were, by and large, variations on a paradigm exemplified by Carrell (1987). In this study, participants were 28 Muslim Arabs and 24 Catholic Hispanics who were ESL students of high-intermediate proficiency enrolled in an intensive English program at a midwestern university. The students each read two texts, one with Muslim-oriented content and one with Catholic-oriented content. Further, each text was presented in either a well-organized rhetorical format or an unfamiliar, altered rhetorical format. After reading each text, students recalled the text in writing and answered multiple-choice comprehension questions about the text. All aspects of data collection were conducted in English. Recall protocols were analyzed for quantity of idea units recalled from the original texts as well as whether recalled ideas were from various levels of the text hierarchy (e.g., main ideas versus details). The protocols were also scored for features such as elaborations and distortions. Answers to the multiple-choice questions were scored for number correct.

The studies were done mainly with university-age participants; only three explored schema issues at seventh grade or below. Most participants were reported to be of intermediate- to advanced-level ESL proficiency, but at least two studies included participants with beginning-level proficiency. Many language groups were represented.

The results of studies in this area resoundingly suggested that schemata affected United States ESL readers' comprehension and recall. In most studies, participants better comprehended and/or remembered passages that either were more consonant with their native cultures or were deemed more familiar (Ammon, 1987; Carrell, 1981, 1987; G. E. Garcia, 1991; Johnson, 1981, 1982; Langer, Bartolome, Vasquez, & Lucas, 1990). There was some further evidence that ESL readers' schemata for content affected comprehension and/or remembering more than did their formal schemata for text organization (Carrell, 1987; Johnson, 1981). For example, in the Carrell (1987) study described in the beginning of this section, participants remembered the most when both the text content and the rhetorical form were familiar. They remembered the least when both the text content and the rhetorical form were unfamiliar. However, when only content or only form was unfamiliar, unfamiliar content presented more difficulty than did unfamiliar form.

No common reasons could be discerned for the lack of schema effects in three studies (Barnitz & Speaker, 1991; Carrell, 1983; Carrell & Wallace, 1983). All were done with older, intermediate- to advanced-level ESL learners, except that Barnitz and Speaker (1991) also included seventh graders (whose ESL level was not stated). All had mixed native language groups. One explanation might be that although the participants were generally designated as intermediate to advanced in ESL proficiency, no evidence was reported that they could read the words in the passages with little difficulty. Inadequate recognition of the passage words could confound results. Another explanation in the Carrell (1983) study might be that the novel passage, "Balloon Serenade" (from Bransford & Johnson, 1973), was simply overwhelmingly bizarre for ESL students. Roller and Matambo (1992), in an English-as-a-foreign-language study (conducted in Zimbabwe), replicated Carrell's (1983) effect and then went on to analyze the "Balloon" passage. They suggested that perhaps the results were contaminated due to a confounding of familiarity (of passage) with other factors, such as difficulty level of the formal structure and noun concreteness. That is, they believed the "Balloon Serenade" passage was more formally consistent and had more concrete nouns than the so-called familiar passage, "Washing Clothes."

(21)   *Studies Emphasizing Text Schemata.*   Paradigms used in the seven reports of studies in this group were variations on what might now be termed classic reading studies on text structure done with English-speaking participants. Participants read texts and then recalled information, for the most part in writing. The structures in texts (e.g., compare-contrast and problem-solving structures in expository text, and standard versus structurally interleaved versions of stories) were identified, and the recalled information was analyzed for variables such as number of propositions recalled, number of high- versus low-level propositions recalled, and recall of temporal sequence of story components. All aspects of the studies were conducted in English.

All the participants in these studies were in ESL-intensive college or precollege matriculation programs, except that there were fourth and fifth graders in one study. All were labeled intermediate- to advanced-level ESL learners. In all studies except one, there were mixed native language groups.

The main overall theme was that different types of text structure affected comprehension and recall—most specifically, quantity of recall (Bean, Potter, & Clark, 1980; Carrell, 1984a, 1984b, though this was not true in Carrell, 1992), type of information recalled (high-versus low-level information) (Carrell, 1984a, 1992), and temporal sequence of recall (Carrell, 1984b).

Another theme was that there may have been differences among language groups as to which text structures facilitated recall better (Carrell, 1984a). For example, Arabs remembered best from expository texts with comparison structures, next best from problem-solution structures and collections of descriptions, and least well from causation structures. Asians, however, remembered best from texts with either problem-solution or causation structures and least well from either comparison structures or collections of descriptions. It remains to be seen whether this interaction of language background with text structure was due to interference/facilitation from known native-language rhetorical patterns (Carrell, 1984a; Hinds, 1983). For example, some have documented a preferred rhetorical Arabic pattern, called "coordinate parallelism" (Kaplan, 1966). Arabs' better performance on texts with comparison structures may have been related to familiarity with "coordinate parallelism" patterns in their native-language texts. However, some other recent work also suggests that culture-specific rhetorical patterns do not transfer to a new language (Connor & McCagg, 1983).

A third theme was that although type of text structure affected the information recalled by ESL students, the students were not highly able to name the organizational plans in the texts they read (Carrell, 1984a, 1992). Finally, there was some minimal evidence that ESL readers with a greater ability to extract nonverbal schemata (on shape-classification tasks) were more able to use text structure to comprehend and recall (Perkins, 1987; Perkins & Angelis, 1985).

(22)   *Relationship Between ESL Reading Proficiency and ESL Oral Proficiency*   Seven studies aimed specifically to address the relationship between ESL reading proficiency and ESL oral proficiency for individuals in the United States. With minor exceptions, investigators in this group typically gave participants several tests (standardized, informal, and/or self-devised) once, or sometimes more than once over a year or so. Occasionally, participants were videotaped conversing in natural settings. Intercorrelations among measures were then examined to determine the extent of relationships. Participants were mainly young (kindergarten through eighth grade in three studies, age 16 through adult in two others). Because both reading and oral language proficiency were main research issues, each was measured, and wide ranges of ability levels were represented. Many different languages were also represented.

These studies produced quite mixed results. Thus, it is not possible to make a simple statement about the relationship between ESL reading proficiency and ESL oral proficiency. Rather, the relationship may have depended on at least three factors: native language, age or grade level, and the type of English oral proficiency measure used. First, native language background mediated the relationship between ESL reading proficiency and ESL oral proficiency (Brown & Haynes, 1985; Tragar & Wong, 1984). Tragar and Wong and Brown and Haynes were the only investigators in this cluster of studies who parsed results by both native language background and grade level. Tragar and Wong worked with 200 Cantonese students and 200 Hispanic students, all of whom had bilingual education in Boston for 1 to 2.5 years. They found a strong positive relationship for Hispanic sixth through eighth graders, and a strong negative relationship for Cantonese sixth through eighth graders. Brown and Haynes found moderately strong positive correlations for adult Arabs and Spaniards, but a negligible correlation for Japanese.

Second, the relationship between ESL reading proficiency and ESL oral proficiency may have been stronger at higher grade levels. Although there was a positive relationship in one study with first-grade Hispanic ESL students (Lara, 1991), there was no significant relationship in two other studies with young children. In contrast to the overall strong correlations just cited for sixth through eighth graders and for adults, as well as in one additional study with adults (Carrell, 1991), no relationship emerged for either Hispanic or Cantonese ESL learners at Grades 3 through 5 (Tragar & Wong, 1984). Likewise, Saville-Troike (1984) found mainly no relationships between ESL reading and ESL oral proficiency (excepting primarily oral English vocabulary) for second through sixth graders with little prior English experience. Even amount of time spent using English orally (with peers and adults) was not related to English reading achievement (Saville-Troike, 1984).

If native language background and ESL-learner age or grade level do mediate the relationship between ESL reading proficiency and ESL oral proficiency, these factors might help to explain mixed results from two other studies. Snow (1991) found mainly positive relationships, and Devine (1987) found some positive and some negative correlations. Only Snow had a large sample; the Devine study had 20 participants. Snow covered kindergarten through eighth grade and two languages. Devine covered 16- to 38-year-olds and five different languages. Results were not reported by age or language background in interpretable ways. It is highly possible that overall false correlations resulted from the combining of subgroups which might have had different correlations.

Third, it may be that a greater number of lower correlations surfaced when less formal and more naturalistic oral proficiency measures were used. For example, where scores were obtained from measures such as interviews, videotapes of natural classroom situations, and conversation tasks (Saville-Troike, 1984; Snow, 1991), a preponderance of, or at least some, near-zero correlations emerged. However, formal, isolated measures of grammar and vocabulary tended to yield strong negative correlations (Devine, 1987).

(23)   *The Relationship Between ESL Reading Proficiency and Variables Other Than English Oral Proficiency.*   Results in this section were from studies which were designed primarily to investigate the relationship between ESL learners' English reading proficiency and selected other vari-

ables, or which secondarily provided information pertinent to these issues. Most of these compared good ESL readers and poor ESL readers, some gave correlational tendencies, and one solely investigated poor ESL readers. A variety of tasks and analyses were used—nearly as wide a variety as is represented by all of the topics in this review. Most of the studies were done with elementary school students, but four were done with college-age or older participants. Most were done with Hispanics, but four studies also included participants from other language backgrounds. Several investigators reported English oral language proficiency levels in addition to English reading proficiencies. Where mentioned, English oral proficiencies ranged from beginning to advanced.

On the whole, results from 14 reports were robust across ages and grade levels, language backgrounds, and oral proficiency levels. There tended to be a positive relationship between English reading proficiency and the variables investigated. The following thematic conclusions were drawn. ESL learners who were more proficient in English reading and those who were less proficient tended to be different in the following ways. The more proficient readers tended to (a) use more schema knowledge (Ammon, 1987); (b) use strategies that were more meaning-oriented (e.g., make more miscues that were syntactically and semantically acceptable [Devine, 1988; Langer et al., 1990] and be more global or top-down in perceiving effective and difficulty-causing strategies [Carrell, 1989]); (c) use a greater variety of metacognitive strategies and use metacognitive strategies more frequently (Anderson, 1991); (d) take more action on plans to solve miscomprehension problems and check their solutions more often (Block, 1992); (e) persist more in the application of metacognitive strategies (Carrell, 1989); (f) make better use of cognates between languages and have more vocabulary knowledge (Ammon, 1987; Garcia & Nagy, 1993; Jimenez et al., 1991; Nagy et al., 1992); (g) make better and/or more inferences (Ammon, 1987; G.E. Garcia, 1991); (h) do better on social studies and science achievement tests (taken in English) (Saville-Troike, 1984); (i) be better readers in their native languages (Carson, Carrell, Silberstein, Kroll, & Kuehn, 1990; Tragar & Wong, 1984), with native-language reading scores best predicting English reading achievement at Grades 3 through 5, but oral English best predicting it at Grades 6 through 8 (Tragar & Wong, 1984); (j) be more proficient in English writing (Carson et al., 1990); and (k) have parents who perceived education to be highly important (Lara, 1991). One study (Carson et al., 1990) suggested that the strength of the relationships between ESL reading achievement and both native-language reading and ESL writing achievement might have been mediated by what the native language was (Chinese vs. Japanese).

However, although the variety and amount of metacognitive-strategy use varied according to English reading proficiency, both more and less proficient ESL readers applied the same most-frequent metacognitive strategies to answer test questions (Anderson, 1991), and identified problems and their sources equally well (Block, 1992). Also, there was no relationship between English reading and (a) math achievement, when tested in English (Saville-Troike, 1984); (b) language background (Saville-Troike, 1984); (c) the extent to which individuals used code switching in oral language (Lara, 1991); (d) a variety of written measures of English language knowledge (excepting one positive correlation) (Saville-Troike, 1984); or, surprisingly, (e) amount of time spent interacting with English text (Saville-Troike, 1984).

(24)   *Similarities Across Learners and Languages.*   In this section, two issues are examined: similarities in cognitive reading processes (a) across United States ESL learners and native English learners and (b) across United States ESL learners' native language and English. To address these two issues, I analyzed only studies which either included and compared both ESL readers and native English readers, or had research designs which allowed inferences about whether the ESL readers used native-language knowledge while they read in English. That is, I analyzed only studies which had data available within the reports to arrive at comparative conclusions. Studies were not included if investigators drew conclusions about similarities or differences in results solely by comparing their results to their (or others') assessments of collective prior work on the given topic.

(25)   *ESL Readers' Processes Compared to Those of Native English Speakers.*   A variety of paradigms was used in this group of 17 reports. Only two studies involved young children (third and fifth

graders); one study involved ninth graders; the remainder included college-age participants. When given, ESL proficiency levels reportedly ranged from beginning to advanced. A variety of native language backgrounds was represented.

The results tentatively suggested that there were some similarities and some differences in aspects of United States ESL readers' processes as compared to those of native English speakers. Qualitatively, or substantively, on the whole, many facets of the processes appeared similar. For the most part, differences tended to be associated with quantitative aspects of using the processes, that is, with the extent to which particular processes were used or with processing speed. No differences in outcomes due to the native language backgrounds of the participants were discernible. One study revealed different outcomes according to proficiency level, and one according to grade level.

Both groups of readers (a) used metacognitive strategies and monitored their reading (Block, 1986a, 1986b, 1992; Padron et al., 1986), (b) generally drew correct inferences from sentences with implicative and factive predicates (Carrell, 1984c), (c) recalled superordinate ideas (Connor, 1984) and propositions in general (Barrera et al., 1986), and (d) identified antecedents and other cohesive signals when reading (Demel, 1990; Duran & Revlin, 1994). (In one study involving antecedents, anaphora was equally difficult for Hispanic ESL fourth-grade readers and for monolingual English-speaking fourth-grade readers [Robbins, 1985].) Like native-English-speaking college students, advanced ESL college learners focused more on content than on function words and appeared to use acoustic scanning (Hatch, Polin, & Part, 1974).

However, with reference to qualitative differences, ESL readers did not use context as well as native English speakers (Carrell, 1983; Carrell & Wallace, 1983). Also, unlike native-English-speaking college students, beginning and intermediate ESL readers relied more on visual cues than on acoustic cues for reading, and focused equally on function and content words (Hatch et al., 1974). Further, at the ninth-grade level, although fluent ESL readers identified cohesive signals as well as native English speakers, they were less able to make use of the information—for example, to make inferences—than were the native English speakers (Duran & Revlin, 1994). However, with college-age participants, there was no difference between groups (Duran & Revlin, 1994).

Quantitatively, compared to native English speakers, the ESL readers tended to (a) use fewer metacognitive strategies (Knight et al., 1985; Padron et al., 1986), (b) use selected metacognitive strategies with different relative frequencies (Knight et al., 1985; Padron et al., 1986), (c) verbalize their metacognitive strategies less (Block, 1992), (d) make proportionately fewer meaningful miscues (Barrera et al., 1986; McLeod & McLaughlin, 1986), (e) have higher error rates for making inferences (Carrell, 1984c), and (f) recall fewer subordinate ideas from text (Connor, 1984). They also tended to monitor their comprehension more slowly (Block, 1992) and perform reading tasks more slowly (Mestre, 1984; Oller, 1972). Further, eye-movement photography revealed that as compared to norms of approximately 12,000 college-level native English readers, ESL college-level readers, though they tended to make about the same number of regressions, differed somewhat in making more fixations with narrower word spans, and differed significantly in that duration of fixation was much longer—about as long as for typical native-English-speaking third or fourth graders (Oller, 1972). This led to the conclusion that a main contrast between the two groups was the speed with which they processed verbal information in short-term memory.

(26)   *Native-Language Transfer to ESL Reading.*   The 17 reports in this group covered a variety of paradigms, with second graders through adults and, where reported, beginning to advanced ESL proficiency levels. The majority of studies involved Hispanic participants, though several other language backgrounds were represented in the remaining studies.

Overwhelmingly, results showed a transfer of native-language knowledge to ESL reading. Six statements supporting native-language transfer can be made. First, there was a positive relationship between ESL and native-language reading ability for readers in the United States (Carrell, 1991; Carson et al., 1990; Saville-Troike, 1984; Tragar & Wong, 1984). Interestingly, for college-age ESL learners in one study (Carrell, 1991), native Spanish reading ability accounted for more variance in English reading than did English oral proficiency. Second, knowledge used to guide comprehension in native-language reading was also used in ESL reading (Carrell, 1984a; Goldman, Reyes, & Varnhagen, 1984; Langer et al., 1990). Third, knowledge of Spanish vocabulary and idioms transferred to ESL reading (Garcia & Nagy, 1993; Irujo, 1986; Jimenez et al., 1991; Nagy et al., 1992). Fourth, participants used the same metacognitive strategies in ESL reading as in their own Spanish reading (Pritchard, 1990). Fifth, at least a minimal number of miscues in ESL oral reading could be attributed to native-language syntactical knowledge (Gonzalez & Elijah, 1979; Romatowski, 1981). And sixth, some participants apparently phonologically recorded their ESL reading into their native language (Muchisky, 1983).

Notably, some transfer could be considered negative, such as omission of articles in English reading when the articles could be omitted in the reader's native language, or such as interference caused by Spanish idioms when the reader came across similar, but not identical, English idioms (Irujo, 1986). On the other hand, much could be considered positive, as in one study where some participants' miscue patterns were the same in ESL and in Spanish reading, but one feature was different: the participants made more miscues on function words than on nouns in Spanish and vice versa in ESL reading (Clarke, 1981).

Only two studies suggested quantitative differences, and these were in the use of comprehension-monitoring and metacognitive strategies in ESL reading as compared to native-language reading. One showed less monitoring in ESL reading (Pritchard, 1990); the other showed more strategy use in ESL reading (Mikulecky, 1991).

(27)   *Miscellaneous.*   I located a handful of studies covering a variety of additional topics. There was some limited evidence that college-age ESL readers used phonological recoding when they read English silently (Muchisky, 1983; see also similar findings on acoustic scanning in Hatch et al., 1974). However, two other studies suggested significant variability in adult beginning and intermediate ESL learners' perceptions of the reading process as sound- versus meaning-centered; this influenced the way they read (Define, 1984, 1988). Also, in the phonological recoding study done by Muchisky (1983), ESL students were able to comprehend well without using phonological recoding. Finally, for adults with intermediate to advanced ESL proficiency, awareness of parts of speech was positively related to reading comprehension (Guarino & Perkins, 1986).

(28)   **SUMMARY AND DISCUSSION**

A partial image of United States ESL readers' cognitive processes emerged. Most notably, there was substantial individual variability in at least two areas: vocabulary knowledge and psycholinguistic strategies. However, on the whole, ESL readers (a) recognized cognate vocabulary fairly well, (b) monitored their comprehension and used many metacognitive strategies, (c) used schemata and prior knowledge to affect their comprehension and recall, and (d) were affected differently by different types of text structures.

Further, tentative images of more proficient versus less proficient ESL readers in the United States were formed. On the whole, more proficient ESL readers (a) made better use of vocabulary knowledge, (b) used a greater variety of metacognitive strategies and used selected strategies more frequently, (c) took more action to solve miscomprehension and checked solutions to problems more often, (d) used psycholinguistic strategies that were more meaning-oriented, (e) used more schema knowledge, and (f) made better and/or more inferences.

(29) *Theoretical Issues*

On the whole, the studies reviewed in this article support the contention that the cognitive reading processes of ESL learners are substantively the same as those of native English speakers. At least, they are more alike than they are different. At the same time, some of the studies reviewed suggested that while the same basic processes may be used, a few selected facets of those processes may be used less or may operate more slowly for ESL learners than for native English readers. Let me first point to two forms of evidence from the present review which support the contention of essential sameness, and then I will summarize the evidence supporting the suggestion that selected facets of cognitive processes may be used less or more slowly by ESL learners.

Findings from a broad array of studies pointed to an image of the cognitive processes of ESL readers (just summarized at the beginning of this section) which was highly similar to portraits of the cognitive processes of native English readers that abound in the more general reading literature. On the whole, the statements made about ESL readers in general and about more proficient ESL readers in the opening to this section could well be made about native English readers.

Also, the results of studies in which United States ESL readers and native English readers were compared indicated that the two groups' cognitive processes were substantively more alike than different. They used similar metacognitive strategies and monitored their comprehension when reading, and identified antecedents in text equally well.

Collectively, these forms of evidence, along with other specific findings from the studies, suggested a relatively good fit to the preexisting native-language reading theories, models, and views many of the studies were grounded in, most specifically to a psycholinguistic view, schema theory, an interactive view of reading, and views of metacognition in reading.

On the other hand, the evidence for the specialness of ESL readers' processes was mainly the amount of use and the length of time to use certain processes. That is, in some instances, ESL readers seemed to use a given process or aspects of it less often, less well, and/or more slowly. On the whole, they used fewer metacognitive strategies and favored some different ones, verbalized metacognitive strategies less, recalled subordinate ideas less well, monitored comprehension more slowly, and did reading tasks more slowly. Less proficient ESL readers did less acoustic scanning and focused more on function words than did others. An additional important specialness was that language background may have affected preferred text structures.

These areas of specialness suggest that the preexisting theories, models, and views might be revisited and modified to account for these data and to specifically allow for explanation of ESL learners' processes. Explorations of the preexisting native-language reading theories, models, and views might address areas such as (a) reasons for decreased use of specific strategies, (b) reasons for depressed recall of subordinate ideas, and (c) what factors account for slower rates of reading for ESL learners as compared to native English speakers.

Whether or not there is a need for a theory of reading specific to ESL or second-language learners is a highly controversial issue. Some second-language researchers believe that second-language reading is "a different phenomenon" from first-language reading (Bernhardt, 1991, p. 226) and, consequently, that a reading theory specific to second-language learners is needed. Others, however, believe that second-language reading is highly similar to first-language reading. For example, Heath's (1986) notion of transferable generic literacies and Krashen's (1984, 1988) reading hypothesis both reveal an underlying assumption that second-language literacy entails the same basic processes as first-language literacy (q.v. Hedgcock & Atkinson, 1993). Another example is the previously mentioned work of Carrell, Devine, and Eskey (1988) on the application of an interactive model of reading to ESL reading. Though the results of the present review on United States ESL readers provide more support for the view that second-language cognitive reading processes are highly similar to those involved in first-language reading, it must be remembered that studies from only one second language and only one country were assessed in this review. It is still possible that quite different results could occur for other second languages or in other situations.

Recall that two second-language acquisition positions tended to be used to ground some of the studies in this review. These were positions widely known in the second-language education community and ones which were not, in themselves, complete theories of the reading process. The findings from studies and the themes in this review indicated a fit to one of the positions, but insufficient information was available to inform about the remaining position. That is, considerable evidence emerged to support the CUP model. United States ESL readers used knowledge of their native language as they read in English. This supports a prominent current view that native-language development can enhance ESL reading.

However, the data were unclear on the separate issue of whether ESL oral proficiency is a prerequisite for ESL reading. The relationship between ESL reading proficiency and ESL oral proficiency may have varied according to age and/or grade level (the relationship may have been stronger at higher grades) as well as according to native language background. Further, the studies were correlational and provided virtually no information about the causal direction of the relationship. Consequently, what their results mean is not clear with regard to the position that English orality must be developed to an optimal level in order for English literacy to fully develop.

(30) *Research Directions*

Earlier comments on the limitations of the research, combined with the images and themes gleaned from the findings, suggest several research directions which can be considered in four areas: research issues to focus on, methodological issues, specific aspects of modifying existing reading theories, and cross-specialty collaboration.

Several factors lead to the belief that a new agenda of research issues might advance the field. First, both the research questions and the methodologies have tended to follow major trends in reading research done with native English speakers, but selectively and 5 to 10 years later. Applying or replicating native-language reading research has been helpful in that it has sometimes enabled comparisons across groups. However, while the questions posed to date have helped us to know something about what United States readers' cognitive processes are, they have provided little insight as to how they happen. Notably absent were studies designed to trace the cognitive development of ESL readers in the United States. Also, reasons for differences between ESL and native-English-speaking readers' use of particular processes, such as why ESL readers' cognitive processing was sometimes slower, were underexplored. Second, the occasional emergence of interactions among reading processes and ESL readers' native language background, age or grade level, and/or ESL proficiency level suggest considerable complexity in some areas of cognitive activity. Third, individual variability in vocabulary knowledge and in the use of psycholinguistic strategies also suggests that pursuing average effects across readers may not be enlightening in some areas of cognitive activity.

It would appear helpful now for researchers to pursue ESL reading research centering around the issues of how and why ESL readers in the United States acquire, deploy, and change their cognitive processes. Such research might examine the following questions. How do ESL readers learn (or fail to learn) about cognates? How do they use cognates when reading? How do beginning ESL readers at various age levels approach text? What accounts for quantitative differences (such as processing speed) in ESL and native-English-speaking readers' processes?

Another important set of neglected research issues centers around the age of participants. There has been very little attention to how cognitive reading processes emerge and develop for preschool through second-grade students in the United States. This is probably due to prior oral primacy beliefs. That is, perhaps United States researchers have tended to think that ESL learners at these young ages cannot or should not acquire ESL literacy, and therefore have not chosen to study children at these ages. However, most literacy researchers would probably agree that we need to know much more now about the early emergence and development of ESL reading. For example, how do ESL cognitive reading processes develop over time, from the inception of learning English onward to some relatively high level of proficiency, and how are the early ESL reading processes similar to, and different from, those of early native English literacy? Further, we need to know much more about how, when, and why ESL reading and ESL oral processes interact, rather than continuing to pursue the more general question of whether they are related. Along similar lines, only one study of United States ESL reading and writing relationships was located. It would also be interesting to pursue "how," "when," and "why" questions about the interchange between ESL reading and writing.

A second suggested area to consider as future research is conducted has to do with methodology. Virtually all of the methodological limitations noted earlier in this review could be addressed in future studies. That is, all investigators should report important characteristics of participants, especially characteristics that might potentially mediate results, including extent of literacy in a native language and ESL oral proficiency level. When participants have mixed backgrounds and/or language/literacy levels, findings should be sorted according to the differences, or analyses should at least account for the differences. Definitions of ESL proficiency should be given, and procedures for determining proficiency should be well-documented. Complete references should be reported for all standardized measures used. Reliabilities and, where possible, validity indexes should be given for all measures.

The agenda of issues given above brings to mind several types of research methods which might be useful. As an example of a way to get at the "howness" of processes, researchers might use a tracking technique similar to "think aloud" protocol analysis, such as that done by Hayes and Flower (1983), to track writers' problem solving. Participants could be videotaped talking aloud while reading, and they could give retrospective interviews. Though "think alouds" have been used in ESL reading research, they have not been used very much, if at all, in conjunction with other methods such as interviews or with videotapes, and they have not been used to actually track or describe the intricacies of how reading processes are used or when they vary.

Alongside tracking techniques, other designs could be formulated to help sort out, or to at least take into account, complexities in reading processes such as native language background. An example is interpretive work in which investigators visit classrooms and follow selected children over a year or longer. Through observation, interviews, and collection of reading samples, and so on, much could be learned about how and when cognitive reading processes develop and are used.

Also, where researchers still wish to pursue questions that involve comparison to native English readers in prior research, it seems imperative that extremely close replications be conducted on selected studies with rigorous designs. If close replications are done, we can more easily compare outcomes across studies.

A third direction is that it would be very useful for theoreticians to select some of the current views on reading and to detail hypothetical points of adaptation for ESL learners. Then a program of research could be conducted to address each of the hypothetical points.

Fourth, and perhaps most importantly, the United States research on ESL reading has tended to be isolated somewhat to the ESL community. Most of the ESL reading research has been published in journals associated with the ESL profession—journals on language, ESL, and/or linguistics. Few ESL cognitive reading research pieces were located in journals known primarily as reading or literacy research journals. This suggests that researchers whose primary specialty is reading might not be doing much work with ESL learners; that if they are studying ESL readers, they are not seeking the audiences of reading research journals; or that ESL reading research, on the whole, has been submitted to literacy journals but has not passed the review process. In any case, if the many communities interested in reading and issues of diversity could cross boundaries and learn and teach with each other, the potential for progress might increase.

③①*Instructional Implications*

As for instruction, the images drawn from the findings in this review strongly imply that for the most part, as least with regard to the cognitive aspects of reading, United States teachers of ESL students could follow sound principles of reading instruction based on current cognitive research done with native English speakers. There was virtually no evidence that ESL learners need notably divergent forms of instruction to guide or develop their cognitive reading processes. This finding runs parallel to results of a recent review of United States research on ESL reading instruction (Fitzgerald, in press). A main conclusion of that review was that results of instructional studies with ESL learners were positive and highly consistent with findings generally reported for native-language participants. Evidence in the present review did suggest, though, that teachers need to be aware of some cognitive processing areas that might deserve extra consideration in ESL learning settings in the United States. For example, ESL learners' slower reading and fewer responses in reading situations, on average, suggest mainly that teachers might display even more than normal patience with ESL learners and that they take extra care when wording questions and making interactive comments in order to maximize the opportunity for activation of thought processes. Another example is that the potential effects of background knowledge suggest that the development of readers' topic knowledge for specific reading selections warrants even more attention from teachers than in other situations.

Chapter 10 Appendix B

① The Effects of Instruction in Solving Mathematical Word Problems for Students With Learning Problems: A Meta-Analysis

② Yan Ping Xin and Asha K. Jitendra

Lehigh University

ABSTRACT

Purpose

Procedure

Results

This article provides a synthesis of word-problem-solving intervention research with samples of students with learning problems (i.e., mild disabilities and at risk for mathematics failure). The effectiveness of word-problem-solving instruction in 25 outcome studies was examined across student characteristics (e.g., grade, IQ); instructional features (e.g., intervention approach, treatment length); methodological features; skill maintenance; and generalization components. Separate analyses were performed for group-design studies and single-subject studies using standardized mean change and percentage of nonoverlapping data (PND), respectively. The overall mean weighted effect size (d) and PND for word-problem-solving instruction were positive across the group-design studies ($ES = 1.89$) and single-subject studies (PND 5 89%). In addition, positive effects for skill maintenance and generalization were found for group design ($ES = 1.78$ and 1.84, respectively) and single-subject studies ($PND = 100\%$). Computer-assisted instruction was found to be most effective for group-design studies. Effects for representation techniques and strategy training were found to be significantly higher than the "other" approach for both group-design and single-subject studies. Long-term (.1 month) intervention effects were significantly higher than short- or intermediate-term interventions for group-design studies, whereas both long-term and intermediate treatments were seen to be more effective than short-term treatments for single-subject studies. Other significant effects found for group-design studies only in terms of student characteristics, instructional features, and methodological features are reported. Finally, implications of the current analysis for future research in the area of word-problem solving are discussed.

Source: From Xin, Y. P., & Jitendra, A. K. (1999). The effects of instruction in solving mathematical word problems for students with learning problems: A meta-analysis. *The Journal of Special Education 32*(4), 207–225. Copyright 1999 by PRO-ED, Inc. Reprinted with permission.

Problem Formation	③

Problems of mathematics underachievement are greatest for students with mild disabilities and those at risk for mathematics failure (Carnine, Jones, & Dixon, 1994; Nuzum, 1987; Parmar, Cawley, & Frazita, 1996; Zentall & Ferkis, 1993). The term mild disabilities refers to students with learning disabilities, mild mental retardation, and emotional disabilities, who are often placed together in classrooms and receive similar curricula. Increasingly, reports point to the difficulties that students with mild disabilities experience in several aspects of mathematics (for reviews see Jitendra & Xin, 1997; Mastropieri, Bakken, & Scruggs, 1991; Mastropieri, Scruggs, & Shiah, 1991; Pereira & Winton, 1991; and Rivera, 1997). Cawley and Miller (1989) reported that the mathematical performance of 8- and 9-year-old students with learning disabilities was equivalent to the first-grade level and that the performance of 16- and 17-year-old students with learning disabilities was equivalent to about the fifth-grade level. In addition, students with mild mental retardation scored significantly lower than age-equivalent students with learning disabilities on four mathematics domains (basic concepts, listening vocabulary, problem solving, and fractions) (Parmar, Cawley, & Miller, 1994). Specifically, word-problem solving is difficult for students with disabilities who evidence problems in reading, computation, or both (Dunlap, 1982). As a result, some of these students reportedly spend more than one third of their resource room time studying mathematics (Carpenter, 1985).

The poor problem-solving performance by students with mild disabilities seems to follow the pattern of lackluster mathematics performance of general education students across the nation. That is, U.S. students are often placed last or next to last in international mathematics comparisons (Anrig & LaPointe, 1989; Gray & Kemp, 1993; LaPointe, Mead, & Phillips, 1989; Stedman, 1994). They have ranked lower than students in other countries in many mathematical areas (e.g., measurement, geometry, data organization), particularly word-problem solving (National Center for Education Statistics [NCES], 1991, 1992). In sum, word-problem solving presents difficulties for students of all ability and age levels (National Assessment of Educational Progress, 1992) and has received considerable attention from the National Council of Teachers of Mathematics (Miller & Mercer, 1993).

Given the relevance of problem solving in today's technologically advanced society, Patton, Cronin, Bassett, and Koppel (1997) recommended teaching students with learning problems to be proficient problem solvers in dealing with everyday situations and work settings. The importance of providing quality word-problem-solving instruction for students with mild disabilities and at-risk students is clear. Although mathematics instruction in general, and word-problem solving in particular, has not received as much in-depth study and analysis as reading (Bender, 1992), a reasonable number of mathematics word-problem-solving intervention studies with samples of students with learning problems is now available. A recent narrative review of word-problem-solving research (Jitendra & Xin, 1997) provided information of practical importance but was limited by its reliance on published studies only, and by a lack of quantitative techniques for analyzing the magnitude of intervention effectiveness. The present review uses a meta-analytic technique to aggregate intervention studies on solving word problems and examine the relationship between study characteristics and intervention outcomes.

Research Questions

Meta-analysis is a statistical analysis technique that provides a quantitative summary of the findings and characteristics of many empirical studies (Glass, 1977). Unlike more traditional narrative and vote-count research syntheses, meta-analysis has the potential to compare the magnitude of different treatment effects across studies to address more macroscopic research questions or high-order interactions on a specified topic. Thus, this technique increases the effective translation of research findings into practice (Kavale, 1984; Kavale & Glass, 1984; Sindelar & Wilson, cited in Mostert, 1996). The present meta-analysis study was designed to ④ answer the following questions.

1. What is the general effectiveness of word-problem-solving interventions (e.g., representation, strategy training, CAI) for teaching students?
2. Is intervention effectiveness related to important student characteristics (i.e., grade/age, IQ level, or classification label)?

3. Are treatment outcomes related to instructional features, such as (a) setting, (b) length of treatment, (c) instructional arrangement, (d) implementation of instruction, (e) word-problem task, and (f) student-directed intervention?

4. Is there a relationship between methodological features (publication bias, group assignment) and effect size?

5. What is the effectiveness of word-problem-solving instruction in fostering skill maintenance and generalization? Are skill maintenance and generalization functions of instructional features (e.g., treatment length)?

METHOD

⑤*Literature Search*

Data Collection

We first conducted a computer search of the Educational Resources Information Clearinghouse (ERIC), 1986 to June 1996, Psychological Abstracts (PsycLIT), 1986 to 1996, and Dissertation Abstracts International (DAI), 1960 to 1996, databases using the keywords problem solving, word problems, disabilities, remedial, and at risk. Following the identification of various articles involving mathematics word-problem-solving instruction designed for students with mild disabilities and those at risk, we searched the references cited in them for more studies. In addition, we hand-searched recent issues (1995–1996) of particular journals (i.e., *Exceptional Children, Exceptionality, Journal of Learning Disabilities, Learning Disabilities Research & Practice, Learning Disability Quarterly, Remedial and Special Education,* and *The Journal of Special Education*) for studies that met the inclusion criteria. The criteria for including a study were as follows: (a) The participants were diagnosed or described as having a disability (e.g., learning disabilities, mental retardation, emotional disturbance) or receiving remedial mathematics instruction, and therefore were deemed to be at-risk; (b) the study investigated the effects of specific word-problem-solving instructional strategies; (c) the study included baseline or pre- and posttreatment assessment data; (d) if of group design, the study reported enough quantitative information (e.g., means, standard deviations, *t* tests or *F* tests) regarding performance outcomes that effect sizes could be calculated; and (e) the study was available in English and either was published in a peer-reviewed journal or was an unpublished research report (e.g., doctoral dissertation).

The studies excluded from this review were those that were descriptive or did not include instruction in solving mathematical word problems. Specifically, studies were excluded when they identified or analyzed the characteristics of difficult-problem solvers (e.g., Liedtke, 1984; Montague, Bos, & Doucette, 1991; Zentall, 1990), assessed learners' mathematics abilities (Parmar, 1992), or examined the influence of task features (e.g., syntax, relevant and/or irrelevant information in word problems) on students' word-problem-solving performance (Englert, Culatta, & Horn, 1987; Wheeler & McNutt, 1983). Two studies had to be excluded from the sample of studies because, although they met most criteria, they did not provide pretreatment assessment data (e.g., Darch, 1982; Miller & Mercer, 1993).

The literature search and selection procedures identified 15 published studies and 10 unpublished doctoral dissertations. All published studies were located in journals between 1986 and 1996, whereas unpublished doctoral dissertations were identified to be from 1980 to 1996. The final sample of 25 studies yielded 14 group-design studies and 12 single-subject studies. The study by Hutchinson (1993) included both a group design and a single-subject design. Tables 1 and 6 present the summary of information from the group and single-subject studies, respectively.

⑥*Computation and Analysis of Treatment Effectiveness*

Data Analysis

Group Design Studies.   The standardized mean change was used to calculate the intervention effect (Becker, 1988). Because a majority of the studies compared the effects of two or more intervention approaches, rather than the effects of one type of intervention versus no intervention, the standardized mean change computed for each sample (experimental or comparison) was deemed to be an appropriate measure of effect size (ES) for within-subject comparisons. As Becker noted, the standardized mean change has several advantages over Glass's effect size: It allows for the direct comparison of data from studies using different designs; in addition, studies without true control groups need not be omitted (Becker, 1988). Another advantage is that because the standardized mean change technique does not entail comparing several intervention conditions to the same control group, such as when numerous intervention conditions are examined in a single study, the violation of independence is not a concern (Becker, 1988; Hunter & Schmidt, 1990). According to Becker, "mean changes from separate samples could be considered independent data points and analyzed using methods of meta-analysis devised for effect-size data" (p. 264). In addition, Becker argued that one could aggregate standardized change measures across studies within treatment or comparison populations and examine the relation of "relevant predictors to the standardized mean changes" (p. 264) by analyzing the independent treatment effects.

The effect size (g) in this study was computed as the difference between the posttest and pretest means for a single sample, divided by the pretest standard deviation. This computation allowed us to treat the pretreatment status as the control group, because the assumption was that the treated group members' pretreatment status was a good estimate of their hypothetical posttreatment status in the absence of a treatment (Glass, 1977). The gs in this study were converted to unbiased ds by correcting them for sampling error artifacts (Hedges & Olkin, 1985). The dependent measure used to calculate effect sizes was either the correct answer in word-problem solving (i.e., operation and computation) or the correct operation chosen. In the event that a study reported both correct answer and correct operation (or correct calculation) scores, only the correct answer was used to calculate the effect size. Effect sizes were calculated for each intervention sample independently within a study, with positive signs given to the ES when the posttreatment was attributed to higher performance. A total of 35 effect sizes were obtained.

In addition to the overall main effect size for the mathematics instruction variable, we calculated effect sizes for the study characteristics (e.g., IQ, label, intervention approach, length of treatment). Furthermore, we tested the homogeneity of effect sizes using Hedges and Olkin's homogeneity statistics Q. The Q statistic has an approximate chi-square distribution with k21 degrees of freedom, where k is the number of effect sizes (Hedges & Olkin, 1985). Using the DSTAT (Johnson, 1989) program, we calculated Q_B and Q_W to estimate the homogeneity of effect sizes between and within classes, respectively. In addition, we used the homogeneity statistics to identify statistical outliers (those that were much larger or smaller than the other effect sizes) that "would result in the largest reduction to the homogeneity statistics" (Johnson, 1989, p. 81). The DSTAT program allows for the stepwise removal of outliers until homogeneity is reached. Such an approach would allow for "stronger conclusions regarding a research literature" (Johnson, 1989, p. 4). In this study, we conducted tests with and without the outliers to examine their influence on the mean effect size. Alpha levels for all analyses of homogeneity of effect sizes in this meta-analysis were set at the .01 level of significance.

Single-Subject Design Studies.   Problems associated with the application of parametric statistical procedures in the estimation and analysis of single-subject research effect sizes make it difficult to directly compare group and single-subject research effect sizes (Scruggs, Mastropieri, & Casto, 1987; White, Rusch, Kazdin, & Hartmann, 1989). Effect sizes have been computed from single-subject studies (Busk & Serlin, 1992) by treating the baseline data points as pretreatment scores and the treatment data points as posttreatment scores. However, the lack of sufficient baseline data points (as few as 3) in the single-subject research on word-problem solving presented problems in terms of the reliability of the effect size procedures and interpretation (Scruggs et al., 1987; White et al., 1989). Instead, we used percentage of nonoverlapping data (PND), a nonparametric approach for synthesizing findings from single-subject design studies (Scruggs et al., 1987). This approach presents a promising alternative to standardized mean difference effect size for quantifying single-subject time series data (Busse, Kratochwill, & Elliott, 1995). PND between treatment and baseline phases of single-subject studies was used to determine treatment effectiveness. PND was computed as the number of treatment data points that exceeded the highest baseline data point in an expected direction, divided by the total number of points in the treatment phase. A positive PND indicated that the intervention scores were higher than the baseline scores. Again, the dependent measure was either the correct answer in word-problem solving (i.e., operation and computation) or the correct operation chosen. We calculated PND scores for each intervention sample independently within a study. When a multiple baseline design across participants was used, individual PND scores were aggregated across participants in a study to obtain an overall treatment effect. Thus, PND scores were aggregated across studies in this review for the main variable of mathematics instruction and for the study characteristics (e.g., IQ, label, intervention approach, length of treatment). A total of 15 PND scores were obtained from the 12 single-subject design studies. One single-subject study (Montague, 1992) involved two groups and the sequential componential analysis of cognitive and metacognitive strategies. Therefore, four treatment effects came from that one study. We also tested for significant differences among variables using Kruskal-Wallis, a nonparametric statistic.

(7) *Coding Study Features*

Coding

The following information was coded from each article to describe the main characteristics of the individual study.

Grade and Age.   This variable refers to three levels: elementary (Grades 1–6, ages 6–12); secondary (Grades 7–12, ages 13–18); and postsecondary (college, ages 19 and above).

IQ.   Two levels of IQ were recorded: IQ lower than 85 and IQ equal to or above 85 (i.e., more than 1 standard deviation above the mean). Given the discrepancy among states in specifying IQ cutoff scores (Frankenberger & Fronzaglio, 1991), especially when describing and identifying students with learning disabilities, we deemed that the criteria of 1 standard deviation below the mean as the cutoff score would help to distinguish the population identified as learning disabled from other categories of disabilities (e.g., mild mental retardation, emotional disturbance).

Classification Label.   Three classes were assigned to this variable: learning disabilities (LD), mixed disabilities (i.e., learning disabilities, mild mental retardation, and emotional disabilities), and at risk (i.e., those in remedial programs).

Intervention Approach.   The orientation of each intervention approach was coded into one of the four categories described below. This grouping of interventions into separate categories does not necessarily indicate mutually exclusive interventions. Instead, it is more likely that approaches overlap or share many similar components. For example, a representational technique or CAI might employ a strategy-training procedure or vice versa. Thus, our classification was based on the primary orientation of the study as determined by the following descriptions.

Representation Techniques.   This approach refers to the interpretation or representation of ideas or information given in a word problem. Representation approaches to solving mathematical problems include pictorial (e.g., diagramming); concrete (e.g., manipulatives); verbal (linguistic training); and mapping instruction (schema-based) (Lesh, Post, & Behr, 1987; Resnick & Omanson, 1987; Swing, Stoiber, & Peterson, 1988).

Strategy Training.   This category refers to any explicit problem-solving heuristic procedures (e.g., direct instruction, cognitive and metacognitive) that lead to the solution of the problem. These may involve explicit teaching or self-regulation of a strategy in isolation or together with other elements (e.g., paraphrasing, visualizing, hypothesizing, estimating the answer) (Montague & Bos, 1986). Direct instruction and cognitive strategies relate to how to solve a problem, whereas metacognitive strategies relate to knowing how to solve a problem and may include self-instruction, self-questioning, and self-regulation procedures (Kameenui & Griffin, 1989; Montague, 1992).

Computer-Aided Instruction (CAI).   This variable refers to an intervention that employs CAI tutorial or interactive videodisc programs.

Other.   This category refers to no instruction (e.g., attention only, use of calculators) or any type of task instruction not included in the above categories (e.g., key word, problem sequence).

Setting.   This variable refers to whether instruction was provided in pull-out settings or classrooms (i.e., resource, self-contained, or remedial). For the purpose of this review, pull-out referred to instruction outside of the special education or remedial classroom in which regularly scheduled mathematics instruction occurred.

Length of Treatment.   Three levels were assigned to this category short (equal to or less than 1 week, 1 to 7 training sessions); intermediate (equal to or less than 1 month, more than seven sessions); and long-term (more than 1 month) interventions. It must be noted that this categorization was arbitrary, in that the mathematics intervention literature does not provide any direction for defining length of treatment.

Implementation of Intervention.   This variable refers to the person (i.e., teacher, researcher, or both) implementing the instruction.

Instructional Arrangement.   This variable refers to whether instruction occurred in groups or individually.

Word-Problem Task.   The word problems used in the reviewed studies were coded into one of three categories: (a) one-step word problems, which required a single mathematical operation to arrive at the correct solution; (b) multistep word problems, which required two or more mathematical operations; and (c) mixed, in which both one-step and multistep word problems were used.

Student Directed.   This category was created to classify studies according to whether or not students were actively involved in strategy regulation. That is, interventions that taught students self-instruction, self-questioning, and/or self-monitoring "to gain access to strategy knowledge, guide execution of strategies, and regulate use of strategies and problem solving performance" (Montague, 1992, p. 231) were coded as high student directed. Those studies that involved teacher-directed instruction only were coded as low student directed.

Publication Bias.   This variable indicates whether the identified study was a published journal article or an unpublished research report.

Group Assignment.   Studies were classified according to the way in which participants were assigned to treatment and comparison conditions. A procedure in which students were randomly assigned to treatment and comparison conditions was coded as "random," a matching technique whereby students were matched on variables and assigned to the treatment and comparison conditions was coded as "matched," and a study that used previously formed groups of students was coded as "intact."

Treatment Integrity.   This variable refers to the presence or absence of treatment integrity information.

Length of Follow-up.   Three categories were identified to disclose when the maintenance tests were given, on the basis of the elapsed time between the termination of the training and the time when follow-up probing was conducted (i.e., 1 to 4 weeks; more than 4 weeks but no more than 10 weeks; and more than 10 weeks).

Type of Generalization.   This category refers to near transfer (similar task transfer or setting generalization) and far transfer (different task transfer). When a study used two different measures at immediate posttesting to compare group performances (e.g., paper and pencil or online in Shiah, Mastropieri, Scruggs, & Fulk, 1995; typical word problems or contextualized problems in Bottge & Hasselbring, 1993), we used the posttest that was dissimilar to the instructional task as the transfer measure.

(8) *Study Characteristics*

Group Design Studies. The 14 group design studies included 9 published studies (64%) and 5 unpublished studies (36%). All published studies were located in journals between 1986 and 1995 (median = 1993), whereas unpublished doctoral dissertations were from 1980 to 1992 (median = 1987). The total number of participants was 581, ranging in age from 8 to 65 years (mean = 14.7). Sample size of the treatment conditions varied from 9 to 37, with a mean sample size of 18.66 and a standard deviation of 7.13. Studies included participants from elementary (34%), secondary (49%), and postsecondary (17%) grades. Only 6 of the 14 studies reported IQ scores; those scores varied from 84.17 to 99.30, with a mean of 92.19 and a standard deviation of 4.94. Of the 35 effect sizes, 444 (76%) of the students were described as having a learning disability, 19 (3%) were identified as having mild disabilities (mixed), and the remaining 118 (20%) were students at risk.

Of the interventions identified in the studies, the most frequent approach was strategy training (46%). Representation techniques constituted 23% of the 35 effect sizes, while CAI and the "other" category constituted 17% and 14%, respectively. In terms of setting, the typical setting for the research intervention was the resource or remedial classroom (71%), whereas instruction in pull-out settings occurred 29% of the time. No instruction was conducted in the general education classroom. The length of interventions varied from 2 days to 4 months, and each session ranged from 30 to 50 minutes. The majority of instruction occurred in small groups (86%); 14% of the instruction was provided individually. The most commonly employed measures were criterion-referenced tests (86%) developed by researchers. Only two studies (14%; Gleason, Carnine, & Boriero, 1990, and Hutchinson, 1993) employed items from standardized tests in addition to criterion-referenced tests. Researcher-implemented treatment (63%) was the most common; studies that reported instruction implemented by the teacher constituted 26% and both teacher and researcher constituted 11%. The most frequent type of word problem tasks used in the studies was one-step tasks (57%), followed by mixed (36%) and multistep problems (7%). In terms of student-directed interventions, the majority of studies reported infrequent student involvement (80%); high student involvement was noted only 20% of the time. For group assignment, most studies involved random assignment (54%), whereas matched and intact group assignments entailed 15% and 31% of the studies, respectively. Seven (50%) of the 14 studies did not report treatment integrity information, and therefore these results were excluded from the analysis.

Single-Subject Design Studies. The 12 single-subject studies included 7 published (58%) and 5 unpublished (42%) studies. All published studies were located in journals between 1986 and 1996 (median = 1993), whereas unpublished doctoral dissertations were from 1981 to 1994 (median = 1987). The total number of participants was 63, ranging in age from 8 to 18 years (mean = 13). Studies included participants from elementary (33%) and secondary (67%) grades. Ten of the 12 studies reported IQ scores; of those, Hutchinson (1993) did not provide individual IQ scores for the 12 students. The IQ scores varied from 70 to 115, with a mean of 93 and a standard deviation of 8.2. The sample included 55 (87%) students with learning disabilities and 8 (13%) identified as mildly disabled.

The two intervention approaches identified from the 15 PND were strategy training (80%) and representation techniques (20%). The length of interventions varied from 5 days to 4 months, and each session ranged from 20 to 55 minutes. Only one study (Hutchinson, 1993) employed items from standardized tests in addition to criterion-referenced tests developed by researchers. Researcher-implemented treatment (87%) was the most common; studies that reported instruction implemented by the teacher constituted 13% and both teacher and researcher constituted 7%. The most frequent type of word-problem tasks used in the studies was one-step (50%), followed by mixed (33%) and multistep problems (17%). In terms of student-directed interventions, the majority of studies reported high student involvement (67%); low student involvement was noted only 33% of the time. Nine (75%) of the 12 studies reported treatment integrity information.

(9) *Interrater Agreement*

The first author coded all studies and calculated effect sizes. A second rater (a doctoral student) independently coded 30% of all selected studies and calculated 30% of all effect sizes. The interrater agreement was defined as the total number of agreements divided by the total number of agreements plus disagreements and multiplied by 100. The interrater agreements for effect size calculation and coding of study features were 100% and 94%, respectively. The disagreements primarily involved coding of the intervention approaches. Therefore, a discussion was held between the author and the second rater, and all discrepancies were resolved following further clarification of the coding definitions.

(10)   **RESULTS: GROUP DESIGN STUDIES**

Reporting Results

Overall Effect of Mathematics Word-Problem-Solving Instruction

All effect sizes in the reviewed studies were calculated from the reported mean and standard deviation scores; no effect sizes had to be calculated from t or F ratios. Table 1 reports the unbiased effect sizes (d). The mean effect size before correction for sample size (g) was 1.92, with a range of 20.43 to 17.23, whereas the unbiased d was 1.89, with a range of 20.42 to 16.77. An examination of Table 1 indicates that the largest effect size ($d = 6.77$) was from the Moore and Carnine (1989) study, and the only two negative effect sizes were from the one study by Walker and Poteet (1989). The homogeneity test for the detection of outliers using the DSTAT statistical software program identified the largest outlier as the one effect size from the Bottge and Hasselbring (1993) study.

   When the homogeneity test for the detection of outliers was conducted on the entire set of selected studies, it resulted in an attrition of approximately 43% of the effect sizes to obtain homogeneity of samples. Because we started with only 35 effect sizes for our analysis and removal of such a large number of outliers would "[defeat] the purpose of metaanalysis which is to draw on the commonality across diverse studies" (Swanson, Carson, & Saches-Lee, 1996, p. 375), we retained the original data set. Instead, we conducted categorical model testing for the rest of the analyses both before and after the outliers were removed within each categorical class to determine the relation between the study characteristics and the magnitude of the effect sizes (B. Johnson, personal communication, January 9, 1997).

(11) *Effect of Intervention Approaches on Word-Problem Solving*

The mean effect size as a function of the intervention approach is shown in Tables 2 and 3 before and after outliers were removed. Results were essentially the same for trimmed data ($k = 27$) and untrimmed data ($k = 35$). CAI yielded the highest effect size ($d = +1.80$), followed by representation ($d = +1.77$), strategy ($d = +.74$), and "other" ($d = .00$) approaches. With the exception of the "other" category, the magnitude of mean effect sizes for all approaches was moderate to large for the trimmed data (range $= +.74$ to $+1.8$). Further simple contrasts indicated significant differences between CAI and strategy training and between CAI and the "other" approach ($p < .01$). Differences between the representation technique and CAI, however, were not significant. In addition, significant differences existed between the representation technique and strategy training ($p < .01$); and the differences between the "other" category and all approaches were significant ($p < .01$).

(12) *Mediator Influences on the Effect of Word-Problem Solving*

The mediator variables related to sample characteristics (e.g., grade/age, IQ, classification label) and instructional features (setting, length of treatment, instructional arrangement,

Table 1   Summary of Group Design Studies Included in the Meta-Analysis

Author	Date	Grade	IQ	Label	TrtA	Setting	InstrA
Published studies							
Bottge & Hasselbring	1993	Sec	NA	At-risk	CAI	Class	Group
Hutchinson	1993	Sec	[greater or equal] 85	LD	Strat	CI	
Gleason, Carnine, & Boriero	1990	Sec	NA	Mixed	CAI Strat	Class	Group
Montague, Applegate, & Marquard	1993	Sec	[greater or equal] 85	LD	Strat Strat Strat Strat Strat Strat	PU	
Moore & Carnine	1989	Sec	NA	At-risk	CAI Strat	Class	Group
Shiah, Mastropieri, Scruggs, & Fulk	1995	Elem	<85	LD	CAI CAI CAI	Class	Group
Walker & Poteet	1988–89	Sec	[greater or equal] 85	LD	Repres	CI	
Wilson & Sindelar	1991	Elem	[greater or equal] 85	LD	Strat Strat Other	Pu	
Zawaiza & Gerber	1993	Postsec	[greater or equal] 85	LD	Repres Repres Other	CL	
Unpublished studies							
Bennett	1980	Sec	NA	LD	Strat	NA	Group
Baker	1992	Elem	NA	LD	Repres Strat	Pull-out	Group
Lee	1992	Elem	[greater or equal]85	LD	Strat	CI	
Marzola	1987	Elem	NA	LD	Strat	Class	Group
Noll	1983	Postsec	NA	At-risk	Repres Repres Repres Repres	Class	Indiv

Author	WPT	StD	GrA	TrtF	Maint (FNa)	Gen.	n	
Published studies								
Bottge & Hasselbring	Mixed	Low	Matched	Yes	NA	Far	15	+
							14	+
Hutchinson	Mixed	High	Random	Yes	2	Far	12	+
Gleason, Carnine, & Boriero	One-step	Low	Random	NA	NA	Near, Far	9	+
						Near, Far	10	+
Montague, Applegate, & Marquard	Mixed	Low	Random	Yes	NA	NA	25	+
		High			NA	NA	23	+
		High			Na	NA	24	+
		High			1, 2, 3	Near	25	+
		High			1, 2, 3	Near	23	+
		High			1, 2, 3	Near	24	+
Moore & Carnine	One-step	Low	Matched	Yes	1	NA	13	+
							16	+
Shiah, Mastropieri, Scruggs, & Fulk	One-step	Low	Random	NA	1	Far	10	+
						Far	10	+
						Far	10	+

continued

Table 1   Continued

Author	WPT	StD	GrA	TrtF	Maint (FNa)	Gen.	n	
Walker & Poteet	One-step	Low	Intact	Yes	NA	NA	33	−
							37	−
Wilson & Sindelar	One-step	Low	Random	Yes	1	NA	21	+
							21	+
							20	+
Zawaiza & Gerber	Multi	Low	Intact	NA	NA	NA	12	+
							13	+
Unpublished Studies								
Bennett	Mixed	High	NA	NA	NA	NA	21	+
Baker	One-step	Low	Random	NA	NA	NA	25	+
							21	+
Lee	One-step	Low	Intact	Yes	1	NA	18	+
						NA	15	+
Marzola	Mixed	High	Intact	NA	NA	NA	30	+
		Low					30	+
Noll	One-step	Low	Random	NA	NA	NA	15	+
							15	+
							15	+
							15	+

Note: TrtA = treatment approach; InstrA = instructional arrangement; TrL = treatment length; Inter = intermediate; TrtI = treatment implemented; TrtF = treatment fidelity; GrA = Group assignment; WPT = word problem task; StD = student directed; n = sample size; d = unbiased effect size; CI = confidence interval; NA = not available.
a 1 = [less or equal] 4 weeks; 2 => 4 weeks but < 10 weeks; 3 = > 10 weeks.
*95% confidence interval contains d = .00.

implementation of instruction, word-problem type, and student direction) were analyzed to explore their influence on math-problem-solving instruction. Again, all categorical model testing was conducted both before and after outliers were removed. The results from both analyses are presented in Tables 2 and 3. Most of the results from the trimmed data in Table 3 yielded an amount of significant results similar to that of the untrimmed data in Table 2. For all categories, the removal of outliers yielded a more homogeneous within-categories effect size.

Grade/Age. Tables 2 and 3 present the results for the category of grade/age before and after outliers were removed. Results of the untrimmed data in Table 2 indicate no significant differences among groups. However, an analysis of the trimmed data in Table 3 reveals a large effect size for the postsecondary group ($d = +1.68$) followed by a moderate effect size for the secondary group ($d = +.78$) and a low effect size for the elementary group ($d = +.47$). Apparently, intervention effects were pronounced with an increase in age. Further simple contrasts revealed that the effect size for the postsecondary group was significantly different from that for the other two groups ($p < .01$). No significant differences were found between elementary and secondary groups. In sum, the inconsistent findings from the two analyses fail to indicate whether this category mediated the intervention effect size.

IQ. Table 2 reports the results for the category IQ, in which only 20 effects sizes were reportedly calculated for the studies. Results of the trimmed data (see Table 3) indicated that the effect size for participants with IQ # 85 was significantly greater ($d = +1.87$) than that for those with IQ # 85 ($d = +.51$, $p < .01$). It seems that IQ did mediate the effect size of the intervention.

Table 2 Summary of Effect Sizes Before Outliers Were Removed

Variable and class	Q[subB]	k	d+	95% CI Lower	95% CI Upper	Q[su
Sample characteristics						
Grade/age	8.34					
Elementary		12	+1.00	+0.80	+1.20	66.05
Secondary		16	+0.73	+0.56	+0.90	165.28
Postsecondary		7	+1.20	+0.88	+1.51	27.15
IQ	19.47 (FN*)					
< 85		3	+1.87	+1.26	+2.49	2.43
>/= 85		17	+0.45	+0.30	+0.60	63.12
Label	74.10 (FN*)					
LD		25	+0.68	+0.55	+0.81	140.04
Mixed		2	+1.96	+1.18	+2.74	1.06
At-risk		8	+2.22	+1.88	+2.56	51.61
Instructional features						
Intervention approach	87.83 (FN*)					
Representation		8	+1.05	+0.79	+1.31	53.55
Strategy		16	+1.01	+0.85	+1.18	78.53
CAI		6	+2.46	+1.97	+2.94	41.19
Other		5	+0.00	−0.26	+0.26	5.72
Setting	1.07					
Pull-out		11	+0.84	+0.66	+1.06	37.24
Classroom		23	+0.97	+0.81	+1.14	225.50
Length of treatment	18.05 (FN*)					
Short		18	+1.10	+0.92	+1.29	101.09
Intermediate		14	+0.62	+0.44	+0.79	110.56
Long		3	+1.25	+0.87	+1.63	37.12
Instructional arrangement	38.26 (FN*)					
Individual		5	+2.18	+1.76	+2.61	9.00
Group		30	+0.78	+0.66	+0.91	219.56
Instr. implemented	48.45 (FN*)					
Teacher		9	+0.50	+0.28	+0.72	70.91
Researcher		22	+0.95	+0.80	+1.10	100.14
Both		4	+2.58	+2.02	+3.13	47.32
Word problem task	5.56					
One-step problems		20	+0.96	+0.80	+1.13	173.48
Multistep problems		3	+0.38	−0.08	+0.83	0.94
Mixed problems		12	+0.89	+0.71	+1.08	67.17
Student directed	0.36					
Low		27	+0.87	+0.73	+1.01	219.61
High		8	+0.95	+0.73	+1.18	46.85
Methodological features						
Publicaton bias	12.72 (FN*)					
Published		24	+0.74	+0.60	+0.89	188.92
Unpublished		11	+1.21	+1.00	+1.42	65.17
Group assignment	76.72 (FN*)					
Random		21	+1.15	+0.99	+1.31	92.41
Matched		4	+2.58	+2.02	+3.13	47.32
Intact		9	+0.31	+0.11	+0.52	47.35

Note: k = number of effect sizes; d+ = effect size corrected for sample size; CI = confidence interval.
Significance of d+ was assessed by the z distribution, and nonsignificant Q reflects homogeneity within category. Q[subB] = homogeneity between-class effect, and Q[subW] = homogeneity within each class.
* p [less or equal] .01.

Table 3   Summary of Effect Sizes After Outliers Were Removed

Variable and class	Q[subB]	k	d+	95% CI Lower	Upper	Q[su
Sample characteristics						
Grade/age	26.25 (FN*)					
Elementary		7	+0.47	+0.23	+0.72	9.73
Secondary		10	+0.78	+0.58	+0.99	20.04
Postsecondary		5	+1.68	+1.29	+2.07	9.82
IQ	17.75 (FN*)					
< 85		3	+1.87	+1.26	+2.49	2.43
>/= 85		15	+0.51	+0.35	+0.67	23.65
Label	58.70 (FN*)					
LD		18	+0.50	+0.35	+0.65	27.08
Mixed		2	+1.96	+1.18	+2.74	1.06
At-risk		6	+1.90	+1.54	+2.26	11.52
Instructional features						
Intervention approach	81.37 (FN*)					
Representation		6	+1.77	+1.43	+2.12	10.72
Strategy		12	+0.74	+0.56	+0.93	19.24
CAI		4	+1.80	+1.27	+2.33	2.66
Other		5	+0.00	−0.26	+0.26	5.72
Setting	51.03					
Pull-out		9	+0.66	+0.46	+0.86	13.48
Classroom		13	+1.83	+1.58	+2.08	24.67
Length of treatment	52.14 (FN*)					
Short		11	+1.72	+1.46	+1.98	17.32
Intermediate		9	+0.73	+0.51	+0.95	16.30
16.30						
Long		2	+2.51	+1.93	+3.09	5.41
Instructional arrangement	51.45 (FN*)					
Individual		5	+2.18	+1.76	+2.61	9.00
Group		20	+0.54	+0.39	+0.68	32.19
Instr. implemented	98.41 (FN*)					
Teacher		5	+1.93	+1.52	+2.34	2.17
Researcher		16	+0.65	+0.49	+0.82	26.24
Both		2	+6.01	+4.77	+7.24	0.91
Word problem task	87.87 (FN*)					
One-step problems		13	+1.89	+1.64	+2.13	16.75
Multistep problems		3	+0.38	−0.08	+0.83	0.94
Mixed problems		9	+0.63	+0.43	+0.83	11.67
Student directed	0.34					
Low		14	+0.59	+0.40	+0.78	21.65
High		6	+0.68	+0.44	+0.92	9.07
Methodological features						
Publication bias	45.02 (FN*)					
Published		16	+0.71	+0.54	+0.88	28.46
Unpublished		8	+1.81	+1.54	+2.08	15.80
Group assignment	157.60 (FN*)					
Random		15	+1.55	+1.35	+1.76	26.13
Matched		2	+6.01	+4.77	+7.24	0.91
Intact		8	+0.11	−0.11	+0.32	10.73

Note: k = number of effect sizes; d+ = effect size corrected for sample size; CI = confidence interval.
Significance of d+ was assessed by the z distribution, and nonsignificant Q reflects homogeneity within category. Q[subB] = homogeneity between-class effect, and Q[subW] = homogeneity within each class.
* p [less or equal] .01.

Classification Label.   An examination of Table 3 indicates that the effect size for students with LD ($d = +.50$) was less than that for students with mixed disabilities ($d = +1.96$) and those at risk ($d = +1.90$). Further post hoc simple contrasts revealed significant differences between the LD and mixed groups and between LD and at-risk groups only ($p < .01$), indicating a mediating influence of this variable on effect size.

Setting.   Tables 2 and 3 report the results for the variable of setting, in which 34 effect sizes were calculated. The categorical model testing for differences before outliers were removed indicated no differences between pull-out and classroom settings. However, the effect size for the classroom setting was significantly greater than that for the pull-out setting ($p < .01$) when outliers were removed. Thus, setting may not have mediated the effect size of the intervention, given the different findings for the trimmed and untrimmed data.

Treatment Length.   Table 3 presents the results for the category of treatment length. The effect sizes for short-term (.7 sessions) interventions were seen to be more effective than intermediate (.7 sessions, .1 month) interventions, but less effective than long-term (.1 month) interventions. Further simple contrasts indicated that these differences were significant ($p < .02$). Treatment duration seemed to mediate the effect size of the intervention.

Instructional Arrangement.   Table 3 reports the results for the category of instructional arrangement. The effect size for individually provided instruction was greater than that for small-group instruction. The categorical model testing revealed significant differences between the two groups ($p < .01$). Thus, instructional arrangement seemed to have a mediating influence on the effect size of the intervention.

Implementation of Instruction.   Tables 2 and 3 present the results before and after outliers were removed for interventions implemented by the teacher, researcher, or both. In general, results from trimmed and untrimmed data seem to indicate that interventions implemented by both teachers and researchers were the most effective. However, these results are based on a small number of effect sizes. Results for interventions implemented by teachers were inconsistent for trimmed and untrimmed data. It seems that teacher-implemented interventions were less effective than those implemented by researchers before outliers were removed (see Table 2). In contrast, results of the trimmed data in Table 3 indicate that interventions conducted by teachers were more effective than those implemented by researchers. Although further simple contrasts showed that the differences among the three groups were significant, we cannot determine whether this category did mediate the effect size of the intervention, given the inconsistent findings before and after outliers were removed.

Word-Problem Task.   Results in Table 3 indicate that the effectiveness of interventions involving one-step word problems was greater than that for multistep and mixed word problems. Also, the effect size of mixed word problems was greater than that of multistep problems. Further simple contrasts revealed that the differences between one-step and multistep problems only were significant ($p < .01$). This variable seemed to mediate the effect size of the intervention.

Student Direction.   Table 3 presents the results for studies categorized by the presence or absence of instruction that was student regulated (e.g., self-instruction, self-questioning). Results indicate that the effect size for student-directed interventions was slightly higher than that for interventions with low student regulation. However, no statistically significant differences were found between these two categories, indicating that this category did not mediate the effect size.

(13) *Other Influences on the Effect of Word-Problem Solving*

Publication Bias.   Tables 2 and 3 provide the results for published and unpublished studies. The removal of outliers yielded a more homogeneous outcome for this category. Both untrimmed and trimmed data analyses indicated that unpublished studies entailed greater effect sizes than published studies, and the differences between them were significant ($p < .01$). The category of publication bias did mediate the effect size of the intervention.

Group Assignment.   Table 3 reports the results for group assignment. The removal of outliers indicated homogeneous within-class effect sizes. For this category of group assignment, both random and matched assignments yielded greater effect sizes when compared with intact group assignment. The differences between the three groups were found to be significant ($p < .01$). Group assignment did mediate the effect size of the intervention.

(14) *Effect of Word-Problem-Solving Instruction on Maintenance and Generalization*

Table 4 presents the results for follow-up length and generalization type. Thirteen of 35 cases (37%) provided follow-up data that allowed for the calculation of effect sizes, and 11 of the 35 cases (31%) included generalization data. The overall unbiased mean effect sizes for maintenance and generalization were +.78 and +.84, respectively. No significant differences for maintenance effects were found in terms of different elapsed time between training and follow-up testing. Also, no significant differences were found between near-transfer generalization (i.e., applying an acquired skill to similar tasks or to different settings) and far-transfer generalization (i.e., applying acquired skills to different tasks). For the remaining analyses of maintenance and generalization by instructional features, we report only the effect sizes because we did not conduct significance tests for differences, given the small sample size in each category.

Maintenance and generalization effect sizes for selected mediator variables related to instructional features (e.g., intervention approach, implementation of instruction, student direction) were computed. Table 5 provides a summary of these results. In terms of intervention approaches, CAI was seen to be more effective in promoting maintenance ($d = +1.53$) than generalization ($d = +.44$). Strategy training was seen to be effective for both maintenance ($d = +.77$) and generalization ($d = +1.09$) of word-problem solving. The category "other" approach included only one sample for maintenance and none for generalization. This class yielded a negative effect size ($d = -.29$) for maintenance. For the representation technique, no data were available for either maintenance or generalization.

Long-term interventions (more than 1 month) were most effective in promoting both maintenance ($d = +3.85$) and generalization ($d = +2.10$). However, the data were limited by only one observation from one study (Hutchinson, 1993). Although short-term (fewer than 7 sessions) interventions were seen to be effective in promoting maintenance ($d =$

**Table 4   Mean Effect Sizes for Maintenance and
                  Generalization**

	n	*d*	95% CI Lower	95% CI Upper
Maintenance				
< 4 weeks	12	+0.78	+0.58	+0.99
> 4 wks – 10 wks	4	+0.89	+0.89	+1.22
> 10 wks	3	+1.12	+0.77	+1.48
Generalization				
Near	5	+1.03	+0.71	+1.34
Far	8	+0.65	+0.34	+0.96

Note: n = number of effect sizes; *d* = effect size corrected for sample
size; CI = confidence interval.

Table 5   Summary of Effect Sizes for Maintenance and Generalization by Instructional Parameters

Variable and class	n	d+	95% CI Maintenance		n	d+	95% CI Generalize	
			Lower	Upper			Lower	U
Intervention approach								
Strategy	8	+0.77	+0.54	+1.01	6	+1.09	+0.80	+
CAI	4	+1.53	+1.03	+2.04	5	+0.44	+0.05	+
Other	1	−0.29	−0.92	+0.33	NA	NA	NA	
Length of treatment								
Short	3	+2.29	+1.63	+2.95	5	+0.64	+0.25	+
Intermediate	9	+0.55	+0.33	+0.76	5	+0.86	+0.58	+
Long	1	+3.85	+2.50	+5.20	1	+2.10	+1.10	+
Instr. implementation								
Teacher	NA	NA	NA	NA	1	+0.94	−0.03	+
Researcher	11	+.86	+0.64	+1.07	8	+0.84	+0.57	+
Both	2	+.36	−0.16	+0.88	2	+0.93	+0.37	+
Student directed								
Low	9	+0.54	+0.29	+0.79	7	+0.76	+0.43	+
High	4	+1.21	+0.87	+1.56	4	+0.95	+0.63	+

Note: NA = not available; n = number of effect sizes; d+ = effect size corrected for sample size; CI = confidence interval.

+2.29), they were less effective than intermediate and long-term interventions of instruction, no data were available on teacher-implemented instruction for maintenance, whereas the results for researcher-implemented instruction ($d = +.86$) indicated a higher effect size when compared with that for instruction implemented by both ($d = +.36$). For skill generalization, teacher-implemented ($d = +.94$) or both teacher- and researcher-implemented instruction ($d = .93$) yielded larger effect sizes than researcher-delivered ($d = +.84$) teaching. For the category student direction, student self-regulated instruction was seen to be more effective than teacher-directed instruction in promoting both maintenance and generalization.

(15)   **RESULTS: SINGLE-SUBJECT STUDIES**

Table 6 summarizes and Table 7 presents the categorical comparisons of single-subject studies. Overall, the median PND score for interventions was 89%, with a range of 11% to 100%. Because PND scores are not always normally distributed, we reported median scores, which are less likely to be affected by outliers than mean scores (Scruggs et al., 1986). An analysis of mediator variables indicated significant differences for intervention approach and treatment length only ($p < .05$).

Representational techniques ($PND = +100$; n = 3) were found to be more effective than strategy training ($PND = +87$; n = 12). Intermediate ($PND = +97$; n = 10) and long-term treatments ($PND = +100$; n = 1) were seen to be more effective than short-term ($PND = +49$; n = 4) treatment. All other categorical comparisons were not statistically significant. Ten of 15 cases (67%) provided follow-up data that allowed for the calculation of PND scores, and 7 of the 15 cases (47%) included generalization data. The overall median PND scores for both skill maintenance and generalization were 100%. Given the small sample size, we did not do further significance tests for differences among instructional features in terms of maintenance and generalization.

Table 6   Summary Characteristics of Single-Subject Design Studies

Author	Date	Grade	IQ	Label	TrtA	TrtL	Trtl	W
Published studies								
Case, Harris, & Graham	1992	Elem	<85	LD	Strat	Short	Res	On
Cassel & Reid	1996	Elem	>/=85	Mixed	Strat	Inter	Res	On
Hutchinson	1993	Sec	>/=85	LD	Strat	Long	Res	Mi
Jitendra & Hoff	1996	Elem	>85	LD	Repres	Inter	Res	On
Marsch & Cooke	1996	Elem	>85	LD	Repres	Inter	Res	On
Montague	1992	Sec	>85	LD	Strat	Short	Res	Mi
		Sec	>85	LD	Strat	Short	Res	Mi
		Sec	>85	LD	Strat	Inter	Res	MI
		Sec	>85	LD	Strat	inter	Res	Mi
Montague & Bos	1986	Sec	>85	LD	Strat	Short	Res	Mu
Unpublished studies								
Huntington	1994	Sec	>85	LD	Repres	Inter	Both	Mu
Nuzum	1983	Elem	NA	LD	Strat	Inter	Res	Mi
Smith	1981	Elem	NA	LD	Strat	Inter	Res	On
Tippins	1987	Sec	>85	LD	Strat	inter	Teacher	Mi
Watanabe	1991	Sec	>85	Mixed	Strat	Inter	Teacher	On

Author	Maint (FNa)	Gen.	n	PND (%)
Published studies				
Case, Harris, & Graham	2	Near	4	39
Cassel & Reid	2	NA	4	95
Hutchinson	NA	NA	12	100
Jitendra & Hoff	1	NA	3	100
Marsch & Cooke	NA	NA	3	100
Montague	NA	NA	3	11
	NA	NA	3	58
	1, 2	Near	3	88
	1, 2	Near	3	89
Montague & Bos	1, 2	Far	6	87
Unpublished Studies				
Huntington	2	Near, Far	3	100
Nuzum	NA	NA	4	100
Smith	1	NA	3	100
Tippins	2	Near	5	86
Watanabe	1	Far	10	73

Note: TrtA = treatment approach; TrtL = treatment length; Inter = intermediate; Trtl = treatment implemented; TrtF = treatment fidelity;
    WPT = word problem task; StD = student directed; n = sample size; PND = percentage of nonoverlapping data; NA = not available.
a1 = [less or equal] 4 weeks; 2 = > 4 weeks but [less or equal] 10 weeks; 3 = > 10 weeks.

Table 7   Summary of Categorical Comparisons for Single-Subject Studies

Variable and class	n	PND+ (%)	Range
Sample characteristics			
Grade/age			
Elementary	6	+100	+39 to +100
Secondary	9	+87	+11 to +100
IQ			
< 85	1	+39	NA
>/= 85	11	+88	+11 to +100
Label			
LD	13	+89	+11 to +100
Mixed	2	+84	+73 to +95
Instructional features			
Intervention approach (FN*)			
Representation	3	+100	+100 to +100
Strategy	12	+87	+11 to +100
Length of treatment (FN*)			
Short	4	+49	+11 to +100
Intermediate	10	+97	+73 to +100
Long	1	+100	NA
Instr. implementation			
Teacher	2	+80	+73 to +86
Researcher	12	+92	+11 to +100
Both	1	+100	NA
Word problem task			
One-step	6	+97	+39 to +100
Multistep	2	+94	+87 to +100
Mixed	7	+88	+11 to +100
Student directed			
Low	5	+87	+11 to +100
High	10	+92	+39 to +100
Methodological features			
Publication bias			
Published	10	+88	+11 to +100
Unpublished	5	+100	+73 to +100

Note: NA = not available; n = number of PND scores; PND+ = median percentage of nonoverlapping data.
*$p<.05$.

(16)   **DISCUSSION AND IMPLICATIONS**

Results of the meta-analysis indicated that word-problem-solving instruction improved the performance of students with learning problems and promoted the maintenance and generalization of the skill. The overall mean effect size after correction for sample size in the group design studies was +.89, while the treatment effect for single-subject studies was 89%. However, the present synthesis is limited in several ways. The effect size measure used in this review was the standardized mean change from preintervention to postintervention test scores. This effect size is a scale-free index of the amount of change due to history, growth, retesting, and treatment (Becker, 1988). As a result, the effect size scores in this study may have been larger than Glass's (1977) traditional effect size, which is the standardized mean difference between the experimental and control group divided by the control group's standard deviation. Moreover, the use of the standardized mean change as an effect size measure may have been one of several factors contributing to the very heterogeneity of effect sizes obtained from the present sample. However, these limitations of the standardized mean change measure do not negate its potential for exploring the relationship between mediating variables and treatment effectiveness. Several limitations of the PND measure used in this review to synthesize single-subject research also are present (Allison & Gorman, 1993). For example, the PND measure can result in a ceiling effect, because the largest possible treatment effect defined by PND is +1.00 (i.e., 100%). Also, a PND measure counts only the percentage of data points in the intervention condition that either exceeds or overlaps with the highest data point in the baseline. Therefore, the measure may not be sensitive to the magnitude of treatment effectiveness and may account for the insignificant findings from the single-subject studies.

Another limitation of the present analysis is that approximately 30% (range: 10%–43%) of the effect sizes had to be removed to establish homogeneity within each class of all categories, resulting in a substantial attrition of data. Due to the heterogeneity within each categorized class, it was necessary to conduct model testing or categorical analyses both before and after outliers were excluded. When the homogeneity within a model's categories is lacking, we cannot interpret the results accurately (Hedges & Olkin, 1985; Johnson, 1989). Therefore, when summarizing the results, we presented the findings both before and after data were trimmed, and for most categories the analyses seemed to yield consistent results (see Tables 2 and 3). At the same time, we exercised caution in interpreting the effects of instruction, because the overall sample size and the number of effect sizes in each class were small. The small number of effect sizes was particularly difficult to interpret when effect sizes were analyzed for the mediator variables and for skill maintenance and generalization components. Given these limitations, the following section presents a discussion of each research question raised in this study. In general, we discuss the findings for group design studies and note only the relevant findings from the single-subject studies.

(17) 1. *What is the general effectiveness of word-problem-solving interventions (e.g., representation, strategy training) for teaching students?*

All intervention approaches, with the exception of the "other" approach, yielded moderate to large mean effect sizes (range 5.74 to 1.80). The largest effect size was obtained from the samples coded as CAI intervention. The effect size of 1.8 for CAI is greater than effect sizes (*ES* = .30 to .53) reported in previous meta-analyses on CAI in general (J. Kulik & C. Kulik, 1987; C. Kulik & J. Kulik, 1991; Niemiec & Walberg, 1987; Schmidt, Weinstein, Niemic, & Walberg, 1985–1986). These differences in effect sizes may be a function of the differences in the manner in which effect sizes were calculated (between-subject vs. within-subject comprisons), content domains (basic skills vs. word-problem solving), type of CAI (e.g., drill and practice vs. tutorial), and population (general education or special education students vs. students with mild disabilities and at-risk students). In the present study, CAI mostly entailed strategy or representation techniques presented via tutorial or videodisc programs. These findings are consistent with those in the literature suggesting that computer-assisted instruction is especially effective when empirically validated strategies and curriculum design principles are incorporated (Carnine, 1994; Jitendra & Xin, 1997; Shiah, Mastropieri, & Scruggs, 1995).

It must be noted that the CAI category included the largest effect size obtained from the Moore and Carnine (1989) study and the largest outlier effect size from the Bottge and Hasselbring (1993) study. One explanation for the large effect sizes may be that these studies combined principles of effective curriculum design with interactive videodisc programs. For example, in the Moore and Carnine study, students were taught ratio and proportion word problems either via an interactive video disc program that used principles of active teaching with curriculum design (ATCD), or by teachers whose instruction was based on active teaching with basals (ATB). Although both groups made significant gains from the pre- to posttest, students in the ATCD group performed significantly higher ($d = 16.77$) than students in the ATB group ($d = 12.95$) on the posttest. In the study by Bottge and Hasselbring, students were taught to solve one-step and multistep addition and subtraction fraction word problems using either contextualized word problems presented on videodiscs (CP) or problems typically found in many basal mathematics textbooks (WP) presented by the instructor. Results indicated that the CP group scored significantly higher ($d = 15.5$) on the contextualized problem posttest than the WP group ($d = +.97$). However, differences between groups on the typical word problem posttest following the intervention were not significant.

Representation technique was seen to be the next most effective approach in facilitating word-problem-solving performance. This finding was supported by the review of single-subject studies that also found it to be the most effective intervention when compared with strategy training. However, the effect sizes for the representation approach were found to be heterogeneous, which, in turn, resulted in substantial differences in effect sizes before and after outliers were excluded (see Tables 2 and 3). The representation technique in one study (e.g., Walker & Poteet, 1989) yielded a negative effect size ($d = 2.04$). One plausible explanation is that the strategy in this study was as simple as having students draw a diagram to represent the problem and failed to make explicit, or teach them to identify, important relationships among key components of the word problem. Clearly, it is important that students develop conceptual understanding in making representational links to be successful problem solvers (Lesh et al., 1987; Prawat, 1989; Resnick & Omanson, 1987; Swing et al., 1988).

In addition, strategy training was found to be moderately effective in facilitating acquisition of problem-solving skills. The single-subject data also indicated strategy training to be an effective intervention. Most strategy training procedures across synthesized studies were similar in that they incorporated explicit instruction and/or metacognitive strategies (e.g., self-instruction, self-questioning, or self-regulation). The present findings seem to support the use of direct instruction, cognitive, and goal-directed strategies to promote student learning (Mercer, Jordan, & Miller, 1994; Pressley, Harris, & Marks, 1992). In this meta-analysis, we did not separate direct instruction from cognitive strategies, as they share many instructional features (Swanson et al., 1996). At the same time, given the limited number of studies, we did not believe that separating them at present would be meaningful. Perhaps with increasing research in problem solving, future investigations should isolate the individual effects of direct instruction and cognitive strategies on student learning.

In contrast, studies classified as "other" (e.g., key word, attention only) were the least effective in improving word-problem-solving performance. In fact, one study (Walker & Poteet, 1989) resulted in a negative effect size ($d = 2.42$) for the key word method typically found in basal mathematics programs. These results support the call for a comprehensive analysis of word-problem-solving instruction in basal mathematics curricula (Carnine, Jitendra, & Silbert, 1997; Carnine et al., 1994; Jitendra, Carnine, & Silbert, 1996; Kameenui & Griffin, 1989; Stein, Silbert, & Carnine, 1997).

(18)   2. *Is intervention effectiveness related to important student characteristics (i.e., grade/age, IQ level, or classification label)?*

It seemed that the variable grade/age did not mediate the effect size of the intervention, whereas the variables IQ and label had a mediating influence on the effect size. Students who had IQ scores below 85 scored higher than students with IQ scores above 85, a finding that is contraintuitive. One reason for the present findings is the limited number of effect sizes: Of the 35 effect sizes, only 20 could be computed for this category because many studies in the sample did not report IQ scores. Additionally, a limited number of observations (i.e., three) were used to calculate the effect size for IQ lower than 85, and the three effect sizes were obtained from one study (Shiah et al., 1995). This study used simple one-step problems, which may explain the benefits associated with the treatment outcomes.

For the variable label, students with LD seemed to benefit less from the intervention than students with mixed disabilities or those at risk. This finding may be explained in terms of instructional arrangement. With the exception of the one study (Hutchinson, 1993) that provided instruction individually and yielded a large effect size ($d = 14.00$), all other studies provided word-problem-solving instruction in small groups for students with LD. Given the heterogeneous nature of LD, it may be that teachers who use group instruction should consider carefully the manner in which these students' individual needs are met (Goldman, 1989; Mercer et al., 1994; Montague, 1993, 1997). However, the treatment effects from the single-subject studies for the various study features did not indicate a mediating influence on effect size.

(19) 3. *Are treatment outcomes related to instructional features, such as (a) setting, (b) length of treatment, (c) instructional arrangement, (d) implementation of instruction, (e) word-problem task, and (f) student-directed intervention?*

Our study seems to indicate that the mediator variables of length of treatment, instructional grouping, and word-problem task did mediate the effect size. The results for treatment length suggest that long-term interventions are more effective than short-term interventions, a finding consistent with the results from the single-subject studies. However, the most short-term interventions (no more than seven sessions) were seen to be more effective than the intermediate-term interventions (more than seven sessions, but no more than 1 month). This finding was different for the single-subject studies, in which intermediate treatment length was seen to be more effective than short-term treatment. It is possible that in the group design studies, some effective interventions, such as the CAI (Shiah, Mastropieri, Scruggs, & Fulk, 1995), resulted in immediate gains after a relatively short period of training, due to the unique, visualized presentation of word-problem-solving instruction. None of the single-subject studies included CAI.

In addition, from the results of this study it would seem that individually provided instruction is more effective than group instruction—a finding that is generally supported in the literature (Mercer et al., 1994; Montague, 1997). However, it must be noted that only five observations were used to calculate the effect size for individual instruction, and they were obtained from two studies (Hutchinson, 1993; Noll, 1983). Thus, interpretation of the present findings may be limited by the small number of effect sizes. Finally, interventions involving simple one-step problems yielded larger effect sizes than multistep word problems or mixed problem types. This finding is consistent with previous research indicating that one-step problems are easier than multistep problems (Stein et al., 1997).

For the variable instructional setting, we cannot at present make the explicit statement that instruction provided in classroom settings is more effective than that provided in pull-out settings, given the inconsistent results before and after outliers were removed. In terms of implementation of treatment, joint researcher- and teacher-implemented interventions were seen to be more effective than either researcher-only or teacher-only interventions. The results of the analysis, after four outliers from three studies (Lee, 1992; Marzola, 1987; Walker & Poteet, 1989) were excluded, yielded more homogeneous within-category effect sizes but altered the findings for teacher- and researcher-implemented instruction in isolation. It seems that interventions implemented by teachers were more effective than the researcher-implemented instruction after outliers were removed, whereas the results were the reverse before outliers were removed. The present finding is not consistent with research results in this area suggesting that when implemented by teachers, intervention effectiveness is questionable on the basis of poor treatment integrity (Allinder, 1996; Fuchs, 1988). One explanation for the inconsistent finding in this study is that the large effect size ($d = +1.93$) was obtained from five observations in two studies (Gleason et al., 1990; Noll, 1983). Of the five observations, four were from the study by Noll, in which all instruction was administered individually. Furthermore, neither study reported any treatment integrity data, which makes it difficult to accurately assess the effectiveness of treatments implemented by teachers.

Instruction involving student self-regulation of strategy did not have a mediating influence on the effect size for word-problem-solving interventions. This finding is not consistent with previous relevant literature suggesting that self-instruction training directly assists students with the process of internalizing the solution sequence and enhances students' word-problem-solving skills (Goldman, 1989; Mercer et al., 1994). One explanation for this finding may be that three of the observations from two studies (Bennett, 1981; Montague, Applegate, & Marquard, 1993) coded as high in student-directed strategy instruction involved a metacognitive strategy. On the one hand, the emphasis on a metacognitive strategy that regulated students' performance but lacked problem-solving-strategy specificity was not sufficient to promote learning. On the other hand, the length of the treatment for cognitive plus metacognitive strategy in the first cycle of strategy training in the Montague et al. study was too short (i.e., seven sessions) for students to internalize the strategy and apply it to effectively solve problems. Again, results of treatment effects from the single-subject studies for the various instructional features, with the exception of treatment length, did not indicate a mediating influence on the PND score.

(20) 4. *Is there a relationship between methodological features (i.e., publication bias, group assignment) and effect size?*

On the basis of results after outliers were removed, it seems that the variables publication bias and group assignment did moderate the effect size. Unpublished studies in this meta-analysis yielded larger overall effect sizes than published studies. This finding seems to be at odds with the popular assumption that published studies generally reflect more positive results. It may be that various factors (e.g., treatment integrity, experimental control) related to the overall quality of a study are critical criteria for publishing a study. For example, whereas 67% of the published studies showed high treatment integrity, only 20% of the unpublished studies reported assessment for treatment integrity. In this meta-analysis, we also examined group assignment, and these results revealed significantly higher effect size scores for matched and randomly assigned groups than for intact groups, thus strengthening the conclusions about the effects of word-problem-solving instruction on student learning. In addition, the findings of single-subject design studies do not indicate a mediating influence of publication bias on the PND score.

(21) 5. *What is the effectiveness of word-problem-solving instruction in fostering skill maintenance and generalization? Are skill maintenance and generalization functions of instructional features (e.g., treatment length)?*

In general, word-problem-solving instruction seemed to positively affect skill maintenance ($d = +.78$) and generalization ($d = +.84$). These findings suggest that students may benefit from specific word-problem-solving instruction for skill maintenance and generalization (Goldman, 1989; Mercer et al., 1994; Pressley et al., 1992) and are supported by the results of maintenance ($PND = 100\%$) and generalization ($PND = 100\%$) effects in single-subject studies.

For the group design studies, with the exception of the "other" category, CAI and strategy training were seen to be effective in promoting skill maintenance and generalization. Although CAI was found to be most effective in promoting maintenance of the skill, it was not as effective when compared to strategy training in promoting generalization (e.g., from online to paper-and-pencil tasks). As Shiah, Mastropieri, Scruggs, and Fulk (1995) noted, it may be that the connection between the online CAI and paper-and-pencil tasks was not well established by students with special needs. Further research in computer-assisted instruction needs to explore and clarify the conditions under which the transfer of acquired skills from online to paper-and-pencil tasks can be achieved. For single-subject studies, although both representation and strategy training approaches were seen to promote skill maintenance and generalization, the database is too limited for the representation category (only two treatment effects) to provide meaningful comparisons.

In the group design studies, generalization was promoted, whether instruction was implemented by teacher, researcher, or both. For single-subject studies, although researcher-implemented instruction (PND = 92%) was seen to be more effective than teacher-implemented instruction (PND = 80%) in improving performance during or after the training, the former was less effective in fostering skill generalization (PND = 69%). It could be that the initial individualized attention provided by the researcher during the study resulted in improved performance on the immediate posttest, but when the researcher's presence in the setting was reduced following the completion of instruction, students' generalization performance was adversely affected. In addition, student performance may have been influenced by various competing factors involved in the generalization setting (i.e., distractions) or the task (e.g., problem complexity, vocabulary, etc.). Results of both group and single-subject studies indicate that maintenance and generalization were influenced by treatment length, in that relatively longer term interventions led to greater benefits than shorter term treatments, indicating the need for students to internalize the strategy steps needed for problem solution. Finally, a high level of student-directed intervention was seen to result in greater levels of maintenance and generalization—a finding supported in the literature (Mercer et al., 1994, Montague, 1997); this finding was supported by generalization effects found in single-subject studies.

(22)   **IMPLICATIONS FOR RESEARCH**

In summary, the effects of varied instructional approaches on student learning are encouraging. Several implications of our analysis for future research in the area of word-problem solving are presented. Our analysis showed that many studies failed to report critical information needed to accurately interpret the study findings. It is important that future research studies provide detailed information of study characteristics that would allow for accurate inferences. This would include identifying data, such as IQ and achievement scores. In addition, clearly defining the population (e.g., LD, mildly disabled, at risk) and providing detailed descriptions of the intervention and comparison conditions are seen as critical to interpreting study findings. Without a description of the comparison group (e.g., Hutchinson, 1993), it is difficult to determine the equivalency of the experimental and comparison groups. It could be that the findings were affected by factors other than the intervention effectiveness. At the same time, details of instructional (e.g., setting, treatment length, task) and methodological features (group assignment, treatment integrity) can be informative. We cannot be certain that many of the approaches implemented by researchers in settings outside of the classroom would be effective in the natural contexts with the existing word-problem-solving database. Furthermore, future studies in this area should address how acceptable interventions are to teachers and students.

This review was further limited by the small number of studies that addressed maintenance and generalization skills. Future research should continue to assess skill maintenance on an ongoing basis (a few weeks to more than a month). The practice of teaching and assessing for generalization of word-problem solving is important. Presenting opportunities to apply the learned skills in new situations and contexts is especially important for students with learning problems. In addition, although different approaches were found to be useful in mathematics word-problem solving, it is important to note that limitations imposed by students' insufficient background or prerequisite skill knowledge can undermine the effectiveness of these approaches. Therefore, future research should assess students' understanding of concepts and skills needed to solve word problems, so as to inform instruction in this area. Finally, further examination of the area of word-problem solving may be warranted when a larger database of primary studies is available. At the same time, future research should explore measures that would allow for a direct comparison of treatment effects from both group and single-subject design studies in order to make a generalized statement about a specific body of research and to effectively translate the research findings into practice.

Locating Information About Research Reports

with
Suzanne Li
City University of New York/Queens College

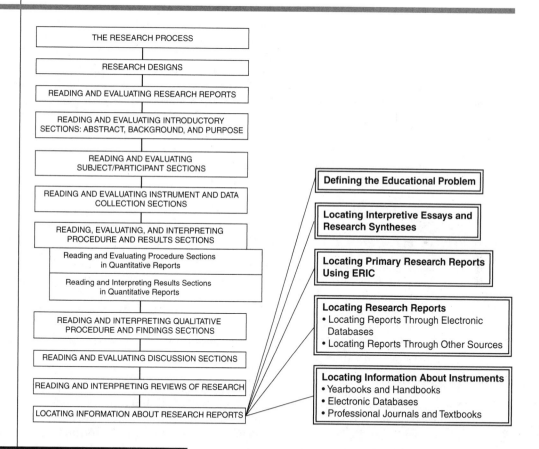

THE RESEARCH PROCESS	
RESEARCH DESIGNS	
READING AND EVALUATING RESEARCH REPORTS	
READING AND EVALUATING INTRODUCTORY SECTIONS: ABSTRACT, BACKGROUND, AND PURPOSE	
READING AND EVALUATING SUBJECT/PARTICIPANT SECTIONS	**Defining the Educational Problem**
READING AND EVALUATING INSTRUMENT AND DATA COLLECTION SECTIONS	**Locating Interpretive Essays and Research Syntheses**
READING, EVALUATING, AND INTERPRETING PROCEDURE AND RESULTS SECTIONS	**Locating Primary Research Reports Using ERIC**
Reading and Evaluating Procedure Sections in Quantitative Reports	
Reading and Interpreting Results Sections in Quantitative Reports	**Locating Research Reports** • Locating Reports Through Electronic Databases • Locating Reports Through Other Sources
READING AND INTERPRETING QUALITATIVE PROCEDURE AND FINDINGS SECTIONS	
READING AND EVALUATING DISCUSSION SECTIONS	
READING AND INTERPRETING REVIEWS OF RESEARCH	**Locating Information About Instruments** • Yearbooks and Handbooks • Electronic Databases • Professional Journals and Textbooks
LOCATING INFORMATION ABOUT RESEARCH REPORTS	

FOCUS QUESTIONS

1. How is an educational problem defined before primary research reports are located?
2. How are research syntheses and essays about research located?
3. How are primary research reports located?
4. Where can information about instruments be located?

To reiterate from chapter 1, educators are decision makers. Whether they are college or university instructors, school practitioners, administrators, or researchers, they are continually making decisions about curriculum, teaching, classroom management, and learning. These decisions are based on their experiences, others' experiences, and their understanding of accumulated knowledge about education. Much of this accumulated knowledge is in the form of research reports and interpretations of research. The sign of a productive profession, such as education, is that its members systematically examine the knowledge base upon which it functions. This text attempts to help educators examine and interpret research from education, psychology, and related areas in the social sciences.

This chapter provides research consumers with some guidance for locating primary research reports, research syntheses, and meta-analyses, as well as evaluations of instruments used in research. Many of the resources for locating these reports, and the reports themselves, can be found on the Internet. Some of the same resources (as well as other resources) can be found in college and university libraries. These resources can also be found in many public libraries. Research consumers need to know *(a)* what resources exist for locating reports and reviews of instruments and *(b)* how to locate research syntheses, primary research reports, and reviews of instruments.

Initially, a consumer needs to identify an educational question or problem. Then, the consumer must decide what kind of information is required to answer the question. To illustrate, a representative educational question is used here. In the following sections, the question's subject area (or topic) is used with the different kinds of resources available to research consumers.

DEFINING THE EDUCATIONAL PROBLEM

The subject used for illustration in this chapter is authentic assessment. The educational questions are "How is authentic assessment used in elementary and middle schools, grades 1–8, for evaluating students' reading and writing?" and "How does authentic assessment provide for more effective student evaluations in reading and writing?" The first step in answering these questions is to be clear about the definitions of key terms. Precise definitions allow research consumers to pose answerable questions and locate relevant studies. Because the target population is defined—first through eighth graders—a key term remains to be defined, that is, *authentic assessment.*

Possible sources of definitions, in addition to definitions that may appear within primary research articles, are textbooks on the subject, dictionaries of educational terms, and educational encyclopedias. Textbooks can be found through libraries' online catalogs under the appropriate subject heading (i.e., *assessment* or *authentic assessment*). Although textbooks may not be a source of research, their authors often include references to (and syntheses of) primary studies. For example, a search of one university library's online catalog did not uncover the subject heading *authentic assessment,* but a keyword search did show several books with the term in their titles. Among them were the following:

Tombari, M. L. (1999). *Authentic assessment in the classroom: Applications and practice.* Upper Saddle River, NJ: Merrill/Prentice Hall.

Collins, M. D., & Moss, B. G. (Eds.). (1996). *Literacy assessment for today's schools: Monograph of the College Reading Association.* Harrisonburg, VA: College Reading Association.

Valencia, S. W., Hiebert, E. H., & Afflerbach, P. P. (Eds.). (1994). *Authentic reading assessment: Practices and possibilities.* Newark, DE: International Reading Association.

In Valencia, Hiebert, and Afflerbach (1994), the aim of authentic assessment of reading and writing is "to assess many different kinds of literacy abilities in contexts that closely resemble the actual situations in which those abilities are used" (p. 9). The on-line catalog showed, as subject headings for these books, educational tests and measurements, case studies, and portfolios in education. These subject headings were noted as possible sources of other materials related to the educational question.

Educational and psychological dictionaries, usually found in libraries' reference sections, contain definitions of technical and professional terms used in these fields. Dictionaries that are important to educators are the following:

The Literacy Dictionary: The Vocabulary of Reading and Writing

A Comprehensive Dictionary of Psychological and Psychoanalytic Terms: A Guide to Usage

Dictionary of Education, Third Edition

Dictionary of Multicultural Education

Dictionary of Philosophy and Psychology

Encyclopedic Dictionary of Psychology

International Dictionary of Education

Longman Dictionary of Psychology and Psychiatry

The Concise Dictionary of Education

In *The Literacy Dictionary,* listed previously, the following definition appears:

authentic assessment A type of assessment that seeks to address widespread concerns about standardized, norm-referenced testing by representing "literacy behavior of the community and workplace" and reflecting "the actual learning and instructional activities of the classroom and out-of-school worlds" (Hiebert et al., 1994), as with the use of portfolios; naturalistic assessment. See also alternative assessment; assessment. Cp. classroom-based assessment. (Harris & Hodges, 1995, p. 15)

Obtaining these definitions and insights from information about authentic assessment, which might be found under headings such as *alternative assessment* and *classroom-based assessment,* is preparatory to seeking summaries and interpretations of the research related to authentic assessment.

LOCATING INTERPRETIVE ESSAYS AND RESEARCH SYNTHESES

Several sources provide interpretive reviews and essays about educational, psychological, and other related social science topics. These sources include the following:

American Educators' Encyclopedia

Encyclopedia of Bilingualism and Bilingual Education

Encyclopedia of Special Education

Handbook of Reading Research, Volumes I, II, III

Handbook of Research on Teaching Literacy Through the Communicative and Visual Arts

Handbook of Research on Teaching the English Language Arts

Handbook of Research on Teaching, Fourth Edition

Review of Research in Education

The Encyclopedia of Education, Second Edition, eBook version

The Encyclopedia of Educational Research, Sixth Edition

The International Encyclopedia of Education

The International Encyclopedia of Education: Research and Studies

The International Encyclopedia of Teaching and Teacher Education

A sampling of the indexes of these handbooks and encyclopedias yields references to the following, among other subject headings (the numbers after the entries refer to the volume and pages in the particular encyclopedia):

In *The International Encyclopedia of Education, Second Edition,* there was no entry for *authentic assessment,* but there was the following:

Assessment
  criterion-referenced
        see *criterion-referenced tests*
  early childhood education 1: 355
        and learning 1: 370–374
  performance
        and educational assessment 1: 369
  grading 10: 5855
  special needs students
        cultural differences 2: 717
  See also
        Evaluation
        Measurement
        Testing
Portfolio assessment
        and cognitive strategy instruction 2: 866
        effects on instruction 7: 3724
Portfolios (background materials) 8: 4617–4623
        and student evaluation 8: 4621

In the essay on page 4622, it was indicated that "portfolios are flexible and well-suited for 'authentic' or 'performance' assessment" (*International Encyclopedia of Education,* Vol. 12).

The *Encyclopedia of Educational Research, Sixth Edition* contained the following index entries:

Authentic assessment, in state assessment programs 1262

Portfolio assessment

> in state assessment programs 1262
>
> of writing 450

Upon referring to the pages noted in the indexes, several interpretive essays are found. In one essay about *authentic assessment,* it was noted that

> The innovation in state assessment that is currently garnering the most attention goes under several different rubrics, including performance assessment and authentic assessment. These terms subsume a variety of different efforts to substantially expand the tasks students perform beyond multiple-choice and similar (such as short-answer and cloze) formats. (Alkin, 1992, p. 1264)

Each of the interpretive essays contains a bibliography of all references discussed within the essay. These bibliographies are excellent sources of additional interpretive essays and research syntheses.

The journal *Review of Educational Research (RER)* is published quarterly by the American Educational Research Association. It is an excellent source of research syntheses and meta-analyses. Research consumers can locate research syntheses in *RER* through the sources discussed in the next section.

LOCATING PRIMARY RESEARCH REPORTS USING ERIC

Educational, psychological, and other social science journals containing primary research reports are usually located in the periodicals sections of libraries. To locate specific research reports—and, for the discussion here, reports about authentic assessment—research consumers need to use sources that index all journal articles (research and nonresearch) and other relevant documents. The *Current Index to Journals in Education (CIJE)* was a monthly print publication with semiannual compilations that indexes and abstracts articles from almost 900 educational journals. A consumer may wish to locate primary research reports and other professional materials that are not published in journals, such as federal and state department of education reports, papers presented at conferences, yearbooks, and even some commercially published books. If so, *Resources in Education (RIE)* offered the same services as *CIJE.* Most of these documents are unpublished and noncopyrighted materials that would otherwise be hard to find. *CIJE* and *RIE* together make up the **ERIC (Education Resources Information Center)** database, which was available in print through 2001, and continues on the Internet and in CD-ROM format. Material is referenced in the ERIC system with an accession, or catalog, number that is called the "ERIC number" in the online formats. Each accession number has a prefix. The prefix "EJ" indicates the material is published in a journal. The prefix "ED" indicates the material is a document, meaning, for example, that it is either an unpublished paper (such as a conference presentation) or material published by a private or public agency (such as a government report).

ERIC is a national network supported by the Institute of Education Sciences (IES) of the U.S. Department of Education. The purpose of ERIC is to provide access to current research results and related information in the field of education. This information appears monthly in ERIC-sponsored Internet Web sites. Most CD-ROM versions of ERIC are updated quarterly. The print formats, *CIJE* and *RIE,* ceased publication in December 2001.

All formats of the ERIC database, whether print, CD-ROM, or Internet, offer the same information for the time they cover; only the presentation and accessibility vary. The ERIC-sponsored Web site offers direct, free public access to the database, although searching is not as efficient as with the CD-ROM formats or the customized commercial Internet versions. The database is accessible, however, even by a research consumer who only has a home computer and Internet access. It can be accessed at http://www.eric.ed.gov/ERICWebPortal/Home.portal?_nfpb=true&_pageLabel=ERIC_ Search. (Note that all Internet Web sites are current as of fall 2004.)

LOCATING RESEARCH REPORTS

To use any format of ERIC, consumers refer first to a guide for determining appropriate subject headings. To maintain uniformity of subject listings, the ERIC system publishes a *Thesaurus of ERIC Descriptors,* which is updated periodically. Descriptors are keywords used in indexing documents. *The Thesaurus* indicates the subject terms that are used to index a topic. For example, checking *The Thesaurus, Fourteenth Edition,* published in 2001, under the listing for *authentic assessment,* the following is noted:

> *Authentic Assessment*
>
> > Use *Performance based assessment*

The entry for *performance based assessment* is shown in Figure 11.1.

The **Scope Note** (SN) for *performance based assessment* shows a definition of the term. The **Related Terms** (RT) list does not include some terms that have appeared in dictionaries and encyclopedias, because those terms entered educational vocabulary *after* this printing of the *Thesaurus.* To keep the database current, other terms that are not yet represented as descriptors in the *Thesaurus* are used in the ERIC subject indexes. Such terms are called **identifiers.**

When a specific subject listing is not in the ERIC *Thesaurus,* research consumers can use a researcher's name to locate references in ERIC. For example, the name "Linda Darling-Hammond" appears several times in the online library catalog, encyclopedic essays, and Education Abstracts/Full Text. When that name is entered in an online search in the author field of the EBSCO version of ERIC, it comes up with 119 records, dating from 1978 to 2003. The first screen of the most recent search results for Linda Darling-Hammond is shown in Figure 11.2. Adding "authentic assessment" to the Linda Darling-Hammond author search and making it a major identifier with the drop down menu brings up the ERIC document "Authentic Assessment in Action: Studies of Schools and Students at Work. The Series on School Reform" shown in Figure 11.3. Clicking on the document title opens another screen with the full entry in Figure 11.4. The subjects covered by the article are in the list of descriptors, including "Student Evaluation" and "Evaluation Methods." "Authentic Assessment" is listed as an identifier, which is a heading that reflects

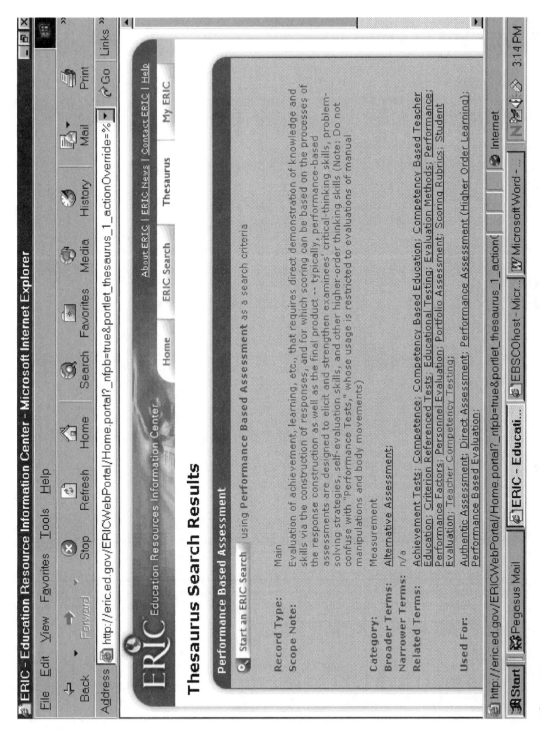

Figure 11.1
Thesaurus Search Results

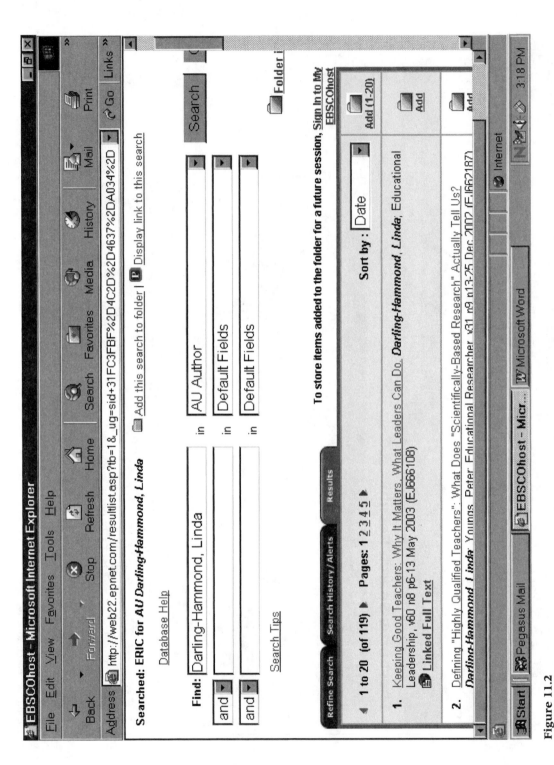

Figure 11.2
Search Results for Linda Darling-Hammond

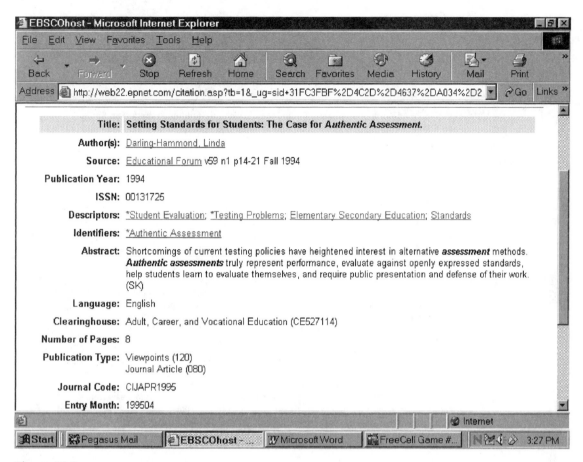

Figure 11.3
ERIC Document, Darling-Hammond's "Authentic Assessment in Action"

terms (currently used by researchers and other authors) that have not been offi-
cially recognized as ERIC descriptors. Clicking on the underlined "Authentic Assessment" will bring up a list of other records with "Authentic Assessment" as an
identifier.

After reading the annotations, the user may select a journal article. If "Linked
Full Text" appears at the bottom of an item in the list of records, as in the 13th record
shown in Figure 11.5, the full text of the selected article can be accessed by clicking
on the phrase. This convenience is because EBSCO, the provider of this version of
ERIC, supplies online access to journals it previously supplied in paper format.
(Other online full text journals may be available from other vendors in the electronic journal list on the library's home page.) Paper format journals can be found
in the periodicals section of the library or on microfilm in the library's microform
section.

ERIC documents can be identified by the same system of descriptors and identifiers; however, document accession numbers are prefixed with "ED" instead of "EJ."

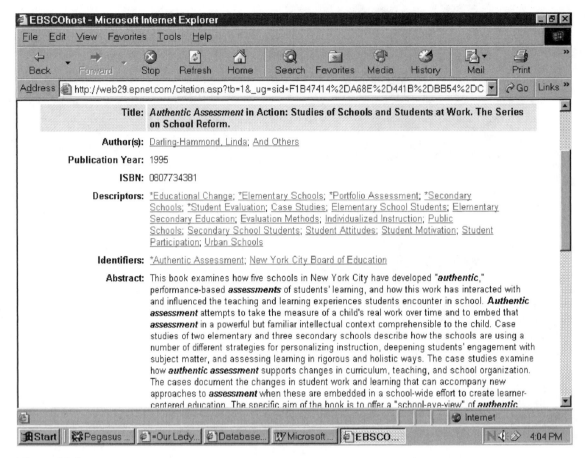

Figure 11.4
Authentic Assessment in Action, Full Entry

After a document has been determined to fit the problem area being searched, the full text can usually be found online by clicking on the underlined phrase in the Availability field: "Full Text from ERIC" if it appears there. (The user's computer must be loaded with the freely available Adobe Acrobat software, version 5 or higher, to read the full text online.) Many libraries also maintain documents on small sheets of microfilm called *microfiche,* which can be read only on special microfiche readers. ERIC microfiche collections (1966–2001) and microfiche readers can be found in college and university libraries and some public libraries. ERIC records also contain information for ordering a document on microfiche or in printed-copy form. In some cases documents, such as commercially published books, are not available from the ERIC document reproduction service. The user may check the library's online catalog for such a book's availability, or request it from a librarian through interlibrary loan.

One of the document entries under authentic assessment is "Authentic Assessment of Self-Concept Through Portfolios: Building a Model With Public Schools," with the accession number ED374085.

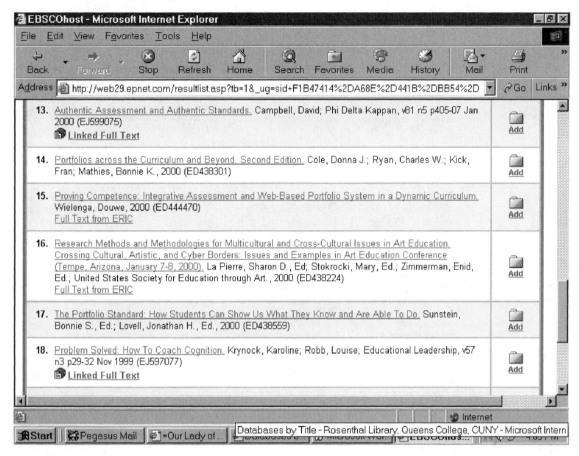

Figure 11.5
Annotations for Authentic Assessment

The noted research project is located in the document resume section. The entry for ED374085 is shown in Figure 11.6. Note the separate listing of descriptors and identifiers.

Because the information in the abstract indicates that this is a study to "investigate the viability of the portfolio model for authentic assessment," the user can tell that this document is relevant to his or her purpose. One can locate the full text of the document by clicking on "Full Text from ERIC" in the Availability field, or in the library's ERIC microfiche collection.

Locating Reports Through Electronic Databases

The ERIC system in electronic format is in two versions: One is found on the Internet; the other is available in libraries on CD-ROMS. Accessing ERIC electronically allows research consumers to search the database more efficiently, because the Internet version and CD-ROMs contain all the terms found in the *Thesaurus of*

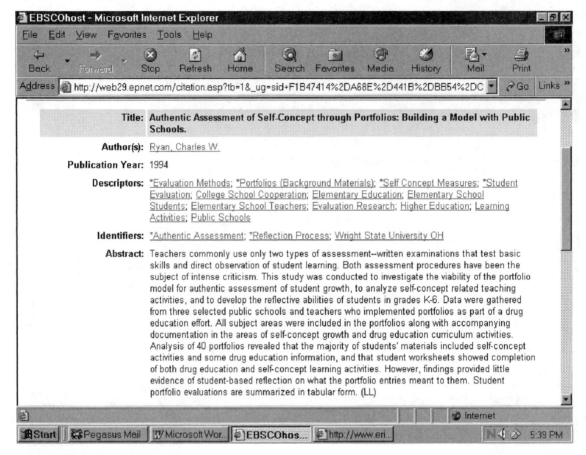

Figure 11.6
Entry for Authentic Assessment

ERIC Descriptors. By combining terms and modifying preliminary searches, the labor of examining compilations of *RIE* and *CIJE* and cross-referencing is eliminated. Whereas the print format can only be searched one subject at a time, for either journal articles or other documents, the CD-ROM and Internet formats can be searched for either articles or documents or both. Also, searches can include other specifications, such as educational level (such as early childhood, elementary, secondary) or publication type (such as journal articles, research reports, curriculum guides).

When a subject is not listed in the ERIC *Thesaurus* and no alternate descriptor is suggested, research consumers can use a CD-ROM or Internet version of ERIC to find references in which the term is used in other parts of the ERIC entry, for example, in the title or abstract of the reference. Figure 11.7 contains an example from a search using the EBSCO Internet version of the ERIC database. Note that *authentic assessment* appears as a phrase in the abstract and *performance based assessment* as a major descriptor (denoted by the asterisk next to the phrase). If the abstract describes the kind of information desired by the research consumer, then one or more of the other de-

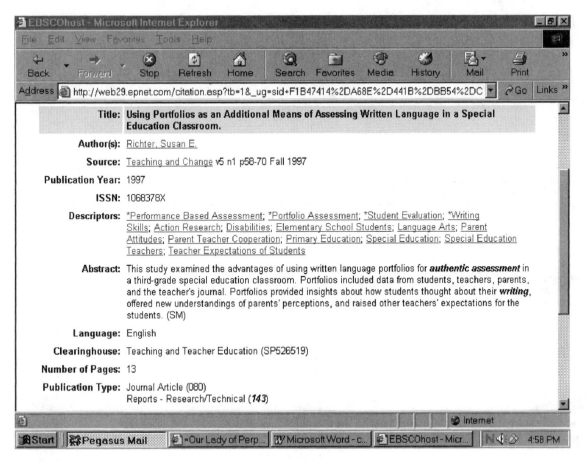

Figure 11.7
Example From a Search Using the EBSCO Internet Version of the ERIC Database

scriptors used in that record, for example, *portfolio assessment,* might be used in extending the search.

Using authentic assessment and the phrase suggested in the current thesaurus, "performance based assessment," a cross-referenced search brings up the information shown in Figure 11.8. Notice that *authentic assessment* appears in the title of the first two entries. Because the following records were identified in the cross-referenced search, the terms will appear elsewhere, most probably in the abstract. To access the abstract, click on the title of the journal article.

The search of the key terms (which include descriptors and identifiers) used in one university's EBSCO version of ERIC revealed that *authentic assessment* and *performance based assessment* had 235 common entries. One of those entries is as follows:

What Works with Authentic Assessment. Burley, Hansel; Price, Margaret; *Educational Horizons,* v81 n4 p193–96 Sum 2003 (EJ669295)

The search can be refined by clicking on the "REFINE SEARCH" key and scrolling down to the Publication Type drop down menu. To limit the search to research,

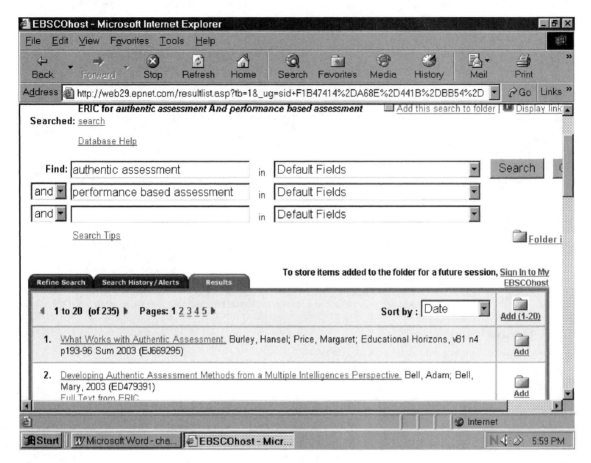

Figure 11.8
Results of a Cross-Referenced Search

scroll down the menu to Reports—Research/Technical, click on the phrase to high-light it, and then scroll back to the top of the screen to click the Search button again. *Authentic assessment* and *performance based assessment in research* will be reduced to 29 records. None of these records refer to authentic assessment and literacy, however. Revising the search to *performance based assessment* and *literacy* and limiting the search to the publication type "reports-research/technical" brings up 18 records, including the following document and journal article:

| Document | *Using Classroom-Based Assessment on a Large Scale: Supporting and Reporting on Student Learning with the Early Literacy Profile.* Falk, Beverly; Ort, Suzanna Wichterle; Moirs, Katie; Columbia Univ., New York, NY. Teachers Coll. National Center for Restructuring Education, Schools and Teaching, 1999 (ED430987). |

| Journal Article | Portfolios Across Educational Contexts: Issues of Evaluation, Teacher Development, and System Validity. Valencia, Sheila W.; Au, Kathryn H.; *Educational Assessment,* v4 n1 p1–35 1997 (EJ559000) |

An important detail to note concerns the different way ERIC identification numbers are listed in print and SilverPlatter CD-ROM and Internet versions. The six-digit identification number is labeled "accession number" in print and on SilverPlatter CD-ROM. For Internet versions, the identification number may be labeled "ERIC No." or "ERIC Identifier." Internet versions also list the ERIC number without any spaces between the letters and numbers.

Remember that ERIC identification numbers (whatever their label) prefixed with "ED" are documents and usually are available on microfiche and becoming increasingly available in full text online. Those prefixed with "EJ" are articles in journals. (Note that more university and college libraries subscribe to electronic databases containing full-text versions of selected journals. Check with your institution's reference librarian about availability.) Information about "Descriptors" and "Identifiers" is laid out similarly in all versions of ERIC.

Locating Reports Through Other Sources

There are other, specialized, abstract compilations and indexes (both in print and electronic formats and not connected with the ERIC system) that research consumers might wish to examine for information related to educational problems or questions. Each of these abstract compilations and indexes uses its own format for subject and author indexes; a full explanation of those systems is contained in each. Several that might be of most interest to educators are *Sociological Abstracts, Psychological Abstracts, State Education Journal Index, Business Education Index, Educational Administration Abstracts, Physical Education Index,* and *Child Development Abstracts and Bibliography.*

If a research consumer requires in-depth educational information published prior to 1995, especially in regard to special education issues, *Exceptional Child Education Resources (ECER)* could complement information found in ERIC. *Education Index* is another source useful for earlier research, when it covered some journals that were not indexed in ERIC. (Its current electronic version now includes abstracts and more full text articles as well, but still not as many as ERIC.)

Dissertation Abstracts International contains abstracts of doctoral dissertations from about 400 participating universities. It is published monthly in two sections. Section A contains dissertations in the humanities and social sciences, which includes education. Section B covers the science areas, which includes psychology. The Internet version includes both sections and is also updated monthly. The dissertations themselves are usually not available, but consumers should check with reference librarians to see whether copies of selected dissertations are available in the universities' microform sections. The index is arranged alphabetically by keyword and alphabetically by title for keywords. The location of abstracts is indicated by page numbers.

LOCATING INFORMATION ABOUT INSTRUMENTS

Information about instruments' format, content, and administration procedures, together with reliability and validity estimates, can be found in yearbooks, handbooks, and professional journals. See other information in chapter 6 about locating information about instruments.

Yearbooks and Handbooks

The major source of information on standardized tests is the *Mental Measurements Yearbooks (MMY)*. These have been published since 1938. The most recent are the *Eleventh Mental Measurements Yearbook* (11th *MMY;* Kramer & Conoley, 1992), the *Supplement to the Eleventh Mental Measurements Yearbook* (11th *MMY*-S; Conoley & Impara, 1994), the *Twelfth Mental Measurements Yearbook* (12th *MMY;* Colony & Impara, 1995), the *Supplement to the Twelfth Mental Measurements Yearbook* (12th *MMY*-S; Conoley, Impara, & Murphy, 1996), the *Thirteenth Mental Measurements Yearbook* (13th *MMY;* Impara & Plake, 1998), the *Supplement to the Thirteenth Mental Measurements Yearbook* (13th *MMY*-S; Plake & Impara, 1999), the *Fourteenth Mental Measurements Yearbook* (14th *MMY;* Plake & Impara, 2001), the *Fifteenth Mental Measurements Yearbook* (15th *MMY;* Plake, Impara & Spies, 2003). They contain reviews of tests and selected bibliographies of related books and journal articles for each instrument.

The purposes of the latest *MMY*s are to provide *(a)* factual information on all known new or reviewed tests in the English-speaking world, *(b)* objective test reviews written specifically for the *MMY*s, and *(c)* comprehensive bibliographies, for specific tests, of related references from published literature. Each volume of the *MMY* contains information on tests that have been published or significantly revised since a previous edition.

The 11th *MMY,* 12th *MMY,* and 13th *MMY* each provide six indexes. The index of titles is an alphabetical listing of test titles. The classified subject index lists tests alphabetically under one or more classification headings, for example, Achievement, Intelligence, Mathematics, Personality, and Reading. This index is of great help to those wishing to locate tests in a particular curriculum area. The publisher's directory and index give the names and addresses of the publishers of all the tests included in the *MMY,* as well as a list of test numbers for each publisher. The index of names includes the names of test developers and test reviewers, as well as authors of related references. The index of acronyms gives full titles for commonly used abbreviations. For example, someone may not know that *DRP* stands for "Degrees of Reading Power." Each entry also gives the population for which the test is intended. The score index gives the subtest scores and their associated labels for each test. These labels are operational definitions of the tests' variables.

The organization of the *MMY*s is encyclopedic: All the test descriptions and reviews are presented alphabetically by test title. To find a particular test, the reader can go right to it without using any index. All test entries are given index numbers that are used in place of page numbers in the indexes.

Entries for new or significantly revised tests in the tests and reviews section (the main body of the volume) include information such as title, author (developer), publisher, cost, a brief description, a description of groups for whom the test is intended, norming information, validity and reliability data, whether the test is a group or individual test, time requirements, test references, and critical reviews by qualified reviewers. Among other things, the reviews generally cite any special requirements or problems involved in test administration, scoring, or interpretation.

The classified subject index is a quick way to determine whether an instrument is reviewed within a particular volume of *MMY.* For example, in the classified subject index of the 11th *MMY* under *achievement* (p. 1079), the following entry (among others) is found:

Comprehensive Tests of Basic Skills, Fourth Edition, grades K.0–K.9, K.6–1.6, 1.0–2.2, 1.6–3.2, 2.6–4.2, 3.6–5.2, 4.6–6.2, 5.6–7.2, 6.6–9.2, 8.6–11.2, 10.6–12.9, see 81.

Remember, the "81" means that the description of the *Comprehensive Tests of Basic Skills* is entry 81 in the main body of the volume; it does not mean that it is on page 81. Page numbers are used only for table of contents purposes.

However, the *Degrees of Reading Power* cannot be found under either *achievement* or *reading* in the classified subject index of the 10th *MMY* or 11th *MMY* because it has not been significantly revised since its original publication. It is found under "reading" in the classified subject index of the 12th *MMY* as

Degrees of Reading Power, Primary: Grades 1–3; Standard: Grades 3–5, 5–8, 8–12 and over, Advanced: Grades 6–9, 9–12 and over, see 101.

A companion source of information about instruments is *Tests in Print (TIP)*, which contains comprehensive bibliographies of instruments that have been reviewed in *MMY*s. The latest edition, *TIP VI* (Murphy, Plake, Impara, & Spies, 2002), is structured in the same way as the classified subject index of *MMY*s. Its value comes not from its reviews of instruments, but from its listings of all tests that were in print at the time of publication, the location of test reviews in *MMY*s 1 through 15, and other writings about the instruments.

There are specialized volumes that contain information about instruments in various curriculum areas. These duplicate *MMY* information and reviews; their value comes from having test information for a particular discipline in a single volume. These monographs are as follows:

English Tests and Reviews

Foreign Language Tests and Reviews

Intelligence Tests and Reviews

Mathematics Tests and Reviews

Personality Tests and Reviews

Reading Tests and Reviews

Science Tests and Reviews

Social Studies Tests and Reviews

Vocational Tests and Reviews

Additional specialized sources of test information reviews are as follows:

A Sourcebook for Mental Health Measures

Advances in Psychological Assessment

Assessment in Gifted Children

Assessment Instruments in Bilingual Education

Bilingual Education Resource Guide

CSE Elementary School Test Evaluations

Directory of Unpublished Experimental Mental Measures

Evaluating Classroom Instruction: A Sourcebook of Instruments

Handbook for Measurement and Evaluation in Early Childhood Education

Handbook of Psychological & Educational Assessment of Children

Instruments That Measure Self-Concept

Language Assessment Instruments for Limited English-Speaking Students

Measures for Psychological Assessment: A Guide to 3,000 Sources and Their Applications

Mirrors for Behavior III

Oral Language Tests for Bilingual Students

Preschool Test Descriptions

Psychological Testing and Assessment

Psychological Testing and Assessment of the Mentally Retarded

Reading Tests for Secondary Grades

Review of Tests and Assessments in Early Education

Scales for the Measurement of Attitudes

Screening and Evaluating the Young Child

Socioemotional Measures for Preschool and Kindergarten Children

Sociological Measurement

Tests and Measurements in Child Development

Tests Used With Exceptional Children

Testing Children: A Reference Guide for Effective Clinical and Psychological Assessments

Valuable companions to the 11th *MMY,* 12th *MMY,* and 13th *MMY* are *Tests: A Comprehensive Reference for Assessment in Psychology, Education, and Business, Third Edition* (Sweetland & Geyser, 1991) and *Test Critiques* (Geyser & Sweetland, 1991). These volumes contain listings and critical reviews of instruments by specialty area.

Electronic Databases

Research consumers can also access electronic databases of test collections, test reviews, and test publishers. Each record provides the title, author, publication date, relevant population, subject terms, ERIC *Thesaurus* terms, availability, and a short abstract about the test's content and form. The test review databases provide index information of volume and test review number for reviews in the *MMY*s and *Tests in Print* (*TIP*) (the *Buros Test Review Locator*), and *Test Critiques* (the *Pro-Ed Test Review Locator*).

The ERIC Clearinghouse on Assessment and Evaluation with its Test Locator hyperlink can be accessed through the Internet at http://ericae.net   .

Some academic libraries also provide Internet and CD-ROM versions of the recent *MMY*s that offer much easier searching and full text of the test reviews. Figure 11.9 shows the result of a search for the Degrees of Reading Power test. By typing "Degrees of Reading Power in tn" in the search box, basic information for the test appears. (The "tn" stands for *test name*.) Clicking on the underlined menu choice "View Complete Record" at the bottom of the brief record brings up a menu of links to the full text available in the print version of the *MMY,* as shown in Figure 11.10. The menu frame on the left of the figure shows the range of information about the test available and allows the user to proceed immediately to the specific information by clicking on the desired underlined choice, such as Test Profile or Review.

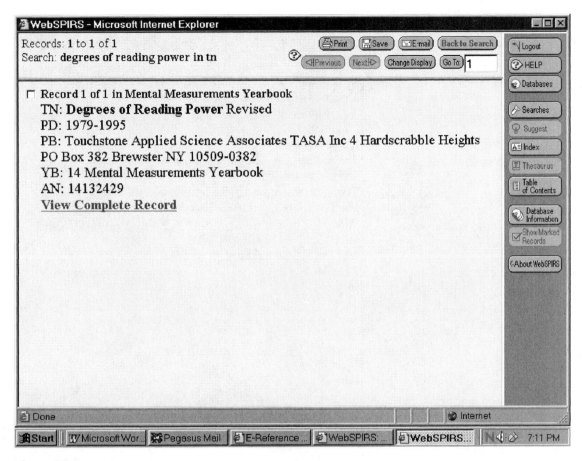

Figure 11.9
Result of a Search for the Degrees of Reading Power Test
Source: © 2005 Ovid Technologies, Inc. All rights reserved.

Professional Journals and Textbooks

A number of professional journals and textbooks contain information and reviews of instruments. Journals such as the *Journal of Educational Measurement, the Journal of Adolescent & Adult Literacy,* and *The Reading Teacher* regularly contain reviews of new and revised instruments. Other journals published by professional associations often contain information about newly published instruments.

Several professional textbooks dealing with educational assessment and evaluation contain information and critiques about various types of instruments. Although the title suggests that the book is intended only for special education, the following textbook is an excellent reference about instruments commonly used in research for measuring academic school performance, learning attributes, classroom behavior, academic areas, and career and vocational interests:

McLoughlin, J. A., & Lewis, R. B. (2005). *Assessing students with special needs* (6th ed.). Upper Saddle River, NJ: Prentice-Hall/Merrill.

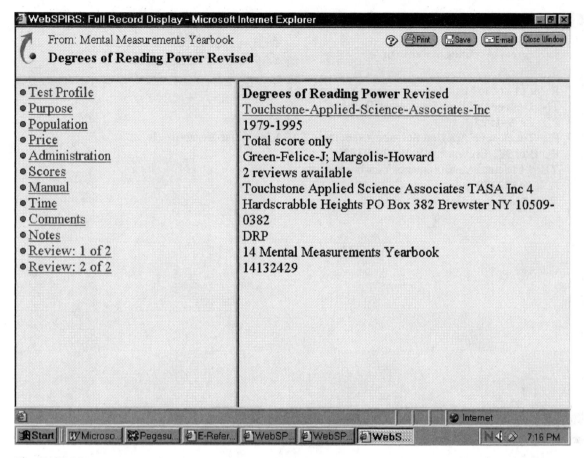

Figure 11.10
Menu of links to full text available in *MMY* print version for *MMY* Degrees of Reading Power Revised
Source: © 2005 Ovid Technologies, Inc. All rights reserved.

SUMMARY

How is an educational problem defined before primary research reports are located?   After considering an educational problem, research consumers should refer to educational dictionaries for specific technical definitions.

How are research syntheses and essays about research located?   Research consumers can locate an educational question in educational encyclopedias and journals specializing in only research syntheses, integrative reviews, and meta-analyses.

How are primary research reports located?   Primary research reports are published in journals or issued by federal, state, and other organizations. They can be located through the electronic versions of the ERIC database, which supplies record items for journal articles containing the article's title, the author's name, the journal's title and volume number, the article's number of pages, the date of publication, document type, and a brief annotation of the contents. Similar information is supplied for non-journal reports. Using ERIC necessitates three steps: (1) referring to the *Thesaurus of*

ERIC Descriptors, (2) combining appropriate subject terms, educational level, and publication type, (3) determining whether the ERIC record refers to a journal article (EJ accession number) or other document (ED accession number). The journals containing the selected articles are then available full text online immediately, or accessed through a library's electronic periodicals list, or located with the library's online catalog. Many of the other documents can be accessed immediately as "full text from ERIC," and most of the other documents can be located in the library's ERIC microfiche document collection using the ED accession numbers. A companion ERIC resource, *Exceptional Child Education Resources (ECER)* and *Education Full Text,* can be used to complement searches in ERIC for older research. Other abstracts produced by specialty areas and for doctoral dissertations in education can also be examined.

These databases can be accessed electronically through CD-ROM formats or by personal computer through the Internet. Electronic access lets the consumer search the databases by using multiple search terms.

Where can information about instruments be located?   Research consumers can find descriptive information and critical reviews about instruments in yearbooks, handbooks, professional journals, and textbooks. The major sources of this information is the *Mental Measurements Yearbook,* available yearly in print and sometimes CD-ROM or through Internet subscription. Searching ERIC can locate information published later than the most currently available *MMY.*

ACTIVITIES

Activity 1

Using either the CD-ROM or print versions of the *Mental Measurements Yearbook* and one or more other sources discussed in the section "Locating Information About Instruments," determine the appropriateness of the following instruments for the indicated research purposes.

   a. Slosson Full-Range Intelligence Test, 1994, ages 5–21
      Research purpose: To identify the learning potential and establish profiles of learning strengths and weaknesses for students with limited English proficiency.
   b. Test of Early Language Development, Third Edition, 1999, ages 2–0 to 7–11
      Research purpose: To compare the language proficiency of primary-grade students with and without language disabilities and to determine the relationship between their language proficiency and beginning reading achievement.
   c. Family Environment Scale, Third Edition, ages 11–adult
      Research purpose: To determine family characteristics that might contribute to children's success in kindergarten and first grade.

Activity 2

   a. Select an education topic related to your teaching situation and locate *(a)* the definition of at least one key term in an educational dictionary; *(b)* one interpretive essay or synthesis of research; *(c)* one primary research report in an educational, psychological, or other social science journal; and *(d)* one primary research report printed "full text from ERIC" or reproduced from an ERIC microfiche document.

b. Using the questions and criteria for evaluating primary research reports, research syntheses, or meta-analyses presented in this text (chapters 3–10), evaluate the selected essays, reviews, and reports.

FEEDBACK

Activity 1

a. For the Slosson Full-Range Intelligence Test, cultural minorities seem to be significantly underrepresented in the sample of the norming group, which is based on data more than 25 years old. Therefore, it might not be appropriate to use the test in a study with individuals with limited English proficiency.

b. The Test of Early Language Development, or TELD-3, was developed for use with normal students; but with certain adjustments in administering and establishing separate forms, the test might be used with special populations. The division of items into Receptive and Expressive Language may be effective for use with special populations. Because it does not contain any reading sections, it might be used in a correlational study with a reading test.

c. The Family Environment Scale (FES) is a norm-referenced instrument with fixed responses. If, in the study, researchers used quantitative research procedures, the instrument might be appropriate. The instrument seems to have appropriate reliability and internal consistency. The instrument seems to have appropriate content validity. However, because there is limited item evidence about the content of the subscales or indexes, a researcher may wish to use caution when intepreting the subscales. Whether the FES has construct validity for the study could be determined by *(a)* examining the framework on which the instrument is grounded, and *(b)* checking the study's sample against the norming group used for the test. FES might not be appropriate to use in a study with qualitative research procedures.

Activity 2

Feedback will be provided by your course instructor.

Representative Quantitative and Qualitative Research Reports

The studies cited in this appendix are representative of studies in the field of education. The studies cited here are suggested studies for applying the interpretive and evaluative information discussed in this text. Further, the studies may be useful to students and instructors who wish to analyze common studies as they undertake activities at the end of various chapters.

Chapter 11 contains specific information about locating primary research studies in print and electronic databases. Students should contact their institutions' reference librarians for additional assistance.

QUANTITATIVE RESEARCH REPORTS IN PRINT JOURNALS

Darch, C., Kim, S., Johnson, S., & James, H. (2000). The strategic spelling skills of students with learning disabilities: The results of two studies. *Journal of Instructional Psychology, 27* (1), 15–27.

Fuson, K. C., Carroll, W. M., & Drueck, J. V. (2000). Achievement results for second and third graders using the standards-based curriculum everyday mathematics. *Journal for Research In Mathematics Education, 31*(3), 277–295.

Gutman, L. M., & Sulzby, E. (2000). The role of autonomy-support versus control in the emergent writing behaviors of African-American kindergarten children. *Reading Research and Instruction, 39*(2), 170–184.

Scott, B. N., & Hannafin, R. D. (2000). How teachers and parents view classroom learning environments: An exploratory study. *Journal of Research on Computing in Education, 32*(3), 401–416.

QUANTITATIVE RESEARCH REPORTS ONLINE

See chapter 11 for information about accessing electronic databases through your institution.

Self-Brown, S. R., & Mathews, S., II. (2003). Effects of classroom structure on student achievement goal orientation. *The Journal of Educational Research, 97*(2), 106–111. Available online through *Education Abstracts/Full Text,* the online version of printed *Education Index.* Available as of spring 2005.

Shapka, J. D., & Keating, D. P. (2003). Effects of a girls-only curriculum during adolescence: Performance, persistence, and engagement in mathematics and science. *American Educational Research Journal, 40*(4), 929–60. Available online through *Education Abstracts/Full Text,* the online version of printed *Education Index.* Available as of spring 2005.

Also, research reports are available on the archived Web sites of federally supported National Research and Development Centers. Those centers, as well as former Research Centers and Institutes, are located at http://www.ed.gov/offices/OERI/ResCtr.html   .

QUALITATIVE RESEARCH REPORTS IN PRINT JOURNALS

Neumeister, K. L. S., & Herbert, T. P. (2003, Spring). Underachievement versus selective achievement: Delving deeper and discovering the difference. *Journal for the Education of the Gifted, 26*(3), 221–238.

Porras Hein, N. (2003). Mexican American parent participation and administrative leadership. *Journal of Latinos and Education, 2*(2), 109–115.

Poston, D., Turnbull, A., Park, J., Mannan, H., Marquis, J., & Wang, M. (2003, May). Family quality of life: A qualitative inquiry. *Mental Retardation, 41*(5), 313–328.

Williams, C. L. (1999). Preschool deaf children's use of signed language during writing events. *Journal of Literacy Research, 31*(2), 183–212.

QUALITATIVE RESEARCH REPORTS ONLINE

See chapter 11 for information about accessing electronic databases through your institution.

Morris, R. N. (2002). A case study on the perspectives of an optional K–5 year-round/ multi-age program in Virginia. ERIC Document No. ED479350. Available in full text from the EBSCO ERIC Data Base. Available as of spring 2005.

Saban, A. (2000, Spring). Professional growth through self-reflection and writing. *Education* (Chula Vista, CA) *120*(3), 512–18. Available online through *Education Abstracts/Full Text,* the online version of printed *Education Index.* Available as of spring 2005.

Skria, L., Reyes, P., Scheurich, J. J. (2000). Sexism, silence, and solutions: Women superintendents speak up and speak out. *Educational Administration Quarterly, 36*(1), 44–75. Available online through *Education Abstracts/Full Text,* the online version of printed *Education Index.* Available as of spring 2005.

Stancavage, F. B., & Reed, E. D. (2003). An investigation of why students do not respond to questions. NAEP Validity Studies: Working Paper Series. Washington, DC: National Center for Education Statistics. ERIC Document No. ED478973. Available in full text at http://nces.ed.gov/ pubsearch/pubsinfo.asp?pubid=200312. Available as of spring 2005.

Also, research reports are available on the archived Web sites of federally supported National Research and Development Centers. Those centers, as well as former Research Centers and Institutes, are located at http://www.ed.gov/offices/OERI/ResCtr.html   .

RESEARCH SYNTHESES AND META-ANALYSES IN PRINT JOURNALS

Note: All issues of *Review of Educational Research* contain research syntheses and, periodically, meta-analyses.

Campbell, J. M. (2003, March-April). Efficacy of behavioral interventions for reducing problem behavior in persons with autism: A quantitative synthesis of single-subject research. *Research in Developmental Disabilities, 24*(2), 120–138.

de Jong, T., & van Joolingen, W. R. (1998). Scientific discovery learning with computer simulations of conceptual domains. *Review of Educational Research, 68*(2), 179–201.

Pirrie, A. (2003, Summer). Spoilsport: On sports and attainment. *Educational Research, 45*(2), 181–188.

Witziers, B., Bosker, R. J., & Kruger, M. L. (2003, August). Educational leadership and student achievement: The elusive search for an association. *Educational Administration Quarterly, 39*(3), 398–425.

RESEARCH SYNTHESES AND META-ANALYSES ONLINE

Contents of current issues of *Review of Educational Research* are available online through *Education Abstracts/Full Text*, the online version of the printed *Education Index*. Check to see if your institution allows access to those sources. Available as of spring 2005.

Baskin, T. W., & Enright, R. D. (2004). Intervention studies on forgiveness: A meta-analysis. *Journal of Counseling and Development, 82*(1), 79–90. Available online through *Education Abstracts/Full Text*, the online version of the printed *Education Index*. Available as of spring 2005.

Jitendra, A. K., Edwards, L. L., & Sacks, G. (2004, Spring). What research says about vocabulary instruction for students with learning disabilities. *Exceptional Children, 70*(3), 299–322. Available online through *Education Abstracts/Full Text*, the online version of the printed *Education Index*. Available as of spring 2005.

Law, J., Zoe, G., & Nye, C. (2004). The efficacy of treatment for children with developmental speech and language delay/disorder: A meta-analysis. *Journal of Speech, Language, and Hearing Research, 47*(4), 924–943. Available online through *Education Abstracts/Full Text*, the online version of the printed *Education Index*. Available as of spring 2005.

Test, D. W., Mason, C., Hughes, C., Konrad, M., Neale, M., & Wood, W. M. (2004, Summer). Student involvement in individualized education program meetings. *Exceptional Children, 70*(4), 391–394. Available online through *Education Abstracts/Full Text*, the online version of the printed *Education Index*. Available as of spring 2005.

Waxman, H. C., & Tellez, K. (2002). Research synthesis on effective teaching practices for English language learners. ERIC Document No. ED474821. Available in full text from the EBSCO ERIC Data Base. Available as of spring 2005.

Standards for Research and Program Evaluation

Ethical Standards of the American Educational Research Association

---

FOREWORD

Educational researchers come from many disciplines, embrace several competing theoretical frameworks, and use a variety of research methodologies. The American Educational Research Association (AERA) recognizes that its members are already guided by codes in the various disciplines and, also, by organizations, such as institutional review boards. AERA's code of ethics incorporates a set of standards designed specifically to guide the work of researchers in education. Education, by its very nature, is aimed at the improvement of individual lives and societies. Further, research in education is often directed at children and other vulnerable populations. A main objective of this code is to remind us, as educational researchers, that we should strive to protect these populations, and to maintain the integrity of our research, of our research community, and of all those with whom we have professional relations. We should pledge ourselves to do this by maintaining our own competence and that of people we induct into the field, by continually evaluating our research for its ethical and scientific adequacy, and by conducting our internal and external relations according to the highest ethical standards.

The standards that follow remind us that we are involved not only in research but in education. It is, therefore, essential that we continually reflect on our research to be sure that it is not only sound scientifically but that it makes a positive contribution to the educational enterprise.

I. GUIDING STANDARDS: RESPONSIBILITIES TO THE FIELD

A. Preamble

To maintain the integrity of research, educational researchers should warrant their research conclusions adequately in a way consistent with the standards of their own theoretical and methodological perspectives. They should keep themselves well informed in both their own

---

and competing paradigms where those are relevant to their research, and they should continually evaluate the criteria of adequacy by which research is judged.

B. Standards

1. Educational researchers should conduct their professional lives in such a way that they do not jeopardize future research, the public standing of the field, or the discipline's research results.

2. Educational researchers must not fabricate, falsify, or misrepresent authorship, evidence, data, findings, or conclusions.

3. Educational researchers must not knowingly or negligently use their professional roles for fraudulent purposes.

4. Educational researchers should honestly and fully disclose their qualifications and limitations when providing professional opinions to the public, to government agencies, and others who may avail themselves of the expertise possessed by members of AERA.

5. Educational researchers should attempt to report their findings to all relevant stakeholders, and should refrain from keeping secret or selectively communicating their findings.

6. Educational researchers should report research conceptions, procedures, results, and analyses accurately and sufficiently in detail to allow knowledgeable, trained researchers to understand and interpret them.

7. Educational researchers' reports to the public should be written straightforwardly to communicate the practical significance for policy, including limits in effectiveness and in generalizability to situations, problems, and contexts. In writing for or communicating with nonresearchers, educational researchers must take care not to misrepresent the practical or policy implications of their research or the research of others.

8. When educational researchers participate in actions related to hiring, retention, and advancement, they should not discriminate on the basis of gender, sexual orientation, physical disabilities, marital status, color, social class, religion, ethnic background, national origin, or other attributes not relevant to the evaluation of academic or research competence.

9. Educational researchers have a responsibility to make candid, forthright personnel recommendations and not to recommend those who are manifestly unfit.

10. Educational researchers should decline requests to review the work of others where strong conflicts of interest are involved, or when such requests cannot be conscientiously fulfilled on time. Materials sent for review should be read in their entirety and considered carefully, with evaluative comments justified with explicit reasons.

11. Educational researchers should avoid all forms of harassment, not merely those overt actions or threats that are due cause for legal action. They must not use their professional positions or rank to coerce personal or sexual favors or economic or professional advantages from students, research assistants, clerical staff, colleagues, or any others.

12. Educational researchers should not be penalized for reporting in good faith violations of these or other professional standards.

II. GUIDING STANDARDS: RESEARCH POPULATIONS, EDUCATIONAL INSTITUTIONS, AND THE PUBLIC

A. Preamble

Educational researchers conduct research within a broad array of settings and institutions, including schools, colleges, universities, hospitals, and prisons. It is of paramount importance that educational researchers respect the rights, privacy, dignity, and sensitivities of their research populations and also the integrity of the institutions within which the research occurs. Educational researchers should be especially careful in working with children and other vulnerable populations. These standards are intended to reinforce and strengthen already existing standards enforced by institutional review boards and other professional associations.

B. Standards

1. Participants, or their guardians, in a research study have the right to be informed about the likely risks involved in the research and of potential consequences for participants, and to give their informed consent before participating in research. Educational researchers should communicate the aims of the investigation as well as possible to informants and participants (and their guardians), and appropriate representatives of institutions, and keep them updated about any significant changes in the research program.
2. Honesty should characterize the relationship between researchers and participants and appropriate institutional representatives. Deception is discouraged; it should be used only when clearly necessary for scientific studies and should then be minimized. After the study the researcher should explain to the participants and institutional representatives the reasons for the deception.
3. Educational researcher should be sensitive to any locally established institutional policies or guidelines for conducting research.
4. Participants have the right to withdraw from the study at any time, unless otherwise constrained by their official capacities or roles.
5. Educational researchers should exercise caution to ensure that there is no exploitation for personal gain of research populations or of institutional settings of research. Educational researchers should not use their influence over subordinates, students, or others to compel them to participate in research.
6. Researchers have a responsibility to be mindful of cultural, religious, gender, and other significant differences within the research population in the planning, conduct, and reporting of their research.
7. Researchers should carefully consider and minimize the use of research techniques that might have negative social consequences, for example, negative sociometrics with young children or experimental interventions that might deprive students of important parts of the standard curriculum.
8. Educational researchers should be sensitive to the integrity of ongoing institutional activities and alert appropriate institutional representatives of possible disturbances in such activities which may result from the conduct of the research.
9. Educational researchers should communicate their findings and the practical significance of their research in clear, straightforward, and appropriate language to relevant research populations, institutional representatives, and other stakeholders.
10. Informants and participants have a right to remain anonymous. This right should be respected when no clear understanding to the contrary has been reached. Researchers are responsible for taking appropriate precautions to protect the confidentiality of both participants and data. Those being studied should be made aware of the capacities of the various data-gathering technologies to be used in the investigation so that they can make an informed decision about their participation. It should also be made clear to informants and participants that despite every effort made to preserve it, anonymity may be compromised. Secondary researchers should respect and maintain the anonymity established by primary researchers.

III. GUIDING STANDARDS: INTELLECTUAL OWNERSHIP

A. Preamble

Intellectual ownership is predominantly a function of creative contribution. Intellectual ownership is not predominantly a function of effort expended.

B. Standards

1. Authorship should be determined based on the following guidelines, which are not intended to stifle collaboration, but rather to clarify the credit appropriately due for various contributions to research.

   a) All those, regardless of status, who have made substantive creative contributions to the generation of an intellectual product are entitled to be listed as authors of that product.

   b) First authorship and order of authorship should be the consequence of relative creative leadership and creative contribution. Examples of creative contributions are: writing first drafts or substantial portions; significant rewriting or substantive editing; and contributing generative ideas or basic conceptual schemes or analytic categories, collecting data which requires significant interpretation or judgment, and interpreting data.

   c) Clerical or mechanical contributions to an intellectual product are not grounds for ascribing authorship. Examples of such technical contributions are: typing, routine data collection or analysis, routine editing, and participation in staff meetings.

   d) Authorship and first authorship are not warranted by legal or contractual responsibility for or authority over the project or process that generates an intellectual product. It is improper to enter into contractual arrangements that preclude the proper assignment of authorship.

   e) Anyone listed as author must have given his/her consent to be so listed.

   f) The work of those who have contributed to the production of an intellectual product in ways short of these requirements for authorship should be appropriately acknowledged within the product.

   g) Acknowledgment of other work significantly relied on in the development of an intellectual product is required. However, so long as such work is not plagiarized or otherwise inappropriately used, such reliance is not grounds for authorship or ownership.

   h) It is improper to use positions of authority to appropriate the work of others or claim credit for it.

   i) Theses and dissertations are special cases in which authorship is not determined strictly by the criteria elaborated in these standards. Students' advisors, who might in other circumstances be deserving of authorship based on their collaborative contribution, should not be considered authors. Their creative contributions should, however, be fully and appropriately acknowledged.

   j) Authors should disclose the publication history of articles they submit for publication; that is, if the present article is substantially similar in content and form to one previously published, that fact should be noted and the place of publication cited.

2. While under suitable circumstances, ideas and other intellectual products may be viewed as commodities, arrangements concerning the production or distribution of ideas or other intellectual products must be consistsent with academic freedom and the appropriate availability of intellectual products to scholars, students, and the public. Moreover, when a conflict between the academic and scholarly purposes of intellectual production and

profit from such production arise, preference should be given to the academic and scholarly purposes.

3. Ownership of intellectual products should be based upon the following guidelines:

    a) Individuals are entitled to profit from the sale or disposition of those intellectual products they create. They may therefore enter into contracts or other arrangements for the publication or disposition of intellectual products, and profit financially from these arrangements.

    b) Arrangements for the publication or disposition of intellectual products should be consistent with their appropriate public availability and with academic freedom. Such arrangements should emphasize the academic functions of publication over the maximization of profit.

    c) Individuals or groups who fund or otherwise provide resources for the development of intellectual products are entitled to assert claims to a fair share of the royalties or other profits from the sale or disposition of those products. As such claims are likely to be contentious, funding institutions and authors should agree on policies for the disposition of profits at the outset of the research or development project.

    d) Author should not use positions of authority over other individuals to compel them to purchase an intellectual product from which the authors benefit. This standard is not meant to prohibit use of an author's own textbook in a class, but copies should be made available on library reserve so that students are not forced to purchase it.

IV. GUIDING STANDARDS: EDITING, REVIEWING, AND APPRAISING RESEARCH

A. Preamble

Editors and reviewers have a responsibility to recognize a wide variety of theoretical and methodological perspectives and, at the same time, to ensure that manuscripts meet the highest standards as defined in the various perspectives.

B. Standards

1. AERA journals should handle refereed articles in a manner consistent with the following principles:

    a) Fairness requires a review process that evaluates submitted works solely on the basis of merit. Merit shall be understood to include both the competence with which the argument is conducted and the significance of the results achieved.

    b) Although each AERA journal may concentrate on a particular field or type of research, the set of journals as a whole should be open to all disciplines and perspectives currently represented in the membership and which support a tradition of responsible educational scholarship. This standard is not intended to exclude worthy innovations.

    c) Blind review, with multiple readers, should be used for each submission, except where explicitly waived. (See #3.)

    d) Judgments of the adequacy of an inquiry should be made by reviewers who are competent to read the work submitted to them. Editors should strive to select reviewers who are familiar with the research paradigm and who are not so unsympathetic as to preclude a disinterested judgment of the merit of the inquiry.

e) Editors should insist that even unfavorable reviews be dispassionate and constructive. Authors have the right to know the grounds for rejection of their work.

2. AERA journals should have written, published policies for refereeing articles.

3. AERA journals should have a written, published policy stating when solicited and non-refereed publications are permissible.

4. AERA journals should publish statements indicating any special emphases expected to characterize articles submitted for review.

5. In addition to enforcing standing strictures against sexist and racist language, editors should reject articles that contain ad hominem attacks on individuals or groups or insist that such language or attacks be removed prior to publication.

6. AERA journals and AERA members who serve as editors of journals should require authors to disclose the full publication history of material substantially similar in content and form to that submitted to their journals.

V. GUIDING STANDARDS: SPONSORS, POLICYMAKERS, AND OTHER USERS OF RESEARCH

A. Preamble

Researchers, research institutions, and sponsors of research jointly share responsibility for the ethical integrity of research, and should ensure that this integrity is not violated. While it is recognized that these parties may sometimes have conflicting legitimate aims, all those with responsibility for research should protect against compromising the standards of research, the community of researchers, the subjects of research, and the users of research. They should support the widest possible dissemination and publication of research results. AERA should promote, as nearly as it can, conditions conducive to the preservation of research integrity.

B. Standards

1. The data and results of a research study belong to the researchers who designed and conducted the study, unless specific contractual arrangements have been made with respect to either or both the data and results, except as noted in II B.4. (Participants may withdraw at any stage.)

2. Educational researchers are free to interpret and publish their findings without censorship or approval from individuals or organizations, including sponsors, funding agencies, participants, colleagues, supervisors, or administrators. This understanding should be conveyed to participants as part of the responsibility to secure informed consent.

3. Researchers conducting sponsored research retain the right to publish the findings under their own names.

4. Educational researchers should not agree to conduct research that conflicts with academic freedom, nor should they agree to undue or questionable influence by government or other funding agencies. Examples of such improper influence include endeavors to interfere with the conduct of research, the analysis of findings, or the reporting of interpretations. Researchers should report to AERA attempts by sponsors or funding agencies to use any questionable influence.

5. Educational researchers should fully disclose the aims and sponsorship of their research, except where such disclosure would violate the usual tenets of confidentiality and anonymity. Sponsors or funders have the right to have disclaimers included in research reports to differentiate their sponsorship from the conclusions of the research.

6. Educational researchers should not accept funds from sponsoring agencies that request multiple renderings of reports that would distort the results of mislead readers.

7. Educational researchers should fulfill their responsibilities to agencies funding research, which are entitled to an accounting of the use of their funds, and to a report of the procedures, findings, and implications of the funded research.

8. Educational researchers should make clear the bases and rationales, and the limits thereof, of their professionally rendered judgements in consultation with the public, government, or other institutions. When there are contrasting professional opinions to the one being offered, this should be made clear.

9. Educational researchers should disclose to appropriate parties all cases where they would stand to benefit financially from their research or cases where their affiliations might tend to bias their interpretation of their research or their professional judgments.

VI. GUIDING STANDARDS: STUDENTS AND STUDENT RESEARCHERS

A. Preamble

Educational researchers have a responsibility to ensure the competence of those inducted into the field and to provide appropriate help and professional advice to novice researchers.

B. Standards

1. In relations with students and student researchers, educational researchers should be candid, fair, nonexploitative, and committed to their welfare and progress. They should conscientiously supervise, encourage, and support students and student researchers in their academic endeavors, and should appropriately assist them in securing research support or professional employment.

2. Students and student researchers should be selected based upon their competence and potential contributions to the field. Educational researchers should not discriminate among students and student researchers on the basis of gender, sexual orientation, marital status, color, social class, religion, ethnic background, national origin, or other irrelevant factors.

3. Educational researchers should inform students and student researchers concerning the ethical dimensions of research, encourage their practice of research consistent with ethical standards, and support their avoidance of questionable projects.

4. Educational researchers should realistically apprise students and student researchers with regard to career opportunities and implications associated with their participation in particular research projects or degree programs. Educational researchers should ensure that research assistantships be educative.

5. Educational researchers should be fair in the evaluation of research performance, and should communicate that evaluation fully and honestly to the student or student researcher. Researchers have an obligation to report honestly on the competence of assistants to other professionals who require such evaluations.

6. Educational researchers should not permit personal animosities or intellectual differences vis-a-vis colleagues to foreclose student and student researcher access to those colleagues, or to place the student or student researcher in an untenable position with those colleagues.

The Program Evaluation Standards: ERIC/AE Digest

Sound evaluations of educational programs, projects, and materials in a variety of settings should have four basic attributes:

- Utility
- Propriety
- Feasibility
- Accuracy

"The Program Evaluation Standards," established by sixteen professional associations, identify evaluation principles that, when addressed, should result in improved program evaluations containing these four attributes. What follows is a summary of the standards.

Guidelines and illustrative cases to assist evaluation participants in meeting each of these standards are provided in the full report (Joint Committee on Standards for Educational Evaluations, 1994). The illustrative cases are based in a variety of educational settings that include schools, universities, medical and health care fields, the military, business and industry, the government, and law.

Utility

The utility standards are intended to ensure that an evaluation will serve the information needs of intended users.

U1 Stakeholder Identification. Persons involved in or affected by the evaluation should be identified so that their needs can be addressed.

U2 Evaluator Credibility. The persons conducting the evaluation should be both trustworthy and competent to perform the evaluation so that the evaluation findings achieve maximum credibility and acceptance.

U3 Information Scope and Selection. Information collected should be broadly selected to address pertinent questions about the program and be responsive to the needs and interests of clients and other specified stakeholders.

U4 Values Identification. The perspectives, procedures, and rationale used to interpret the findings should be carefully described so that the bases for value judgments are clear.

U5 Report Clarity. Evaluation reports should clearly describe the program being evaluated, including its context, and the purposes, procedures, and findings of the evaluation so that essential information is provided and easily understood.

U6 Report Timeliness and Dissemination. Significant interim findings and evaluation reports should be disseminated to intended users so that they can be used in a timely fashion.

U7 Evaluation Impact. Evaluations should be planned, conducted, and reported in ways that encourage follow-through by stakeholders so that the likelihood that the evaluation will be used is increased.

Source: ERIC Clearinghouse on Assessment and Evaluation. Washington DC, Eric Document No. ED 385 612; 1995

Feasibility

The feasibility standards are intended to ensure that an evaluation will be realistic, prudent, diplomatic, and frugal.

F1 Practical Procedures. The evaluation procedures should be practical to keep disruption to a minimum while needed information is obtained.

F2 Political Viability. The evaluation should be planned and conducted with anticipation of the different positions of various interest groups so that their cooperation may be obtained and so that possible attempts by any of these groups to curtail evaluation operations or to bias or misapply the results can be averted or counteracted.

F3 Cost Effectiveness. The evaluation should be efficient and produce information of sufficient value so that the resources expended can be justified.

Propriety

The propriety standards are intended to ensure that an evaluation will be conducted legally, ethically, and with due regard for the welfare of those involved in the evaluation, as well as those affected by its results.

P1 Service Orientation. Evaluations should be designed to assist organizations to address and effectively serve the needs of the full range of targeted participants.

P2 Formal Agreements. Obligations of the formal parties to an evaluation (what is to be done, how, by whom, and when) should be agreed to in writing, so that these parties are obligated to adhere to all conditions of the agreement or formally to renegotiate it.

P3 Rights of Human Subjects. Evaluations should be designed and conducted to respect and protect the rights and welfare of human subjects.

P4 Human Interactions. Evaluators should respect human dignity and worth in their interactions with other persons associated with an evaluation so that participants are not threatened or harmed.

P5 Complete and Fair Assessment. The evaluation should be complete and fair in its examination and recording of strengths and weaknesses of the program being evaluated so that strengths can be built upon and problem areas addressed.

P6 Disclosure of Findings. The formal parties to an evaluation should ensure that the full set of evaluation findings along with pertinent limitations are made accessible to the persons affected by the evaluation and any others with expressed legal rights to receive the results.

P7 Conflict of Interest. Conflict of interest should be dealt with openly and honestly so that it does not compromise the evaluation processes and results.

P8 Fiscal Responsibility. The evaluator's allocation and expenditure of resources should reflect sound accountability procedures and otherwise be prudent and ethically responsible so that expenditures are accounted for and appropriate.

Accuracy

The accuracy standards are intended to ensure that an evaluation will reveal and convey technically adequate information about the features that determine worth of merit of the program being evaluated.

A1 Program Documentation. The program being evaluated should be described and documented clearly and accurately so that the program is clearly identified.

A2 Context Analysis. The context in which the program exists should be examined in enough detail so that its likely influences on the program can be identified.

A3 Described Purposes and Procedures. The purposes and procedures of the evaluation should be monitored and described in enough detail so that they can be identified and assessed.

A4 Defensible Information Sources. The sources of information used in a program evaluation should be described in enough detail so that the adequacy of the information can be assessed.

A5 Valid Information. The information gathering procedures should be chosen or developed and then implemented to ensure that the interpretation arrived at is valid for the intended use.

A6 Reliable Information. The information gathering procedures should be chosen or developed and then implemented to ensure that the information obtained is sufficiently reliable for the intended use.

A7 Systematic Information. The information collected, processed, and reported in an evaluation should be systematically reviewed and any errors found should be corrected.

A8 Analysis of Quantitative Information. Quantitative information in an evaluation should be appropriately and systematically analyzed so that evaluation questions are effectively answered.

A9 Analysis of Qualitative Information. Qualitative information in an evaluation should be appropriately and systematically analyzed so that evaluation questions are effectively answered.

A10 Justified Conclusions. The conclusions reached in an evaluation should be explicitly justified so that stakeholders can assess them.

A11 Impartial Reporting. Reporting procedures should guard against distortion caused by personal feelings and biases of any party to the evaluation so that evaluation reports fairly reflect the evaluation findings.

A12 Metaevaluation. The evaluation itself should be formatively and summatively evaluated against these and other pertinent standards so that its conduct is appropriately guided and, on completion, stakeholders can closely examine its strengths and weaknesses.

Approved by the American National Standards Institute as an American National Standard. Approval date: March 15, 1994.

FURTHER READING

Hansen, J. B. & Patton, M. Q. (1994). The Joint Committee on Standards for Educational Evaluation's "The program evaluation standards: How to assess evaluations of educational programs". [Book review]. *Educational and Psychological Measurement, 54*(2), 550–567.

Joint Committee on Standards for Educational Evaluation (1994). *The program evaluation standards: How to assess evaluations of educational programs.* Thousand Oaks, CA: Sage (available from ERIC/AE).

Stufflebeam, D.L. (1987). Professional standards for assuring the quality of educational program and personnel evaluations. *International Journal of Educational Research, 11*(1), 125–143.

Thompson, B. (1993, April). *The revised program evaluation standards and their correlation with the evaluation use literature.* Paper presented at the annual meeting of the American Educational Research Association, New Orleans, LA. ERIC Document No. 370 999.

Glossary

abstract A complete overview of the research report.

accessible population A group that is convenient to the researchers and representative of the target population. Practical considerations that lead to the use of an accessible population include time, money, and physical accessibility.

action research See **participatory action research.**

analysis of covariance (ANCOVA) A statistical procedure based on analysis of variance (ANOVA), allowing researchers to examine the means of groups of subjects as if they were equal from the start. They do this examination by adjusting the differences in the means to make the means hypothetically equal.

analysis of variance (ANOVA) A statistical procedure used to show differences among the means of two or more groups of subjects, or two or more variables. It is reported in F ratios. The advantage in using an ANOVA is that several variables (as well as several factors) can be examined. In its simplest form, ANOVA can be thought of as a multiple t test.

authentic assessment Assessment of students' work and the products of their learning by comparing their performance and products (such as oral reading, writing samples, art or other creative output, and curriculum-related projects) to specified levels of performance. The materials and instruction used are true representations of students' actual learning and their activities in the classroom and out-of-school worlds. (See **criterion-referenced tests.**)

authenticity criteria Criteria by which the work of researchers with a constructivist perspective can be judged.

background section The section of the research report that contains (a) an explanation of the researchers' chosen problem area, (b) its educational importance, (c) summaries of other researchers' results that are related to the problem (called a *literature review*), and (d) strengths from the related research that were used and weaknesses or limitations that were changed.

baseline measure The pretest in single-subject research; it can take the form of one or several measurements. It is the result to which the posttest result is compared, to determine the effect of each treatment.

best evidence A concept by which research consumers can select and review studies for inclusion in research reviews only if the studies are specifically related to the topic, are methodologically adequate, and are generalizable to a specific situation.

case study A form of single-subject research, undertaken on the premise that someone who is typical of a target population can be located and studied. In case studies, the individual's (a) history within an educational setting can be traced, (b) growth pattern(s) over time can be shown, (c) functioning in one or more situations can be examined, and (d) response(s) to one or more treatments can be measured.

causal-comparative research Research that seeks to establish causation based on preexisting independent variables. Researchers do not induce differences in an experimental situation; instead they seek to identify one or more preexisting conditions (independent variables) in one group that exist to a lesser degree in the other. When one or more conditions are identified, they can attribute causality. (Also called *ex post facto research.*)

causative research See **experimental research.**

central tendency, measure of The middle or average score in a group of scores. The middle score is called the *median;* the arithmetic average score is called the *mean.* The most common score is called the *mode.*

chi-square test A nonparametric statistic used to test the significance of group differences between observed and expected outcomes when data are reported as frequencies or percentages of a total, or as nominal scales.

cluster sampling The procedure by which intact groups are selected because of convenience or accessibility. This procedure is especially common in causal-comparative research.

comparative research Research that seeks to provide an explanation about the extent of the relationship between two or more variables, or examines differences or relationships among several variables. These variables might represent characteristics of the same group of subjects or those of separate groups.

concurrent validity The extent to which the results show that subjects' scores correlate, or are similar, on two instruments administered during the same time period.

constructivism   Researchers with this theoretical perspective argue that knowledge and reality do not have an objective or absolute meaning. Knowledge is constructed, not reproduced. Goals and objectives of a research project are derived by the participants in negotiation with the researchers. To them, an individual interprets and constructs a reality based on his or her experiences and interactions with the environment. Constructivists have the idea that things and events vary, rather than thinking of what is true in terms of being equal with the so-called real world.

construct validity   The quality obtained when an instrument's creator demonstrates the instrument as representing a supportable theory.

content validity   The quality obtained when an instrument's creator demonstrates that the specific items or questions used in the instrument represent an accurate sampling of specific bodies of knowledge (such as curricula or courses of study).

control   Use of procedures by researchers to limit or account for the possible influence of variables not being studied.

control group   The group of subjects in experimental research not receiving the experimental condition or treatment (sometimes called the *comparison group*).

correlation   A measure of the extent to which two or more variables have a systematic relationship. (See **product-moment correlation**.)

correlation of coefficient   The result of an arithmetic computation done as part of a product-moment correlation. It is expressed as *r*, a decimal between −1.0 and +1.0 (See **product-moment correlation** and **Pearson product-moment correlation**.)

counterbalanced design   The research design in which two or more groups get the same treatment; however, the order of the treatments for each group is different and is usually randomly determined. For this type of design to work, the number of treatments and groups must match. Although the groups may be randomly selected and assigned, researchers often use this design with already existing groups of subjects, such as all classes in a grade level.

criterion-referenced test   An instrument that measures students' performances in terms of expected learner behaviors or to specified expected levels of performance. Scores show students' abilities and performances in relation to sets of goals or to what students are able to do. Scores do not show subjects' rankings compared with others, as norm-referenced tests do. A standardized criterion-referenced test is one for which the administration and scoring procedures are uniform, but the scoring is in relation to the established goals, not to a norm group. (See **authentic assessment.**)

cross-validation   The procedure in which researchers investigate using the same purpose, method, and data analysis procedure, but use subjects from a different population.

data   The information obtained through the use of instruments by quantitative researchers.

degrees of freedom   The number of ways data can vary in a statistical problem.

dependent variable   The variable researchers make the acted-upon variable. It is the variable whose value may change as the result of the experimental treatment (the independent variable).

derived scores   Test scores that are converted from raw scores into other scores, such as grade equivalents, normal curve equivalents, percentiles, or stanines.

descriptive research   Research that seeks to provide information about one or more variables. It is used to answer the question "What exists?" This question can be answered in one of two ways: using quantitative methods or qualitative methods.

descriptors   Key words found in the *Thesaurus of ERIC Descriptors* and used in such indexing documents as *Resources in Education* and *Current Index to Journals in Education.*

directional hypothesis   A statement of the specific way one variable will affect another variable when previous research evidence supports it. (Also called a *one-tailed hypothesis*.)

direct observation   The research procedure in which researchers take extensive field notes or use observation forms to record information. They categorize information on forms in response to questions about subjects' actions or categories of actions. Or, they tally subjects' actions within some predetermined categories during a time period.

discussion section   A section of the research report that contains the researchers' ideas about the educational implications of the research results (also called *conclusions section*).

effect   The influence of one variable on another.

effect size   An indication of the magnitude (meaningfulness or importance) of statistical results by providing a measure in relation to the standard deviation of the data gathering instrument. Effect size is commonly reported as a decimal fraction of the standard deviation. In meta-analyses, it is shown as a ratio derived from the combined mean scores of the experimental and control groups and the standard deviations of the control groups. It shows the size of the difference between the mean scores of the experimental and control groups in relation to the standard deviations.

equivalent forms reliability Reliability determined by correlating the scores from two forms of an instrument given to the same subjects. The instruments differ only in the specific nature of the items. (Sometimes called *parallel forms reliability.*)

ERIC or **Education Resources Information Center** A national network supported by the Institute of Education Sciences of the U.S. Department of Education. Its purpose was to provide access to current research results and related information in the field of education. It was a decentralized system composed of about 16 clearinghouses, each specializing in a major educational area.

ethnographic research Educational researchers have borrowed some of the practices of ethnographic research from researchers in cultural anthropology and sociology. Ethnographic research, like other qualitative inquiries, emphasizes firsthand field study. Ethnographic research designs stress the study of "culture" within a group that shares a culture, examining "shared patterns of behavior, belief and language." Often used synonymously with *qualitative research,* although some researchers consider ethnography a subtype of qualitative research.

evaluation research The application of the rigors of research to the judging of the worth or value of educational programs, projects, and instruction. It extends the principle of action research, which is primarily of local interest, so that generalizations may be made to other educational situations. And, although undertaken for different reasons than is experimental research, the quantitative research method used in evaluation research is based on that of experimental research.

experimental condition The condition whereby the independent variable is manipulated, varied, or subcategorized by the researcher in experimental research. (Also called *treatment.*)

experimental group The group of subjects in experimental research receiving the experimental condition or treatment.

experimental research Research that seeks to answer questions about causation. Researchers wish to attribute the change in one variable to the effect of one or more other variables. The variables causing changes in subjects' responses or performance are the independent variables. The variables whose measurements may change are the dependent variables. The measurements can be made with any instrument type: survey, test, or observation.

external validity Validity based on researchers' assurance that results can be generalized to other persons and other settings.

extraneous variables Variables that might have an unwanted influence on, or might change, the dependent variable. Researchers can restrict the influence of extraneous variables by controlling subject variables and situational variables.

F **ratio** The way in which analysis of variance (ANOVA) and analysis of covariance (ANCOVA) are reported.

face validity The extent to which an instrument appears to measure a specific body of information. In other words, "Does the instrument look as if it would measure what it intends to measure?"

factorial designs Research designs in which there are multiple variables and each variable is subcategorized into two or more levels, or factors. The simplest factorial design involves two independent variables, each of which has two factors. This format is called a "2 × 2 factorial design." Factorial designs can have any combination of variables and factors.

feminist research Researchers using this strategy believe that what makes feminist research uniquely feminist are the motives, concerns, and knowledge brought to the research process. This is a diverse group of researchers who study the ways in which gender does and ought to influence people's conceptions of knowledge, the knowing subject, and practices of inquiry and justification. Feminist researchers come from a perspective, not a method. They see the organizing of the social world by gender.

field notes Written narratives describing subjects' behaviors or performances during an instructional activity. These notes are then analyzed and the information categorized for reporting. The analysis can start with predetermined categories, and information from the notes is recorded accordingly. Or, the analysis can be open-ended in that the researchers cluster similar information and then create a label for each cluster.

fieldwork The collection of data during qualitative studies in particular educational settings.

focus groups Focus groups involve the explicit use of group interaction to produce data and insights that would be less accessible without the interaction found in a group. There are no specific rules for the creation or use of focus groups, nor are there specific guidelines for determining group size, membership, or selection procedures. Most often, focus group membership is a purposeful sample: Researchers create group membership to gain the greatest amount of information. A group usually has no more than ten representative people. The discussion, guided by a facilitator, is given focus by a series of topic or task-related questions. The aim is to draw information from local experience and traditions and to provide understanding about the impact of the project on those involved (that is, the stakeholders).

generalizability The ability of results to be extended to other students or the target population. That means a research consumer in a different place can have confidence in applying the research producers' results.

grounded theory research Researchers using a grounded theory approach apply a set of systematic guidelines to the information they collect to identify key themes and patterns, in order to inductively build theoretical frameworks. This strategy is in contrast to one in which a theory is the consequence of deduction, that is, the creation of a theory before information or data is collected, and then a search is undertaken for evidence to support it. Grounded theorists use an extensive coding system, applying tags and labels to the primarily narrative data collected. Such coding enables the data to be systematically explored. Researchers use these coding labels to group their data into categories and develop conceptual relationships between and among categories, looking for commonalities, differences, patterns, and themes. Although many researchers use qualitative methodology in grounded theory research, some researchers feel grounded theory is a general methodology that can be used with either quantitative or qualitative data, or with both in combination.

hierarchical linear models (HLM) A technique related to multiple correlation technique. HLM is based on the premise that many subjects within a group are more similar to each other than they are to subjects randomly sampled from the entire population.

hypothesis A tentative statement about how two or more variables are related. A hypothesis is the researchers' conjectural statement of the relationship between the research variables and is created after the investigators have examined the related literature, but before they undertake their study. It is a tentative explanation for certain behaviors, phenomena, or events that have occurred or will occur. It can be either directional or nondirectional.

identifiers Keywords used in indexing documents that are not yet represented as descriptors in the ERIC *Thesaurus of ERIC Descriptors.*

independent variable The influencing variable in experimental research, the one to which researchers wish to attribute causation. (Sometimes called the *experimental variable.*) When the independent variable is an activity of the researcher, it is called a *treatment variable.*

information collection procedures The specific activities qualitative researchers engage in to record and analyze information. Basically, the information-gathering activities are observing people and events, interviewing people, and examining documents. After information is collected, it is sorted and categorized. The information-analyzing activities are primarily coding the information and developing themes.

instruments A broad range of specific devices and procedures for collecting, sorting, and categorizing information about subjects and research questions.

instruments section A subsection of the method section of a research report, containing a description of the data collection instruments: observation forms, standardized and researcher-made tests, and surveys.

integrative review of research See **research synthesis.**

interaction effect The effect in experimental studies of two or more variables acting together. Interactions are expressed as F ratios within ANOVA or ANCOVA tables and can be shown in a graph.

internal consistency reliability Reliability determined by statistically comparing the subjects' scores on individual items with their scores on each of the other items, and with their scores on the instrument as a whole. (Sometimes called *rationale equivalence reliability.*)

internal validity Validity based on researchers' assurance that changes to dependent variables can be attributed to independent variables.

interrater/interjudge reliability See **scorer reliability.**

interval scale The statistical form presenting data according to preset, equal spans and identified by continuous measurement scales: raw scores and derived scores such as IQ scores, percentiles, stanines, standard scores, and normal curve equivalents. It is the most common form of data reporting in educational and social science research and it is the way data from most tests are recorded.

interview An instrument used to obtain structured or open-ended responses from subjects. It differs from a questionnaire in that the researcher can modify the data-collection situation to fit the respondent's responses.

inventory A questionnaire that requires subjects to respond to statements, questions, or category labels with a "yes" or "no" or asks subjects to check off appropriate information within a category.

Likert-type scale A scale that uses forced choices of response to statements or questions; for example, "Always," "Sometimes," or "Never." Each response is assigned a value; a value of 1 represents the least positive response.

literature review A subsection of the background section of a research report, containing summaries of related research; in it, researchers indicate strengths from the related research that were used in their study, and weaknesses or limitations that were changed.

matched groups design The research design in which the experimental and control groups are selected or assigned to groups on the basis of a single-subject variable, such as reading ability, grade level, ethnicity, or special disabling condition.

mean The arithmetical average score.

median The middle score in a group of scores.

meta-analysis A critical examination of primary research studies in which quantitative data analyses were used. Research reviewers use meta-analysis as "analysis of analyses" (statistical data analysis of already-completed statistical data analyses). In them, the reviewers convert the statistical results of the individual studies into a common measurement so they can obtain an overall, combined result.

method section The section of the research report usually composed of three subsections: subjects, instruments, and procedures.

microfiche Small sheets of microfilm containing images of documents that can be read only on special microfiche readers.

mode The most frequent (common) score in a distribution of scores.

multiple correlation A statistical technique used to examine the relationships among more than two variables. The procedure is interpreted similarly to a single correlation coefficient. It can also be used to make predictions. The technique is used frequently in causal-comparative experimental research. (Also called *multiple regression*.)

narrative research Researchers taking a narrative inquiry approach focus on people's lives and lived experiences. They point to the "storied" nature of human understanding, arguing that stories have always been one of the most basic ways that people make meaning of the world. They consider the deliberate attempt to story and re-story experiences (including educational experiences) a good way to understand human experiences and their meaning for those who participate in them. Narrative researchers collect and tell stories of people's lives, describe people's lived experiences, and analyze participants' explanations of what they do, why, with whom, and in what context. They attempt to understand and portray the complexity of these experiences and to interpret them in ways that can help make those experiences relevant and meaningful to others.

nominal scale The statistical form reporting as numbers of items, or as percentages of a total. Data from surveys and observations are often recorded in this way.

nondirectional hypothesis A statement used when researchers have strong evidence from examining previous research that a relationship or influence exists but the evidence does not provide indications about the direction (positive or negative) of the influence. (Also known as *two-tailed*.)

nonequivalent control group design The research design in which the groups are not randomly selected or assigned, and no effort is made to equate them statistically.

nonparametric statistics Statistical procedures used with data that are measured in nominal and ordinal scales. These statistics work on different assumptions than do parametric statistics and are used for populations that do not have the characteristics of the normal distribution curve.

norm See **normal distribution curve.**

normal curve equivalent (NCE) A normalized standard score with a mean of 50 and a standard deviation of 21.06. NCEs of 1 and 99 are equivalent to percentiles 1 and 99.

normal distribution curve A distribution of scores or other measures that in graphic form present a distinct bell-shaped appearance. In a normal distribution, the measures are distributed symmetrically around the mean. In a normal distribution, the mean, median, and mode are identical.

norming group The individuals used in researching the standardization of the administration and scoring of norm-referenced tests.

norm-referenced test An instrument that measures an individual's performance compared with a standardization, or norming, group.

one-tailed hypothesis See **directional hypothesis.**

operational definition A definition of a variable that gives the precise way an occurrence of that variable is viewed by researchers.

ordinal scale The statistical form showing the order, from highest to lowest, for a variable ranking. There is no indication as to the value or size of differences among items in a list; the indication is only to the relative order of the scores.

parallel forms reliability See **equivalent forms reliability.**

parametric statistics Statistical procedures used with data measured in interval scales and based on certain assumptions, all of which are related to the concept of a normal distribution curve.

participant observer A qualitative researcher who goes to the particular setting being studied and participates in the activities of the people in that setting. Researchers functioning in this role try to maintain a middle position on a continuum of complete independence as an observer, to complete involvement in the people's activities.

participants The individuals involved in qualitative constructivist research. They are not considered just subjects, because they actively engage with researchers in the progress of the study. Such researchers are not concerned about meeting any strict standards of randomization. The selection procedure may even be considered recursive. That is, constructivist qualitative researchers may not stay with their original sample; they may add or change participants as they redefine their target population, or as the scope of their study changes because of information gained through data collection procedures.

participatory action research *Action research, teacher research, collaborative inquiry,* and *participatory action research* are all terms to describe a systematic inquiry in which professional (i.e., academic) researchers conduct research with (rather than on or for) teachers, administrators, and even sometimes parents and students. It is a research process that weaves together both professional research knowledge and "local" (e.g., teacher, practitioner) knowledge. The professional researchers and other participants collaborate in setting research concerns and share in the control of the research processes and products. See **teacher-as-researcher research** for comparison.

Pearson product-moment correlation The most common correlation coefficient. (See **product-moment correlation** and **correlation of coefficient.**)

pilot study A limited research project, usually with a few subjects, that follows the original research plan in every respect. By analyzing the results, research producers can identify potential problems.

population A group of individuals having at least one characteristic that distinguishes them from other groups. A population can be any size and can include people from any place in the world.

positivism Researchers with this theoretical perspective look at knowledge as an awareness of objects that are independent of any subject. According to this view, objects and events have intrinsic meaning, and knowledge is an explanation of an as-

sociation with what is real. A statement is meaningful to them if it can be shown to be supported by means of the experience; this is considered the verifiability principle. Positivists consider a statement as supportable only when the conditions under which the statement is verified is known. In this way, knowledge should represent a real world that is thought of as existing, that is, separate and independent of the researcher; and, this knowledge should be considered true only if research results accurately explain that independent world.

posttest The second and subsequent measurements after a pretest.

posttest-only control group design The research design in which the experimental and control groups are not pretested. An example of this design is two or more randomized groups being engaged in comparison activities without being given a pretest.

practical significance A determination about how useful research results are. To determine this, research consumers need to answer: "How effectively can the results be used in my teaching situation?"

predictive validity The extent to which an instrument can predict a target population's performance after some future situation. It is determined by comparing a sample's results on the instrument to their results after some other activity.

pretest The test given to the subjects to collect initial, or baseline, data.

pretest-posttest control group design The research design in which all groups are given the same pretest and posttest (survey, observation, or test).

procedure section A subsection of the methods section of a research report, containing a detailed explanation of how the researchers conducted their study.

product-moment correlation Refers to the quantified relationship between two sets of scores for the same group of subjects. The result of the arithmetic computation is a correlation coefficient, which is expressed as *r*, a decimal between 21.0 and 11.0. The most common interval scale correlation coefficient is the Pearson product-moment correlation. Correlations show whether two or more variables have a systematic relationship of occurrence—that is, whether high scores for one variable occur with high scores of another (a positive relationship), or whether they occur with low scores of that other variable (a negative relationship). The occurrence of low scores for one variable, with low scores for another, is also an example of a positive relationship. A correlation coefficient of zero indicates that the two variables have no relationship with each other (that is, are independent of each other).

purpose section The section of the research report that contains the specific goal (or goals) of the research project. A goal may be expressed as a statement, a question, or an hypothesis.

qualitative research Research using a broad range of strategies that have roots in the field research of anthropology and sociology. It involves collecting data within natural settings, and the key data collection instruments are the researchers themselves. Qualitative research data are verbal, not numerical. Because qualitative researchers are just as concerned with the process of activities and events as they are with results from those activities or events, they analyze data through inductive reasoning rather than by statistical procedures.

quantitative descriptive research Designs that deal with statistically explaining the status or condition of one or more variables or events. Research consumers should be concerned that information is valid, objective, and reliable, and that variables or events are portrayed accurately.

quantitiative research Research using procedures involving the assignment of numerical values to variables. The most common quantitative descriptive measures researchers use are the mean (a measure of central tendency) and the standard deviation (a measure of the variability of the data around the mean).

questionnaire An instrument that necessitates the respondent either writing or orally providing answers to questions about a topic. The answer form may be structured in that there are fixed choices, or the form may be open-ended in that respondents can use their own words. Fixed-choice questionnaires may be called *inventories.*

randomization An unbiased, systematic selection or assignment of subjects. When randomization is used, researchers assume that all members of the target population have an equal chance of being selected for the sample, and that most human characteristics are evenly distributed among the groups.

random sampling Based on the principle of randomization, whereby all members of the target population have an equal chance of being selected for the sample. The subjects that are finally selected should reflect the distribution of relevant variables found in the target population.

rationale equivalence reliability See **internal consistency reliability.**

ratio scale The statistical form showing relative relationships among scores, such as half-as-large or three-times-as-tall. In dealing with educational variables, researchers do not use these scales much.

reference section The section of the research report that contains an alphabetical listing of the books, journal articles, other research reports, instructional materials, and instruments cited in the report.

reliability The extent to which tests scores are consistent; that is, the degree to which the test scores are dependable or relatively free from random errors of measurement. Reliability is usually expressed in the form of a reliability coefficient. Or, it is expressed as the standard error of measurement derived from the reliability coefficient. The higher the reliability coefficient, the better. A test (or set of test scores) with a reliability of 1.00 would have a standard error measurement of 0, and thus the test would be perfectly reliable. The reliability coefficient (usually expressed as r) can range from .00 to 1.00.

reliability coefficient The number expressing an instrument's reliability, expressed in decimal form, ranging from .00 to 1.00. The higher the coefficient, the higher the instrument's reliability.

replication The procedure in which researchers repeat an investigation of a previous study's purpose, question, or hypothesis.

representative The quality of a sample in which the researchers' results are generalizable from the sample to the target population.

research The systematic attempt not only to collect information about an identified problem or question, but also to analyze that information and to apply the evidence thus derived to confirm or refute some prior prediction or statement about that problem. Educational research is not unique within the total research community; it is the application of some generally accepted systematic procedures to examine the knowledge base of education.

research design The overall strategy or plan used by researchers for answering their research questions.

research methods The activities researchers use within their research design.

research report A full description of researchers' purposes, rationalizations, activities, and findings.

research synthesis A critical examination of research producers' methods and conclusions in primary studies and of the generalizability of their combined findings. Also referred to as *integrative review of research* and *research integration.*

results section The section of the research report that contains the results of the researchers' data analyses; it contains not only the numerical results (often presented in tables and charts) but also an explanation of the significance of those results.

sample A representative group of subjects; it is a miniature target population. Ideally, the sample has the same distribution of relevant variables as found in the target population.

sampling error   Any mismatch between the sample and the target population.

scales   Methods of measurement that measure variables related to attitudes, interests, and personality and social adjustment. Usually, data are quantified in predetermined categories representing the degree or intensity of the subjects' responses to each of the statements or questions. Unlike data from tests, which are measured in continuous measurements (e.g., stanines 1 through 9, or percentiles 1 through 99), data from scales are discrete measurements, forcing respondents to indicate their level of reaction. Common forced choices are "Always," "Sometimes," or "Never." This type of data quantification is called a *Likert-type scale.*

scientific research   An investigative activity that makes possible two things: (*a*) the discovery that our world is (or is not) organized as our preconceptions lead us to expect and (*b*) the theories to understanding our world.

scorer or rater reliability   Reliability determined by comparing the results of two or more scorers, raters, or judges. Sometimes presented as a percentage of agreement or as a coefficient. (Sometimes called *interrater* or *interjudge* reliability.)

simple experimental design   An experimental design with one independent variable, or that uses a subject selection procedure that limits the generalizability of its results. (See **experimental research.**)

single-subject research   Any research in which there is only one subject or one group that is treated as a single entity (e.g., when an entire school is studied without regard to individual students' performances). Single-subject research may be descriptive or experimental. The case study is a form of single-subject research.

situational variable   A variable related to the experimental condition (i.e., a variable outside the subjects) that might cause changes in the subjects responses relating to the dependent variable.

Solomon four-group design   The research design in which four groups are formed using random selection and random assignment. All four groups are posttested, but only two groups are pretested. One pretested group and one nonpretested group are then given the experimental condition.

split-half reliability   A form of internal consistency reliability determined by dividing the instrument in half and statistically comparing the subjects' results on both parts. The most common way to split a test is into odd- and even-numbered items.

standard deviation   A measure of the variability of the data around the mean. SD is based on the normal curve. It shows how scores were distributed around the mean. It is the way variability is usually reported.

standardized test   An instrument that has been experimentally constructed. The test constructor uses accepted procedures and researches the test's (*a*) content, (*b*) procedures for administration, (*c*) system for recording and scoring answers, and (*d*) method of turning the results into a usable form. A standardized test is one for which the methods of administering, recording, scoring, and interpreting have been made uniform. Everything about the test has been standardized so that if all its directions are correctly followed, the results can be interpreted in the same manner, regardless of where in the country the test was given.

statistical regression   The tendency of extreme high and low standardized test scores to move toward the group arithmetic mean.

statistical significance   The probability of results being caused by something other than mere chance; this situation occurs when the difference between the means of two sets of results exceeds a predetermined chance level. When results are significant, researchers know that they can be confident about the conclusions they may make from their findings.

statistics   Numerical ways to describe, analyze, summarize, and interpret data in a manner that conserves time and space. Researchers select statistical procedures after they have determined what research design and types of data will be appropriate for answering their research question.

stratified random sample   A sample whose subjects are randomly selected by relevant variables in the same proportion as those variables appear in the target population.

subjects   The particular individuals or objects used in the research.

subjects section   A subsection of the method section of a research report, containing a description of the individuals or objects used in the study. The section gives general information about age, sex, grade level, intellectual and academic abilities, and socioeconomic level. The section also contains the number of subjects and an account of how the subjects were selected and assigned to groups.

subject variable   A variable on which humans are naturally different and that might influence their responses in regard to the dependent variable.

t **test**   A statistical procedure used when there are two sets of scores to determine whether the difference between the means of the two sets of scores is significant. The significance is reported as numbers such as t = 1.6 or t = 3.1. After determining the value of *t*, researchers consult a statistical table to determine whether the value is a significant one.

target population The specific group to which the researchers would like to apply their findings. It is from the target population that the researchers select the sample, which become the subjects of their study.

teacher-as-researcher synthesis of research A review of research produced for local educational use.

teacher-as-researcher research Teacher-as-researcher research is directed to studying local educational practice and to producing practical, immediately applicable findings. The questions or problems studied are local in nature (e.g., a specific class) and generalizability to other educational situations is not important to the researchers. Often teacher-as-researcher research is a collaboration between classroom teachers without research expertise and trained researchers. Sometimes this process is called *action research.* See **action research** and **participatory action research** for comparison.

test-retest reliability Reliability as determined by administering the same instrument again to the same subjects after a time period has elapsed (also referred to as *test stability*).

treatment See **experimental condition** and **independent variable.**

triangulation A procedure of collecting information from several different sources about the same event or behavior; it is used in qualitative research for cross-validating information.

trustworthiness The accuracy and consistency of qualitative research. The qualitative researchers' aim is to provide enough supporting evidence that the consumer of the research has confidence in the researchers' findings.

two-tailed hypothesis See **nondirectional hypothesis.**

validity The extent to which an instrument measures what it is intended to measure. (See **concurrent validity, construct validity, content validity, external validity, face validity, internal validity,** and **predictive validity**).

validity generalization The procedure in which researchers use the same purpose, method, and data analysis procedure, but they use subjects from a unique population.

variability The extent to which scores cluster about the mean. The variability of a normal distribution is usually reported as the standard deviation (SD).

variable Anything in a research situation that varies and can be measured. It can be human characteristics (of students or teachers), or it can be characteristics of classrooms, groups, schools and school districts, and instructional materials.

volunteer subjects Volunteers are different by nature from nonvolunteers because of some inherent motivational factor. Results from the use of volunteer subjects might not be directly generalizable to the target population containing seemingly similar (but nonvolunteer) individuals or groups.

References

Abdal-Haqq, I. (1998). *Constructivism in teacher education: Considerations for those who would link practice to theory.* Washington, DC: Office of Educational Research and Improvement, ERIC Clearinghouse on Teaching and Teacher Education. (ERIC Document Reproduction Service No. ED426986)

Abrami, P. C., Cohen, P. A., & d'Apollonia, S. (1988). Implementation problems in meta-analysis. *Review of Educational Research, 58,* 151–180.

Aksamit, D. L., & Alcorn, D. A. (1988). A preservice mainstream curriculum infusion model: Student teachers' perceptions of program effectiveness. *Teacher Education and Special Education, 11,* 52–58.

Alexander, P. A., Kulikowich, J. M., & Jetton, T. L. (1994). The role of subject-matter knowledge and interest in the processing of linear and nonlinear texts. *Review of Educational Research, 64*(2), 201–252.

Alkin, M. C. (Ed.). (1992). *The encyclopedia of educational research* (6th ed.). Upper Saddle River, NJ: Prentice Hall.

Allen, J. D. (1986). Classroom management: Students' perspectives, goals, and strategies. *American Educational Research Journal, 23,* 437–459.

Anderson, E. (2003, Fall). Feminist epistemology and philosophy of science. In E. N. Zalta (Ed.), *The Stanford encyclopedia of philosophy, 1.* Retrieved March 15, 2003, from http://plato.stanford.edu/archives/fall2003/entries/feminism-epistemology/

Anfara, Jr., V. A., Brown, K. M., & Mangione, T. L. (2002). Qualitative analysis on stage: Making the research process more public. *Educational Researcher, 31*(7), 28–38.

Annie E. Casey Foundation, The. (2002). *Local learning partnership guidebook: Making connections.* Baltimore, MD: Author.

Applefield, J. M., Huber, R., & Moallem, M. (2000–2001). Constructivism in theory and practice: Toward a better understanding. *The High School Journal, 84*(2), 35–53.

Ardovini-Brooker, J. (2002). *Feminist epistemology: The foundation of feminist research and its distinction from traditional research.* Retrieved March 15, 2004, from the Advancing Women™ Web site, http://www.advancingwomen.com/awl/spring2002/ARDOV~CG.HTM

Babad, E., Bernieri, F., & Rosenthal, R. (1987). Nonverbal and verbal behavior of preschool, remedial, and elementary school teachers. *American Educational Research Journal, 24,* 405–415.

Ballenger, C., & Rosebery, A. S. (2003). What counts as teacher research? Investigating the scientific and mathematical ideas of children from culturally diverse backgrounds. *Teachers College Record, 105*(2), 297–314.

Bangert-Drowns, R. L., & Rudner, L. M. (1991, December). *Meta-analysis in educational research: An ERIC digest.* Washington, DC: ERIC Clearinghouse on Tests, Measurements, and Evaluation. (ERIC Document Reproduction Service No. ED339748)

Barron, A. E., Hogarty, K. Y., Kromrey, J. D., & Lenkway, P. (1999). An examination of the relationships between student conduct and the number of computers per student in Florida schools. *Journal of Research on Computing in Education, 32*(1), 98–107.

Baumann, J. F., Allen, J. B., & Shockley, B. (1994). *Research questions teachers ask: A report from the National Reading Research Center school research consortium* [Online]. Retrieved October 1, 2004, from http://curry.edschool.virginia.edu/go/clic/nrrc/ques_r30.html

Beck, I. L., McKeown, M. G., & Worthy, J. (1995). Giving a text voice can improve students' understanding. *Reading Research Quarterly, 30*(2), 220–238.

Benito, Y. M., Foley, C. L., Lewis, C. G., & Prescott, P. (1993). The effect of instruction in question-answer relationships and metacognition on social studies comprehension. *Journal of Research in Reading, 16,* 20–29.

Berkowitz, S. (1997). Analyzing qualitative data. In J. Frechtling & L. Sharp (Eds.), *User-friendly handbook for mixed method evaluations.* Washington, DC: Directorate for Education and Human Resources, The National Science Foundation. Retrieved June 1, 2004, from http://www.ehr.nsf.gov/EHR/REC/pubs/NSF97-153/CHAP_4.HTM

Berliner, D. C. (1987). Knowledge is power: A talk to teachers about a revolution in the teaching profession. In D. C. Berliner & B. V. Rosenshine (Eds.), *Talks to teachers: A festschrift for N. L. Gage* (pp. 3–33). New York: Random House.

Biklen, D. (1993). *Communication unbound: How facilitated communication is challenging traditional views of autism and ability/disability.* New York: Teachers College Press.

Bisesi, T. L., & Raphael, T. E. (1995). Combining single-subject experimental designs with qualitative research. In S. B. Neuman & S. McCormick (Eds.), *Single-subject experimental research: Applications for literacy* (pp. 104–119). Newark, DE: International Reading Association.

Bissex, G. L. (1994). Teacher research: Seeing what we are doing (pp. 88–104). In T. Shannahan (Ed.), *Teachers thinking, teachers knowing: Reflections on literacy and language education.* Urbana, IL: National Conference on Research in English and National Council of Teachers of English.

Bogdan, R. C., & Biklen, S. K. (2003). *Qualitative research for education: An introduction to theory and methods* (4th ed.). Boston: Allyn & Bacon.

Borgia, E. T., & Schuler, D. (1996). *Action research in early childhood education.* ERIC Digest. Urbana, IL: ERIC Clearinghouse on Elementary and Early Childhood Education. [ERIC Document Reproduction Service No. ED401047]

Boston, C. (2004). *Effective size and meta-analysis.* ERIC Digest. Retrieved October, 1, 2004, from http://www.ericdigests.org/2003–4/meta-analysis.html

Brayton, J. (2004). *What makes feminist research feminist? The structure of feminist research within the social sciences.* Retrieved March 15, 2004, from http://www.unb.ca/web/PAR-L/win/feminmethod.htm

Brooks, M. G., & Brooks, J. G. (1999). The constructivist classroom: The courage to be constructivist. *Educational Leadership, 57*(3), 18–24.

Burns, J. M., & Collins, M. D. (1987). Parents' perceptions of factors affecting the reading development of intellectually superior accelerated readers and intellectually superior nonreaders. *Reading Research and Instruction, 26,* 239–246.

Burns, R. B., & Mason, D. A. (1998). Class formation and composition in elementary schools. *American Educational Research Journal, 35*(4), 739–772.

Bursuck, W. D., & Lesson, E. (1987). A classroom-based model for assessing students with learning disabilities. *Learning Disabilities Focus, 3,* 17–29.

Burton, F. R. (1991). Teacher-researcher projects: An elementary school teacher's perspective. In J. Flood, J. M. Jensen, D. Lapp, & J. R. Squire (Eds.), *Handbook of research on teaching the English language arts* (pp. 226–230). Upper Saddle River, NJ: Prentice Hall.

Burton, F. R., & Seidl, B. L. (2003). Teacher researcher projects: From the elementary school teacher's perspective. In J. Flood, D. Lapp, J. R. Squire, and J. M. Jensen (Eds.), *Handbook of research on teaching the English Language Arts* (2nd ed., pp. 225–231). Mahwah, NJ: Lawrence Erlbaum Associates.

Campbell, D. T., & Stanley, J. C. (1971). *Experimental and quast-experimental designs for research.* Chicago: Rand McNally.

Carlberg, C. G., Johnson, D. W., Johnson, R., Maruy-ama, G., Kavale, K., Kulik, C., Kulik, J. A., Lysakowski, R. S., Pflaum, S. W., & Walberg, H. J. (1984). Meta-analysis in education: A reply to Slavin. *Educational Researcher, 13*(8), 16–23.

Charles, C. M. (1995). *Introduction to educational research* (2nd ed.). White Plains, NY: Longman.

Charmaz, K. (2000). Grounded theory: Objectivist & constructivist methods. In Norman Denzin & Yvonna S. Lincoln (Eds.), *Handbook of qualitative research* (2nd ed., pp. 509–535). Thousand Oaks: Sage.

Clandinin, D. J., & Connelly, F. M. (2000). *Narrative inquiry: Experience and story in qualitative research.* San Francisco, CA: Jossey-Bass.

Clements, D. H., & Nastasi, B. K. (1988). Social and cognitive interactions in educational computer environments. *American Educational Research Journal, 25,* 87–106.

Clery, E. (1998). Homeschooling: The meaning that the homeschooled child assigns to this experience. *Issues in Educational Research, 8*(1), 1–13. Retrieved October 1, 2004, from http://cleo.murdoch.edu.au/gen/iier/iier8/clery.html

Connelly, F. M., & Clandinin, D. J. (1990). Stories of experience and narrative inquiry. *Educational Researcher, 19*(5): 2–14.

Conoley, J. C., & Impara, J. C. (Eds.). (1994). *Supplement to the eleventh mental measurements yearbook.* Lincoln: The Buros Institute of Mental Measurements/University of Nebraska-Lincoln.

Conoley, J. C., Impara, J. C., & Murphy, L. L. (Eds.). (1996). *Supplement to the twelfth mental measurements yearbook.* Lincoln: The Buros Institute of Mental Measurements/University of Nebraska-Lincoln.

Conoley, J. C., & Kramer, J. J. (Eds.). (1989). *Tenth mental measurements yearbook.* Lincoln: University of Nebraska Press.

Conoley, J. C., & Kramer, J. J. (Eds.). (1995). *Twelfth mental measurements yearbook.* Lincoln: University of Nebraska Press.

Conoley, J. C., Kramer, J. J., & Mitchell, J. V., Jr. (Eds.). (1988). *Supplement to the ninth mental measurements yearbook.* Lincoln: University of Nebraska Press.

Cooper, H. M. (1982). Scientific guidelines for conducting integrative research reviews. *Review of Educational Research, 52,* 291–302.

Cooper, H. M. & Lindsay, J. J. (1998). Research synthesis and meta-analysis. In L. Bickman & D. J. Rog

(Eds.), *Handbook of applied social research methods* (pp. 315–341). Thousand Oaks, CA: Sage.

Corbin, J., & Strauss, A. (1990). Grounded theory research: Procedures, canons, and evaluative criteria. *Qualitative Sociology, 13,* 3–21.

Cornbleth, C. (2002). Images of America: What youth do know about the United States. *American Educational Research Journal, 29*(2), 519–552.

Creswell, J. W. (1998). *Qualitative inquiry and research design: Choosing among five traditions.* Thousand Oaks, CA: Sage.

Creswell, J. W., & Miller, D. L. (2000, Summer). Determining validity in qualitative inquiry. *Theory Into Practice, 39*(3), 124–130.

Davis, A., Clarke, M. A., & Rhodes, L. K. (1994). Extended text and the writing proficiency of students in urban elementary schools. *Journal of Educational Research, 86*(4), 556–566.

DeLain, M. T., Pearson, P. D., & Anderson, R. C. (1985). Reading comprehension and creativity in black language use: You stand to gain by playing the sounding game! *American Educational Research Journal, 22,* 155–173.

Denzin, N. K., & Lincoln, Y. S. (2000). Introduction: The discipline and practice of qualitative research. In N. K. Denzin & Y. S. Lincoln (Eds.), *Handbook of qualitative research* (2nd ed., pp. 1–29). Thousand Oaks, CA: Sage.

Dick, B. (2002). *Grounded theory: A thumbnail sketch.* Retrieved August 1, 2004, from http://www.scu.edu. au/schools/gcm/ar/arp/grounded.html

Donnelly, J., Capeling-Alakija, S., Lopes, C., Benbouali, A., & Diallo, D. (1997). *Who are the questionmakers? A participatory evaluation handbook.* OESP Handbook Series. New York: Office of Evaluation and Strategic Planning, United Nations Development Programme. Retrieved June 1, 2004, from http://www.undp.org/eo/documents/who.htm

Donoahue, Z., Van Tassell, M. A., & Patterson, L. (Eds.). (1996). *Research in the classroom: Talk, texts, and inquiry.* Newark, DE: International Reading Association.

Duffelmeyer, F. A., & Adamson, S. (1986). Matching students with instructional level materials using the Degrees of Reading Power system. *Reading Research and Instruction, 25,* 192–200.

Edwards, B. (2002). Deep insider research. *Qualitative Research Journal, 2*(1), 71–84. Retrieved August 1, 2004, from http://www.latrobe.edu.au/aqr/previousJournals.htm

Eisenhart, M. (1999). On the subject of interpretive reviews. *Review of Educational Research, 68*(4), 391–399.

Eisner, E. W. (1991). *The enlightened eye: Qualitative inquiry and the enhancement of educational practice.* Upper Saddle River, NJ: Merrill/Prentice Hall.

Erickson, F. (1986). Qualitative methods in research on teaching. In M. C. Wittrock (Ed.), *Handbook of research on teaching* (3rd ed., pp. 119–161). Upper Saddle River, NJ: Prentice Hall.

Esterberg, K. G. (2002). *Qualitative methods in social research.* New York: McGraw-Hill.

Fagan, W. T. (1988). Concepts of reading and writing among low literate adults. *Reading Research and Instruction, 27,* 47–60.

Feldman, A., & Capobianco, B. (2000). *Action research in science education.* ERIC Digest. Columbus OH: ERIC Clearinghouse for Science Mathematics and Environmental Education. [ERIC Document Reproduction Service No. ED463944]

Fieser, J., & Dowden, B. (Eds.). (2004). *The internet encyclopedia of philosophy.* Retrieved March 15, 2004, from http://www.iep.utm.edu/

Finn, J. D., Gerber, S. B., Achilles, C. M., & Boyd-Zaharias, J. (2001, April). The enduring effects of small classes. *Teachers College Record, 10*(32), 145–184.

Firestone, W. A. (1987). Meaning in method: The rhetoric of quantitative and qualitative research. *Educational Researcher, 17*(7), 16–21.

Firestone, W. A. (1993). Alternative arguments for generalizing from data as applied to qualitative research. *Educational Researcher, 22*(4), 16–23.

Fitzgerald, J. (1995). English-as-a-second-language learners' cognitive reading processes: A review of research in the United States. *Review of Educational Research, 65*(2), 145–190.

Fleisher, B. M. (1988). Oral reading cue strategies of better and poor readers. *Reading Research and Instruction, 27,* 35–60.

Frechtling, J., & Sharp, L. (1997). *User-friendly handbook for mixed method evaluations.* Washington, DC: Directorate for Education and Human Resources, The National Science Foundation. Retrieved June 1, 2004, from http://www.ehr.nsf.gov/EHR/REC/pubs/NSF97-153/start.htm

Fuchs, D., & Fuchs, L. S. (1986). Test procedure bias: A meta-analysis of examiner familiarity effects. *Review of Educational Research, 56,* 243–262.

Fuchs, D., & Fuchs, L. S. (1989). Effects of examiner familiarity on black, Caucasian, and Hispanic children: A meta-analysis. *Exceptional Children, 55,* 303–308.

Fuchs, D., Fuchs, L. S., & Fernstrom, P. (1993). A conservative approach to special education reform: Mainstreaming through transenvironmental programming and curriculum-based measurement. *American Educational Research Journal, 30*(1), 149–177.

Gall, J. P., Gall, M. D., & Borg, W. R. (1999). *Applying educational research: A practical guide* (4th ed.). New York: Addison Wesley Longman.

Gall, M. D., Gall, J. P., & Borg, W. R. (2002). *Educational research: An introduction* (7th ed.). Boston: Allyn & Bacon.

Gay, L. R., & Airasian, P. (2003). *Educational research: Competencies for analysis and application* (7th ed.). Upper Saddle River, NJ: Merrill/Prentice Hall.

Geyser, D. J., & Sweetland, R. C. (1991). *Test critiques.* Austin, TX: Pro-Ed.

Giangreco, M. F., & Taylor, S. J. (2003). "Scientifically based research" and qualitative inquiry. *Research & Practice for Persons With Severe Disabilities, 28*(3), 133–137.

Gillis, M. K., Olson, M. W., & Logan, J. (1993). Are content area reading practices keeping pace with research? In T. V. Rasinski & N. D. Padak (Eds.), *Inquiries in literacy learning and instruction.* The Fifteenth Yearbook of the College Reading Association (pp. 115–123). Pittsburg, KS: College Reading Association.

Glass, G. V. (1976). Primary, secondary, and meta-analysis of research. *Educational Researcher, 5*(10), 3–8.

Glass, G. V. (2000). *Meta-analysis at 25.* Retrieved October 1, 2004, from http://glass.ed.asu.edu/gene/papers/meta25.html

Glaser, B. G., & Strauss, A. L. (1967). *The discovery of grounded theory.* Chicago: Aldine.

Glazer, B. G. (2004). *An interview with Dr. Bernard G. Glazer conducted by Dr. Andy Lowe.* Retrieved March 15, 2004, from the Web site of The Grounded Theory Institute, http://www.groundedtheory.com/index.html

Golafshani, N. (2003). Understanding reliability and validity in qualitative research. *The Qualitative Report, 8*(4, December), 597–607. Retrieved June 1, 2004, from http://www.nova.edu/ssss/QR/QR8-4/golafshani.pdf

Goodson, I. F. (1993, March). The devil's bargain: Educational research and the teacher. *Education Policy Analysis Archives, 1*(3). Retrieved October 1, 2004, from http://olam.ed.asu.edu/epaa/v1n3.html

Graue, M. E., & Walsch, D. J. (1995). Children in context: Interpreting the here and now of children's lives. In J. A. Hatch (Ed.), *Qualitative research in early childhood settings.* Westport, CT: Praeger.

Greenwood, D., & Levin, M. (1998). *Introduction to action research: Social research for social change.* Thousand Oaks, CA: Sage.

Guba, E. G., & Lincoln, Y. S. (1989). *Fourth generation evaluation.* Newbury Park, CA: Sage.

Guthrie, L. F., & Hall, W. S. (1984). Ethnographic approaches to reading research. In P. D. Pearson, R. Barr, M. L. Kamil, & P. Mosenthal (Eds.), *Handbook of reading research* (pp. 91–110). New York: Longman.

Guthrie, L. F., Seifert, M., & Kirsch, I. S. (1986). Effects of education, occupation, and setting on reading practices. *American Educational Research Journal, 23,* 151–160.

Hancock, B. (1998; Updated: 2002). *Trent focus for research and development in primary health care: An introduction to qualitative research.* Nottingham, England: Trent Focus Group. Retrieved June 1, 2004, from http://www.trentfocus.org.uk/Resources/Qualitative%20Research.pdf

Harding, S. (1991). *Whose science? Whose knowledge? Thinking from women's lives.* Ithaca, NY: Cornell University Press.

Harris, J. B., & Grandgenett, N. (1996, Spring). Correlates among teachers' anxieties, demographics, and telecomputing activity. *Journal of Research on Computing in Education, 28,* 300–317.

Harris, T. L., & Hodges, R. E. (Eds.). (1995). *The literacy dictionary: The vocabulary of reading and writing.* Newark, DE: International Reading Association.

Hartley, J., & Chesworth, K. (1998, July). *Qualitative and quantitative methods in research on essay writing: No one way.* Paper presented at "Higher Education Close Up," an international conference at the University of Central Lancashire, Preston, United Kingdom. Retrieved October 1, 2004, from http://www.leeds.ac.uk/educol/documents/000000682.htm

Hatch, J. A. (1995). Studying childhood as a cultural invention: A rationale and framework. In J. A. Hatch (Ed.), *Qualitative research in early childhood settings* (pp. 117–133). Westport, CT: Praeger.

Hevern, V. W. (2003, May). *Philosophical perspectives. Narrative psychology: Internet and resource guide.* Retrieved April 1, 2004, from the Le Moyne College Web site: http://web.lemoyne.edu/~hevern/nr-constr.html

Hevern, V. W. (2003, June). *Education. Narrative psychology: Internet and resource guide.* Retrieved April 1, 2004, from the Le Moyne College Web site: http://web.lemoyne.edu/~hevern/nr-educ.html

Hiebert, E. H., Valencia, S. W., & Afflerback, P. P. (1994). Definitions and perspectives. In S. W. Valencia, E. H. Hiebert, & P. P. Afflerback (Eds.), *Authentic reading assessment: Practices and possibilities* (pp. 6–21). Newark, DE: International Reading Association.

Hill, J. W., Seyfarth, J., Banks, P. D., Wehman, P., & Orelove, F. (1987). Parent attitudes about working conditions of their adult mentally retarded sons and daughters. *Exceptional Children, 54,* 9–23.

Hillocks, G., Jr. (1992). Reconciling the qualitative and quantitative. In R. Beach, J. L. Green, M. L. Kamil, & T. Shanahan (Eds.), *Multidisciplinary perspectives on literacy research* (pp. 57–65). Urbana, IL: National Conference on Research in English/National Council of Teachers of English.

Hirtle, J. S. (1993). Connecting to the classics. In L. Patterson, C. M. Santa, K. G. Short, & K. Smith

(Eds.), *Teachers are researchers: Reflection and action* (pp. 137–146). Newark, DE: International Reading Association.

Homan, S. P., Hines, C. V., & Kromrey, J. D. (1993). An investigation of varying reading level placement on reading achievement of Chapter 1 students. *Reading Research and Instruction, 33*(1), 29–38.

Hughes, C. A., Ruhl, K. L., & Gorman, J. (1987). Preparation of special educators to work with parents: A survey of teachers and teacher educators. *Teacher Education and Special Education, 10,* 81–87.

Hunsucker, P. F., Nelson, R. O., & Clark, R. P. (1986). Standardization and evaluation of the Classroom Adaptive Behavior Checklist for school use. *Exceptional Children, 53,* 69–71.

Husen, T., & Postlethwaite, T. N. (Eds.). (1994). *The international encyclopedia of education,* 2nd ed. New York: Pergamon/Elsevier Science.

Impara, J. C., & Plake, B. S. (Eds.). (1998). *Thirteenth mental meansurements yearbook.* Lincoln: The Buros Institute of Mental Measurements/University of Nebraska-Lincoln.

Jackson, G. B. (1980). Methods for integrative reviews. *Review of Educational Research, 50,* 438–460.

Jacob, E. (1987). Qualitative research traditions: A review. *Review of Educational Research, 57,* 1–50.

Jacob, E. (1988). Clarifying qualitative research: A focus on traditions. *Educational Researcher, 17*(1), 16–24.

Jacob, E. (1989). Qualitative research: A response to Atkinson, Delamont, and Hammersley. *Review of Educational Research, 59,* 229–235.

Jacobs, J. E., Finken, L. L., Griffin, N. L., & Wright, J. D. (1998). The career plans of science-talented rural adolescent girls. *American Educational Research Journal, 35*(4), 681–704.

Jansen, G., & Peshkin, A. (1992). Subjectivity in qualitative research. In M. D. LeCompte, W. L. Millory, & J. Preissle (Eds.), *The handbook of qualitative research in education* (pp. 681–725). San Diego: Academic Press/Harcourt Brace.

Johnson, B. (1993). *Teacher-as-researcher.* ERIC Digest. Washington DC.: ERIC Clearinghouse on Teacher Education. [ERIC Document Reproduction Service No. ED355205]

Johnson, R. W. (1993). Where can teacher research lead? One teacher's daydream. *Educational Leadership, 51*(2), 66–68.

Joint Committee on Standards for Educational Evaluation. (1981). *Standards for evaluation of educational programs, projects, and materials.* New York: McGraw-Hill.

Joint Committee on Standards for Educational Evaluations. (1994). *The Program Evaluation Standards: How to assess evaluations of educational programs.* Thousand Oaks, CA: Sage (available from ERIC/AE).

Jones, I. (1997, December). Mixing qualitative and quantitative methods in sports fan research. *The Qualitative Report* [Online serial], *3*(4). Retrieved October 1, 2004, from http://www.nova.edu/ssss/QR/QR3-4/jones.html

Jovanovic, J., & King, S. S. (1998). Boys and girls in the performance-based science classroom: Who's doing the performing. *American Educational Research Journal, 35*(3), 477–496.

Joyce, B. (1987). A rigorous yet delicate touch: A response to Slavin's proposal for "best-evidence" reviews. *Educational Researcher, 16*(4), 12–14.

Kamberelis, G., & Bovino, T. D. (1999). Cultural artifacts as scaffolds for genre development. *Reading Research Quarterly, 34*(2), 138–70.

Kamil, M. L., Langer, J. A., & Shanahan, T. (1985). *Understanding research in reading and writing.* Boston: Allyn & Bacon.

Kerlinger, F. N. (1973). *Foundations of behavioral research: Educational, psychological, and sociological inquiry* (2nd ed.). New York: Holt, Rinehart & Winston.

Konopak, B. C. (1988). Eighth graders' vocabulary learning from inconsiderate and considerate text. *Reading Research and Instruction, 27,* 1–14.

Kramer, J. J., & Conoley, J. C. (Eds.). (1992). *Eleventh mental measurements yearbook.* Lincoln: The Buros Institute of Mental Measurements/University of Nebraska-Lincoln.

Kuhn, T. (1970). *The structure of scientific revolutions* (3rd ed.). Chicago: University of Chicago Press. Retrieved October 1, 2004, from http://oak.ucc.nau.edu/jgr6/eng522_kuhn.htm

Lacey, A., & Luff, D. (2001). *Trent focus for research and development in primary health care: An introduction to qualitative analysis.* Sheffield, England: Trent Focus. Retrieved June 1, 2004, from http://www.trentfocus.org.uk/Resources/introduction_qualitative_research.htm

Ladas, H. (1980). Summarizing research: A case study. *Review of Educational Research, 50,* 597–624.

Lancy, D. F. (1993). *Qualitative research in education: An introduction to the major traditions.* New York: Longman.

Langer, J. A. (1984). The effects of available information on responses to school writing. *Research in the Teaching of English, 18,* 27–44.

Langer, J. A., Campbell, J. R., Neuman, S. B., Mullis, I. V. S., Persky, H. R., & Donahue, P. L. (1995). *Reading assessment redesigned: Authentic texts and innovative instruments.* Washington, DC: U.S. Department of Education, Office of Educational Research and Improvement.

Lass, B. (1984). Do teachers individualize their responses to reading miscues? A study of feedback during oral reading. *Reading World, 23,* 242–254.

Lazarowitz, R., Hertz-Lazarowitz, R., & Baird, J. H. (1994). Learning science in a cooperative setting: Academic achievement and affective outcomes. *Journal of Research in Science Teaching, 31,* 1121–1131.

LeCompte, M. D., & Goetz, J. P. (1982). Problems of reliability and validity in ethnographic research. *Review of Educational Research, 52,* 31–60.

LeCompte, M. D., Millory, W. L., & Preissle, J. (Eds.). (1992). *The handbook of qualitative research in education.* San Diego: Academic Press/Harcourt Brace.

LeCompte, M. D., Preissle, J., & Tesch, R. (1993). *Ethnography and qualitative design in educational research* (2nd ed.). San Diego: Academic Press.

Lee, O. (1999). Science knowledge, world views, and information sources in social and cultural contexts: Making sense after a natural disaster. *American Educational Research Journal, 36*(2), 187–219.

Lemke, J. L. (1998). Analysing verbal data: Principles, methods, and problems. In K. Tobin & B. Fraser (Eds.), *International Handbook of Science Education.* London: Kluwer Academic Publishers, 1175–1189. Retrieved August 1, 2004, from http://academic.brooklyn.cuny.edu/education/jlemke/papers/handbook.htm

Leinhardt, G., & Pallay, A. (1982). Restrictive educational settings: Exile or haven? *Review of Educational Research, 52,* 557–578.

Lincoln, Y. S., & Guba, E. G. (1985). *Naturalistic inquiry.* Beverly Hills, CA: Sage.

Linn, R. L. (1994). Performance assessment: Policy promises and technical measurement standards. *Educational Researcher, 23*(9), 4–14.

Lloyd, L. (1999). Multi-age classes and high ability students. *Review of Educational Research, 69*(2), 187–212.

Lyytinen, P., Rasku-Puttonen, H., Poikkeus, A. M., Laakso, A. L., & Ahonen, T. (1994). Mother-child teaching strategies and learning disabilities. *Journal of Learning Disabilities, 27,* 186–192.

MacColl, G. S., & White, K. D. (1998). *Communicating educational research data to general, nonresearcher audiences.* ERIC/AE Digest. Washington, DC: ERIC Clearinghouse on Assessment and Evaluation. (ERIC Document Reproduction Service No. ED422406)

Madden, N. A., & Slavin, R. E. (1983). Mainstreaming students with mild handicaps: Academic and social outcomes. *Review of Educational Research, 53,* 519–169.

Maeroff, G. I. (1982, March 30). Specific TV shows tied to child's achievement. *The New York Times,* p. C9.

Mahoney, C. (1997). Common qualitative methods. In J. Frechtling & L. Sharp (Eds.), *User-friendly handbook for mixed method evaluations.* Washington, DC: Directorate for Education and Human Resources, The National Science Foundation. Retrieved June 1, 2004, from http://www.ehr.nsf.gov/EHR/REC/pubs/NSF97-153/start.htm

Mandoli, M., Mandoli, P., & McLaughlin, T. F. (1982). Effects of same-age peer tutoring on the spelling performance of a mainstreamed elementary LD student. *Learning Disability Quarterly, 5,* 185–189.

Manning, M., Manning, G., & Cody, C. B. (1988). Reading aloud to young children: Perspectives of parents. *Reading Research and Instruction, 27,* 56–61.

Manzo, A. V., Manzo, U. C., & McKenna, M. C. (1995). *Informal reading-thinking inventory.* Fort Worth: Harcourt Brace College.

Marshall, C., & Rossman, G. B. (1995). *Designing qualitative research* (2nd ed.). Thousand Oaks, CA: Sage.

Martin, L. E., & Reutzel, D. R. (1999). Sharing books: Examining how and why mothers deviate from the print. *Reading Research and Instruction, 39*(1), 39–70.

Masters, J. (1999). The history of action research. *Action Research Electronic Reader.* Retrieved March 15, 2004, from http://www.scu.edu.au/schools/gcm/ar/arr/arow/rmasters.html#AR%20what

Maxwell, J. A. (1992). Understanding and validity in qualitative research. *Harvard Educational Review, 62*(3), 279–300.

Maxwell, J. A. (1998). Designing a qualitative study. In L. Bickman & D. J. Rog (Eds.), *Handbook of applied social research methods* (pp. 69–100). Thousand Oaks, CA: Sage.

Mays, N., & Pope, C. (Eds.). (2000). *Qualitative research in health care* (2nd ed.). London: BMJ Books. Retrieved June 1, 2004, from http://www.bmjpg.com/qrhc/index.html

McBrien, J. L., & Brandt, R. S. (1997). *The language of learning: A guide to education terms.* Alexandria, VA: Association for Supervision and Curriculum Development.

McCarthy, P., Newby, R. F., & Recht, D. R. (1995). Results of an early intervention program for first grade children at risk for reading disability. *Reading Research and Instruction, 34*(4), 273–294.

McCormick, S. (1995). What is single-subject experimental research? In S. B. Neuman & S. McCormick (Eds.), *Single-subject experimental research: Applications for literacy* (pp. 1–31). Newark, DE: International Reading Association.

McFarland, K. P., & Stansell, J. C. (1993). Historical perspectives. In L. Patterson, C. M. Santa, K. G. Short, & K. Smith (Eds.), *Teachers are researchers: Reflection and action* (pp. 12–18). Newark, DE: International Reading Association.

McKeown, M. G., Beck, I. L., Sinatra, G. M., & Loxterman, J. A. (1992). The contribution of prior knowledge and coherent text to comprehension. *Reading Research Quarterly, 27*(1), 78–93.

McNemar, B. S. (1998). The everyday literacy behavior of an adolescent mother for whom English is a second language. In T. Shanahan & F. V. Rodriquez-Brown (Eds.), *47th yearbook of the National Reading Conference* (pp. 274–284). Chicago: National Reading Conference.

Mehra, B. (2003). Lives in transition: Stories of three foreign elementary students from India. *The Qualitative Report, 8*(3), 377–407. Retrieved June 1, 2004, from http://www.nova.edu/ssss/QR/QR8-3/mehra.pdf

Messick, S. (1994). The interplay of evidence and consequences in the validation of performance assessments. *Educational Researcher, 23*(2), 13–23.

Meyers, M. D. (1997, June). Qualitative research in information systems. *MIS Quarterly, 21*(2), 241–242. MISQ Discovery, archival version, retrieved June 1997, from http://www.misq.org/discovery/MISQD_isworld/ MISQ Discovery, updated version, last modified: February 27, 2004. Retrieved June 1, 2004, from www.qual.auckland.ac.nz

Mifflin, L. (1995, May 31). Study finds educational TV lends preschoolers even greater advantages. *The New York Times*, p. B8.

Mitchell, J. V., Jr. (Ed.). (1983). *Tests in print III: An index to tests, test reviews, and the literature on specific tests.* Lincoln University of Nebraska Press.

Mitchell, J. V., Jr. (Ed.). (1985). *Ninth mental measurements yearbook.* Lincoln University of Nebraska Press.

Moore, J. (1999, January). *Some basic concepts in meta-analyses.* Paper presented at the annual meeting of the Southwest Educational Research Association, San Antonio, TX. (ERIC Document Reproduction Service No. ED426101)

Morgan, D. L. (1988). *Focus groups as qualitative research.* Newbury Park, CA: Sage.

Morris, R. N. (2002). *A case study on the perspective of an optional K–5 year-round/multi-age program in Virginia.* (ERIC Document Reproduction Service No. ED479350)

Morrow, L. M. (1988). Young children's responses to one-to-one story readings in school settings. *Reading Research Quarterly, 23*, 89–107.

Moustafa, M. (1995). Children's productive phonological recoding. *Reading Research Quarterly, 30*(3), 464–476.

Murphy, L. L., Impara, J. C., & Plake, B. S. (Eds.). (1999). *Tests in print V: An index to tests, test reviews, and the literature on specific tests* (Vols. I and II). Lincoln: The Buros Institute of Mental Measurements/University of Nebraska-Lincoln.

Nassar-McMillan, S. C., & Borders, L. D. (2002, March). Use of focus groups in survey item development. *The Qualitative Report, 7*(1). Retrieved June 1, 2004, from http://www.nova.edu/ssss/QR/QR7-1/nassar.html

Nattiv, A. (1994). Helping behaviors and math achievement gain of students using cooperative learning. *The Elementary School Journal, 94,* 285–297.

Nelson, J. R., Smith, D. J., & Dodd, J. M. (1994). The effects of learning strategy instruction on the completion of job applications by students with learning disabilities. *Journal of Learning Disabilities, 27,* 104–110.

Neuman, S. B. (1999). Books make a difference: A study of access to literacy. *Reading Research Quarterly, 34*(3), 286–311.

Newman, R. S., & Schwager, M. T. (1995). Students' help seeking during problem solving: Effects of grade, goal, and prior achievement. *American Educational Research Journal, 32*(2), 352–376.

Nielsen, H. B. (1995). Seductive texts with serious intentions. *Educational Researcher, 24*(1), 4–12.

Nist, S. L., & Olejnik, S. (1995). The role of context and dictionary definitions on varying levels of word knowledge. *Reading Research Quarterly, 30*(2), 172–195.

Okagaki, L., & Frensch, P. A. (1998). Parenting and children's school achievement: A multiethnic perspective. *American Educational Research Journal, 35*(1), 123–144.

Olson, M. W. (1990). The teacher as researcher: A historical perspective. In M. W. Olson (Ed.), *Opening the door to classroom research* (pp. 1–20). Newark, DE: International Reading Association.

Osborne, J. W. (2000). Advantages of hierarchical linear modeling. *Practical Assessment, Research & Evaluation, 7*(1). Retrieved August 1, 2004, from http://PAREonline.net/getvn.asp?v-7&n-1

Osborne, S. (1985). Effects of teacher experience and selected temperament variables on coping strategies used with distractible children. *American Educational Research Journal, 22,* 79–86.

Pandit, N. R. (1996, December). The creation of theory: A recent application of the grounded theory method. *The Qualitative Report, 2*(4). Retrieved August 1, 2004, from http://www.nova.edu/ssss/QR/QR2-4/corbin

Pascarella, E. T., Pflaum, S. W., Bryan, T. H., & Pearl, R. A. (1983). Interaction of internal attribution for effort and teacher response mode in reading instruction: A replication note. *American Educational Research Journal, 20,* 269–276.

Patterson, L., & Shannon, P. (1993). Reflection, inquiry, action. In L. Patterson, C. M. Santa, K. G. Short, & K. Smith (Eds.), *Teachers are researchers: Reflection and action* (pp. 7–11). Newark, DE: International Reading Association.

Peshkin, A. (1993). The goodness of qualitative research. *Educational Researcher, 22*(2), 24–30.

Pitman, M. A., & Maxwell, J. A. (1992). Qualitative approaches to evaluation: Models and methods. In M. D. LeCompte, W. L. Millory, & J. Preissle (Eds.), *The handbook of qualitative research in education* (pp. 729–770). San Diego: Academic Press/Harcourt Brace.

Plake, B. S., & Impara, J. C. (Eds.). (1999). *Supplement to the thirteenth mental measurements yearbook*. Lincoln: The Buros Institute of Mental Measurements/ University of Nebraska-Lincoln.

Plake, B. S., Impara, J. C., & Spies, R. A. (2003). *The fifteenth mental measurements yearbook*. Lincoln: The Buros Institute of Mental Measurements/ University of Nebraska-Lincoln.

Popham, W. J., & Sirotnik, K. A. (1973). *Educational statistics: Use and interpretation* (2nd ed.). New York: Harper & Row.

Pretty, J. N. (1994). Alternative systems of inquiry for sustainable agriculture. *IDS Bulletin, 25*(2), 37–48. University of Sussex: IDS.

Putney, L. G., Green J. L., Dixon, C. N., & Kelly, G. J. (1999). Evolution of qualitative research methodology: Looking beyond defense to possibilities. *Reading Research Quarterly, 34*(3), 368–377.

Qin, Z., Johnson, D. W., & Johnson, R. T. (1995). Cooperative versus competitive efforts and problem solving. *Review of Educational Research, 65*(2), 129–143.

Reinking, D., & Schreiner, R. (1985). The effects of computer mediated text on measures of reading comprehension and reading behavior. *Reading Research Quarterly, 20*, 536–552.

Richgels, D. J. (1986). Grade school children's listening and reading comprehension of complex sentences. *Reading Research and Instruction, 25*, 201–219.

Rolón-Dow, R. (2004). Seduced by images: Identity and schooling in the lives of Puerto Rican girls. *Anthropology & Education Quarterly, 35*(1), 8–29.

Rosenshine, B., & Meister, C. (1994). Reciprocal teaching: A review of the research. *Review of Educational Research, 64*(4), 479–530.

Rudner, L. M., & Shafer, W. D. (2001). *Reliability*. ERIC Digest. College Park, MD: ERIC Clearinghouse on Assessment and Evaluation. (ERIC Document Reproduction Service No. ED458213)

Santa, C. M. (1988). Changing teacher behavior in content reading through collaborative research. In S. J. Samuels & P. D. Pearson (Eds.), *Changing school reading programs: Principles and case studies* (pp. 185–204). Newark, DE: International Reading Association.

Sauvage, G. M. (2003). Positivism. *The Catholic Encyclopedia*, Vol. XII. (Transcribed by D. J. Potter). Retrieved March 15, 2004, from www.newadvent.org/cathen/12312c.htm

Schwandt, T., A. (1997). *Qualitative inquiry: A dictionary of terms*. Thousand Oaks, CA: Sage Publications.

Seidman, I. (1998). *Interviewing as qualitative research: A guide for researchers in education and the social sciences* (2nd ed.). New York: Teachers College Press.

Seymour-Rolls, K., & Hughes, I. (1999). Participatory action research: Getting the job done. *Action Research Electronic Reader*. Retrieved March 15, 2004, from http://www.scu.edu.au/schools/gcm/ar/arr/arow/rseymour.html

Shanahan, T. (2000). Research synthesis: Making sense of the accumulation of knowledge in reading. In M. L. Kamil, P. B. Mosenthal, P. D. Pearson, & R. Barr (Eds.), *Handbook of reading research* (Vol. III, pp. 209–226). Mahway, NJ: Lawrence Erlbaum Associates.

Singh, S., & Richards, L. (2003). Missing data: Finding 'central' themes in qualitative research. *Qualitative Research Journal, 3*(1), 5–17. Retrieved August 1, 2004, from http://www.latrobe.edu.au/aqr/previousJournals.htm

Slavin, R. E. (1984a). Meta-analysis in education: How has it been used? *Educational Researcher, 13*(8), 6–15.

Slavin, R. E. (1984b). A rejoinder to Carlberg et al. *Educational Researcher, 13*(8), 24–27.

Slavin, R. E. (1986). Best-evidence synthesis: An alternative to meta-analytic and traditional reviews. *Educational Researcher, 15*(9), 5–11.

Slavin, R. E. (1987a). Best-evidence synthesis: Why less is more. *Educational Researcher, 16*(4), 15–16.

Slavin, R. E. (1987b). Mastery learning reconsidered. *Review of Educational Research, 57*, 175–213.

Slavin, R. E. (1992). *Research methods in education* (2nd ed.). Boston: Allyn & Bacon.

Smith, J. K., & Heshusius, L. (1986). Closing down the conversation: The end of the quantitative-qualitative debate among educational inquiries. *Educational Researcher, 15*(1), 4–12.

Smith, M. L. (1987). Publishing qualitative research. *American Educational Research Journal, 24*, 173–183.

Solomon, D., Watson, M. S., Delucchi, K. L., Schaps, E., & Battistich, V. (1988). Enhancing children's prosocial behavior in the classroom. *American Educational Research Journal, 25*, 527–554.

Sommers, R. (2003). "Real" middle school teachers. *The Qualitative Report, 8*(4), 530–538. Retrieved June 1, 2004, from http://www.nova.edu/ssss/QR/QR8-4/sommers.pdf

Sparks, G. M. (1986). The effectiveness of alternative training activities in changing teaching practices. *American Educational Research Journal, 23*, 217–225.

Spindler, G., & Spindler, L. (1992). Cultural process and ethnography: An anthropological perspective. In M. D. LeCompte, W. L. Millory, & J. Preissle (Eds.), *The handbook of qualitative research in education* (pp. 53–92). San Diego: Academic Press/Harcourt Brace.

Stock, W. A., Okun, M. A., Haring, M. J., Miller, W., Kinney, C., & Ceurvost, R. W. (1982). Rigor in data synthesis: A case study of reliability in meta-analysis. *Educational Researcher, 11*(6), 10–14.

Swanson, B. B. (1985). Teacher judgments of first-graders' reading enthusiasm. *Reading Research and Instruction, 25,* 41–36.

Swanson, D. B., Norman, G. R., & Linn, R. L. (1995). Performance-based assessment: Lessons from the health professions. *Educational Researcher, 24*(5), 5–11, 35.

Sweetland, R. C., & Geyser, D. J. (1991). *Tests: A comprehensive reference for assessment in psychology, education, and business* (3rd ed.). Austin, TX: Pro-Ed.

Tallent-Runnels, M. K., Olivarez, A., Jr., Lotven, A. C. C., Walsh, S. K., Gray, A., & Irons, T. R. (1994). A comparison of learning and study strategies of gifted and average-ability junior high students. *Journal for the Education of the Gifted, 17,* 143–160.

Taylor, S. J., & Bogdan, R. (1998). *Introduction to qualitative research methods: A guidebook and resource* (3rd ed.). New York: John Wiley & Sons.

Thompson, M. S., Entwisle, D. R., Alexander, K. L., & Sundius, M. J. (1992). The influence of family composition on children's conformity to the student role. *American Educational Research Journal, 29*(2), 405–424.

Thompson, R. L. (1999, January). *Reliability generalization: An important meta-analytic method, because it is incorrect to say, "the test is unreliable."* Paper presented at the annual meeting of the Southwest Educational Research Association, San Antonio, TX. ERIC Document No. ED434121.

Trochim, W. (2001). *The research methods knowledge base* (2nd ed.). Cincinnati, OH: Atomic Dog Publishing.

Valencia, S. W., Hiebert, E. H., & Afflerbach, P. P. (Eds.). (1994). *Authentic reading assessment: Practices and possibilities.* Newark, DE: International Reading Association.

VanDeWeghe, R. (1992). What teachers learn from "kid watching." *Educational Leadership, 49*(7), 49–52.

Van Maanen, J., Dabbs, J. M., Jr., & Faulkner, R. R. (1982). *Varieties of qualitative research.* Beverly Hills, CA: Sage.

Van Scoy, I. J. (1994). Differences in teaching between six primary and five intermediate teachers in one school. *The Elementary School Journal, 94,* 347–356.

Vaughn, S., Schumm, J. S., Klingner, J., & Saumell, L. (1995). Students' views of instructional practices: Implications for inclusion. *Learning Disability Quarterly, 18,* 236–247.

Vukelich, C. (1986). The relationship between peer questions and seven-year-olds' text revisions. In J. A. Niles & R. V. Lalik (Eds.), *Solving problems in literacy: Learners, teachers, and researchers* (pp. 300–305). Thirty-fifth Yearbook of the National Reading Conference. Chicago: National Reading Conference.

Wadsworth, Y. (1998). What is participatory action research? *Action Research International,* Paper 2. Retrieved March 15, 2004, from www.scu.edu.au/schools/gcm/ar/ari/p-ywadsworth98.html

Webb, N. M., Ender, P., & Lewis, S. (1986). Problem-solving strategies and group processes in small groups learning computer programming. *American Educational Research Journal, 23,* 243–261.

West, S. L., & O'Neal, K. K. (2004). Project D.A.R.E. outcome effectiveness revisited. *American Journal of Public Health, 94*(6), 1027–1030.

Wiersma, W. (1995). *Research methods in education: An introduction* (6th ed.). Boston: Allyn & Bacon.

Wilkinson, I., Wardrop, J. L., & Anderson, R. C. (1988). Silent reading reconsidered: Reinterpreting reading instruction and its effects. *American Educational Research Journal, 25,* 127–144.

Wilkinson, L., & APA Task Force on Statistical Inference. (2000). Statistical methods in psychology journals: Guidelines and explanations. *American Psychologist, 55*(7). Retrieved March 15, 2004, from www.apa.org/journals/amp/amp548594.html

Wilson, S. (1977). The use of ethnographic techniques in educational research. *Review of Educational Research, 47,* 245–265.

Wolcott, H. F. (1992). Posturing in qualitative inquiry. In M. D. LeCompte, W. L. Millory, & J. Preissle (Eds.), *The handbook of qualitative research in education* (pp. 3–52). San Diego: Academic Press/Harcourt Brace.

Writing@CSU. (2004). *Writing@CSU: Writing guides. Overview: Ethnography, observational research, and narrative inquiry.* Retrieved March 15, 2004, from http://writing.colostate.edu/references/research/observe/printFormat.cfm?printformat-yes

Xin, Y. P., & Jitendra, A. K. (1999). The effects of instruction in solving mathematical word problems for students with learning problems: A meta-analysis. *The Journal of Special Education, 32*(4), 207–225.

Yopp, H. K. (1988). The validity and reliability of phonemic awareness tests. *Reading Research Quarterly, 23,* 159–177.

Young, S. A., & Romeo, L. (1999). University and urban school district collaboration: Preschoolers and preservice teachers gain literacy skills. *Reading Research and Instruction, 38*(2), 101–114.

Zutell, J., & Rasinski, T. (1986). Spelling ability and reading fluency. In J. A. Niles & R. V. Lalik (Eds.), *Yearbook of the National Reading Conference: Solving problems in literacy: Learners, teachers, and researchers* (pp. 109–112). Chicago: National Reading Conference.

Name Index

Subject Index